A History of Political Murder in Latin America

SUNY series in Global Modernity

Arif Dirlik, editor

A History of Political Murder in Latin America

Killing the Messengers of Change

W. John Green

SUNY PRESS

Cover art: *Masacre en Colombia* by Fernando Botero, courtesy of the Museo Nacional de Colombia.

Map images © Brian Wrigley

Published by State University of New York Press, Albany

Printed in the United States of America

For information, contact State University of New York Press, Albany, NY
www.sunypress.edu

Production, Jenn Bennett
Marketing, Kate R. Seburyamo

Library of Congress Cataloging-in-Publication Data

Green, W. John, 1963–
A history of political murder in Latin America : killing the messengers of change / W. John Green.
pages cm. — (SUNY series in global modernity)
Includes bibliographical references and index.
ISBN 978-1-4384-5663-8 (hc : alk paper)—978-1-4384-5664-5 (pb : alk. paper)
ISBN 978-1-4384-5665-2 (e-book)
1. Political violence—Latin America—History—20th century. 2. Murder—Latin America—History—20th century. 3. Assassination—Latin America—History—20th century. 4. Disappeared persons—Latin America—History—20th century. 5. Massacres—Latin America—History—20th century. 6. Political persecution—Latin America—History—20th century. 7. State-sponsored terrorism—Latin America—History—20th century. 8. Political culture—Latin America—History—20th century. 9. Latin America—Politics and government—20th century. 10. Latin America—Social conditions—20th century. I. Title.
F1414.G75 2015
306.2098—dc23 2014027596

10 9 8 7 6 5 4 3 2 1

Contents

Preface and Acknowledgments

On the morning of November 17, 1991, I went for a hike that began along the Circunvalar, a winding road that threads its way through the Parque Nacional on the eastern edge of Bogotá, where the city crowds against Mount Monserrate. After rounding a secluded bend, my companions and I saw a group of military police milling about a grassy bank. Spread upon it lay the bodies of two young men, neatly arranged side by side. Each had been shot in the chest several times and obviously moved there later. As we passed, one of the soldiers joked, "No están durmiendo." ("They're not sleeping.") Before I left Colombia in late July 1992, I ran across the publically displayed bodies of people violently killed on two other occasions.

The early to mid-1990s were the final years of the bloody and highly successful offensive by paramilitary groups against the leftist Unión Patriótica party, a political organization with ties to the Revolutionary Armed Forces of Colombia, the FARC, Colombia's largest guerrilla army. One might say that this project began with those sightings, but it also grows out of my long-term research interest in popular political mobilizations and the repression they often face. My first book explored Colombian Gaitanismo in the 1920s, '30s, and '40s, a populist movement that ended with its leader's assassination in 1948 and the violent suppression of its adherents in the years that followed.

This venture is, admittedly, ambitious in its scope. I examine the phenomenon of political murder throughout modern Latin America, focusing on many different countries in some depth, with quicker but significant glances at most of the rest. Given the number of such killings in Latin America, the aim is necessarily more thematic and comparative than encyclopedic. I build on an expansive literature composed of monographs on individual countries and their regions. And though a growing number of excellent collections now compare and contrast the various "dirty wars" since the late 1960s, they are multiauthored and invariably structured as a series of separate country studies that sometimes seem like an exercise in parallel play. In contrast, this book flips the focus from country histories to political murder itself, pulling the broader literature together to let the various cases illuminate the phenomenon in concert and thematically. Obvious disparities exist among the different countries' experiences, but what really jump out are the similarities. This is important to recognize because many specialists tend to see "their" country or subregion (Mexico, Central America, the Caribbean, the Andes, the Southern Cone, Brazil) as unique or the "worst" case, while others might insist that their countries are "not as bad." This project is, therefore, a regional history that should be of use to the wider scholarly community, yet it is also aimed at a general audience. I present a broad portrait of political murder in Latin America and offer a unified thesis about its causes and practices. My goal is comparative synthesis.

Many Latin Americanist scholars attest to the value of comparative history, but few actually attempt it. One explanation for this situation, as Charles Bergquist noted in his own ambitiously comparative *Labor in Latin America*, is that historians revere studies rooted deeply in primary sources, and rightly so. But this laudable preference can unfortunately reinforce a tendency toward excessively focused specialization, with contentious territorial undertones, even in an interconnected field like Latin American studies. The result is a palpable timidity regarding forays onto other people's turf. Not surprisingly, most works of history dealing with the postindependence period still revolve around the nation-state. It is also true that many "big" comparative books can have problems. Some are better at presenting lots of details and entertaining vignettes than at outlining a coherent interpretation, while others are long on interpretation but short on evidence. Both of these undesirable outcomes dissuade authors.

Finally, historians can be divided broadly by disposition into splitters and lumpers. The more extreme splitters object to overarching comparisons. They want to focus on the individual cases, separate regions, and very different countries during neatly defined periods. As with the insistence on primary documents, this healthy impulse can also be taken to absurd levels. Regional history is more unwieldy, to be sure, but Mexico, Colombia, Peru, Argentina, Brazil, etc., are themselves large, complex, culturally and regionally diverse nations. Given that all political boundaries are to some degree artificial constructs, should we also avoid talking about *them* as "wholes"? Another extreme that would be absurd in the present circumstance is seeing every murder and massacre as a separate, unique, atomized occurrence, unrelated and uncomparable. Certainly the timing, scale, or intensity of political murder is tied to the individual political story of a country or one of its regions. The details and context matter. But even giving the splitters their due, we can recognize parallels and similarities. Whether consistent or sporadic, recourse to political murder across the region reveals a broader phenomenon. Countries with intense histories of political murder turn out to be examples of a larger experience rather than exceptional cases. The splitters love monographs on narrow topics. So, in fact, do lumpers, but they see them as building blocks, and believe that we should use them to construct larger interpretive structures (ones that can stand straight and true, of course).

I should also note that despite the importance of political murder, and my own fascination with the topic, I feel a certain trepidation about writing such a book as this one. A real danger exists that readers with little or no personal experience of Latin America will come away with an unduly negative image of the region, or have old stereotypes reinforced. This problem came up the first time I taught this material to undergraduates, at the University of South Carolina at Columbia, where no one in that particular class had ever traveled in the region. Subsequent classes at Hampden-Sydney College and Washington and Lee University confirmed my fear that people who have not been to Latin America are more likely to develop a negative impression, though I should also point out that these were all popular classes, and students from each expressed desires to go there when the courses were completed.

The compelling beauty of Latin America's varied locales and the hospitality of its peoples are widely acknowledged, and I've spent a big chunk of my adult life wandering there in the years since 1980. Many Latin Americanists began as I did, when they traveled in the region as young people. So as I worked on this project, I liked to remind anyone who would listen that in Latin America most people, most of the time, do not witness or experience overt political murder. Yet when I remembered those young men on the Circunvalar, and considered that most Latin Americans have *some* firsthand experience of political murder, I pressed on with the task. Though I would like to look away, as many good people there do much of the time, I can't escape a basic fact: in the twentieth century, to differing degrees, the phenomenon was nearly ubiquitous, and it has yet to disappear. We should also remember that millions of Latin Americans constantly and heroically resist all forms of political repression, and to appreciate their struggle, we must understand what they are up against.

In the spirit of full disclosure, I acknowledge that for several years I served as a Colombia country specialist for Amnesty International USA. I was, however, already fully immersed in the study of political murder when I started volunteering for them. Also, for many years I was a Senior Research Fellow with the Council on Hemispheric Affairs (COHA) in Washington, D.C., editorializing periodically about human rights issues. Be that as it may, this is not an "activist" book. For sure, I hope activists will read it. I also wouldn't be unhappy if others who read it started thinking along activist lines. I believe there is a point to telling this story, beyond academic history. But I also want to get the story right, no matter where it takes me, and regardless of whether or not human rights activists agree with all my conclusions.

This is an enormous topic, spread over a long period, touching on many countries. Thus, in an effort to avoid stupid errors and ignorant misstatements, I asked many people for feedback over the course of several years, and a good number of them responded generously. Darrel Hamlin long encouraged me to pursue a topic that he as a political scientist believes is both interesting and important. In an early phase of the project, Alan Knight waded through a thick swamp of possible elements and concepts I hoped to address in the study, and with a few quick strokes of his analytical machete, helped me see my way forward. At COHA, Larry Birns, Fred Mills, and Farzin Illich provided ample encouragement. Keith Sprouse presided over uncounted sessions of "porch stog therapy" to let me think out loud (at times repetitively and rather obsessively) about the job at hand. Sarah Hardy reminded me of the relevance of Carolyn Forché's work, and listened to more than her share of my sometimes graphic reflections on political murder. Jamie Sanders, Jane Rausch, Victoria Sanford, Geoff Jensen, Ken Lehman, Nicole Greenspan, Mark Drumbl, David Bello, Jon Eastwood, Roxann Prazniak, Bill Cooper, Leah Carroll, Hendrik Kraay, Thomas Fischer, Brian Turner, Lizardo Herrera, and SUNY's anonymous readers read part or all of various versions of the manuscript and provided invaluable insight and very constructive criticism. My older sister, Kelly Green, served as frontline editor and "educated general reader" sounding board. Arif Dirlik, as series editor, gave generous and insightful feedback, guidance, critique and encouragement. Finally, my wife and fellow Latin Americanist Jana DeJong, who was with me on that November hike in 1991, endured the most intimate relationship with my intellectual journey through a very dark land, and somehow didn't kick me out of the house. For that, and much more, I thank her.

I benefited enormously from a residential fellowship at the Virginia Foundation for the Humanities in Charlottesville. The VFH is not just a good place to work but also a place full of helpful people. Thanks to the comments, suggestions, and critiques offered by the other fellows and staff, the material truly coalesced while I was working there. I should note as well that I gained a great deal from presenting portions of the work at various conferences and forums. These included a talk at the Center for the Study of Democracy, St. Mary's College of Maryland; a paper at the Cultural Studies Colloquium, Washington and Lee University; a talk at the symposium "Nicaragua: Insurrection and Revolution," Hampden-Sydney College; a talk at the Fundación Global Democracia y Desarrollo FUNGLODE, Santo Domingo, Dominican Republic; a paper at the XVI Congreso de la Asociación de Colombianistas; a paper at the symposium "Mataron a Gaitán" 60 Años, Universidad Nacional de Colombia, Bogotá; a talk at the Biblioteca El Tintal Manuel Zapata Olivella, Bogotá, Colombia; a training session for Department of Homeland Security asylum attorneys regarding Colombia, Manhattan Office, Federal Plaza; a training session for Department of Homeland Security asylum officers regarding Colombia, Newark Office; a brown-bag presentation at the Latin American Studies Program of the University of South Carolina at Columbia; and a paper at the Georgia Political Science Association Conference in Savannah, Georgia. For everyone involved in these presentations, I have nothing but gratitude.

And as much as I would like to avoid the blame for any errors, oversights, or boneheaded analysis, I must bow to the inevitable and embrace them all.

Mexico and Central America
Mexico
Mexico City
Cuba
Havana
Dominican Republic
Santo Domingo
Haiti
Port-au-Prince
Belize
Belmopan
Honduras
Tegucigalpa
Guatemala
Guatemala City
El Salvador
San Salvador
Nicaragua
Managua
Panama
Panama City
Costa Rica
San Jose

South America
Venezuela
Caracas
Guyana
Georgetown
Suriname
Paramaribo
French Guiana
Cayenne
Colombia
Bogota
Ecuador
Quito
Peru
Lima
Brazil
Brasilia
Bolivia
La Paz
Paraguay
Asuncion
Chile
Santiago
Uruguay
Montevideo
Argentina
Buenos Aires

Key Terms and Acronyms by Country

Argentina

AAA—*Alianza Anticomunista Argentina* (Argentine Anticommunist Alliance), more commonly known as the *Triple A*

Asociación Madres de Plaza de Mayo—The Mothers of the Plaza de Mayo, which expanded with a sister organization, the *Asociación Civil Abuelas de Plaza de Mayo* (The Grandmothers of the Plaza de Mayo)

Campo de Mayo—Army base also known as *El Campito*, the organizational point of the Army's intelligence task forces

El Cordobazo—Uprising in the city of Córboba in 1969

Desaparecidos—The Disappeared, from the verb *desaparecer*

ERP—*Ejército Revolucionario de Pueblo* (People's Revolutionary Army)

ESMA—*Escuela Superior de Mecánica de la Armada* (Naval Petty-Officers School of Mechanics), the focal point of the Navy's dirty war activity and a notorious torture center

Ezeiza Massacre of 1973

Grupos de Tarea—Task forces, also known as GTs

Guerra Sucia—Dirty War, the term used by the Argentine military to describe their "struggle against subversion"

Junta Militar—Military government led by representatives of the different branches of the armed forces

Liga Patriótica—Patriotic League, 1919

La Mazorca—"The Ear of Corn," the armed branch of the *Sociedad Popular Restauradora* in the 1830s and 1840s

Los Montoneros—The armed movement of the Peronista left-wing youth movement

Nunca Más—Never Again, a title used by various truth commission reports in various countries

Peronismo—Popular name of the *Partido Justicialista* founded by Juan Domingo Perón

El Proceso—The short version of *Proceso de Reorganización Nacional* (Process of National Reorganization), the official designation for the period of military rule from the coup of 1976 until 1983

BOLIVIA

Banzerato—Term designating the period of dictatorial rule by General Hugo Banzer (1971–1978)

COB—*Central Obrera Boliviana* (Bolivian Labor Central)

DIN—*Departamento de Investigación Nacional* (Department of National Investigation)

Falange Socialista Boliviana—Bolivian Socialist Falange

Massacre of Tolata—Also known as the Massacre of the Valley of 1974

MIR—*Movimiento de Izquierda Revolucionaria* (Movement of the Revolutionary Left)

MNR—*Movimiento Nacionalista Revolucionario* (Revolutionary Nationalist Movement)

Revolution of 1952

SES—*Servicio Especial de Seguridad* (Special Security Service)

BRAZIL

CIE—*Centro de Informaçoes de Exército* (Army Information Center)

CNS—*Conselho Nacional de Segurança* (National Security Council)

Os Coronéis—The Colonels, regional elites and local political bosses in late nineteenth and early twentieth centuries

EM—*Esquadrão Motorizada* (motorized police), also short for *Esquadrão da Morte* (death squad)

Estado Novo—New State of Getúlio Vargas (1937–1945)

GDE—*Grupo de Diligencias Especiais* (Special Diligence Group)

Getulismo—Political movement of Getúlio Vargas

GOE—*Grupo de Operações Especiaís* (Special Operations Group)

Os Homens de Ouro—The Men of Gold

Jagunçoes—Enforcers, hired gunmen

Justiciero—Vigilante
Military Coup of 1964
Pistoleiro—Hired gunman
Polícia Especial—Special Police, also called the "Tomato Heads" because of their red berets
RONE—*Rondas Nocturnas Especiais da Polícia* (Motorized Nocturnal Civil Police)
Scuderie Detective Le Cocq—Shield of Detective Le Cocq
SNI—*Serviço Nacional de Informaçoes* (National Intelligence Service)

CHILE

La Caravana de la Muerte—The Caravan of Death
Chilean Way of Socialism—Chilean governmental policy after the 1970 election of Salvador Allende
CNI—*Central Nacional de Informacion* (National Information Center)
DINA—*Dirección de Inteligencia Nacional* (National Intelligence Directorate)
El 11 de Septiembre 1973—The 11th of September, date of the coup against Salvador Allende
Operación Cóndor—Operation Condor

COLOMBIA

ACCU—*Autodefensas Campesinas de Córdoba y Urabá* (Peasant self-defense forces of Córdoba and Urabá)
AUC—*Autodefensas Unidas de Colombia* (United Self-Defense Forces of Colombia)
Autodefensas—Self-Defense Forces, a euphemism for right-wing paramilitary groups
Las Bananeras—Banana Massacre of 1928
Bloque de Búsqueda—Search Bloc
El Bogotazo—Uprising in Bogotá and other cities beginning on April 9, 1948
Chulavitas—Conservative partisan police from the department of Boyacá during La Violencia
Contrachusmas—Conservative police "auxiliaries" from the department of Antioquia during La Violencia
CONVIVIR—Rural Vigilance Cooperatives

DAS—*Departamento Administrivo de Segurida* (Administrative Department of Security)
El 9 de Abril 1948—The 9th of April, day on which Jorge Eliécer Gaitán was murdered
ELN—*Ejército de Liberación Nacional* (Army of National Liberation)
FARC—*Fuerzas Armadas Revolucionarias de Colombia*, (Revolutionary Armed Forces of Colombia)
Gaitanismo—Political movement of Jorge Eliécer Gaitán
Hereditary Hatreds—Name for the intense rivalry between the Liberal and Conservative parties
MAS—*Muerte a Secuestradores* (death to kidnappers)
M-19—*Movimiento 19 de Abril* (19th of April Movement) Guerrilla movement that evolved into the *Alianza Democrática M-19*, a political party
Pájaros—Birds, nickname for Conservative party assassins during La Violencia
Paras—Short for *Paramilitares* (paramilitaries)
Los PEPES—*Los Perseguidos por Pablo Escobar* (People Persecuted by Pablo Escobar)
Sicarios—Drug business hired killers
UP—*Unión Patriótica* (Patriotic Union Party)
La Violencia—Period of civil war, violence, and political repression (1946–1966)

Cuba

Bay of Pigs Invasion of 1961
Cuban Revolution of 1959
Foco—Focal Point or Revolutionary Cell, referred to in Che Guevara's theory of revolution, known as *foquismo*
Movimiento 26 de Julio—26th of July Movement
Revolution for Export

Dominican Republic

El 42—"The 42" Death Squad
Frente Democrático Anticomunista y Antisubversiva—Anticommunist, Antisubversive Democratic Front, also known as *La Banda*
La Masacre del Perejil—The Parsley Massacre of 1937
SIM—*Servicio de Inteligencia Militar* (Military Intelligence Service)
Trujillato—Term designating the period of rule by General Rafael Leonidas Trujillo (1930–1961)

El Salvador

ANSESAL—*Agencia Nacional de Securidad Salvadoreñva* (Salvadoran National Security Agency)
ARENA—*Alianza Republicana Nacionalista* (National Republican Alliance)
FMLN—*Frente Farabundo Martí para la Liberación Nacional* (The Farabundo Martí National Liberation Front)
GN—*Guardia Nacional* (National Guard)
Massacre at El Mozote of 1981
La Matanza—The Slaughter of 1932
ORDEN—*Organización Democrática Nacionalista* (National Democratic Organization)
PH—*Policía de Hacienda* (Treasury Police)
PN—*Policía Nacional* (National Police)

Guatemala

EGP—*Ejército Guerrillero de los Pobres* (The Guerrilla Army of the Poor)
FAR—*Fuerzas Armandas Rebeldes* (Rebel Armed Forces)
G-2 or *Las Dos*—Military Intelligence
Guardia de Hacienda—Treasury Police
Mano Blanca—White Hand death squad
MLN—*Movimiento de Liberación Nacional* (Movement of National Liberation)
Movimiento Revolucionario de Noviembre 13—13th of November Revolutionary Movement
Operación Ceniza—Operation Ashes
Operation PBSUCCESS
ORPA—*Organización Revolucionario del Pueblo en Armas* (The Revolutionary Organization of the People in Arms)
PGT—*Partido Guatemalteco del Trabajo* (Guatemalan Communist Party)
PMA—*Policía Militar Ambulante* (Military Police)
URNG—*Unidad Revolucionaria Nacional Guatemalteca* (The Guatemalan National Revolutionary Unity)
La Violencia—Period of repression and civil war (1960s through the 1990s)

Honduras

Battalion 3-16
FUSEP—*Fuerzas de Seguridad Pública* (Public Security Forces)

Mexico

Acteal Massacre of 1997
Los Bravi—Enforcers for Profirio Díaz
Camisas Doradas—Gold Shirts
Camisas Rojas—Red Shirts
Cardenismo—Political movement of Lázaro Cárdenas
Cuerpo de Policía Auxiliar Ganadera—Auxiliary Ranch Police
Defensas Sociales—Paramilitary organizations
EZLN—*Ejército Zapatista de Liberación Nacional* (Zapatista Army of National Liberation), also known as the *Zapatistas*
Guardias Blancas—White Guards
Los Halcones—The Falcons (enforcers)
Ley de fuga—"Law of Flight," as it is often expressed in English; otherwise known as "shot trying to escape"
Mapaches—Raccoons (enforcers)
Maximato—Term designating period of rule and influence by Plutarco Eliás Calles between 1924 and 1934
Mexican Revolution of 1910
MRM—*Movimiento Revolucionario del Magistrado*a (Revolutionary Teachers Movement)
PAN—*Partido Acción Nacional* (National Action Party)
Paz y Justicia—(Peace and Justice)
PdlP—*Partido de los Pobres* (Party of the Poor)
Pistolero—Hired gunman
PNR—*Partido Nacional Revolucionario* (National Revolutionary Party)
Porfiriato—Term designating the period of rule and influence by Porfirio Díaz (1876–1911)
PRI—*Partido Revolucionario Institutional* (Institutional Revolutionary Party)
Los Rurales—National Rural Police force during the *Porfiriato*
Tlatelolco Massacre of 1968

Nicaragua

Los Contras—Popular name for the FDN *Fuerza Democrática Nicaraguense* (Nicaraguan Democratic Front) based in Honduras, and the ARDE *Alianza Revolucionaria Democrática* (Democratic Revolutionary Alliance) in Costa Rica

FSLN—*Frente Sandanista de Liberación Nacional* (Sandinista National Liberation Front) also known as *Los Sandanistas*
GN—*Guardia Nacional* (National Guard)
Legión 15 de Septimebre—Legion of the 15th of September
Revolution of 1979

Panama

Batallones de la Dignidad—Dignity Battalions
The Civic Crusade
Los Dobermans—Nickname for the Company of Public Order Police Unit
FDP—*Fuerzas de Defensa de Panamá* (Panama Defense Forces)
GN—*Guardia Nacional* (National Guard)
Operation Just Cause Invasion of 1989
Los Sapos—The Toads, Intelligence agents and thugs, also known as the F-8 death squad

Paraguay

Partido Colorado—Colorado Party
Los Pyragués—"The Hairy Feet" in Guaraní
Stronato—Term designating the military dictatorship of Alfredo Stroessner (1954–1989)
La Técnica—Popular name of the secret torture facility housed at the old *Dirección Nacional de Asuntos Técnicos* in Asunción.

Peru

Auto Coup—Self-Coup of President Alberto Fujimori 1992
APRA—*Alianza Popular Revolucionaria Americana* (American Popular Revolutionary Alliance) also known as *Aprismo*
Comités de Auto Defensa—Self-Defense Committees
Grupo Colina—Military paramilitary death squad
MRTA—*Movimiento Revolucionario Túpac Amaro* (Túpac Amaro Revolutionary Movement)
PCP—*Partido Comunista Peruana* (Peruvian Communist Party)
Sendero Luminoso—Shining Path

Uruguay

CNT—*Confederación Nacional de Trabajadores* (National Confederation of Labor)

Tupamaros—*Movimiento de Liberación Nacional* (Movement of National Liberation)

Introduction

A Political Culture of Murder

Colonel Aureliano Buendía, a central character in Gabriel García Márquez's seminal *One Hundred Years of Solitude*, led thirty-two unsuccessful rebellions in an unnamed Latin American country. He also had seventeen sons, by seventeen women, and each was named "Aureliano" followed by his mother's surname. Years after making peace with the central government, an elderly, disillusioned, and injudicious Colonel Buendía grew irritated at the influence of U.S. interests in his hometown, Macondo. He shouted in public that, "one of these days I'm going to arm my boys so we can get rid of these shitty gringos!" Over the next week, García Márquez tells us, Buendía's sons were "hunted down like rabbits by invisible criminals." One was stabbed with an icepick. Another was knocked into a boiling caldron. Most were shot. Only one, Aureliano Amador, escaped into the mountains. Decades later, near the end of the novel, the fugitive returned to Macondo to seek refuge at his father's old home. There "two policemen," who had chased Aureliano Amador "like bloodhounds across half the world," stepped out from behind some almond trees and shot him between the eyes.[1] Easily one of the most famous passages in Latin American literature, the massacre of the sons of Colonel Buendía is no whimsical exaggeration springing from García Márquez's so-called "magical realism." It evokes a very real tradition.

Political murder has served the interests of Latin America's most powerful and privileged citizens rather well. Certainly political murder was widely employed in the twentieth century, and its use shows no sign of abating in the early twenty-first. Such murder generally seeks to eliminate the bearers of ill tidings for hegemonic structures, to kill the messengers of change.[2] Naturally there are other traditions of political violence in Latin America, including struggles among political factions, revenge killings, tyrannicide, and terrorism for revolutionary purposes.[3] This study does not pretend to explain all political violence in Latin American history. It will, however, examine a virulent strain that can be found across time and throughout the region. Indeed one can safely argue that this, the most widely exercised form of political murder, has been carried out by states, elites, or their proxies, against a variety of closely related enemies. These have included the unnervingly popular leaders of mass political movements, politically minded former revolutionaries and demobilized guerrillas, pesky agitators, intellectuals, artists, journalists, academics, subversive activists and ambitious labor organizers, troublesome lawyers, prosecutors and judges, and even crusading priests and nuns. In other words, power elites aimed to purge their societies of all "bad influences," and the individuals whom they considered the cause of any social or political unrest fell into that category.[4] Important sectors of the Latin American elites simply do not want to hear their messages of change. As a result, the practice of political murder has broadened at times through the region's various "dirty wars" into the wholesale slaughter of entire categories of "subversives," mutating into the attempt to kill the rank and file as well, moving beyond killing the messengers to killing anyone who might heed their message. This book, then, is the history of a proclivity.

It is true, of course, that throughout Latin American history elites have enjoyed considerable success in maintaining nonviolent, but powerfully "hegemonic," control over their respective societies. The idea of hegemony encompasses the many subtle forms of social, cultural, ideological, and political manipulation that elites utilize, and hegemonic forces have a long record of achievement in Latin America.[5] Yet the pendulum of interpretation might have swung too far. In the valuable effort to tease out ideological subtleties, we might be in danger of downplaying the importance of more direct and obvious methods of political and social control. The brutal reality is that elites have also skillfully used homicide as a mechanism of domination. There is no denying, at any rate, that Latin America has experienced high degrees of overt repression and political murder.

Some observers might maintain, and with some justification, that cultural/ideological hegemony and political murder are ostensibly exclusive techniques, and that political murder happens when hegemony breaks down or is absent. But in Latin America, they very often seem to work together for the same end. To begin with, even the most successful systems of ideological control need occasional dollops of corrosive enforcement. At the same time, some degree of acquiescence and consent must exist in even the worst dictatorships. In his study of the Rafael Trujillo regime in the Dominican Republic, Richard Lee Turits reminds us that "numerous political philosophers from Niccolò Machiavelli to Antonio Gramsci have affirmed the need for forms of consent in all political systems."[6] Even brutal dictatorships like Trujillo's, one of the region's most notorious, could not rely exclusively on the stick. A combination of repression and degrees of consent is perhaps the most stable mix for nondemocratic regimes, though violence is at times the dominant partner.[7]

In many ways hegemony and political murder have formed a bond in Latin America that often allows elites to murder people they perceive as threats, and get away with it. Across the world, people of the establishment find opposing voices annoying or threatening. Many members of these elites would like to physically eliminate such troublemakers, but cannot do so with impunity, and thus must rely on more subtle methods to silence voices of change. It is simply the case that, in Latin America, certain elites are prone to kill, not just attack or discredit such voices. They seldom worry about creating martyrs since the institutions that could punish such blatant abuses of power have historically been absent or weak. Consequently, power can be exercised much more nakedly. The complicated interactions of hegemony are in play, but political murder is a viable option, and for many in the elite, it is the first choice.

This relationship between hegemony and political murder brings the role of the state to center stage. Many students of political violence in Latin America generally credit states with carrying out most if not all political murders. They focus on the "regime of terror organized by those who are already in control of institutions of power."[8] Taking a global view, R.J. Rummel argued that when governments acquire absolute power, "state murder" will follow. He noted that millions of people were killed by governments in the twentieth century, which endured "a plague of power, not germs," and that "the more power a government has the more it can act arbitrarily according to the whims and desires of the elite."[9] Some students of violence, however, have questioned whether all this murder is the result of rampant power. Raymond Duvall, Michael Stohl, and Ted Robert Gurr all employ some variation on the "weak state" hypothesis to explain why death squads are deployed. But whether the state is weak or strong, political murder can be tricky and costly to use. Miles Wolpin has argued that death squads "are particularly likely to be employed against strong, urban-based opposition groups and where deniability is considered necessary for domestic and/or international reasons."[10] Unfortunately for elite interests, Bruce Campbell has pointed out problems with "plausible deniability," which "can hardly be maintained domestically for long, if it even works at all." Internationally, many observers in foreign governments, NGOs, and news outlets are difficult to fool. Though "states wishing to use extreme forms of extralegal violence thus have every reason to appear uninvolved," in the end, "the charade doesn't usually last very long,"[11] even if some states seem to believe that it lasts long enough for their general purposes.

There is also the question of what kind of a state is in power. Ted Robert Gurr stresses that "democratic values and traditions" inhibit violence.[12] Perhaps this is so, though almost all Latin American states have used political murder from time to time—not just military dictatorships, but also democracies. It is true that in Latin America it has been the more authoritarian states and societies that were prone to a continuing reliance on political murder, yet at times what some observers might call the "façade" of democracy allows for the use of murder in ways not open to dictatorships. It is hidden in plain sight, yet there are fewer obvious targets for protest. Governments can claim ignorance, or an inability to stop it. Deploying the paramilitary model of diffuse groups is in this sense an advance over direct state repression in that it makes for a much harder target for political protest. This is a dangerous game, however, because there is usually more room in democracies for messengers of change to operate. In the end, Latin American states that employ political murder can be weak or strong, democracies or dictatorships.

But to truly understand the impact of political murder, we must move beyond a fixation on "state" violence and pay more attention to elites in general, since some elites are prone to violence all on their own. This tendency is exacerbated by the fact that states themselves are hardly monolithic actors with absolute control (indeed Max Weber's idea that "the state" claims a monopoly on the legitimate use of violence is often only an aspiration). States are often fractured among branches and agencies, or along national, regional, or local lines, as William Stanley reminds us for the case of El Salvador.[13] And what is true of states is even more apparent with elites. Obviously, there are numerous factions among Latin American elites, and not all of them are given to using political murder. But a very significant subset in most countries of the region has been known to employ it. These can be called the murderous elites. They are a rather blood-thirsty Latin American branch of what C. Wright Mills indentified in 1956 as "the power elite." These included the new managerial class of executives running big U.S. corporations and seeking greater and greater levels of profit, top generals and admirals of the U.S. military (whom he called "warlords"), and high-level politicians (especially in the executive branch), all of whom had merged to dominate the economic and political establishment of the United States. Mills argued that to the degree that "national events are decided, the power elite are those who decide them."[14] Latin American elites' penchant for homicide is a variation on this theme. Tulio Halperín Donghi echoed Mills when he noted that the elements of the murderous elite, the class interests and forces behind repressive regimes in the region, include "the military hierarchy, the national economic elite, and the transnational corporations."[15]

And since not all Latin American elites participate, it is essential to create a profile of the murderous elites. At times this seems rather straightforward, as once again in the case of El Salvador, where one U.S. State Department observer characterized elites as a "bunch of murderous thugs."[16] The problem is that representatives of all elites can be found among the murderously inclined, which are like the mythological hydra. These elites are international, national, regional, local, political, economic, social, criminal, military (sometimes working for civilian elites, sometimes for themselves), and of course, "state." Decisions to murder can be made in the offices of the president, the military central command, the local headquarters of political parties, small-town mayors' offices, local army barracks, police stations, swanky cafes and social clubs, cooperate headquarters or local branch offices, and hacienda great rooms, among other places, including Washington D.C. The hydra's many heads are diverse and not particularly unified, except in their agreement about the usefulness of political murder. The murderous elites do not form a "class" in the Marxian sense, given that they have not historically shared a common relationship to the "means of production." Nor is there a global cabal of interests (e.g., international capitalism) or some continuously organized regional conspiracy behind all the political murders (though, as Operation Condor and other actions of its ilk showed, there can be plenty of coordination among Latin American countries and the United States.) Even in individual countries, there is no consistent economic class or political elite or armed representative at the root of the practice. Landed elites might have played an outsized role in the practice of political murder in Mexico, Colombia, and Central America but have not been as predominant in Argentina, Brazil, Chile, or Uruguay.[17] Perhaps the murderous elites represent more of a Weberian class, linked not only by their prestige and power, education, and social groupings (or desire to enter the highest realms thereof) but also by their take on how to defend their status. In Latin America these elites partake of a shared worldview that privileges the murder of troublesome gadflies in what can still be called, with some qualifications, a version of "class struggle."

There are two unifying elements of the elite "perp" profile. The first is a pronounced reactionary intolerance of any social, economic, or political change that will diminish their "civilizing" power relative to the "barbarous" masses. This is a key component for understanding elite attitudes toward political murder, since it was the widespread development of republican culture and democratic popular mobilization in the nineteenth century that drove repressive elites in the twentieth.[18] This is, in fact, an old tendency. For over three hundred years the Spanish and Portuguese colonial regimes encouraged elites to view their Indigenous, African, and mixed race subjects as decidedly inferior. Though Iberian colonialism justified its practices of domination with the goal of spreading Christian "civilization," elites continued to view the humanity of the subjugated inhabitants of the Americas with suspicion. Not surprisingly, from soon after independence both liberal and conservative elites "interpreted their societies in terms of a struggle between civilization and barbarism." They also tended to envision even constitutional forms of government in terms of firm authority, hierarchy, and restricted control of institutions and resources.[19] This perennial struggle of Latin American elites fighting against the "barbarism" of "los de abajo" (Spanish for the *hoi polloi* or "the great unwashed," literally, "those from below") was still quite clear in 1845 as the publication of *Facundo*, Domingo Faustino Sarmiento's classic work of history and polemic, demonstrated. Many of the same concerns were raised in even more dramatic ways during the Mexican Revolution after 1910. As the pace of change accelerated in Latin America over the course of the twentieth century, driven by industrialization, urbanization, the rise of mass politics, and population growth, elites became increasingly frightened and threatened by the barbarians at the gates.

Ultimately, all notions of change came to be considered "radical" in certain quarters. While many students of the classical age of populism, from the 1920s through the 1960s, stress its controlled and co-opted nature, elites experienced enormous anxiety over Mexican Cardenismo, Argentinean Peronismo, Peruvian Aprismo, Colombian Gaitanismo, and other movements. Even more upsetting were the overtly socialist and "revolutionary" movements, especially the Cuban Revolution of 1959, the election of Salvador Allende in Chile in 1970, the Nicaraguan Revolution of 1979, and insurgencies in Guatemala, El Salvador, Mexico, Colombia, Argentina, Peru, and other countries. These periods of popular mobilization in Latin America also generated serious concern in the United States throughout the twentieth century, but especially during the Cold War years stretching from the 1940s to the implosion of the Soviet Union.

Wedded to the murderous elites' hatred of change and fear of the rising tide of popular movements across the region during the nineteenth and twentieth centuries, therefore, is a second and also key element of their profile: an historic willingness to use violence to thwart these phenomena. The basic point is that social and political change in Latin America is sometimes violent, and sometimes not, but has typically been met with various forms of repression, especially political murder. In the twentieth century elites grew tired of trying to co-opt and contain populist movements, and were deeply afraid of violent revolutionary change. Political murder, therefore, has been about derailing these impulses toward mobilization. And, just as important, elites greatly benefited from the elimination of populist politics, a process that created expanded opportunities for capital accumulation. It is hardly surprising that elites came to encompass new violent elements, such as what Nazih Richani refers to in the Colombian case as the "narcobourgeoisie," which have made dramatic land grads displacing untold thousands of smallholders over several decades.[20]

So while Latin America has significant traditions of popular mobilization, these are mirrored by practices of repression that date to its Colonial origins. Latin America elites in the modern period have used violence to suppress voices of change, whatever the effect on political structures.[21] Dirk Kruijt and Kees Koonings have noted that "pro-status quo social movements and political parties have been setting up armed groups throughout the past century." These endeavors were typically "backed by economic elites for whom armed groups served to defend property, to repress social protests or to carve out space in (local) political arenas."[22] Marcia Esparza contends that societies plagued by deep divisions, often the consequence of colonialism, "offer the necessary conditions" for repressive methods. Political murder on the grand scale, she argues, results from conscious decisions made by elites (state and nonstate, one should add) who want to protect their control of resources.[23] Indeed, many Latin American elites have often been happy to dispense with democratic structures. As Luis Roniger argues, "the breakdown of civilian rule" in the second half of the twentieth century largely resulted from "the lack of democratic conviction" among significant portions of the elite.[24] Finally, Patrice McSherry argues that Latin American militaries "overthrew civilian governments and destroyed other centers of democratic power in their societies (parties, unions, universities, and constitutional sectors of the armed forces) precisely when the class orientation of the state was about to change or was in the process of change, shifting power to non-elite social sectors. Preventing such transformations of the state was a key objective of Latin American elites."[25] And this has long been the case.

For the murderous elites, then, containing popular political impulses is about combat, organized conflict, and class struggle. Many do not want to share, and they are aware of their options. As E.V. Walter pointed out in 1969, elites often eliminate individuals who pose threats to their control, and this use of terror is also designed to intimidate those sectors of the broader society who would welcome change.[26] David Mason and Dale Krane have asserted that political murder (in the form of death squads) is "most prevalent in societies where an authoritarian alliance between the military and powerful economic elite is faced with a serious challenge to its legitimacy and authority. What the ruling elite fear most is an opposition movement that can mobilize the rural and urban poor behind efforts to redistribute political power and economic resources."[27] But these threats are not always violent, and the regimes are not always authoritarian and military, and indeed, are often fairly secure. On a continuum, it can be said that Mexico (during the late Porfiriato), Guatemala, El Salvador, and Nicaragua (under the Somozas) were more threatened by popular and revolutionary forces than Mexico (under the PRI), Colombia, Argentina, or Brazil; in Chile the threat was electoral. But in all these places (and times), elites still believed in political murder. In Latin America, political murder is often the default mode for some elites, used for all threats, big or small. With considerable insight, Krujit and Koonings note that "Latin America's political culture is characterized by its roughness."[28]

In fact, the ever-present counterrevolutionary impulse against both popular politics and revolutionary movements provides evidence of a historically ingrained political culture of murder in Latin America. The murderous elites have repeatedly demonstrated its existence when they directed their attention to social, political, and economic threats from below. The widespread use of political murder under both "authoritarian" and "democratic" regimes seems to imply a deeper process, an enforcement mechanism that forms a part of the inherent logic of hegemony in the Americas.[29] While not detached from regional differences or the contingencies of any historical moment, this propensity to kill troublemakers continued throughout much of modern Latin American history. Of course Latin American countries have different societies and economies, and varying relationships with the United States, so some other variable seems to be at work. Elites in other parts of the world and at other times have practiced political murder, but its ubiquity in Latin America calls out for examination. If one rules out simplistic and even racist assertions about their "character," and avoids recreating them with similar takes on the "nature" of their societies, there is still this glaring and undeniably high incidence of political murder in Latin America. Ultimately, one returns to questions of power, elite struggles against popular threats, and to the political culture of murder.

Many historians and social scientists regard the concept of "culture" as amorphous and problematically vague, the font of many dubious claims, and perhaps more trouble than it is worth. Latin Americanists have produced many thoughtful arguments about the benefits and drawbacks of the cultural analysis of political phenomena, and have yet to reach a consensus.[30] Despite the potential interpretive conundrum that recognizing them creates, however, similar cultural processes clearly stretch across various societies, especially related ones. Clifford Geertz defined culture "as a set of control mechanisms—plans, recipes, rules, instructions (what computer engineers call 'programs')—for the governing of behavior."[31] Culture dictates what is "obvious" and "natural," and is usually invisible to and unquestioned by its adherents. In a process that parallels dynamics, as noted by Thomas S. Kuhn in his study of scientific communities, the murderous elites created a cultural "paradigm," or "matrix," of likeminded individuals.[32]Finally, in one of its more extreme formulations, cultural interconnectedness has been described in terms of a "meme" (a word coined by Richard Dawkins to sound like "gene,") a unit of cultural transmission, imitation, and reproduction, a self-replicating cultural belief, idea, or practice. These cultural units can be transmitted from one individual or group to another, and reflect the spread of behaviors.[33]

Critics of Dawkins' "meme" object to the idea of a "discrete unit" of culture, pronouncing the notion as too simplistic, one dimensional, reductionist, and mechanistic. They have a point. And regarding political murder, it is not just an "idea" or a "self-replicating pattern of information" but a whole set of assumptions, practices, and variations on a theme. Yet in its diffusion across Latin America, the political culture of murder does have some meme-like qualities. Certainly the connections between culture and political violence have not gone unnoticed. Aldo Lauria-Santiago has argued that we should "pose deeper questions about the contradictory contexts from which state violence emerges, the assumptions and origins of the agents of violence," and, one can add, its backers. The goal should be to understand how political violence "is mediated by ideological and cultural constructs."[34] To this end, in linking "violence to broader considerations about Mexican politics and society in the revolutionary period," Alan Knight looked to Pierre Bourdieu's usage of "habitus," which "denotes a historically determined set of assumptions and practices governing social life, which do not require conscious direction or awareness, which fix the parameters of what is normal, 'reasonable,' and 'common-sensical.' " He used Bourdieu's "habitus" (others might use the word "culture") as "a convenient shorthand denoting the bundle of practices and assumptions characteristic of Mexico in the 1920s and 30s." To be sure, there was not a single, homogenous political culture. Yet there were "common characteristics shared by much of Mexico, one of them being a sad familiarity with political violence," an experience found in "developed" regions as well as rural back waters.[35]Knight could also be speaking of the rest of Latin America, virtually all of which has demonstrated these characteristics at various times.

The political culture of murder, then, is not a static, immutable, universal presence in the region. It is subject to expediency and happenstance. Yet it clearly reflects the obstinate elite inclination to hold onto political and economic power at all costs. It is this single-minded focus that drives the practice and causes it to loom so large in the broader political culture.[36] As a consequence, the rise of democracy can supercharge elite fears and drive the use of political murder. And Latin America is not an anomaly in this regard. There are abundant classical and historical precedents of elites resisting the rise of real or potential popular mobilizations with murder. In Athens, the democratic reformer Ephialtes "was the victim of patrician wrath, engendered by anti-aristocratic reforms." His murderers "almost certainly acted on behalf of the secret societies of oligharchs." In Sparta, the necessary route to full citizenship and membership in the hoplite battle line was a period spent living off the land and murdering individuals among the subject population of Helots, a practice meant to maintain Spartan domination. And one should also mention the murders of the Gracchi, Tiberius Sempronius, and Gaius Sempronius Gracchus, "Tribunes of the People" in the late Roman Republic. In their cases, murdered as they were for advocating various reforms, the reactionary Roman Senators themselves did the deed, showing the way for countless generations of murderous elites.[37]

A final important issue that should be mentioned at the outset concerns the relationship of guerrilla war to political murder in Latin America. Ted Robert Gurr argues that it is often "the existence of a class, group, or party that the ruling elite see as a threat to its continued rule" that makes the elite prone to use death squads.[38] It is also true that death squads and political murder are "intrinsic to internal warfare" against armed opposition and guerrilla movements.[39] There is an obvious connection between the existence of guerrilla movements and the use of political murder in Latin America, but it is not necessary or automatic. Certainly in many cases political murder was used to crush insurgencies, and then its practice spilled over into broader use. Yet while the existence of guerrilla movements facilitated extensive reliance on political murder, they did not make it inevitable. Nor does if follow that if no guerrilla threat exists there will be no political murder. At various points, peaceful political mobilizations were crushed by the murder of their leaders and supporters. And, in fact, the demobilization of guerrillas can drive the practice of dirty war, as Mauricio Romero has argued in the case of Colombia, where various efforts to include former guerrillas in politics have led to heightened use of political murder.[40] Finally, it is also well established that many people who are clearly not guerrillas get killed, often before there are insurgent movements in their regions. And their murders then help generate and sustain guerrilla movements. In such cases, political murder drives the creation of guerrilla movements, not vice versa.

The presence of guerrilla movements is, assuredly, a great justification to use murder, and also allows elites to intentionally blur the lines between guerrillas/insurgents and civilians (who might or might not be supporting them). Yet there is not always a clear arrow of causality running from the existence of guerrillas to the use of political murder. In the end, the reason that some Latin American elites embraced political murder was not the existence of guerrilla movements but rather the political culture of murder. As Edelberto Torres-Rivas has pointed out, terrorism of the state (or, again, one can add, of nonstate elites) "was not a merely contingent phenomenon directly produced by popular insurgency; rather it arose out of a long established tradition."[41]

The distinguished French sociologist Daniel Pécaut has thrown up his hands and argued that no real political content remains in the lingering regime of violence that plagues Colombia, the unnamed homeland of Colonel Aureliano Buendía. Instead he portrays a "banality of violence" so generalized and diverse that political patterns and motivations are no longer discernible. Similar arguments have been made for Mexico and El Salvador.[42] Yet as a history of Latin American politics through the prism of political murder, this study will demonstrate that ample violence in the region still conforms to patterns of elite repression against popular movements. In fact, it is important to remember that the political culture of murder developed as a reaction to the many widespread and powerful popular mobilizations that occurred throughout the region during the nineteenth and twentieth centuries. Latin American political history has witnessed elites flipping back and forth between first attempting to violently crush egalitarian and democratic impulses from below, and then striving to co-opt, control, and indirectly repress them. The point is, there simply would not be a reactionary political culture of murder if there were not also a profoundly democratic and popular impulse for political mobilization among the common peoples of Latin America. Returning to the fictional sons of Colonel Buendía, it is important to stress what they represent: the spirit of rebellion and potential for popular mobilization that many elites hate, fear, and all-too-commonly confront with murderous violence.

Political murder and violent repression, sanctioned by the state (and/or by elites) and targeting agents of transformation, has been an undeniably consistent phenomenon across Latin America. Despite diversity of countries, cultures, and societies, murderous elites around the region have demonstrated a similar inclination to murder messengers of change that threaten the status quo of hierarchy, authority, and wealth distribution (or even elite visions for the future that naturally provide little space for assertive popular classes). To this end, the killing has in many cases extended to the audience for the messages of change. Whether carried out by direct representatives of the central state, thinly veiled surrogates, defiant regional leaders, or other groups wielding power, murders, assassinations, disappearances, and bloody massacres evolved together into the preferred, often default, set of instruments that a significant portion of Latin America's elites would take out of their tool kit to deal with popular threats to their hegemony. The political culture of murder that drives the phenomenon (that is, the package of assumptions, attitudes, and practices of deadly force generated by the widespread elite reactionary antagonism toward any change that could reduce their degree of political and economic control) offers a useful window for viewing the general political cultures of Latin America in the twentieth century. The murderous elites that partake of this cultural paradigm are united around the region and across time by their agreement that political murder, used in conjunction with more conventional methods of hegemonic control, is an indispensable and effective tool of power.

The book is arranged in two main parts, with a supplemental third section provided as an appendix.

Part I explores the practice of political murder. To this end, Chapter 1 examines the victims, namely, who gets killed (as a matter of course) and why. The similarities between victims through time and across Latin America definitively tie the phenomenon of political murder together as a regional trend. Chapter 2 lays out the mechanics of individual assassination and mass-directed dirty war. While the victims are consistent across the region, the practice of political murder has been as varied as the different countries themselves. Each country or period has its own styles and methods—its own particular route to the common destination of killing the messengers of change. There are, however, clear and recurring patterns. Chapter 3 focuses on the victims' bodies. Killing thousands of people has many physical implications. The corpses literally begin to pile up. How each national or regional elite has dealt with this problem is instructive. Bodies, and their ultimate resting places and conditions, were and remain an important symbolic element of the practice of political murder.

Part II addresses the justifications for political murder, the associations among those individuals and nations that practice it, and finally its legacies around the region and around the world. Chapter 4 allows dirty warriors to speak for themselves. The practitioners of political murder tend to be proud of their work, but even when they are not, they have not proven reluctant to talk about it. The chapter examines the justifications for dirty war, and thoughts about its practice, as expressed by generals, regional elites, paramilitary commanders, and other apologists. Chapter 5 examines the networks of regional cooperation. Such arrangements do not imply an organized conspiracy of Latin American elites, but the networks of cooperation created by Latin American governments strongly indicate that many members of the various elites have long been in basic agreement about the general usefulness of political murder. The chapter also considers the role played by the United States, and explores the idea that the elites of Latin America do not need the Gringos (or Yankees, depending on how far south one goes) to show them how to kill and disappear their "subversives." Many studies begin with the assumption, implicitly or explicitly, that U.S. government and corporate interests are the driving force behind the practice of political murder in Latin America. In fact, the United States has not followed a consistent policy. But just because the United States is not the root of all political evil in Latin America does not mean that it is off the hook; for a country that sees itself as a paragon of democratic virtue and an example to the rest of the world, the U.S.'s record is problematic. Chapter 6 rounds out the study by considering the current state of the political murderer's art in Latin America, and where the different countries seem to be headed. The chapter turns to the effects that political murders have had on Latin American societies, in particular on their political institutions, and to the wide range of popular responses. Differing degrees of lingering impunity have created a continuum from Guatemala, El Salvador, and Colombia, through Mexico and Brazil, and on to Chile and Argentina. The chapter also examines the impact of human rights groups, campaigns, and the evolution of international law. To conclude, the chapter explores the prospects for continued use of political murder, while putting it in a global context.

Finally, readers will find an appendix that breaks with the thematic structure of the book and provides a country-by-country overview. No master narrative of political murder exists for Latin America. Each country has its own history of the practice, some with long traditions and others with standout moments or passing flare-ups. Assembled together, however, these individual histories produce a colossal and integrated mosaic that tells a consistent story, and reinforces arguments made in Parts I and II. What is more, without a parallel series of narratives laying out the general details of each country's experience, and the different political contexts in which similar political murders were committed, some readers might end up with a hopeless jumble of ungrounded and uncontextualized impressions. And while these narratives lay out the general history of political murder in seventeen countries that have significant traditions (only presenting the big picture for each nation), their level of detail might seem rather daunting for readers unfamiliar with modern Latin American history. Readers can, therefore, approach the appendix in different ways. They can look on it as a high hill to climb at the beginning of the journey, from which they can see their meandering trail laid out before them. Or they can go around it and plunge into the network of thematic chapters, returning to the overview at the end of the trek, or at various points along the way.

PART I

The Practice of Political Murder in Latin America

CHAPTER 1

TARGETS AND VICTIMS

His dance of death was famous. In 1463, Bernt Notke painted a life-sized, thirty-meter-long "Totentanz" that snaked around the chapel walls of the Marienkirche in Lübeck, the picturesque port town outside Hamburg in northern Germany. Individuals covering the entire medieval social spectrum were represented, ranging from the Pope, the Emperor and Empress, and a King, followed by (among others) a duke, an abbot, a nobleman, a merchant, a maiden, a peasant, and even an infant. All danced reluctantly with grinning images of the reaper in his inexorable procession. Today only photos remain. Allied bombers destroyed the church during World War II.

If Notke were somehow transported to Latin America five hundred years later to produce a new version, he would find no less diverse a group to portray: a popular politician, Jorge Eliécer Gaitán, shot down on a main thoroughfare in Bogotá; a churchman, Archbishop Oscar Romero, murdered while celebrating mass in San Salvador; a revolutionary, Che Guevara, summarily executed after his surrender to the Bolivian army; journalists Rodolfo Walsh and Irma Flaquer, disappeared in Argentina and Guatemala; an activist lawyer and nun, Digna Ochoa, murdered in her office for defending human rights in Mexico; a soldier, General Carlos Prats, murdered in exile for standing up for democratic government in Chile; a pioneering human rights organizer, Azucena Villaflor, disappeared from in front of her home in Buenos Aires never to be seen again. They could all dance together, these and many other messengers of change cut down by this modern plague. We can imagine them all linked hand in hand—hundreds of thousands of victims—gyrating in a seemingly endless political dance of death, threading its way through modern Latin American history. And reminiscent of the Black Death, political murder in Latin America does not discriminate. Expanding beyond the leaders of popular movements, it will take all those deemed sufficiently subversive, threatening, or prone to challenge the status quo. But even they will not satisfy its appetite. Peasants trying to stay clear of conflict, children anywhere, and the elderly—all these have been its victims. At its most extreme, political murder in Latin America avoids nuance and fine distinctions, erring on the side of excess. When in doubt, kill them all. As a military intelligence operative in Guatemala explained, spontaneous, chain-reaction killings are often necessary: "I am an element of the government and I am seen abducting someone, and [a witness] later recognizes me and shouts out, 'He's the one! He's the one!' Well, that person, very prudently, very cautiously, must be eliminated."[1]

And yet, patterns can be discerned. The similarities among victims through time and across Latin America make the case most strikingly that something rather generalized is going on. In country after country, the same kinds of people have been marked for death.[2] This is Latin America's grand tradition of political murder. The sampling presented here must necessarily be a humble slice of the overall number of people killed, but even at that, the patterns jump out. Quoting from Amnesty International reports, Jeffrey Sluka noted that "year after year" victims of political murder turn out to be "government opponents, members of ethnic and religious groups, and civilians living in areas of military operations." Groups lumped in as "terrorists" and "subversives" (those guilty of "any activity or idea that challenges the status quo") usually include "clergy, labor organizers or trade unionists, human rights activists, indigenous peoples and minorities asserting their rights, teachers, students, health and social workers, journalists, and so on." The typical target of death squad activities, as one U.S. diplomat put it in 1984, "is anybody with an idea in his head." Expansion of the victim category in "social cleansing" operations to "undesirables" (that is, homeless people, street kids, drug addicts, squatters, prostitutes, homosexuals) was evident in Guatemala, Argentina, Brazil, Colombia, Mexico, and other countries.[3] Likewise, David Mason and Dale Krane have noted that the targets of death squads tend to be leaders of opposition parties or movements, rank and file of said opposition, and random members of the public. This highlights for all to see that alliance with the opposition is dangerous.[4]

There is indeed wide, wide agreement on this point in the broad literature on political violence in Latin America. The types of people targeted for political murder are astonishingly consistent. In fact, they quickly become numbingly familiar. And while in most cases investigators focus on individual countries, we can easily connect the dots of a larger pattern that ties the region together.

People caught in the net of El Proceso in Argentina naturally included anyone suspected of sympathizing with the guerrillas, but also anyone unlucky enough to have his or her name in the wrong address book. Journalists were especially targeted, of course, but so also were doctors and social workers who ventured into suspect neighborhoods, as well as lawyers filing writs of habeas corpus.[5] Alan Knight noted that the Mexican PRI used a good deal of violence against "dissident political groups . . . independent unions . . . journalists . . . students . . . and, pervasively and endemically, against peasants, both individually and collectively." He was echoed by Julie Mazzei, who avowed that "individuals and groups who threaten the dominance of the PRI and the traditional, regionalized political system" were most likely to be targeted by paramilitary groups in Chiapas.[6] Kees Koonings examined victims of repression in Brazil, noting that those murdered included "not only the (known) perpetrators of armed opposition" but also members of "a wide range of political and social organizations" who might be deemed a threat to "national security."[7] Joan Kruckewitt characterized people disappeared in Honduras as refugees from El Salvador, students, labor leaders and union activists, secondary teachers and college professors, journalists, peasant leaders, and of course, leftists and their sympathizers. Americas Watch agreed, observing that the victims included anyone suspected of supporting guerrillas, the political left, students, union members, attorneys defending political prisoners, and activists working for land reform.[8] Abderrahman Beggar showed that Peruvian state and paramilitary forces targeted "intellectuals, unionists, journalists, professors, students, and peasants."[9] Examining the victims of political murder in Colombia, Jasmin Hristov noted the "selective assassination" of "members of social movements and human rights organizations . . . educators, academics, and students . . . politicians and journalists," as well as the social cleansing of "disposables" (desechables.)[10] And Piero Gleijeses, examining the Violencia in Guatemala, recognized that "journalists, university professors, priests, and men and women of the political center lost their lives. . . . They died alongside members of rural cooperatives, grassroots organizers, labor leaders, left wing students, and armed guerrillas." Tellingly, "periods of selective repression alternated with waves of greater violence."[11] The lists of comparable groups go on and on.[12]

What follows is a taste, a small, controlled tap of the keg. If the spigot were opened wide, the resulting torrent of victims would overwhelm the discussion, and require a chapter many thousands of pages long.

REVOLUTIONARIES AND FORMER GUERRILLAS

The desire to eliminate the most obvious emissaries of change—the revolutionaries, guerrillas, and insurgent leaders, those actively seeking the reordering of society through violent means—is perhaps the easiest to understand. It seems natural that elites would want them dead.

The model for dealing with this category of troublemakers was clear by the time of the Mexican Revolution. Revolutions are inevitably messy, and lots of key participants end up assassinated, for a variety of reasons. A practice emerged during the Mexican Revolution, however, that would be repeated in later conflicts throughout the region. In many ways this pattern was established, of course, with Francisco Madero, the upper-class leader of a generalized opposition to the long hegemony of the Porfiriato. After President Porfirio Díaz had been removed, Madero became president. Yet the remnants of Pofirian regime, in the person of General Victoriano Huerta, rose against Madero and murdered him, thus instigating the truly momentous stage of the revolution, from 1913 through 1917.

Madero's murder was followed by those of the "popular" leaders of the revolution. Emiliano Zapata, the quintessential popular revolutionary commander, had risen quickly at the outset of the revolution in 1910 to command the Ejército Libertador del Sur (Liberation Army of the South) in Morelos. After Diaz's defeat, Zapata pushed Madero, with little success, to implement significant land reform. Frustrated, Zapata and his followers relocated to the mountains of southern Puebla and promulgated the more radical Plan de Ayala. The Zapatistas resisted outside forces in their region with considerable bravado, taking on all comers from Huerta to Venustiano Carranza (leader of the "Constitutionalist" faction), until 1919. After helping drive the last remnants of the Porfiriato from power, Zapata fell out with the victorious Constitutionalists and refused to cooperate. Unable to eradicate the Zapatistas in battle, the Carranza government demonstrated the lengths to which it would go to engineer a successful ambush. After a feigned defection by a Carranza follower (involving a real attack on a Federal column that killed fifty-seven soldiers), Zapata agreed to a meeting on April 10, 1919, at the Hacienda de San Juan in Chinameca. He was greeted by concentrated rifle fire. After Zapata, the other most important popular leader of the revolution was Doroteo Arango Arámbula, known to history by his nom de guerre, Francisco "Pancho" Villa. As a youth, Villa led a colorful life that crisscrossed the boundaries between lawful and outlaw life. During the struggle he served Madero's forces as a resourceful guerrilla leader, and rose to command the successful Divisiòn del Norte. Villa also served as the provisional Governor of Chihuahua from 1913–1914. Though he never endorsed a revolutionary plan like Zapata's, he spoke of reform and distributed land to his troops. After being defeated by the Constitutionalists in pitched battle, and giving the U.S. General "Black Jack" Pershing fits in his redeveloped role as a guerrilla commander, Villa eventually made peace with the new president, Adolfo de la Huerta, and retired to his hacienda.

In 1923, however, the politically ambitious Villa was ambushed while riding in his open-air car.[13]

The Mexican murders were followed by those of other prominent guerrilla leaders and revolutionaries throughout the twentieth century. One important victim was Augusto "César" Sandino in Nicaragua, the illegitimate son of a well-to-do landowner. As a young man in the 1920s Sandino spent time in Honduras, Guatemala, and especially Mexico. In Mexico he imbibed a motley assortment of intellectual influences, ranging from spiritualism to communist radicalism to the revolutionary regime's homegrown ideology of *mestizaje*, which stressed the importance of the indigenous heritage in the racial and cultural mix of Latin American societies. He returned to Nicaragua in time to bootstrap his way into a position of command on the Liberal party side in the Constitutionalist War of 1926. After other Liberal leaders, pressured by the United States, signed a truce with the Conservative government in 1927, Sandino declared war on the "Colossus of the North" as "the enemy of our race" and began attacking the U.S. Marines sent to enforce the peace. Fighting in the name of "Indo-Hispanic" America, Sandino's campaign drew admiration from across Latin America, as well as from the Soviet Union and the Comintern. Though his forces often suffered at the hands of the Marines, Sandino survived and effectively resisted U.S. forces with guerrilla tactics until their withdrawal in January of 1933. Sandino vowed his loyalty to the new Nicaraguan President and disbanded his followers, in return for which he and his people were granted amnesty and control over the territory they were given to establish agricultural cooperatives. But Sandino also had political ambitions. Thus in February 1934, Anastasio Somoza García had Sandino kidnapped by the Guardia and executed. The next day the Guardia fell on Sandino's followers and massacred them.[14]

Another victim was Guadalupe Salcedo, one of the most successful Liberal guerrilla leaders of the Violencia in Colombia. Salcedo was certainly the best known of those operating in the eastern plains, or Los Llanos, between 1949 and the 1953 amnesty offered by General Gustavo Rojas Pinilla. Official repression was especially harsh in "Liberal" areas such as the Llanos. Salcedo was a cowboy and expert horseman, unsurpassed in his own environment. He developed into a master of guerrilla tactics, and was renowned for the defeat he inflicted on the army at Orocué in 1952, where he wiped out an entire column. Yet after the June 13, 1953, "golpe de opinion," in which the reunited Liberal and Conservative elites backed the new Rojas Pinilla government, Salcedo responded to the offer of a cease fire and amnesty. In September Salcedo led three hundred followers to sign a peace accord. Unfortunately, there were insufficient guarantees for the safety of demobilized Liberals (a pattern that would repeat itself). Salcedo retired to his finca, but did not cease all political activities. On June 6, 1957, he was assassinated in a Bogotá cantina in the south of the city. Surrounded by the police, he came out with his hands up. The police opened fire, killing him and his companions. Salcedo was "exploring the possibilities of coordinating guerrilla solidarity" with Liberals in the Sumapaz region when he was killed.[15]

A later example from Panama was that of Hugo Spadafora Franco. A Panamanian medical doctor, Spadafora fought with guerrilla fighters in West Africa, served as Vice-Minister of Health under the Omar Torrijos regime, and formed a group to fight the Somoza regime in neighboring Nicaragua. After the 1979 Revolution, he joined the Sandanistas, though he later went back to Panama to oppose Manuel Noriega, and publically criticized the dictator for his drug connections. Noriega's regional commander, who grabbed and tortured Spadafora, referred to him as a "rabid dog." Noriega asked him if he knew what to do with a dog with rabies. Spadafora was beheaded.[16]

But easily the most famous case was that of Ernesto "Che" Guevara. An Argentine by birth, a medical doctor, intellectual, theorist on economic, political, and military affairs, and one of the most influential guerrilla leaders in history, Guevara was among the key leaders of the Cuban revolution of 1959. But more important, he came to be associated with the idea of world revolution. Guevara spoke of creating "one, two, many Vietnams," in the effort to overburden leading capitalist states (especially the United States) and overthrow them. Perhaps even more than Fidel Castro, El Che became the most prominent embodiment of the leftist ideal of revolution in the 1960s, an advocate of armed struggle against class exploitation, and a true believer in the importance of freeing mankind's innate morality in order to create a new society. To the elites of his day, Guevara was the most dangerous messenger of change in the world. As a peripatetic medical student and young physician, Guevara witnessed the social and economic inequalities of Latin America and came to rage against the forces of "monopoly" capitalism and "imperialism." He joined Fidel Castro's band of revolutionaries as a medic but quickly became a successful guerrilla commander in his own right. After the fighting ended, Guevara served in various high-level posts in the revolutionary government, wrote memoirs and manuals on guerrilla warfare, and traveled as a diplomat with rock star status. Yet he saw his true calling as a guerrilla commander. After an unsuccessful attempt to export revolution to the Congo, he returned to Latin America to prove his "foco" theory.

The outlines of his disastrous incursion into Bolivia are well known. Guevara did not count on the effectiveness of U.S. anti-insurgent training. He also expected assistance from the Bolivia Communists, and from Cuba, none of which materialized. Thus, despite some early victories, his small force of fifty guerrillas quickly found itself outmatched by the Bolivian army, which had received training form the CIA and U.S. Army Rangers (indeed, U.S. personnel were on hand for his capture). With a large part of his force destroyed, and given his bad personal relations with the Bolivian Communist party, Guevara found himself in desperate straits by October of 1967. After an informant betrayed his location, the Bolivian army captured Guevara on October 7. They held him for two days before Bolivian President René Barrientos ordered his execution. Guevara was shot so as to appear to have died in a firefight.

Che seems to have had a death wish most of his life. From an early age he had suffered from acute asthma, and always felt near death. In a poem the young Guevara wrote in 1947, he indicated that he wanted to overcome the "destiny" of a "drowning" death, and "to die fighting." In 1952 he wrote that "I see myself being sacrificed to the authentic revolution." Che went to Bolivia to do or die, seemingly "finding death on the battlefield preferable to an agonizing death" as a Cuban bureaucrat. He told the head of the Bolivian Communist Party that "the only way I will leave is dead."[17] The murderous elites happily obliged him.

POPULAR POLITICIANS

Populist and leftist politicians who call for change, often times members of the elite who speak for the pueblo, can have almost as short a life expectancy as demobilized revolutionaries. Some have been killed under murky circumstances.[18] Yet taken together they represent a disturbing pattern; if not, then this history points to an improbable number of "lone gunmen."

Jorge Eliécer Gaitán was the pivotal political figure in Colombia during the twentieth century. He rose to political prominence as the champion of banana workers mowed down by government machine guns in Ciénaga, Magadalena on December 6, 1928.[19] Emerging from the left wing of the Liberal party, Gaitán came to embody the hopes and demands of the working- and middle-class pueblo and threaten the stable workings of the two-party system from 1928 through 1948. While some students have questioned whether Gaitán's death was the product of an actual oligarchic plot,[20] his death did show how effectively an assassination, or a whole slew of them, could derail a big political movement. Kennedyesque mysteries about "who" killed someone in Latin America are relatively rare (the case of Gaitán is one of the few) because for such murders to have political value perpetrators generally prefer for it to be widely "known" who was behind them, to discourage other such messengers of change. Obscurity can also be effective, but aficionados of political murder generally assume that "dark forces of reaction" are in play and rarely accept "single shooter" or "random act" theories.

Indeed, running for president in Colombia can be particularly dangerous. After Gaitán, the single most traumatic assassination was that of Luís Carlos Galán, a Colombian journalist turned Liberal politician. Born in 1943, his father was persecuted for being a Liberal after Gaitán's murder and moved the family to Bogotá in 1949. From his student days, Galán was politically active on the Liberal left, and was even jailed for a night as a fourteen-year-old after attending a rally against the government of General Rojas Pinilla. As a student at the Jesuit Universidad Javeriana he became a more centrist Liberal and gravitated toward journalism. After graduation in 1965, he started writing for *El Tiempo* of Bogotá, as well as the weekly *Nueva Frontera*. He often railed against the influences of the emerging drug trade, old-boy politics, and the loss of collective values. He also became involved in socially progressive Liberal politics, beginning in 1970 when President Misael Pastrana appointed him Minister of Education. He went to Italy as Colombian ambassador, served as Senator for the department of Santander, and was elected city councilman for Bogotá. He started a new faction of the Liberal party known as "Nuevo Liberalismo" and ran for president in 1982, losing to Belisario Betancur, and coming in third behind the official Liberal candidate, former president Alfonso López Michelsen. After returning to the Liberal fold in 1987, Galán became ever more popular as a result of his loud condemnations of drug traffickers and calls for their extradition to the United States. When he announced his new presidential campaign in July 1989, his popularity with voters surged. A much-concerned Pablo Escobar began a campaign of threats against Galán and his family, and finally, on August 18, 1989, Escobar's hit men shot him down before television cameras at a rally in Soacha, Cundinamarca.[21] Galán, though not much of a threat to traditional elites, nor a clear agent of change to the established status quo, nevertheless threatened newer, more violent, criminal elite sectors. And his campaign for extradition of narcos represented popular frustration with growing narco power.

What is dangerous for Liberals proved even more deadly for leftist candidates. Jaime Pardo Leal was the presidential candidate of the Unión

Patriótica in the 1986 elections. At that moment, the entire movement was being targeted by paramilitaries. He came in third, with only 4.5 percent of the vote. But even that showing was too much of a threat. On October 11, 1987, Pardo Leal was shot by a fourteen-year-old sicario with connections to the drug trade and its paramilitary wing. Bernardo Jaramillo, who took over the leadership of the UP after the murder of Pardo Leal, moved to distance the party from the FARC. He was killed in Bogotá on March 22, 1990, during his presidential campaign. A similar fate befell the dashing and charismatic leader of the M-19, Carlos Pizarro Leongómez. After periods of study at the Universidad Javeriana and the Universidad Nacional, this son of a Colombian admiral joined the FARC at age eighteen. Thereafter, because of disagreements with FARC leaders, he helped found the M-19 in 1973. He was captured by the military in 1979, and tortured. He was amnestied under Betancur in 1982, and though he returned to guerrilla struggles periodically throughout the rest of the 1980s, he also made attempts at negotiated peace. He finally helped demobilize the guerrilla movement in December 1989, and subsequently founded the new M-19 political party. As the M-19's presidential candidate, Pizarro was assassinated while traveling on a commercial flight on April 26, 1990.[22]

Of course, this was not just a Colombian phenomenon. The most famous case of murder of a political leader was that of Salvador Allende in Chile, though it should be included with qualifications. It is widely accepted that Allende likely committed suicide as the Chilean army attacked the presidential palace, but to exclude him would be letting Augosto Pinochet and his comrades off on an unreasonable technicality. In a court of law, Allende's death would be manslaughter at least, or more likely felony murder.

JOURNALISTS, ACADEMICS, INTELLECTUALS, ARTISTS, AND TEACHERS

People associated with ideas, and their transmission, are also natural targets. Isaiah Berlin spoke of the "Russian" concept of intelligentsia, in which the natural and even necessary role of the artist is to criticize the status quo. Latin American intellectuals in the twentieth century largely agreed with this view. Elites were less enamored of it.

Journalists in particular have been targeted consistently. Perhaps the best-documented murder of a journalist was that of Bill Stewart, a television reporter for ABC news. On June 20, 1979, Stewart was driving in Managua, followed by his camera crew, when they were stopped at a checkpoint by the Guardia Nacional. As his crew filmed (unnoticed by the soldiers), an officer ordered Stewart and his interpreter, Juan Espinosa, out of their vehicle. After Stewart presented his official press credentials, he was taken a few feet away and forced to lie face down on the ground. The officer put his rifle to the back of Stewart's head and fired. Then Espinosa was killed as well. The video was aired on all the major U.S. networks and around the world. It had a clear impact on the United States government's decision to openly turn against Somoza. The soldiers undoubtedly knew that Stewart was an American. Perhaps he was shot because the regime was collapsing, and the soldiers were tired, angry, and badly led, or perhaps it was because they did not appreciate (or care about) the damage the murder would inflict on government. But in all likelihood Stewart's murder was also a matter of policy.

One of the most iconic murders of a journalist was the killing of Rodolfo Walsh in Argentina. Born in 1927 of Irish descent on a farm in Rio Negro Province, Walsh studied philosophy at the University for a short time but left school to work at a wide range of odd jobs. At age eighteen he got a spot as a proofreader for a newspaper. He became a writer of detective novels but is also regarded as the father of Argentine investigative journalism. His 1957 book *Operación Masacre* probed the summary execution of Peronistas after an aborted attempt to reinstall the caudillo to power in 1956. After the Cuban revolution, Walsh became a believer in the *foquista* style of revolutionary struggle advocated by his famous countryman Che Guevara, and joined the Montoneros in 1970. On the first anniversary of the coup, March 24, 1977, Walsh published his "Open Letter from a Writer to the Military Junta," which was praised by novelist Gabriel García Márquez as "one of the jewels of universal literature." In the letter Walsh called the military out for toppling an elected government, for banning political parties, attacking labor unions, destroying industries by design (to weaken the left), freezing wages and raising prices, silencing the press, and initiating the worst wave of terror that Argentines had ever known. He attested that they had illegally detained and imprisoned thousands (putting them in concentration camps out of reach of lawyers, judges, journalists, and international observers), tortured their prisoners, and ultimately killed them. The "Triple A" death squad, he argued, was now the army, navy, and air force. The day after Walsh's open letter was published, a squad from ESMA, the Naval Mechanics School, led by Alfredo Astiz tried to kidnap him off the streets of downtown Buenos Aires. He thwarted their plan by pulling out a .22 caliber Walther PPK pistol and wounding a policeman in the group. He was killed on the spot by massive return fire. Prisoners at the ESMA later saw his bullet-riddled body, and some believe it was burned.[23]

Another of the most internationally recognized cases was that of Pedro Joaquin Chamorro in Nicaragua, a journalist, editor, and publisher of the family-owned *La Prensa*, the main opposition paper to challenge the Somoza regimes. Scion of the powerful Chamorro clan, grandson of one president and cousin or nephew to others, he began his career of vocal opposition as a law student protesting the government of Anastasio Somoza García, and was jailed temporarily in 1944. Soon thereafter *La Prensa* was closed down, and the Chamorros went to Mexico, where Pedro Joaquin studied journalism. The family eventually returned to Nicaragua and resumed publication of *La Prensa*, and with the death of his father in 1952, Pedro Joaquin became editor. He was repeatedly jailed, tortured, and eventually exiled. He participated in a failed rebellion against Luís Somoza Debayle in 1959, and was consequently imprisoned until 1969, when he took up the editorship of *La Prensa* once again. He continued the struggle against the last of the clan to hold power, Anastasio Somoza Debayle. Pushing for human rights and democracy, *La Prensa* was routinely censored. Chamorro wrote to Somoza in 1975 that he was waiting for his attack. In January of 1978 it finally came. Chamorro was killed in his car by concentrated shotgun fire.[24]

Finally, one can add other example to this hard-headed tribe, the dramatic case of Irma Flaquer in Guatemala. Flaquer was a psychologist, editor, and journalist, and the founder of Guatemala's first human rights commission (which she later disbanded in frustration). She stubbornly refused to take the hint and be silent about official connections to political repression. In her newspaper columns in *La Hora* and later in *La Nación,* she became one of the government's most high-profile critics. As an advocate for social justice and democracy she also had various connections to insurgent groups. In 1970 she survived a hand grenade attack on her car, and continued on with both her roles as public critic of the regime and a covert operative of the guerrillas. She was also beaten and shot at. Finally, on October 16, 1980, as she was driving home with her son from her grandson's birthday party (purportedly one day before she was to leave for exile in Sandinista-controlled Nicaragua), their car was boxed in by a jeep and a minivan. After firing into the car (hitting her son in the head), Flaquer's attackers dragged her into a waiting car and she was disappeared.[25]

It should be noted that the huge majority of journalists do not have connections to insurgent groups (though murderous regimes often assert such links). Just doing their job is enough to get them killed. Ironically, the murder of journalists tends not to be big news. Their deaths, like the leftover radiation of the Big Bang, form a constant background static.[26] They are regularly joined by academics, especially those who study politics and violence. Anthropologist Myrna Mack worked with some of the 1.3 million IDPs (Internally Displaced Persons) in Guatemala in the late 1980s. She was one of the few Guatemala scholars who ventured out into the countryside (foreign researchers were not as likely to be killed and could do more fieldwork). On the evening of September 11, 1990, she was waylaid as she left her office in downtown Guatemala City and stabbed 27 times by a soldier in civilian clothes. Her murder had been ordered by Col. Juan Valencia Osorio, who worked on the presidential security detail. In Guatemala in the 1980s "more than one hundred university professors and researchers were murdered." Mack once famously quipped that in the United States academics say "publish or perish," whereas in Guatemala, "if we publish, we perish."[27] Her point was valid beyond Guatemala. Hernán Henao was also an anthropologist, professor, and dean at the Universidad de Antioquia in Medellín, Colombia, who fell afoul of the wrong people. He published extensively on political violence, internally displaced people, and human rights, and was a major critic of Colombian political repression. After various death threats, he declared the university campus a "territorio de paz" (territory of peace). On May 4, 1999, two men and a woman pulled him out of a meeting, took him to a nearby room, and shot him. He was the seventh professor from the Universidad de Antioquia to be killed in ten years.[28] And there was nothing new about this phenomenon. Basque nationalist and veteran of the Spanish Civil war Jesús de Galíndez fled to the Dominican Republic in 1939. He eventually became a Trujillo critic and had to flee, once again, in 1946, to New York City. There he became a graduate student and faculty member in political science at Columbia University. He wrote a dissertation on Trujillo that was critical of his regime, with "sober and damning analysis," entitled "The Era of Trujillo." He also penned a well-known and humorous depiction of his years in the DR. On March 12, 1956, he was snatched off a subway platform, flown to the DR in a private plane, and reportedly tortured and murdered.[29]

As the Galíndez case made clear, it can be dangerous to make jokes, because the murderous elites are not known for their sense of humor. Another example was that of Jaime Garzón, a Colombian journalist, politician, and comedian whose forte was political satire. After a stint as the appointed mayor of Sumapaz (a small rural settlement connected to Bogotá), and a period of work for the Gaviria administration, Garzón began a career as a television political satirist. He was especially known for his show "Quac El Noticero" between 1995 and 1997. His characters were popular and immediately recognizable throughout Colombia. In 1998 he negotiated for the release of FARC kidnapping victims, and his success raised suspicions in certain circles. General Jorge Enrique Mora Rangel called for an investigation, and even accused Garzón of collaboration with the guerrillas. On August 13, 1999, Garzón was gunned down in front of his studio by a pair of assassins on a motorcycle (a classic Colombian method). Investigators later concluded that the hit was ordered by paramilitary leader Carlos Castaño.[30]

Church Men and Women

Church hierarchies in Latin America have been known to support the status quo and give comfort to ruling elites. Yet there have also been dissenting voices from within the Catholic Church, and these tend to be dealt with according to the general pattern.

The most famous case by far was that of Archbishop Oscar Romero in El Salvador, to whom the faithful there now often refer to as "San Romero." Romero served as a parish priest from the mid-1940s until 1966, when he was appointed as Rector to the inter-diocese seminary of San Salvador. He also became editor of the archdiocesan publication *Orientación*, and betrayed a clear conservative bent, seemingly at odds with the emerging "Liberation Theology" of the leftist priests of Latin America. It was thus understandable that his elevation to Archbishop of San Salvador in 1977 would be less than welcome to such churchmen. Yet his consciousness was ripe for raising. After the murder of his friend, left-leaning Jesuit Rutilio Grande, Romero decided that he would "have to walk the same path." Archbishop Romero began denouncing poverty and social injustice, as well as political murder, bringing him international notoriety. He also chided the United States for its role. Predictably, on March 24, 1980, the day after he delivered a sermon calling on members of the Salvadoran defense forces to act like Christians and cease carrying out repressive and murderous orders, he was himself murdered as he celebrated mass at a hospital chapel. At his funeral a week later, which brought out two hundred fifty thousand mourners and protesters, gunmen firing from government buildings (including the presidential palace) caused panic, and killed between thirty to fifty people.[31]

Romero was not the last high churchman to be killed. Cardinal Juan Jesús Posadas Ocampo, archbishop of Guadalajara, was murdered on May 24, 1993, in the parking lot of the Guadalajara International airport. Seated in his car, he was shot fourteen times. A hastily convened investigation by the PRI government concluded unconvincingly that Posadas Ocampo was "mistaken" for a drug lord in a firefight between opposing cocaine gangs. When the PRI's decades-long hold on power was broken by Vicente Fox in 2000, he immediately moved to reopen several prominent murder cases, including that of Posadas Ocampo, which had been plagued by the disappearance of documents, police interference, and death threats to prosecutors. The new investigation ruled out the drug shoot-out version of the story and proposed a new theory—that members of the Carlos Salinas administration had the Cardinal killed because of information he had uncovered regarding government links to drugs and prostitution.[32] And in Guatemala, Bishop Juan Gerardi was known for his work with indigenous communities. During the 1970s he pushed for government recognition of Mayan languages. As president of the Guatemalan Conference of Bishops, he denounced the fire and massacre at the Spanish embassy in 1980. Consequently, he traveled to Rome and was not permitted to reenter the country until 1982. In 1988 the Conference of Bishops assigned him to serve on the National Reconciliation Commission, work that helped bring about the REMHI (Recovery of Historical Memory Project), which eventually produced the report *Guatemala: Nunca Más*. The report placed the blame for most of Guatemala's political murder on the government and the army. On April 26, 1998, two days after the report's publication, Bishop Gerardi was beaten to death in the garage of his residence. Three army officers were convicted for his murder in 2008.[33]

There were also the posthumously famous church women from the United States who were murdered in El Salvador. These four women—the two Maryknoll sisters, Maura Clarke and Ita Ford, Ursuline sister Dorothy Kazel, and their lay missionary companion, Jean Donovan—became persons of interest to the Salvadoran Guardia Nacional because of their "subversive" work with destitute Salvadoran nationals. On December 2, 1980, Donovan and Kazel picked up Clarke and Ford from the airport as they returned from a Maryknoll conference in newly Sandinista Managua, Nicaragua. They were followed by plain-clothed guardsmen, who intercepted them as they left the airport. The women were driven to an isolated location, raped, beaten, and killed with automatic weapons. Their white van was left with its headlights and radio on, though it was set on fire later that evening.[34] Their deaths demonstrated that, at times, literally no one was safe. Nine years later, little had changed. During a government offensive against the FMLN at Universidad de Centro America (UCA), six prominent Jesuits were killed on November 16, 1989. These included Ignacio Ellacuría, rector of the university, and Ignacio Martín-Baro, the vice rector. They and the other priests (as well as their cook and her daughter) were murdered execution style. Though the university was in territory controlled by the government and the forces responsible wore military uniforms, the killers left a note implicating the guerrillas. It fooled no one. The Salvadoran Right had long characterized the UCA as "a hotbed of Marxist ideas," a platform for plotting guerrilla operations, and a poisonous influence on the nation's youth.[35]

Finally, there is the case of nun and human rights lawyer Digna Ochoa in Mexico. A graduate of law school in Jalapa, the capital of Veracruz, Ochoa got a job in the State Attorney General's office, though she was also a sympathizer with political opposition groups. She had the misfortune to run across a "black list" of union leaders and political dissidents. She was subsequently abducted and raped by a group of men she claimed were state police officers, but there was no investigation of the incident. Traumatized, she entered a Dominican convent from 1991 through 1999. When she returned to legal work in Mexico City, she was abducted again in August 1999. Her captors drove her around in a car and threatened her, but released her. Then in October she was abducted yet again and held overnight. The Inter-American Human Rights Court recommended her for state protection, and in 2000 she left for voluntary exile in Washington, D.C., where she received Amnesty International's "Enduring Spirit" award. In March 2001, she returned to work in Mexico City, even though the government discontinued her protective detail. She began representing political dissidents and victims of human rights violations by the Mexican army in particular. When she was killed on October 19, 2001, she was defending peasant ecologists from Guerrero. She was found in her law offices, shot twice, in the left temple (she was right-handed) and in the thigh. Originally declared a homicide, government officials later ruled her death a suicide, over vocal objections from many quarters.[36]

GENERALS, DIPLOMATS, JUDGES, AND LAWYERS

Even members of the established regime can fall prey to murderous conspiracies if they seem inclined to allow, or heaven forbid, work for change. The Chilean professional military man, Carlos Prats González, is a prime example. Graduating at the top of his class at the Chilean Military Academy, Prats was commissioned an officer in the artillery in 1935. He moved up steadily, teaching at the Academy and serving as an adjunct military attaché to the United States and as military attaché to Argentina. In 1967 Prats was given command of the III Army Division, and in 1968 was promoted to Brigade General and chief of the army staff. In 1969 he was made Division General. When coup-minded elements of the military assassinated General René Schneider, out-going president Eduardo Frei Montalva named Prats his replacement as Commander-in-Chief of the army in October 1970. Prats picked up the mantle of leadership for the "constitutionalists," as the followers of the "Schneider Doctrine" of nonpolitical interference were known. Yet Prats went further and became a clear supporter of the Allende government, serving in his cabinet in various capacities. Thus he angered both the anti-Allende forces and the constitutionalists in the armed forces. He also lost face with the officer corps after a bizarre episode in which he fired shots at a woman's car after a traffic altercation. The "Alejandrina Cox Incident" helped generate a minor coup attempt known as the "Tanquetazo," in which a column of tanks motored up to the Presidential Palace. The final straw was the public protest in front of his house by wives of his officers. These women called Prats a coward and repudiated him for failing to restore "order" to Chile. Prats resigned as both Army Commander and as Interior Minister the next day. Prats was replaced by Augusto Pinochet (believed to be loyal to Allende) just weeks before the September 11, 1973, coup. Following the coup, Prats went with his wife into voluntary exile in Buenos Aires, and set himself up as a possible head of a restored constitutional government for Chile. On September 30, 1974, he and his wife were killed by a car bomb outside their apartment by DINA agent Michael Townley.[37]

Salvador Allende's trusted lieutenant Orlando Letelier became the next recipient of Pinochet's unwelcome attention. Letelier was born in Temuco, Chile, in 1932, and as a teenager was trained as a cadet at the Chilean Military Academy. But after secondary school he opted for a legal education at the Universidad de Chile, graduating in 1954. He worked until 1959 as an analyst for the copper industry. That year he joined the Chilean Socialist Party and supported Allende's unsuccessful second bid for the presidency. As an upshot, he was fired. He moved with his family to Venezuela, becoming a copper consultant. Later he became a senior economist for the Inter-American Development Bank. After Allende was elected president in 1970, he appointed Letelier as ambassador to the United States, thanks to his years working in Washington D.C. Letelier also served as Minister of Foreign Affairs, Interior, and Defense, and given his expertise, played an important role in the expropriation of the copper industry. During the 1973 coup, he was arrested as he arrived at his office in the Defense ministry. He was imprisoned for a year and tortured repeatedly. International pressure finally secured his release, granted on the condition that he left Chile. By 1975 he had moved to Washington, D.C., where he became a senior fellow at the Institute for Policy Studies and a professor at American University. Most important, after the murder of General Prats, Letelier became the best-known critic of Pinochet's regime, and even helped scuttle several loans for Chile's military government. On September 21, 1976, Letelier and his assistant Ronni Moffitt were killed by a car bomb on Sheridan Circle, also placed by the well-traveled Michael Townley.[38]

Lawyers who try to extend the rule of law to would-be agents of change have also been considered fair game. Many have died in Guatemala. On November 26, 1970, law professor Julio Camey Herrera was killed on the streets of Guatemala City. A member of the committee studying a reportedly corrupt mining deal the government was pushing, Camey Herrera was caught up in the state of siege and suspension of constitutional guarantees. Government forces occupied the University of San Carlos, and hours later he was dead. A similar fate befell Adolfo Mijangos López, a lawyer, congressman, and well-respected intellectual who had stood openly against Carlos Castillo Armas in 1954. Though paralyzed in an accident while he was studying in Europe in 1958, he remained a force in Guatemalan politics. On January 13, 1971, he was shot in his wheelchair on a crowded street in downtown Guatemala City while onlookers watched in horror.[39] In El Salvador, Roberto D'Aubisson used his infamous television show to finger Attorney General Mario Zamora Rivas (a Christian Democrat) as an operative of the guerrillas. Zamora protested and filed a libel suit but clearly underestimated the threat against him. On February 22, 1980, while Zamora was conducting a meeting with other high-level Christian Democrats in his home, masked and armed men stormed in, separated him from the rest, and shot him in a bathroom.[40] Likewise Rodrigo Lara Bonilla, Colombian Minister of Justice under Belisario Betancur, was assassinated on April 30, 1984, by henchmen working for Pablo Escobar. Often attributed solely to the prosecution of cocaine traffickers, Lara Bonilla's murder was also driven by Betancur's ill-fated attempt to negotiate with the Colombian guerrillas.[41] In Honduras, the extrajudicial execution of "well-known attorney" Gerardo Salinas took place in front of his office in Tegucigalpa on June 6, 1980. Salinas was representing three Hondurans accused of purchasing weapons for the Salvadoran guerrillas.[42] In Peru, Manuel Febres Flores worked for the AAD (the Association of Democratic Lawyers), an organization that defended people accused of terrorist acts. Many supporters of Peru's paramilitary forces believed that the AAD was the "legal arm" of the guerrillas. Febres Flores was murdered by paramilitaries on July 28, 1988.[43]

Human Rights Activists, Labor and Community Leaders, Students

Dirty warriors take a special interest in groups that resist their program with collective forms of mobilization, whether through human rights activism, community groups, or labor organizing.

The modern incarnation of Latin American human rights activism was born in Buenos Aires's Plaza de Mayo, in front of the Casa Rosada, the seat of Argentina's executive branch. It was there that a group of mothers and grandmothers of the disappeared began their weekly protests on April 30, 1977. They wore white head scarves to symbolize the baby shawls of their missing children. Though initially viewing the Madres de Plaza de Mayo as an annoyance, the junta began to target them in late 1977, a few months after they emerged. Alfredo Astiz, a young and handsome naval officer (known later as the "blond angel of death") befriended and infiltrated Las Madres, posing as "Gustavo Niño," the supposed brother of a disappeared boy. (Astiz, who had led the team attempting to abduct Rodolfo Walsh, was also infamously responsible for the shooting of Dagmar Hagelin, a seventeen-year-old Swedish-Argentine girl). It was Astiz who selected The Madres' Vice President, Azucena Villaflor de Vicenti for abduction, scooped up in front of her home as she went to buy a newspaper. Two of the other founding members of the Madres, Maria Ponce de Bianco and Esther Balestrina de Creaga, were violently kidnapped from a meeting at the Santa Cruz church in the San Cristobál neighborhood of Buenos Aires, along with French nuns Sister Alicia Doman and Sister Léonie Dunquet and several of the Madres rank and file.[44] We can also mention another famous Argentine case, that of Augusto Vandor, the Peronista union leader. Perón doubted his loyalty (Vandor had pushed for Peronismo without Perón) and reportedly engineered his murder by the Peronist left.[45]

Guatemalan elites have also demonstrated a savage bent toward such activist groups over the years. Rogelia Cruz Martínez (a former Miss Guatemala) was murdered in 1968 for her left-wing political views. Her case was not helped by the fact that she was also the girlfriend of labor leader Leonardo Costillo Johnson.[46] By the end of 1972, most of the leaders of the Partido Guatemalteco del Trabajo (PGT) had been captured and killed. Later, in October 1978, the Ejercito Secreto Anticomunista (the Secret Anti-Communist Army), or ESA, a death squad with clear government ties, published a list of 38 opposition leaders it had marked for death. At the top of the list was Oliverio Castañeda de León, Secretary General of the University Student Association, who was gunned down after speaking at a rally, in sight of dozens of passively on-looking police. This was a signature killing, and demonstrative of the impunity with which the forces of the status quo could eliminate critics. Added to the list in 1979 were the assassinations of high-profile opposition politicians Alberto Fuentes Mohr and Manuel Argueta. By 1984, new human rights organizations began to replace the ones wiped out in the repressions of the 1970s, and these became targets of a new wave of death squad activity. Also targeted, predictably, were labor leaders and student activists. The Grupo de Apoyo Mutuo (Mutual Support Group), or GAM, a support group for the families of the disappeared established in 1984, saw its public relations director, Héctor Gómez Calito, and another "outspoken leader," María Rosario Godoy de Cuevas, both tortured and murdered. He was snatched from a bus stop in March 1985; she was kidnapped in April, along with her younger brother and two-year-old son. Their mutilated bodies were later identified.[47]

In Mexico, guerrilla, political activist, and labor organizer Rubén Jaramillo was assassinated in 1962, after many prior attempts on his life. Jaramillo had been a leader in Zapata's "Army of the South" and in the 1940s was involved in labor activism. He had organized a party, the Partido Agrario Obrero Morelense (Agrarian Labor Party of Morelos), or PAOM, and in 1943 launched a new guerrilla movement in Morelos. He was amnestied in 1944, and after he founded PAOM, ran for governor, claiming that victory had been stolen in 1945. In 1946 his followers were tortured and murdered, many believed by state Judicial Police and thugs paid by the sugar barons. He then renewed his insurgency, which lasted for years. In 1958 he took another amnesty, and in early 1960s was once again leading rural workers in land occupations. On May 23, 1962, his home was surrounded by federal troops and Judicial Police, and he and his family were taken prisoner. Later their bodies, filled with bullets, were dumped on a road near Xochicleo.[48]

In the Dominican Republic, the Mirabal sisters, known as Las Mariposas, were perhaps the most famous dissidents to defy Trujillo. Patricia Mercedes, Minerva, Maria Teresa, and Debé were products of the Dominican social and economic upper crust. Cultured, educated, married to other prominent citizens, they still expressed intense opposition to Trujillo's regime. Minerva received a law degree but was not permitted to practice after she spurned Trujillo's creepy romantic advances. She led the charge but was soon followed by her sisters. They formed a group known as the "Fourteenth of June Movement." Minerva's code name was "butterfly." She and Maria Teresa were repeatedly jailed and tortured. Three of the Mirabals' husbands were also locked up in an unsuccessful attempt to silence the sisters. On November 25, 1960, as they returned from a visit with their husbands in prison, they were stopped by Trujillo's henchmen, taken to a cane field (the traditional location in the DR for such things) and savagely beaten and strangled.[49]

Themes get repeated, and the killing can be rather extensive, as the murder of local leaders and union organizers in Colombia demonstrated. A very partial but representative list of those murdered or disappeared between

2000 and 2004 included presidents of the community action committees, presidents of peasant associations, leaders of "peace" communities, union leaders, the founder of a human rights group devoted to the families of the disappeared, and the leader of a black and indigenous women's group.[50]

Mass Slaughters

Many victims, though part of a targeted group, were killed individually, and their numbers do add up. The emotional weight of collective killing, however, can be overwhelming in comparison. Mass slaughters can be localized and quick, or spread over entire countries for years at a time. They represent the shift toward attacking the message of change through the murder of its possible audience. They express the ultimate logic of repression and dirty war in all its varieties. This killing is less focused and more indiscriminate, but no less politically motivated. Whether the victims are urban leftists in Argentina, Uruguay, or Chile, Mayan villagers in Guatemala, Communist party members or sympathizers in El Salvador, Colombian militants of Liberal and leftist movements, or potential peasant supporters of guerrilla bands, the underlying concept remains the same: people with alternative ideas about society who are considered threats to the social, economic, and political status quo must be eliminated.

Elimination is often aimed at entire political movements. In Colombia this happened first on a massive scale with the Gaitanistas in the 1940s and 1950s. History repeated itself on a smaller scale with the destruction of the UP in the 1980s and 1990s. Fidel Castaño, cocaine business associate of Pablo Escobar, invested heavily in cattle and land. He became a para leader around 1987, and "armed his own private army" to carry out "dirty war" against the UP, the political "unarmed branch of subversion." A "scorched earth" campaign treated leaders, activists, and leftist fellow travelers as supporters of subversion—the Castaños assumed all had "automatic and direct connection" to the guerrillas.[51]

Whole ethnic groups could be targeted, such as the Maya in Guatemala, with entire villages wiped out. In Guatemala, the overall numbers of victims seem more akin to those of African genocides. A representative example is the May 1978 massacre in Panzós, Alta Verapaz. In the 1970s there had been significant economic change in the area of Panzós. Campesinos were being pushed off their land to facilitate mining and increased cattle production, both of which led to land concentration. Campesinos organized to get titles to their land, and elite landowners retaliated. On May 29, seven-hundred Kekchi Indians from nearby villages walked to Panzós to present a letter of protest to the mayor. Armed men in the town hall opened fire with automatic weapons, killing men, women, and children.

The potential for Indian mobilization was not lost on the forces of the status quo, and Co-ops became prime targets. During Operation Ashes, Co-op membership rolls were used as death squad lists to facilitate the killing of the most activist Indians and leaders, and "suspected" guerrillas. Another prime example was the July 1982 massacre at Finca San Francisco in Nentón, Huehuetenango. High-ranking army officers claimed land near the finca in order to pursue lucrative ranching and hydroelectric endeavors, as well as rumored petroleum reserves. The EGP (Guerrilla Army of the Poor) was active in the area, and the army used this as a convenient excuse to accuse the campesinos of collaboration. At eleven a.m. on July 17, the army entered San Francisco and called the inhabitants into the plaza. More than three hundred were massacred, their bodies mutilated.[52]

In Argentina, El Proceso liquidated the Montoneros and the ERP (People's Revolutionary Army) and all suspected supporters. The military insisted that when fighting guerrillas you have to take out the roots as well, eliminating all supporting structures. This extended to adolescent school kids. In a famous massacre known as the Night of the Pencils, members of a high school group in the city of La Plata called the Unión de Estudiantes Secundarios (Secondary Student Union), or the UES, ranging in age from sixteen to eighteen years old, were targeted over several days beginning on September 16, 1976. Ten were abducted and held in several of the various illegal detention centers the military had created, and six were executed in January 1977, according to Pablo Díaz, one of the survivors. While a couple of the students apparently had some contact with the wider networks of the ERP and the Montoneros, the group's main activity had been its participation in protests demanding free public transportation for students. The military, however, was not inclined to take chances, even with a group of teenagers.[53]

In Guerrero, Mexico, in the early 1990s, a campesino organization, the Organización Campesina de la Sierra del Sur (OCSS; Southern Sierra Campesino Organization), agitated for credit and other agricultural aid from the government. In the wake of the Chiapas mobilization, the group faced increased government opposition and in turn became more confrontational. On June 28, 1995, a group of OCSS members was stopped at a state police roadblock at a spot known as Aguas Blancas, east of Atoyac de Alvarez. The campesinos were on their way to a rally to protest the disappearance of one of their own. The intimidating actions of the police rapidly escalated the situation. Ultimately, the police opened fire, killing seventeen. A police video of the scene seemed to provide evidence that the victims had been engaged in an armed clash with the police, but later investigation by the National Human Rights Commission concluded that state police authorities had edited the tape, and even planted evidence, namely weapons they claimed were wielded by the OCSS militants. Three of the killed were shot in the head, as if executed.[54]

Mass killings can also hide in plain sight. The slow-motion slaughter of young "criminals" by police death squads in Brazil is a case in point. The victims were "typically male, in their early twenties, and poor. They are nearly always working class, and often nonwhite."[55] Was this just about "crime," or was it the elimination of potential revolutionaries?

Words on the Lesser Tradition

Of course, some forces on the political left, especially those advocating violent revolutionary struggle, have also used political murder. They have assassinated "enemy" leaders, both civilian and military, weeded out "traitors" and rivals of various stripes, and perpetrated massacres. But there are key differences in scale and effectiveness; popular forces have not done it nearly as much nor as well.[56] A graphic image makes the point. If one were to make two stacks of bodies, first of those murdered by states and elites, and second of those murdered by revolutionaries, it is clear which would be larger—much larger. Many observers have noted the difference of scale, among them Noam Chomsky, who contrasted "the 'wholesale terror' practiced by states and 'retail terror' practiced by anti-state individuals and insurgent groups."[57] States and elites, the forces of the status quo, have historically killed the most by far. They have also had more luck with the practice.

There is a reason for this difference, with its own Darwinian logic. Political murder as a strategy does not work so well for would-be "popular" movements. The history of Latin America suggests that it is politically counterproductive, or even suicidal, for movements that claim wider appeal to use political murder. And it is clear that groups and movements that have used it were largely divorced from the necessities of the political realm. This was the case with the biggest offender, the Sendero Luminoso in Peru, the singular instance in which an insurgent group outkilled (by some reckonings) the government and its elite paramilitary allies. Enrique Obando has noted that Sendero's "brutality provoked a great rejection by the Peruvian population." The Peruvian armed forces thus "managed to achieve a certain popular support as fighters against senderista terrorism."[58] Sendero was, as a consequence, clearly unpopular when their leader "Presidente Gonzalo" was captured, and the movement largely imploded. The armed Argentine left of the 1970s also practiced assassinations and bombing, regardless of popular feelings. It was thus scarcely surprising that most Argentines were not dramatically opposed to the coup of 1976, since most people initially believed the military line that it had been carried out to "restore order." And the Colombian guerrilla army, the FARC, has long enjoyed massive amounts of cash from the narco economy, allowing it to function and survive without political popularity.[59] This dynamic was even apparent in the German parallel of the 1970s and 1980s, when the RAF (Red Army Faction) lost its Robin Hood image as it became more violent.

The point is that political murder works better for repressing popular movements than for propagating them. What is more, the so-called "forces of reaction" are better at it, so much so that using it takes the fight onto the elites' preferred battleground. It is extremely difficult to beat them at this game, especially under conditions of urban guerrilla warfare, where police forces have most of the advantages. So, seen in Darwinian terms, it is clear why the use of political murder by the left is a smaller, less successful tradition. Leftist groups that employ political murder to seek power tend to be "selected against," unless there are special circumstances that allow them to break the rules of politics, such as the FARC still enjoy.[60] The crux of this argument, however, is not concerned with left or right political divisions, exactly, though it often falls out that way. It is more about the proclivities of those in power who employ political murder in Latin America. Leftists have used it, and in the process demonstrated the breadth of the political culture of murder, though to date the Left in power (a fairly rare occurrence until recently, anyway) has not used it as often nor as much.

In Cuba, after the revolution of 1959, groups of people connected to the Fulgencio Batista regime were executed, fifteen to seventeen thousand, by some estimates, though scholars believe those numbers are greatly inflated, putting the number of individuals executed by the Castro government at somewhere "between three hundred and seven hundred."[61] This experience followed old Latin American traditions going back to the nineteenth century, albeit on a large scale, as after civil wars losers were often sent to the wall. John Lee Anderson has also noted an evolution in the thinking of Che Guevara toward a more sympatric stance regarding the use of assassination.[62] With these actions the new revolutionary elite demonstrated that they also knew how to deal with dissenting voices. Yet over the decades, the Castro regime, while clearly authoritarian and undemocratic, has not used political murder on a large scale the way most of its neighbors in the region have at one point or another. It has been, rather, more given to imprisoning dissidents or sending them into exile. Omar Torrijos in Panama certainly killed some dissidents, and the PRI (which had some leftist pretensions and leanings in its early years) used political murder against the usual messengers of change. These examples go to show the ubiquitous nature of the political culture of murder among ruling elites, and its broad influence beyond political ideology.

On the other hand, the Sandinista government in Nicaragua during the 1980s did not give in to the use of political murder, despite enormous pressure from the United States and the Contras. In Chile, the Allende administration, until recently the most clearly "socialist" government in the region after Cuba, decidedly did not employ political murder. In Venezuela, President Hugo Chávez was known to be quite ugly to his opponents. Yet during more than a decade in power he had no need of political murder, since he consistently won elections and skillfully outmaneuvered the opposition.[63] This is also true of his most famous "socialist" contemporaries in the so-called "pink tide" of leftist governments in Latin America, presidents Evo Morales of Bolivia and Rafael Correa of Ecuador. In fact, political murder is not popular among ruling elites who really seem to believe in democracy.

As with the Black Death, the phenomenon of political murder does not recognize political frontiers. Bernt Notke could draw on almost any Latin American country for a new totentanz, using the examples mentioned here, or many tens or hundreds of thousands of others. This representative series of portraits serves simply to establish the patterns. While such a degree of monotonous repetition may be a sin against good writing style, thus is the history of political murder in Latin America. From the "big" murders of individual messengers of change, those known nationally and internationally, to the slaughter of the rank and file, the story is extraordinarily similar in country after country. This study must be more than just a roll call of famous assassinations, a list of massacres, or a series of sociological categories and abstract typologies. It must bear witness that those murdered were people—not abstractions. The enormity of the phenomenon forces us to take refuge in metaphors, or even clichés. This is a forest. The best we can do is to chart its boundaries and, while wandering through, describe some of the trees in detail. These famous examples of political murder allow us to view the tips of the proverbial icebergs. One could add a whole host of lesser known or virtually unknown individuals on the regional and local levels, from students, activists and labor leaders, to local politicians, journalists, priests and nuns, academics, artists, and intellectuals. For the murderous elites it is important kill both conveyors of the message of change and the potential audience. In the process, they hope to make people afraid to transmit such ideas, and equally afraid to receive them.

Chapter 2

Dirty War Mechanics

On a chilly winter evening in 1977, Evel Aztarbe de Petrini answered her front door bell. Outside stood ten armed men clothed in black. They claimed to be searching for a thief, and asked who was in the house. After she replied that only she and her sons were home, the men pushed their way in and dragged her sons out to the patio, where they began kicking them in the groin. They ransacked the house and stole various household goods and articles of clothing. They claimed to find bomb-making materials, and then asked which of her sons was Sergio. As they hauled him away, Sergio begged to know why they were taking him, and his mother implored them to take her instead. In answer, they roughly smacked Evel, put a pistol to Sergio's head, and kicked her younger son, who was still on the floor, jeering that he should stay and look after his mother. The men then shoved Sergio into a truck and drove away into the Argentine night. That was the last anyone ever saw of Sergio. He had been disappeared.[1] This episode, with its band of armed men preying on defenseless civilians (whom they spirit away into the night), provides an iconic illustration of dirty war technique in Latin America. But it really only represents a single tactic in a big lumpy satchel of lethal practices.

Known matter-of-factly as "wet work" among intelligence professionals, the mechanisms of murder, disappearance, assassination, and mass killing are diverse. While the victims of political homicide have been consistent across the region, how they were dispatched has been as astoundingly complex as the different countries themselves. Thus the repressive apparatus that a state or part of a state or elite might employ can vary widely, as can the actual methods of butchery. Jeffrey Sulka pointed out that the victims of political murder have been "gunned down in groups and shot individually, blown up with bombs and artillery, stabbed, strangled, hacked to death, or poisoned." They are often "tortured to death" or "sexually abused before being killed."[2] There is, consequently, no single "Latin American style" of killing. Latin Americans are inventive, and in this context their creativity unfortunately translates into processes that are messy and convoluted by design. No one is ever supposed to sort it all out. Each country or period has its own favored routes to the common destination of killing the messengers of change, or the members of their potential audience. There is, however, an important caveat: variations tend to get repeated. Certain techniques, tried and true, find widespread employment. So while there is no single organizational method or means of slaughter, there seems to be a shared playbook, evident in the recurring patterns found across Latin America.

The basic building block, of course, has been the death squad. Bruce Campbell defined death squads as "clandestine and usually irregular organizations, often paramilitary in nature, which carry out extrajudicial executions and other violent acts . . . against clearly defined individuals or groups of people. Murder is their primary or even sole activity." He argues that death squad members tend not to wear uniforms and strive to give governments "deniability"; regimes routinely disavow any connection to them. At the same time, however, Campbell stresses that death squads generally "operate with the overt support, complicity, or acquiescence of government, or at least some parts of it."[3] Looking at the case of Brazil, Martha Huggins offered support for this view. Whether they were informal groups of private security gunmen and "off duty" police, or official active-duty police in elite units, she contends that death squads in Brazil were carrying out planned policy. They were not merely random or spontaneous formations. She insisted that "rather than being an outgrowth of 'deviant' premodern social disorganization, Brazil's death squads have been firmly rooted in modern police organization."[4] Gonzalo Sánchez and Mary Roldán described a parallel process in Colombia during the 1950s. For Sánchez, the Violencia did not spontaneously materialize in various regions—it "arrived" with the death squads. Roldán maintained that the Violencia was not "an organic development," but rather the result of official efforts to carry out political repression.[5]

Yet there has been plenty of variation on the death squad theme. In fact, one can identify a continuum that begins with regular military operations, in which the various services act like death squads (or form smaller covert units for that purpose, peopled by active-duty soldiers and sailors) and encompasses police detachments hunting subversives or weeding out undesirables; political parties fielding their own partisan civilians or henchmen; mixed-membership hit squads with multiple connections; paramilitary organizations in the pay of national or local government or regional elites (both "legitimate" and "criminal"); paramilitary proxy armies funded from abroad; and, finally, stretches to freelancers and rogue players, professional paid assassins, often working in pairs from the backs of speeding motorcycles (a practice known in Colombia as the parrillero), with loyalties that are frequently unclear.

Considering this spectrum, two things are apparent. First, while the general categories are clear enough, some groups and individuals can fall into more than one. Untidy historical reality laughingly defies crisp typologies. Overlap is particularly apparent regarding membership in death squads which, like the categories themselves, can be quite fluid. The practitioners are skilled specialists in high demand (including the ones with criminal backgrounds), moving from group to group, while many military, police, and paramilitary organizations, along with various death squads in between, have often operated in closely coordinated fashion, and even in combined squads. In Argentina, El Salvador, and Guatemala, for instance, an assortment of units from the army, navy, various police agencies, and even the customs and treasury services had their own groups, and were known to treat each other as rivals. But in practice they often hunted together.

The second thing we can say about death squads is that their relationships to the state are far from consistent or completely predictable. Admittedly, some students stress the connections. Sulka noted that death squads are "usually linked directly or indirectly with the regular security forces," though sometimes "they are part of paramilitary 'defense' forces, civilian right-wing paramilitary groups who kill people the state wants, or doesn't mind being, killed." But he insisted that "there is always overlap in membership and other forms of direct or indirect collusion between death squads and the army and police, and the death squads are usually directly or indirectly under official or unofficial state control." He contended that though they are "outside the law," death squads enjoy impunity and "are generally and secretly fully integrated into the state's regular security network."[6] This, however, is something of an exaggeration in that it overemphasizes the role of the state at the expense of nonstate elites. While Kees Koonings and Dirk Kruijt have reasonably argued that all death squads have a common tendency "to defend or restore established interests by applying violence to 'undesired' social categories and political opponents," it does not follow that death squads only do this work for "the state." Indeed, Campbell recognized a "mix of state and private interests" behind death squads.[7] As noted earlier, states are not monolithic entities. Regional governments and security forces within central governments might have varying degrees of involvement, and can also be decidedly independent. The relationships death squads have to the state are thus usually close but also complex. They experience ruptures and discontinuities and, once again, exhibit a spectrum ranging from direct, government-sponsored and -organized varieties to indirect "private" enterprises serving other power players who might at times operate against the wishes of a particular national government.

Though invented as a specific coinage for the Argentine context, "dirty war" serves as a good general designation for this endeavor. It is "unclean" politically, in the sense of being impure, without honor, or polluted. It is grimy like a muddy windshield, and not particularly transparent. It is also a "war" in that the goal is generally the same—to kill persons deemed hazardous to the status quo and advocates of change whom members of the elite find threatening. This chapter thus explores the many different ways that dirty war has been waged.

Precursors and Innovators

Before discussing the dirty war mechanics of the last century or so, it is necessary to give a nod to some of the more important nineteenth-century death squad pioneers. Repressive violence in the political process has been a central theme in Latin American history. The patterns were well established before, and decidedly not the products of, the twentieth century, though they were certainly perfected and expanded enormously after 1900. In almost every country, later forms of political murder have been based on earlier native forms, mixed in with new elements drawn from North American and European models as well as from other Latin American countries.

In many fundamental ways, the modern Latin American death squad was born wholly formed in the 1830s, like a blood-thirsty Athena springing forth fully clad in armor from the head of a demented Zeus. Such was the band of terror experts loyal to Juan Manuel de Rosas, Governor of Buenos Aires Province in Argentina, which was the prototype for later death squads. Called La Mazorca, literally "the ear of corn," because of their cohesiveness, this group was the armed branch of Rosas's Federalist society, the Sociedad Popular Restauradora. Tellingly, the word "mazorca" was punned in Spanish as "más horca," or "more gibbet." Though the Mazorca was occasionally employed to police Federalista followers and weed out "dissidents" (as it was in 1832–1833), it served primarily to eliminate members of the Unitario opposition. The Mazorca generally did not indulge in indiscriminate mass terror but tended to target Unitario leaders. It was known, however, to carry out random murders for their demonstrative effects, and to exterminate prisoners of war; it was given to displaying the heads of its victims on stakes. Fanatically loyal to Rosas, the leader of the Sociedad explained (paraphrased by John Lynch) that they were "dedicated to 'exterminating' the savage Unitarians and any other opponents whom Rosas might indicate." As the lance and the knife were "ingrained" in Argentina's rural culture, it followed that the "lance thrust" and "throat-cutting" were the preferred methods of killing. As Domingo Faustino Sarmiento noted during the Mazorca's heyday, killing by "cutting the throat with a knife instead of by shooting, is the result of the butcher's instinct which Rosas has exploited to give executions a more gaucho-like form and more pleasure to the assassins." The Mazorqueros typically went from house to house looking for victims, arresting, torturing, and killing. They even threatened members of the legislature, brandishing knives "in the very galleries of the House of Representatives." They were recruited "from the police and the *serenos* (corps of nightwatchmen), and they included professional cutthroats and delinquents." They were "a force of urban irregulars who were on the state payroll and received secret service money" though "not a department of the state." Yet they worked with the police "and there was evidently a degree of joint membership."[8] Thus the Mazorca exhibited the basic features that characterize its more modern descendents, right down to its relationship with the state and its coercive forces, which was close but vague, as well as its utilization of violent criminals.

Echoes of the Mazorca reverberated throughout the nineteenth century, most famously in Mexico under Porfirio Díaz. The Rurales, modeled after the Spanish Guardia Civil, were "a federal police agency [that had been] established under the Benito Juárez regime." It became known for generous use of the so-called "Ley de fuga," or the law of flight, as it is often expressed in English. It covered individuals who were "killed trying to escape." The Rurales used it "to intimidate Mexicans into submission."[9] According to Lesley Byrd Simpson, the Rurales were given "the power to shoot on sight, and no questions asked." As he noted, they dealt with "troublesome Indian caciques, striking workmen, indiscreet speakers and writers."[10] The Ley de fuga has been employed by most, if not all, Latin American police forces and militaries, which have had no trouble appreciating its usefulness, though in recent decades an updated version has evolved alongside the original; now the dead are purportedly "killed in a gun battle with" police, the army, etc. Díaz also employed a goon squad known as the Bravi. Its members served many functions, including as presidential bodyguards and intelligence agents, but were most useful for intimidating and liquidating his political rivals. This "private army of thugs" excelled at "terrorizing dissenters" and "could be counted on to wreck newspapers and remove suspected opponents in their own way."[11] Mexican regional leaders during the Porfiriato had their own pistolero versions of the Rurales and the Bravi.[12]

Other countries repeated these models ad nauseam. In nineteenth-century El Salvador (as in other parts of Latin America) the tightly knit elites employed private security and militias that pointed the way for later paramilitary groups (indeed, hiring armed bands of retainers was a traditional precaution employed by landed elites worldwide). In 1895, the Rural and Mounted Police forces were established. This Rural Police evolved into the National Police but never completely replaced the private groups, which served the additional purpose of lending a hand during conflicts and turf battles. In 1912, the National Guard was established, known as Las Guardias. It soon became a brutal protector of elite interests, but even the Guard did not replace the private militias. In 1917, future president Alfonso Quiñóez Molina started the Liga Roja to co-opt the labor movement and bring it under elite control. It had its own goon squads to ensure oligarchy-friendly election results and attack politically "subversive" organizations.[13] In Argentina, in 1909, around 100 strikers were shot by Buenos Aires police. Paramilitary squads such as the Liga Patriótica aided the army during the repression in Buenos Aires during the "semana tragic" of 1919, and in the rural slaughter of strikers in Patagonia in 1920.[14] Finally, regional elites and local political bosses in late nineteenth- and early twentieth-century Brazil were known as Os Coronéis, or the Colonels, since landowners were typically given the rank of Colonel in the National Guard, allowing them to do their own policing. They employed groups of *pistoleiro* enforcers to maintain control of their estates and of local politics. These armed men, known as jagunçoes, dealt in vengeance and blood feuds, since power struggles among elite families were the rule. Indeed, in political competition on the local level, "violence was a necessary part." Richard Graham argues that while elites strove to win elections and gain appointments, "force was the only genuine source of power."[15] In 1880s Rio de Janeiro, an organization called the Mão Negra (Black Hand) reportedly killed "marginals."[16]

Rosas's innovations in the first decades after independence helped set the tone for later generations of murderous elites in modern Latin America. He was the epitome of a rich landowning class given to using violent repression to craft a world to its liking. And while he worked on a larger scale than many of his descendents, he showed them the way.

DIRECT MILITARY OPERATIONS

Whether tightly focused or brutally indiscriminate, the intentional and wanton slaughter of noncombatant civilian populations by military units is political murder. Such actions aspire to repress threats to the existing economic, political, and social establishment on the large scale, and to uproot and eliminate support for insurgent and rebel groups. Overt government use of military assets against political opponents in Latin America has taken many and varied forms. In most countries, this is how the largest numbers of the murdered were actually killed. It represents the most efficient method by far, to turn armies themselves into über death squads of the whole. It is also important to note that since Roman times, at least, rulers have known that the best way to defeat a guerrilla force is with a combination of persistence and ruthless repression. To grind down resistance and bring about exhaustion and capitulation militaries have employed scorched earth strategies that included the poisoning of wells, the burning of fields and villages, the slaughter of livestock, the leveling of towns and cities, and the enslavement and massacre of whole populations.

Thus an appropriate starting point is the Salvadoran "Matanza." While El Salvador is rightly infamous for its numerous variations on the death squad (see below), the majority of people killed there, in both the earlier and later periods of murder, died at the hands of the Salvadoran military, in direct operations. As Cynthia Arnson points out, "the overwhelming number of abuses were committed by the military and security forces themselves."[17] After they had secured the major towns in 1932, government forces went on the offensive, killing several rebel leaders in battle and executing those they captured in the fighting. Other leaders were later hunted down in Guatemala and Honduras, and within days the killing extended to most leftist leaders, whether or not they had participated in the rebellion. The rebels suffered from an ugly combination of few modern weapons and bad tactics, namely a propensity for wave attacks against machine gun crews. Once the rebellion was crushed, a broader butchery ensued, with savage full-scale repression across western El Salvador. The army, police, and Guardia went on a sustained campaign of murder against all "communists," namely any campesino who did not have a landowner to swear that he (or she) was not a rebel. They rounded up any and all probable or even possible rebels. Rural common people, campesinos or indios, can be hard to sort from the less discerning elite point of view, so the killers made arbitrary decisions. Individuals were presumed guilty if they had strong indigenous facial features, dressed as campesinos, or—most damning—carried a machete (it did not matter that the machete is the necessary and universal tool from Mexico to northern South America). In Izalco, and then in Juayuá, and finally all over the west of the country, invitations were sent to the general population who had not participated in the rebellion to appear in person and receive clearance papers. Many of those unfortunate enough to conform to Salvadoran rural norms were arrested. As was the custom in El Salvador, the condemned were tied together by their thumbs in groups of fifty and led to the walls of churches for liquidation by firing squads. Others were forced to dig massive graves and were then mowed down into them by truck-mounted heavy machine guns. All were killed—men, women, children, and even the dogs that had followed their owners.[18] The army itself moved to purge its ranks of rebel sympathizers, when an "entire company of the First Cavalry was executed by firing squad," with "similar executions in the First Infantry Regiment and the air force."[19]

The post-1977 Salvadoran military regime also used its repressive power with a vengeance. The most infamous and symbolic of its operations came to be known as the El Mozote Massacre. It took place as part of an anti-guerrilla strategy known as "killing by zone," where the military assumed that the majority of a region's inhabitants were guerrillas, or so close to them as not to matter. The general principle was that "in this bloody war, in the red zones, there was really no such thing as a civilian." On December 11, 1981, men of the Atlacatl Battalion assembled the inhabitants of the village of El Mozote, in the department of Morazan. After interrogating and torturing the men, and raping the women and older girls, the soldiers opened fire with automatic weapons. They killed everyone they could find, including the children, many of whom had been locked in the church—they were shot through the windows. The next day, some of the El Mozote people who had fled to the nearby village of Los Toriles were also rounded up and shot.[20]

Yet while the massacre at El Mozote was certainly emblematic of its kind in El Salvador and other parts of Latin America, it could not compare in scale with the bloody operations of the Guatemalan military in the late 1970s and early 1980s. During those years the Guatemalan army massacred the inhabitants of hundreds of Mayan villages. The number of massacres of Indians increased dramatically in May 1978 and remained high through 1982. CIA reports spoke of the "indiscriminate" slaughter of civilians, where soldiers were instructed "to fire on anything that moved" and were "expected to give no quarter to combatants and to non-combatants alike."[21] In mid-1981 the army attacked rebels in the coffee regions of the West Coast and in the food-producing zones near the capital. From November 1981 into 1982 they pushed on under Operación Ceniza (Operation Ashes). As the name implied, this was clearly a scorched earth strategy. The army used massacres and the destruction of entire villages to dominate the Pan-American Highway, and then push to the Mexican border through southern Quiché; fifteen thousand soldiers made a "slow sweep" through the entire department. The guerrilla forces used hit-and-run tactics from mountain hideouts, but the region's civilian inhabitants became the army's real targets.

The military's operation was the product of intense research and meticulous planning. The army identified villages based on their perceived infection with subversive influence, and color coded them as "white" (those thought to be free of insurgent influence, which were spared), "pink" (indicating some leftist presence, but largely spared, after enough murders had been committed to eradicate any infection), and finally, "red"—villages that were infected to the point they had to be wiped from the earth. "By the early 1982 peak of terror, troops regularly burned villagers' houses and crops and killed their farm animals in a 'scorched earth' policy designed to depopulate the zones of guerilla operations. What had been a selective campaign against guerrilla sympathizers turned into a mass slaughter designed to eliminate support or potential support for the rebels, and included widespread killing of children, women, and the elderly."[22] Some towns witnessed horrors that seemed to spring from the Old Testament, where "troops murdered children by beating them on rocks or throwing them into rivers as their parents watched . . . they gutted living victims, amputated genitalia, arms, and legs, committed mass rapes, and burned victims alive."[23]

Similar patterns were apparent in Colombia across the decades. The most infamous of Colombia's many massacres was the "Banana Massacre" of December 6, 1928, at Ciénaga, near Santa Marta in the Department of Magdalena. Banana workers had been striking for a month against the operations of the United Fruit Company, demanding written contracts, an eight-hour work day, and the end of payment in company script. The Conservative government in Bogotá sent the army to end the "subversive" action, which they did by installing machine gun crews at the corners of the main plaza, where thousands of workers and their families had congregated that Sunday after mass. After closing off the main streets and issuing a five-minute warning, the soldiers opened fire, killing hundreds of people.[24] Another well-known incident occurred in April 1952, when the Batallón Colombia, fresh from the battlefields of Korea, carried out a massacre of campesinos near El Líbano, Tolima. The army had, for the most part, maintained a degree of neutrality in the early Violencia. Political murder was more of a "police" activity. But in the mid-1950s, the army was pulled into conflict in a few spots.[25] In response to a brutal ambush in April 1952, when Liberal guerrillas tried to assassinate the governor of Tolima, but ended up killing women and children passengers in his car (the governor was in the lead jeep, which escaped), the national government was moved to "exterminate" the "bandits" (read: Liberal guerrillas) near Líbano. A joint force of national police and soldiers from Batallón Colombia swept across eastern Líbano. The so-called "Battle of Líbano" saw the slaughter of at least 1,500 country folk (some estimates were higher by thousands). More than a thousand farm houses were destroyed, to deny any sanctuary to the guerrillas. "On the slightest pretext, campesinos were shot, houses burned, crops as well as food stuffs destroyed. The underlying assumption was that every farmer was a 'bandit,' or potentially one, and should be treated as such. The fight was not considered to be between Colombians, but between the forces of order and a subversive, perhaps communist, rabble."[26] Though extreme, this was common in the worst years of the Violencia, when army and police units targeted civilians.[27] The army also fired on students engaged in protests at the Universidad Nacional in June 1954, killing thirteen.[28] These traditions were still alive fifty years later, as the massacres of the 1990s and later demonstrated. Individually they were small, but their numbers added up. On May 1, 2003, soldiers of the army's 18th Brigade, Navos Pardo Battalion supposedly disguised themselves (by wearing AUC and ACCU paramilitary armbands) to attack the indigenous community at Betoyes, killing four and raping three others. And on February 21, 2005, at the Peace Community of San José de Apartado, the Bolívar Company, Vélez Battalion, 17th Brigade killed eight, including three children.[29]

In Nicaragua the Somoza-dominated Guardia Nacional, even more than most Latin American militaries, functioned, at regular intervals from the time of its inception, like an overarching death squad. Since most of the people of the northern mountains were considered "potential bandits" (and, indeed, likely bandits), the Guardia reasoned that "almost the entire civilian population" should be targeted. They found that "murder was a powerful tool." Most deaths were not combat deaths; in fact "all evidence indicates" that the U.S. Marines and the Guardia had a "shoot first" policy, and from 1927 to 1933 employed a "semi-scorched" earth strategy. In their fight against Sandino, Guardia patrols would fire into "suspicious" houses, because even if the inhabitants were not "bandits," they were surely aiding them. In fact, Guardia members generally assumed that the entire population in some regions supported the Sandinistas; their "collective guilt" made them worthy of "collective punishment." Both Guardia units and their

Marine allies bombed and machine-gunned suspicious individuals, groups, and structures. After Sandino's assassination, the Somoza-led Guardia would often return to its brutal large-scale operations, especially as opposition to the regime consolidated in the late 1970s. In September 1978 the Guardia initiated "Operation Mop Up." They shot people (including children) in their own homes and in the streets, but the serious numbers of dead were generated when Somoza's air force bombed civilian urban populations. Estimates of those killed ranged from five thousand to ten thousand, and wounded from ten thousand to twenty thousand.[30]

In Argentina, the military responded brutally to the ERP guerrilla campaign of May 1972, led by Mario Roberto Santucho in the remote, heavily forested, and mountainous province of Tucumán in northwest Argentina. The ERP believed that by following the "glorious" examples of leftist insurgencies in Vietnam and Cuba they could bring the Perón government to its knees, and then seize power. They would carve out "liberated zones" from which the revolution would spread, garnering popular support and driving the government's representatives and armed forces before them. After being holed up in towns and cities, government forces would eventually be pushed back to Buenos Aires, and then out of the country altogether. Unfortunately for the ERP, General Acdel Edgardo Vilas, who was chosen to lead "Operación Independencia," had also read Mao and Che Guevara, as well as various counterinsurgency thinkers. General Vilas (who did not command enough troops to have a huge advantage over the relatively well-armed insurgents) refused to pick up the gauntlet the guerrillas had thrown down and immediately follow them into the rough, mountainous, and thickly jungled terrain of the *monte*. He chose instead to attack their networks of material and ideological support in the province's towns. His strategy aimed to exterminate local ERP supporters and scare off their would-be replacements. Though Vilas also instituted programs to garner local support among the region's long-time residents, his program relied heavily on repression. Vilas's troops and local police arrested anyone who was young and from the outside world: labor organizers, teachers and students, leftists of all stripes, journalists in particular. The operation's impressive efficiency was a result of painstaking intelligence efforts. Basically, anyone considered suspicious was rounded up and sent to one of fourteen makeshift interrogation centers. Most detainees were "disappeared." And while Vilas's political murder campaign progressed in the towns, his troops carried out a careful counteroffensive in the *monte*. It pressured the already stressed guerrillas, who then had to make dangerous trips into town to resupply. By November 1975 the ERP in Tucumán was a spent force, seeking to escape.[31]

Other notable instances of military repression throughout the region are not hard to find. One of the largest slaughters, comparable in size to the Salvadoran Matanza, was the 1937 "Parsley massacre" of Haitians in the Dominican Republic, also known as El Corte. Desiring a firmer border between the two countries, Dictator Rafael Trujillo decided to annihilate the roughly twenty thousand Haitians living in the DR. Over several days in early October, Dominican troops hunted them down, often asking them if they could pronounce "perejil" (parsley), since Haitians were believed to be incapable of pronouncing it correctly. The soldiers shot them, stabbed them, and hacked them. To augment their murderous effectiveness, the Dominican authorities closed the main bridge connecting the countries.[32] Another infamous massacre took place in Mexico, on October 2, 1968, in the Plaza de Tres Culturas, in the Tlatelolco section of Mexico City. Months of political unrest had fermented against the backdrop of a worldwide student protest movement. President Gustavo Díaz Ordaz wanted to quell the Mexican chapter of the student movement before the Olympics, and sent the army to occupy UNAM (the National Autonomous University of Mexico) in late September, and the resulting beatings and arrests only fueled student demonstrations, which grew in protest. On October 2, over fifteen thousand students from different universities marched through Mexico City. By early evening, five thousand students and lookers-on had assembled in the Plaza de Tres Culturas. Police and Army units, backed up by tanks and machine-gun-mounted armored vehicles, surrounded the Plaza and began to fire. The slaughter continued for hours as soldiers searched nearby apartment houses.[33] In Peru, an excellent example was the Cayara Massacre of May 14, 1988. An Army unit moved into the town of Caryara in Ayacucho and slaughtered twenty-nine campesinos. They then hid their bodies, and went on to kill more in the following days. The army originally claimed that the perpetrators were guerrillas, but surviving witnesses argued that the army had killed unarmed civilians in revenge for an earlier Sendero ambush. Many of the witnesses also subsequently disappeared. Investigators and judges were threatened and attacked. The case was called "the epitome of government impunity."[34] In Bolivia, as well, the army carried out the massacres of San Juan and of Tolata. In a winter night in June 1967, striking miners were celebrating the festival of San Juan at mining camps in northern Potosí. Under the cover of darkness, army units surrounded the revelers (men, women, and children) and opened fire, killing eighty-seven people. In 1974, during the Hugo Banzer dictatorship, the army carried out the Massacre of the Valley, also known as the Massacre of Tolata in Cochabamba, killing peasants who were protesting an International Monetary Fund–mandated currency devaluation and removal of subsidies on basic goods. The cost of living had risen 39 percent, though wages rose much more slowly, and prices on consumer goods had roughly doubled. The peasants set up roadblocks in protest. The army went in to clear the roads and in the process "took the lives of more than one hundred peasants."[35]

COVERT MILITARY DEATH SQUAD OPERATIONS

Official efforts can also metastasize as covert, small-unit, but still official military operations, with firm if somewhat obscured chains of command. Their tactics run to the more clandestine side, working out of view. These squads also emphasize the quick grab and the disappearance.

A good example of a small yet official force whose sole purpose was murder germinated early in the regime of Augusto Pinochet in Chile. Between October 4 and 19 of 1973 (roughly a month after the coup against Salvador Allende), General Sergio Arellano Stark commanded a team of officers that flew in Puma helicopters to five cities in Chile: Cauquenes to the south of Santiago, and La Serena, Copiapó, Antofagasta, and Calama to the north. Their trek came to be known as The Caravan of Death. Pinochet had ostensibly sent Arellano, the real organizational force behind the overthrow of Allende, to "standardize" the sentences of political prisoners arrested after the coup. In reality this "standardization" entailed selecting various individuals for extrajudicial execution. Seventy-five prisoners whose sentences were judged to be too "lenient" were killed.[36] Most of the people arrested were guilty of holding political views—be they liberal, leftist, socialist, or communist—deemed subversive by the Chilean military. In most cases the local media were told (and then duly reported) that the prisoners had been killed "trying to escape." The Chileans had a classic sense of history. After the early months of the regime, when killings had been somewhat indiscriminate, a new secret military security organization, DINA, evolved under Colonel Manuel Contreras. Though better controlled, DINA was still a brutal military death squad organization, largely independent of military oversight and answerable directly to Pinochet. U.S. intelligence officers called it a "modern day Gestapo," though DINA also had clear connections to the CIA, especially training it received from the Gringos in "interrogation techniques." DINA embarked on "an orgy of mass murder," both in Chile and abroad.[37]

Yet arguably the classic manifestation of Latin American "military" death squads can be found in the Argentine Proceso, during which soldiers and sailors on active duty disappeared people off the streets and from their homes. In many ways it set the standard for coordination and military bureaucratization (though precision was not the goal—in fact, there were lots of collateral victims, and that was just fine with the juntas' leadership). The groundwork for the operation had been laid in the years before the 1976 coup, when federal police, Buenos Aires Provincial police, and military intelligence units had meticulously prepared lists of all the usual suspects. The actual abductions were generally carried out by "grupos de tarea" (task forces), or GTs, of armed men in units ranging from small groups of four or five to larger squads of ten to twenty. Sergeant Victor Ibañez, who served from 1976 to 1980 at Campo de Mayo (known as El Campito—the organizational point of the army's intelligence GTs), extrapolated on dirty war tradecraft. They dressed as civilians and carried only side arms. Their operations were well-planned snatch maneuvers during which the "situation area" was controlled with plenty of personnel.[38] Police were informed ahead of time and told to stay clear. These were unmistakably official operations—the street would be blocked off, and it was not unusual for the electricity in the whole neighborhood to be shut off. If the victim was on the street, he or she would be bum rushed, overwhelmed, quickly blindfolded, handcuffed, and shoved into a waiting car (frequently one of the infamous green Ford Falcons.) If the victim targeted was at home, the operation would usually take place at night. The building would be surrounded, and then the grupo would smash into the house or apartment. If the target was not in, anyone there might be held hostage. In a two-part process, most of the people who had been "chupado" ("sucked up") were sent to one of the hundreds of detention centers around the country for interrogation and torture. When the interrogators were finished with them, most of the victims were "transferred"—dirty war speak for killed. Neither Franz Kafka nor George Orwell could have expressed it better.

At the beginning of the Proceso, a section of army intelligence Battalion 601 was created to integrate and coordinate the work of the various army, navy, air force, and police GTs. It was based at the Domingo Viejobueno Arsenal and commanded by Col. Alberto Valín. There was a general division of dirty war labor: the GT1, controlled by the First Army Corp, was especially devoted to eliminating ERP guerrillas; the GT2, which represented the air force, focused on an assortment of smaller leftist groups; the GT3, commanded by the navy, primarily targeted the Montoneros; and finally, the GT4, dominated by the federal police, also specialized in Montoneros. Later, other grupos de tarea were created to target union activists, students, religious leaders, and political parties. The army GTs were often led by army personnel but largely composed of federal or provincial police officers, former members of the Triple A, or even violent criminals working off their sentences. Naval units were first dispatched from ESMA, the infamous Naval Mechanics' School, manned by naval officers, noncommissioned officers, common sailors, and retired personnel.[39] From a purely military point of view, the Argentine tactic of disappearing people suspected of ties to the guerrillas made sense, as it "sowed great uncertainty among the revolutionary organizations." They often did not know which of their cadres were dead or alive, which had deserted, or whether someone missing was in a detention center giving up everything they knew under torture.[40]

Perhaps less iconic than the Argentine case was that of Guatemala, though it was every bit as organized and official. In fact, while most of Guatemala's dirty war dead were killed by regular army units in the countryside, the military there carried out extensive covert urban death squad operations, and easily disappeared more victims than the Argentines. Army intelligence, often known as "the unelected, parallel government of Guatemala," began to take shape after the 1954 coup, with significant input from the CIA and the U.S. military. It also received extensive training and technical support from Argentine and Israeli sources. It specialized in "tracking, controlling, and eliminating both armed and unarmed opposition" and began compiling lists of "suspected communists" and other political targets. Jennifer Schirmer noted that Guatemala's "powerful Medusa-headed and clandestine intelligence bureaucracy," generally characterized as "Army intelligence," was split into three sections in the 1980s—the D-2 for Directorate of Intelligence, the S-2 for Sectional Intelligence, and G-2 for group patrols—but as a whole it continued to be referred to as G-2 or Las Dos. A G-2 operative she interviewed, speaking from personal experience, described Guatemala military intelligence as "a death squad that exists only to kill." As it evolved from the 1960s to the 1980s, G-2 coordinated death squads in military units, police forces, and paramilitary groups. These entities had clear links to the highest echelons of the military command. By the 1978–1982 period, "executive involvement in political repression reached new heights." Representatives of President (General) Lucas García, the Interior Minister, the Army Intelligence Command, and the National Police met "to draw up hit lists."[41]

Other cases abound. In El Salvador, as noted, death squads killed a fairly small share of those murdered (perhaps 10 percent). But they proved very effective in spreading terror and were a key to the "repressive machinery of the state." The CIA recognized that "rightist terrorist cells . . . use both active duty and retired military personnel in their campaigns." El Salvador's armed forces' death squads included units from the First Brigade in San Salvador, the Army Signal Corps, and the Second Brigade in Santa Ana.[42] Even the Honduran army got into the game with its Argentine-style knockoff, the Battalion 3-16 (known by various names). Schooled by U.S. trainers referred to as "Mr. Bill" and "Mr. Mike," in August 1980 twenty-five Hondurans were also trained in Texas by the CIA and FBI. Once they were back in Honduras they received more training by Argentines in torture and disappearing techniques. It was a classic urban death squad; they dressed in civilian clothes and wore disguises. They followed their victims and whisked them away in double-cab Toyota pickups with tinted windows and false license plates.[43] The Brazilian military government likewise saw any political unrest as the result of subversive influences and a direct challenge to its authority. It thus embraced the spirit of the age. In 1968, as repression increased, thousands of "subversives" were jailed, and many killed, by joint civil/military units of handpicked police and soldiers. In Rio, the Grupo de Operações Especiaís (GOE; Special Operations Group) went to war with subversion. It received training from Brazilian, U.S., Arab, and Algerian instructors. And, in July 1969, Operação Bandeirantes-OBAN (OBAN-Bandeirant Operation), a private program, was also started for the São Paulo region that employed federal, state, and military police, as well as active-duty military personnel. It was created to eliminate subversive groups.[44] Finally, in Peru, the Grupo Colina was responsible for several massacres, two of which stand out. On November 3, 1991, a group of six armed and masked men descended on a house in the Barrios Altos neighborhood of Lima, where a cookout was in progress. After making the guests lie on the ground, the gunmen fired at the group for over two minutes. Fifteen people were killed, including an eight-year-old child. After the killing, the shooters returned to their jeeps (apparently police vehicles) and sped away, sirens blaring. Early attempts by the Peruvian Congress to investigate were stymied by President Alberto Fujimori's "auto coup" against his own government in April 1992, in which Congress was dissolved. Later investigations indicated that the killers were military intelligence officers affiliated with Grupo Colina who believed they were targeting a group of Sendero guerrillas (which was, in fact, assembled on the second floor). Grupo Colina's other most infamous mass murder was the La Cantuta Massacre, carried out in July 1992 at the Universidad Nacional de Educación Enrique Guzmán y Valle, known colloquially as La Cantuta, after the neighborhood in which it is found. La Cantuta was founded in 1822 as a normal school and by the 1960s had come to be known as a focal point of leftist politics. Shut down in 1977 by the military, it was allowed to reopen in 1980. This time the targets were both the Sendero and the Túpac Amaru Revolutionary Movement (Peru's other important guerrilla group, though the Senderistas were dominant). On July 18, 1992, two days after the Sendero committed a deadly bombing, members of the Grupo Colina (most of whom were also members of the Army Intelligence Service and the Army Directorate of Intelligence) abducted professor Hugo Muñoz Sánchez and nine students, none of whom were ever seen again.[45]

POLICE DEATH SQUADS

In many, if not most, Latin American countries, police forces have long been used for purposes of general repression, and have willingly opened fire on demonstrators and protesters. It is an old tradition, also practiced in Europe and the United States, and it does not inevitably lead to death squads. But such police practices, if continually employed, might indicate a predisposition toward the use of death squads. In Latin America, in any case, police death squads predate their military versions in most countries, and there is also little doubt about the widespread and long-term involvement of Latin American police forces in such endeavors. Sometimes police worked as autonomous killers, and other times they acted under military command. Often they formed the backbone of urban death squads. Piet Van Reenen notes that police can also have "helpers," called "extensions." Some extensions, such as death squads, are illegal—"policing by way of illegal extensions is exerting power in an illegal, uncontrolled and most of the time violent way." The brutality employed by police and their helpers in Latin America "is a specialized, small-scale activity" that amounts to "killing or maiming or the threat" to do so. Van Reenen also argues that "a common element is that they are political tools for elites in their countries." Finally, police are known to share their helpers with other government entities or nongovernmental groups—political parties, the army, security firms, and business interests.[46]

Early forms of police death squads were especially tied to local politics. Alan Knight observes that much political violence in Mexico during the 1920s and 1930s was carried out by local police at the behest of local elites. These constabularies were described as "chiefly composed of criminals," and "notorious for opening fire on citizens as they pleased."[47] In El Salvador, in 1932, the police used voter registration rolls to round up those who had probably voted communist. These groups were shot and buried in large unmarked graves.[48] And in Brazil, the "history of the police," Van Reenen insists, "is a history of violence." In particular, it has been a history of "violence directed against the masses of poor people." Regarding police death squads, it is clear that "the military dictatorship did not create this phenomenon." Rather, it "found an existing method and instrument to threaten and kill without official involvement and responsibility which could quite easily be used against political opponents." Likewise, Paulo Sérgio Pinheiro notes that in Rio de Janeiro and São Paulo, "the State police have always helped to maintain the order imposed by the ruling classes" by repressing strikes and any popular protests.[49] Indeed, in the Brazilian countryside the pattern was an old one, consisting mainly of "force and threat of force by hired hands of landowners" who worked closely with police. Whether they worked as resident muscle on the property, or as professional pistoleiros, their victims were "mostly landless people," laborers, union organizers, and human rights activists. The hired guns were used to remove land occupiers or to "punish and discipline" workers. Police and pistoleiro interaction in Brazil evolved over decades—sometimes they would work together, in coordinated fashion, with police standing back and observing, facilitating impunity. Less commonly, police would inhibit pistoleiros.[50]

In mid-twentieth-century Colombia, state-sponsored killing also tended to be carried out by groups that were generally identified as "police." These were called Contrachusmas or Chulavitas, depending on their region of origin. In fact, even before the 1946 election, the Liberal establishment (which, given the appointment power of the executive, controlled police forces down to the municipal level) often acted in league with Conservatives to attack the left-Liberal Gaitanistas. After their electoral victory, and their subsequent control of police forces throughout Colombia, Conservatives began to create a legal framework that would allow bands of armed civilians to do elite bidding. Liberals were kicked out of local police departments and replaced by ultra-Catholic Conservative partisans, such as the country folk from the Chulavita district of Boyacá (especially from Boavita and Soatá). After Gaitán's assassination on April 9, 1948, the practice expanded. Trusted Conservatives from Boyacá, Nariño, and Antioquia were dispatched to Liberal areas, where violence did not start but "arrived" with the Chulavitas and their brethren, who served as "police" shock troops in Liberal departments and municipalities.[51] In particular, Chulavitas were sent to regions where Gaitanismo was strongest, such as in Valle de Cauca and Tolima. They were known as specialists in savage "collective massacres."[52]

Conservatives also moved quickly to install civilian-staffed "auxiliary" police units at the local level. These Contrachusmas (literally "antiscum" fighters), as they were known in the department of Antioquia, were sent to carry out partisan violence. These "reserve officers" were selected on the basis of their rabid Catholic views (like the Chulavitas, who dedicated their activities to the Virgen de Carmen) and loyalty to the Conservative Party. Using Conservative civilians gave the government plausible deniability, and training these forces amounted to little more than handing out .38 specials. Conservative mayors, many of whom had criminal records, and partisan police, in league with local Conservative extremists, drove the violence. Assassins were aided by police, mayors, party bosses, and even priests, all calling for more such units. Liberal guerrillas were often displaced Gaitanistas, mobilized in many places by attacks and massacres (Contrachusmas were much more likely to attack civilians than to actually fight guerrillas). In a familiar pattern, terror made it next to impossible for guerrillas to demobilize. After Gaitán's death, partisan Conservative police in Antioquia targeted labor unions, while followers of Laureano Gómez funded the organization of additional Contrachusmas to quash Liberal mobilization, because they felt that the regular police were not sufficient; their philosophy was "a sangre y fuego" ("for blood and fire").[53] The appointed Conservative Governor of Valle de Cauca, Nicolás Borrero Olano, met with large landowners and other members of the elite there who also pushed for a "private" police force to protect their economic interests. Not surprisingly, these early private police were former property protectors in the employ of hacendados. Such groups carried out the October 22, 1949, massacre at the Casa Liberal in Cali, a Gaitanista, left-Liberal organization. (The Conservatives particularly hated it, calling its members a collection of "miserable reds.") The Casa Liberal in Cali was also a refuge for Liberals fleeing the violence in the countryside. On the day of the killings, Liberals had congregated there to hear speeches by Liberal políticos. As the speakers and audience began to leave around seven p.m., police began firing from adjacent buildings. The Liberal speakers escaped in their cars, while most of the Liberals hid in the Casa. The police attacked the building, firing rifles and machine guns at anyone and everyone. Twenty-six were killed and more than fifty wounded. Soldiers from the nearby army post arrived three hours later.[54] In fact, such partisan police became a fact of life throughout Colombia. In July 1952, the new Conservative governor of Antioquia, Dionisio Arango Ferrer, was such a big believer in auxiliary police that he even made Contrachusma groups responsible for a large share of the department's public order.[55]

Later forms of police death squads were often connected to the efforts of military governments. An Argentine police commissioner interviewed in August 2003 noted that when the military took over the police after the 1976 coup, they did so to make use of the skills sets specific to law-enforcement organizations. The police understood "how to operate in the terrain of a neighborhood." Police officers know better than soldiers how "to move in an urban setting." Thus "the military sent the police to the front lines of 'the war against subversion.'" In Guatemala, as well, "the police became the main pillar of state terrorism under the control of and alongside the army." Their auxiliaries were involved in the basics of "carrying out killings, issuing threats, and making people disappear." Guatemalan police squads, such as the Policía Militar Ambulante (PMA) were linked to military intelligence, and the Guardia de Hacienda, an independent police force, was also deeply involved in intelligence operations.[56] In El Salvador, the Policía Nacional (National Police), or PN, employed one of the country's more secretive death squads, formed in 1979 or earlier, mostly from the criminal investigation, special political investigation, and narcotics sections. The CIA noted that the PN sought to avoid "high profile" targets, and aimed to leave "no indication of responsibility." The uniformed branch of the Policía de Hacienda (the treasury police) was as murderous as any of El Salvador's security forces but also had a covert death squad.[57] In Brazil, under Law 317 of 1967 and Law 667 of 1969, the military government moved to place all police power under national military control. Law 317 subordinated municipal and state police to military-appointed officials. Law 667 was designed especially to wage an "internal war" on the forces of leftist subversion. In São Paulo, the Departamento Estadual de Investigacoes Criminais (DEIC; State Department of Criminal Investigation) had a secret unit to deal with the most important cases; it was said they were a tough group that really enjoyed the job of assassination.[58] And during the 1970s, the main forces deployed against "subversion" and the "internal enemy" were "specialized mobile shock units with the military police." In São Paulo, these units were called Rondas Ostensivas Tobias de Aguiar, or ROTAS. They were used after 1968 against urban guerrillas, anyone suspected of "subversion," and even common criminals.[59] Finally, after the 1980 coup in Bolivia, General Luis García Meza created a branch of the Departamento de Investigación Nacional (Department of National Investigation) called the Servicio Especial de Seguridad (SES; Special Security Service). This branch carried out one of the most infamous political massacres of his regime—the assassination of eight important members of the MIR in January 1981. The SES was also deployed to kill other political and labor leaders.[60]

But police death squads have existed under democratically elected governments as well. As Mark Bowden has argued, the "Search Bloc" searching for Pablo Escobar in Colombia was itself acting like a death squad in that it did not really seem to be letting anyone surrender. As 1992 drew to a close, "twelve major players in Pablo's organization . . . had been killed in 'gun battles'" with its officers. Driven by retaliatory murders of police by

Escobar's sicarios, the $2000 bounty he offered for such killings, and his bombing campaign in Bogotá, they were also frustrated by the fact their efforts were clearly wracked by inside informants who alerted Pablo within minutes of new intelligence on his whereabouts. American and Colombian agents listening to Pablo's communications were struck by how calm and confident he sounded. Many wondered if perhaps something could be done to make him less comfortable. In January 1993, rural homes and estates owned by Escobar and his family were burned in succession, while car bombs exploded in Medellín in front of apartment buildings where his family lived. Also, "bodies of Pablo's associates began turning up all over Medellín and Bogotá." They often wore signs left by "Los PEPES"—People Persecuted by Pablo Escobar. The PEPES targeted Escobar's bankers, lawyers, family members, and business associates. They issued cash rewards for information, and targeted "Pablo's most prized properties and assets, his antique cars, his country homes, his apartment houses, his air craft and air ports." They killed several of his lawyers, blew up their fincas, kidnapped their families, tortured and killed them. Other of Escobar's associates resigned. People with the most tenuous connections to Escobar and his family were kidnapped, tortured, and murdered.[61]

According to Carlos Castaño, he and his brother Fidel, along with Adolfo Paz, were the directors of Los PEPES. One of the most famous, and certainly the most focused, death squads in Colombian (and maybe Latin American) history, Los PEPES was an excellent demonstration of the method's usefulness—here was a big threat eliminated, with his whole organization brought down. They proved that political murder was not just effective against leftists but could be used against rogue elites as well. This victory was a clear police/auxiliary operational success story, and Castaño wanted credit: "Pablo Escobar was dead thanks to Los PEPES and its union with the state." Castaño insisted that Los PEPES was "the first paraestatal group in Colombian history." Of course it was not, and indeed it represented an old tradition in Colombian history. Yet he pointed out correctly that the PEPES seemed to be tolerated by the attorney general, the police, the army, the DAS, and by the president, César Gaviria. "Even journalists silently applauded, and that's how it had to be!" On the "many contacts" between Castaño's "antisubversive" struggle and the state, he noted that "all my life I have had friends in the armed forces, who communicated by various means; if not talking directly to me, they talked to my people, among whom where ex-military and ex-police." Castaño gave an insider's view of how a death squad works in conjunction with the state. The PEPES carried out "irregular operations" in which they "found the enemy and enemies and executed them." The Bloque de Búsqueda carried out other operations, "with our information." The PEPES "never carried out operations with the police," and in this they "were very careful." They "did not want to cause problems for the institution." But the PEPES were "tactical allies." Tellingly, Castaño argued that "if the PEPES had not come forward, the police would have invented a similar group."[62]

Political Party Death Squads

Closely connected to police death squads were those associated with local politicians and political parties. As the Mazorca demonstrated, these were some of the oldest varieties in Latin America.

In Mexico, "freelance pistoleros" were a phenomenon that dated to well before the 1920s, but the Revolution increased their use in "the hot, dense, often dirty undergrowth" of local politics. Such muscle was "found in the service of governors, caciques, judges, and even officials of . . . Arbitration Boards" who presided over labor disputes. Yet the later years of the revolutionary decade (1910–1920) also generated new armed bands, "the ubiquitous *defensas sociales.*" They "became a fact of political life" and could be "highly influential in local politics," quickly outliving the lawless context in which they emerged. Rather than provide order, "their political role remained, underpinning local cacique power." These armed men were used to coerce election results, commit various types of robbery and extortion, and of course, to murder troublesome opponents.[63] Mexico was hardly an anomaly, and had parallels all over Latin America. As noted earlier, these were well-established traditions from the nineteenth century that involved local and regional caudillos, patronage networks, and bands of clients serving as private armies of retainers. These operated as proto-death squads, especially during elections, when "coercive capacities frequently determined electoral outcomes." Conservative party gangs in Nicaragua, for instance, could be excessively violent. These bands ranged "from five to 50 or more" and were employed to intimidate, harass, and kill "their political foes and their foes' family members, clients, and allies." One of the most notorious was that of Anastacio Hernández. In 1927, Hernández and his death squad killed at least forty-nine people, but in all likelihood, hundreds more. Knowing that the Liberals were "virtually guaranteed" power in the 1928 elections, "the Conservative power holders sought to diminish the voting power of the Liberal party," most directly by "murdering prospective Liberal voters and by sending thousands fleeing into Honduras."[64]

And, of course, it is no surprise that the Colombians would also be innovators in political party death squads, given the history of the "hereditary hatreds." In fact, Colombia provides one of the classic examples of partisan civilians in the pay of local government and regional elites with the *pájaros* (or "birds") of the Violencia. They were especially active in Valle de Cauca, where they perfected their style, but also made their presence felt in Old Caldas, Tolima, and Cauca. The early pájaros were part-time assassins working in small groups of two or three, often alongside police, but always in collaboration with the local Conservative political establishment. At first they focused on Liberal political notables and the party's landed and moneyed elite, but soon moved on to a variety of Liberal targets. They were Conservative loyalists, small tradesmen and farmers, who were based in known cafes and directly employed by mayors and departmental organizations. They would leave their day jobs to form a "flock," carry out a specific assassination ("hacer un trabajito"—do a "little job"), and then "fly away." They were known professionally by their nicknames, such as Pájaro Azul (Bluebird), Pájaro Verde (Greenbird), and Pájaro Negro (Blackbird)."[65] Their work was directed by Conservative elected officials and gamonales (political bosses), such as Governor Nicolás Borrero Olano of Valle de Cauca, who was a personal friend of later infamous pájaro assassins Lamparilla and Pájaro Verde. In addition to the obvious local and national políticos, other collaborators with pájaros included priests, military officers, local attorneys, and departmental legislators. And naturally there was overlap with the Chulavitas and Contrachusmas as Conservatives moved to convert local police forces into the arms of the Conservative party after the election of 1946.[66]

The most infamous Conservative assassin, the so-called "prince" of the pájaros, was León María Lozano of northern Valle, more widely known as El Cóndor.[67] A small-scale businessman and white-collar employee from Tuluá, Valle, Lozano was a fanatically Catholic and thoroughly partisan Conservative stalwart. Among all the pájaros, he was singled out by the Conservative party establishment close to Borrero Olano to do their bidding. He worked closely with other infamous assassins such as Lamparilla, El Vampiro, El Loco Atehortúa, El Indio Carmona, and El Jorobado, among others. Lozano was photographed next to future military president Gustavo Rojas Pinilla when the latter commanded the Third Brigade in Valle. Rojas Pinilla declared his "neutrality" regarding the rising sectarian violence, granting El Cóndor and his followers unfettered autonomy to put down rebellious Gaitanistas in 1948 and later. Working with Chulavita police units, El Cóndor's pájaros terrorized the Liberals of the department. El Cóndor was especially infamous for the murders of the "suicide squadron." A group of prominent citizens in Tuluá signed a letter to *El Tiempo* of Bogotá on July 10, 1955, denouncing Lozano and other pájaro leaders. These brave souls were sentenced to death by the pájaros (hence their sobriquet), and many were hunted down. The slaughter was so outrageous (even by the standards of the Violencia) that El Cóndor lost some of his political cover. He removed himself to Barranquilla, where he was eventually gunned down by the son of one of his first victims. Though El Cóndor's network was broken up, pájaros survived and prospered (leading directly to sicarios and para death squads in later decades). These more professional later versions of the pájaros moved freely in the light of day, using the main roads unmolested by police or army. They were used to homogenize towns (as were the Contrachusmas in Antioquia) and to "conservatize" them.[68]

Later practitioners in El Salvador modernized the political party death squad model and blurred the definitional lines. In the 1960s, General José Alberto "Chele" Medrano (who was also the head of ANSESAL, El Salvador's principal security agency) forged an entity called ORDEN, the Organización Democrática Nacionalista (National Democratic Organization) that was part political party and part paramilitary organization. ORDEN specialized in rural "counterintelligence." The CIA pointed out that it, like other purported intelligence-gathering organizations, "effectively institutionalized vigilantism." ORDEN mobilized thousands of rural folks to act as agents of the land-owning classes for the purposes of identifying and eliminating "real and suspected enemies of the regime." It intimidated and murdered individuals "suspected of involvement with the extreme left."[69] It was also clearly integrated with El Salvador's intelligence agencies and armed forces and shared their goals of "completely demobilizing and eliminating dissent." There was plenty of "membership overlap" because personnel were recruited directly from military. Moonlighting was common, as ORDEN sections enjoyed cordial relations with regional elites and locally stationed military units. Business and agricultural associations established other death squads with ties to ORDEN, like FALANGE, with its obvious nod to fascist Spain (Fuerzas Armadas de Liberación Nacional—Guerra de Exterminación), established in 1975; Mano Blanco (White Hand) that grew out of ANSESAL; GAS (Gremio Anti-Comunista Salvadoreño) that worked "alongside the armed forces;" and finally, UGB (Unión Guerra Blanca), founded in 1976, which was famous for its slogan: "Be a patriot, Kill a Priest."[70]

ORDEN was disbanded in 1979, but its work lived on as its networks remained intact, and its agents and specialists migrated to other security agencies or maintained death squads such as the Mano Blanco.[71] They also took its work in a more decidedly political direction. One of the most prominent actors to emerge from ORDEN was Roberto D'Aubuisson, who founded ARENA, the far-right political party that would come to dominate Salvadoran politics. The CIA characterized D'Aubuisson as the "principal henchman for wealthy landowners" and as the lynch pin of "right-wing death squads." A protégé of Medrano, as a military intelligence officer he was too right-wing even for El Salvador's army. After being kicked out of the military for involvement in an aborted coup, D'Aubuisson, as the CIA noted, believed in terminating "anyone not supportive of the traditional status quo." Funded by big Salvadoran money while in exile in Guatemala, he founded a political group that eventually became, in October of 1981, ARENA. D'Aubuisson was first elected to the constituent assembly, and then as its president. ARENA even had its own affiliated death squads, such as the ESA, Ejercito Secreto Anticomunista (Secret Anticommunist Army), operated by D'Aubuisson's underling, Héctor Antonio Regalado. (One of Regalado's early efforts in the 1970s was a faux "Boy Scout" troop of young assassins, who were themselves eliminated after 1980 for knowing too much.) The ESA's operatives were drawn from old ORDEN networks, as well as the Treasury and National Police forces. From 1981 to 1983 it specialized in killing suspected rebels and Christian Democratic Party workers and elected officials. ESA generally sought to make headlines, despite its name. Members of the intelligence section of the Guardia Nacional (GN), D'Aubuisson's old unit, ran a death squad that maintained close ties to ARENA. The CIA observed that GN assassinated individuals who were "thought to support leftist causes." Led by Major Mario Denis Morán, earlier director of the UGB, its big kill was Rodolfo Viera, along with the American advisors Michael Hammer and Mark Pearlman.[72]

The pájaros of Colombia and ORDEN of El Salvador were direct forebears of the paramilitaries.

Paramilitaries

Paramilitary organizations offer the most evasive subset within the broader death squad realm. There have been various efforts to provide descriptions and definitions ever since the term "paramilitary" was coined by British journalists attempting to characterize "Nazi-sponsored groups of enforcers that policed movement rallies and disrupted those of their opponents" in the 1930s. They were also called "military-style groups."[73] The use of the prefix "para" gives the sense of proximity and approximation yet also implies deviation, and irregularity, of being close but not winning the proverbial cigar.[74] Clouding the picture even more is the fact that this image of non-conformity is often a careful construct. Andrew Scobell and Brad Hammitt offer a definition of "paramilitary force" that involves armed, normally uniformed, groups with characteristics of both military and police organizations. This force usually serves to some degree as an instrument of state policy, using repressive policing functions aimed to suppress the opposition. Its command structures are often linked to police or military, with which it typically shares personnel.[75] Kruijt and Koonings' definition likewise recognizes "an organized form of coercive (military) capacity that is modeled upon a military format but does not belong to the official, hence legitimate, domain of the security forces." In general, paramilitaries can be contrasted with "more had hoc, loosely organized" death squads, yet "the boundaries between paramilitary forces and death squads are in practice often hazy."[76]

Even more than with other varieties of death squads, paramilitary relations to the state are a matter of interpretive contention. Ostensibly autonomous, they are usually semiofficial in nature and often intimately linked to government forces while serving as their clear proxies. U.S. Defense Department analysts in the late 1990s, for instance, noted that while "distinct from the armed forces of any country," paramilitaries resembled them in "organization, equipment, training, or mission." The Defense analysts also found it reasonable to assume that a paramilitary group is "an agent of the state."[77] For Kruijt and Koonings, paramilitary groups "operate in the interface of politics and violence," and "employ violence, coercion, and terror to back up certain economic, social, or political objectives."[78] They do not, however, *necessarily* do this for the state, any more than other death squads. In fact, the key points for Scobell and Hammitt in determining the nature of any particular paramilitary group are the differing degrees of loyalty it has to the state as well as its level of autonomy.[79] Nevertheless, some students stress connections to state forces. Jasmin Hristov lumps paramilitaries in as an integral, indeed, seamless part of "the state's coercive apparatus," alongside the military, police, intelligence services, and other "death squads." She characterizes "paras" as "the invisible hand" of the state, "a clandestine and illegal extension" of its repressive capacities.[80] Patrice McSherry argues as well that, in Latin America, paramilitary forces are almost invariably "state-sponsored" supplements to regular military forces. She stresses state control and direction of paramilitary groups as part of what she calls the "parastatal structures," that is, "forces and infrastructure of 'black world' special operations."[81]

Such a pronounced emphasis on paramilitary connections to the state could be seen as an understandable interpretive reaction to absurd government denials of any connections whatsoever. But in fact paramilitaries do repeatedly emerge with tenuous state control, or evolve in that direction. Mauricio Romero recognizes that paramilitary "impresarios of coercion" are generally clandestine arms of the state and "violent defenders of the status quo." Yet in Colombia a "divorce" between military brass and civilian leaders facilitated the rise of "paras" on the regional level during the various peace processes that repeatedly drove a wedge between regional and national elites. It was the perceived danger to local elite interests that spawned paramilitary groups there.[82] Julie Mazzei argues along similar lines, and characterizes paramilitaries as extra-state "noninstitutional" actors who use violence "to protect the established order" but denies that they carry out "state-sponsored violence." Rather, they usurp the state's "monopoly over the legitimate use of violence." This happens (whether the state allows it, choosing to "overlook" the usurpation of its prerogatives, or is indeed at times unable to stop it) because of divisions among the elite.[83] For both Romero and Mazzei, the key to paramilitary development is the existence of powerful elites that feel the state has allowed too much reform and opened the door to too much change.[84]

As these differing interpretations make clear, scholars do not completely agree regarding paramilitary autonomy vis a vis the authority of the state. As with any death squad, relationships are complex, given that regional elites or governments are often at odds with national governments. Yet while this is a large, fluid category, it has some unique characteristics. In particular, paramilitary organizations have been more visible than classic death squads—in the size and quasimilitary ordering of their units, in that they generally wear uniforms, and finally, in their open and friendly relationships with regular military and police forces. Yet, like other death squads, they are largely unrecognized by their patrons. Paramilitaries provide distance and degrees of plausible deniability, even though they inhabit legal frameworks of occasional legality and legitimacy.

Varied cases of paramilitarism in Latin America demonstrate what a catch-all category it can be. Sometimes the elites have even been known to take care of business for themselves, and a prime example can be found during the Matanza of 1932 in El Salvador. After the rebel attacks on Sonsonate were repulsed, General José Tomás Calderón encouraged the leading local citizens to form "civic guards." Landowners and other propertied individuals who had things to lose in a social revolution joined these units, and got into the spirit of the enterprise. As historian Thomas Anderson noted, "most of them appear to have been decked out to play in a jungle movie, with riding breeches, high boots, open-neck shirts, and a pith helmet or a wide-brimmed cowboy hat." Though legend credits these groups with numerous massacres, the guardia did the real heavy lifting in the Matanza. The "civic guards" were more prone to carrying out isolated lynchings, and were reminiscent of fascist units in 1930s Italy, or Falangists in Spain.[85]

On rare occasions paramilitary-style organizations have actually been established for popular class "self-defense." In Peru, the Rondas represented "a new relationship binding the peasantry to the armed forces" against the increasingly unpopular and homicidal Sendero Luminoso.[86] But "popular" participation in paramilitary groups has more commonly been coerced, as in the case of Guatemalan Patrullas de Autodefensa Civil, or PACs, where there were "900,000 forcibly recruited (indigenous) peasants in paramilitary units under local army command."[87]

Paramilitaries can also look like straight-up death squads. The term paramilitary in Peru (as well as other places) "can refer to death squads, private justice, armed 'self-defense' groups, 'cleanup operations' (aimed against prostitutes, beggars, homosexuals, etc.) or simply an extension of official state repression."[88] Or they can conform to long-established traditions of political repression. In Mexico, for instance, the federal government was directly involved with paramilitary groups such as the Halcones (the Falcons), a semiofficial group founded in September 1968 that was organized, trained, and financed by the federal district government with the specific purpose of repressing troublesome leftist students. Described as "thugs" and "toughs," their forte was attacking unarmed demonstrators. Their use against students in 1971 proved that President Luis Echeverría's purported commitment to making peace with youth movements in the aftermath of Tlatelolco was short-lived. On June 10, 1971, ten thousand students in Mexico City, demonstrating in sympathy for UNAM students in Monterrey, marched down the Avenida San Cosme, straight into what would become known as the Corpus Christi Massacre. Dozens of young men armed with chains and clubs jumped out of pick-up trucks and vans to attack the demonstrators. After hours of savage fighting, twenty-five students were dead, and many others were wounded. This was perhaps their most famous attack, but the Halcones had also used bamboo sticks to squash a rally on November 4, 1970, in which leftist students were celebrating the victory of Socialist Salvador Allende in the Chilean presidential election. The Echeverría government claimed that the Halcones had no official support, and were merely the natural outgrowth on the right of antileftist feeling, but connections to the Mexican government were known to U.S. embassy officials.[89]

Certainly one of the most notorious organizations that fell into the definitional cracks between death squads and paramilitaries, and which refuses to stay obediently on one side or the other of the state control divide, was the infamous Triple A (short for the Alianza Anticomunista Argentina, or Argentine Anticommunist Alliance). Really a hodgepodge of various allied groups on the far right, it was the creature of Juan Perón's close advisor José López Rega, and spawned a series of namesakes in other countries. Donald Hodges notes that the Triple A was "generally believed to have been organized behind Perón's back." But, he points out, Perón set the process of repression into motion with moves against Peronist governors who had fallen from favor and with the murder of Peronist militants on the left. Also, given Perón's longstanding conflicts with the armed forces, he "had no other choice in combating subversion than to build a secret army with police recruits under police direction." Establishing the model used during the Proceso, "its ranks included not only army officers and police officers on active duty, but also discharged police officers, enlisted criminals, and cadres of the right-wing Peronist Youth of the Argentine Republic (JPRA) and the quasifascist Peronist Trade Union Youth (JSP.)"[90] Patrice McSherry notes the suspect timing of Triple A's emergence after the coup in Chile, and that while it was technically nonstate, its close ties to the Peronist right and the Argentine intelligence community through José María Villone, head of SIDE, Secretaría de Inteligencia del Estado (Secretariat of State Intelligence), and Alberto Villar (who was appointed by López Rega to head the federal police), made it seem like a state agent.[91]

Gunmen working for the Triple A made their first high-profile statement on June 20, 1973, during the Ezeiza Airport Massacre. Standing alongside members of the police forces and representatives of the Ministry of Social Welfare, they were sent to fire on the Montoneros and Peronist Youth who planned to occupy the area directly in front of the platform where Perón was supposed to address the enormous crowd waiting to welcome him home. More than 200 were killed, and even Montonero critics doubted that they returned fire in any serious way—most carried banners.[92] Triple A also made an impact on the national consciousness in November 1973, when members tried, and failed, to assassinate Senator Hipólito Solari Yrigoyen with a car bomb. They came into their own targeting Montonero militants and sympathizers and ERP cadres. They also murdered judges, lawyers, professors, priests, police chiefs, labor organizers, and community leaders with leftist views. The Army Commander in Chief, Jorge Rafael Videla, clearly approved of Triple A activities, as the Argentine army aided and abetted their activities. In their short period of ascendance from 1974 to 1976, they got the dirty war going by killing over two thousand people who right-wing Peronists found offensive. When Triple A was disbanded, its practitioners were absorbed by the state's official repressive apparatus.[93]

Paramilitaries can also be proxy armies funded from abroad, like the Nicaraguan Contras. Though the Contras eventually evolved into a somewhat broader movement, they had originally morphed form the remnants of Somoza's Guardia Nacional. First trained by Argentine dirty warriors, the CIA later sustained them as a paramilitary army. Terror, mayhem, brutality, rape, and murder were their business. Their routine was to arrive at a poorly defended town or village or state farm, assemble all people foolish or unfortunate enough to remain, and murder anyone they suspected of Sandinista sympathy. In the words of one affiliated mercenary, they would slaughter people "like hogs."[94] The period from December 1981 to January 1985 saw many hundreds of attacks by units ranging in size from a dozen or so to a few hundred. They almost always killed at least one person but usually three or four. Occasionally they massacred larger groups of ten to twenty, or even more, as in the October 18, 1983, attack on Pantasma, Jinotega, where they destroyed most of the town and murdered forty civilians and seven defenders. They occasionally paused to inflict ritualistic mutilation on the bodies of their victims. Whether in small or large bands, they tended to target unarmed civilians (the strong suit of the old Guardia Nacional) or attack very small Sandinista defense force outposts. They loved the ambush and were constantly grabbing and/or murdering people on the roads and attacking state farms. They targeted Sandinista neighborhood committees, election commissions, missionary groups, state electric and telecommunications companies, ministries of Agriculture, Natural Resources, and Construction, and even individual farmhouses and towns. Their basic bag of tricks included kidnapping, burning, blowing things up, assassination, mass rapes, torture, and mutilation. State employees were especially vulnerable, but anyone was game, including women, children, and the aged.[95] They were led by "dozens of colorful and ruthless contra leaders" with nicknames like Suicida, Comandante Bravo, Krill, Cancer, and the Jackal. These were "men whose visceral hatred of the Sandinista revolution manifested as systemic terror" against all things Sandinista. Greg Grandin argues that the U.S. cold warriors knew what they were getting with the Contras. They were, according to one Pentagon advisor, "just a bunch of killers."[96] By the end of their run they had killed the huge majority of the thirty thousand civilians killed in the struggle.

Finally, and most important, regional elites have played enormous roles in creating and sustaining paramilitary movements. Mexico, of course, has a long tradition of such groups. Landowners in Chiapas reacted to, and successfully thwarted, land and labor reforms proposed during and after the Revolution of 1910 by creating armed paramilitary bands called Mapaches

(Raccoons). These groups were legalized in the 1950s by the governor of Chiapas, Efraín Arana Osorio, who created the Cuerpo de Policía Auxiliar Ganadera (Auxiliary Ranch Police). Composed of ranch hands, it was used primarily to attack squatters. Soon thereafter landowners began using "private security guards" for similar purposes (giving their preferred answer to popular desires for reform). In 1961, governor Samuel León Brindis legalized the use of these private armed groups, which came to be known as Guardias Blancas, or White Guards. They excelled at murdering peasant leaders, as well as other repressive activities. By the late 1980s, their existence was causing trouble for the national PRI elite, particularly in their negotiations for NAFTA. The Guardias Blancas' legal status was repealed, but they continued to operate, even in conjunction with police units.[97] Paramilitary groups were also deployed for the political "reconquest" of the Loxicha area of Oxaca. Loxicha communities in the 1980s had united to drive out the local political caciques. The caciques counterattacked with their own version of Guardia Blanca paramilitaries, acting in league with judicial police and the Mexican army to "terrorize and subdue the local population."[98]

It was in response to the Zapatista "uprising" in Chiapas in 1994, however, that Mexican elites showed their true mettle by forming at least twelve different paramilitary groups to thwart popular mobilizations. In the years since, these groups have killed in excess of fifteen thousand people. The process began when the PRI government made a pact with the EZLN and angered a constellation of actors. Indeed, in May 1994, CIA analysts noted that portions of the PRI, the Mexican military and local Chiapan elites, wanted to step up counterinsurgency against Zapatistas. They took matters into their own hands and created various paramilitary groups. These groups had obvious ties to local rancher and business elites, and to police and locally stationed military units, which supplied training, equipment, and even salaries. In addition, the Mexican army drew up the Plan of Campaign Chiapas 94. This plan identified groups that could be called on to form paramilitary units, especially ranchers and small-property owners of a "patriotic" bent. The largest of these organizations was named (with dark irony) Paz y Justicia (Peace and Justice). Others included Los Chinchulines (also known by other names, such as United Front and Ejido Members), the Moviminento Indígena Revolucionaria Anti-Zapatista (MIRA; Indigenous Revolutionary Anti-Zapatista Movement), La Máscara Roja (The Red Mask), and Los Puñales (The Daggers). In a typical attack, in 1996, Los Chinchulines struck Bachajón after a local election result that was unfavorable to local elites. They killed six and burned a school, a Jesuit mission, a local indigenous rights center, and various homes.[99] After 1996, in the Loxicha region of Oaxaca, government and paramilitary forces waged a preventative "brutal, low-intensity war" against the local population who might have sympathies for the Zapatista guerrillas. As Kristin Norget describes it, the evolution of "Mexico's 'militarized democracy' . . . has involved a delicately balanced construction of a semblance of a 'rule of law' on the one hand and unchecked police violence on the other." Through the use of disappearances and murders, the military and their paramilitary allies worked to limit the public space for activity by the political opposition.[100]

The most notorious paramilitary massacre in Chiapas, and in Mexico, took place in December 1997 at the village of Acteal. It was bigger than most para attacks, and the lack of government response (police and local military units ignored calls for help) was glaring.[101] The attack occurred in the midst of PRI attempts to reassert control of the region in November, and was preceded by an assassination attempt on Bishop Samuel Ruiz. Many villagers had been killed, and others sought refuge in Acteal. On December 22, Paz y Justicia moved in and butchered forty-five people (nine men, twenty-one women, fifteen children). They targeted members of Las Abejas, a Christian indigenous group. Most were shot in the back, shot as they prayed, and shot as they fled. The killing went on for over five hours. Bodies were hacked with machetes. Police, who could hear gunfire at their station, did not respond until it was over, and then let the paras leave with their weapons. President Ernesto Zedillo went on TV to denounce the attack (and many PRI old-guard "dinosaurs" felt betrayed), though Jorge Madrazo, the Federal Prosecutor General blamed the attack on "inter-communal conflicts."[102]

Yet clearly Latin American paramilitarism enjoyed its most vibrant flowering to date in Colombia, where the role of regional elites was paramount. There have been more than 100 paramilitary groups in Colombia in recent decades, and some became major players in national politics, controlling huge territories.[103] Paramilitary groups in Colombia represent the culmination of several parallel lines of development, going back to the beginning of the Violencia. The first came out of the "police" death squad and pájaro traditions of the 1940s and 1950s. After 1949, pájaros became full-time professionals and more urban in their target base. The second was the 1960s state organizational effort (exhibited in Decree 3398 of 1965 and Law 48 of 1968), which was driven by national security doctrines and cold war ideologies. In the 1960s and 1970s, landowners used this type of group to kill peasant land-reform leaders and activists (though in the 1970s the Colombia state tended more to use arbitrary detention). In the 1980s, murder, extrajudicial execution, and disappearances reemerged in full flower with the third and ultimate incarnation of Colombian paramilitariam, during which the landed narco elite and their private armed groups made an "unholy alliance" with emerald miners and smugglers, the Colombian military, and multinational corporations.[104] In the area around Puerto Boyacá, paramilitary groups evolved in the late 1980s and 1990s into armies.

In the early 1980s, the organization known as Muerte a Secuestradores (MAS, Death to Kidnappers) was the first model that regional elites, reinforced by their new entrepreneurial recruits from the narcotics business, hit upon to protect their interests as guerrilla groups increasingly targeted them for kidnapping, extortion, and "war taxes." Yet death squads operating under the MAS mantel soon evolved in a more institutionalized direction. This evolution was driven as much by central government attempts to negotiate with guerrilla forces and the political left as it was by actual security concerns. Thus elites throughout the north sought to restore "order" and eliminate the possibility of democratization. They were aided by local military units, especially the 14th Brigade of the Army in the Magdalena River valley.[105] In particular, the Castaño family stepped in to give the movement a strong political focus. The Castaños controlled a large finca named Las Tangas in a "liberated" zone in Córdoba. Beginning in 1987, Las Tangas became a training camp that spawned a paramilitary group known as Los Tangüeros. Fidel Castaño deployed this band of more than one hundred fighters to hunt guerrillas and, more specifically, their support groups.[106] Under Fidel and his brothers Carlos and Vicente, Los Tangüeros evolved, after 1994, into the ACCU, which continued to focus, not surprisingly, on the various guerrilla movements' bases of support and sympathy. Though the ACCU was the largest paramilitary organization, it was joined by others, such as those of José Gonzalo Rodríguez Gacha (a.k.a. "El Mexicano") and Henry Pérez, who formed the Autodefensas Campesinas del Magdalena Medio, Víctor Carranza in Boyacá, who led the Autodefensas de las Llanos Orientales, as well as Autodefensa groups in César, Santander, and Cundinamarca, among others. As these groups became more decidedly political in their orientation, they excelled at murdering leftist mayors, especially of the UP party, in waves from the late 1980s to the late 1990s.[107] Finally, in April 1997, Carlos Castaño united the various "bloques" into a general, if rather loose, confederation called the AUC, which had very clear connections to the Colombian army. While an "influx of drug money" allowed Colombian paramilitaries "to develop offensive military capabilities with large numbers of troops, in some cases better financed than the military," it is also clear that these organizations were more creatures of right-wing politics and their "antisubversive project" in support of the status quo than of straight narcotics trafficking.[108] In zones controlled by the AUC in the northeast and in the Magdalena Medio, they remade their regions through murder and displacement. Economic and political power was concentrated in the hands of the business and agrarian elite, while public protest and discussion of issues were severely restricted.[109]

Colombian "paras" of all stripes enjoyed intimate relations with individual military and police units. Many commentators have noted that they were comfortable operating "within startlingly close proximity" to army installations.[110] In fact, they habitually used army transports, passed at will through checkpoints, and placed their bases next to military bases. What is more, paras were principally active in the most heavily militarized zones, neutralizing the guerrilla "auxiliaries." Police and military patrols saw nothing, apparently, of the one-hundred-member-strong para units that passed by on land and on the Magdalena River.[111] The military was involved through its noninterventions into paramilitary attacks and its late arrivals at massacres. They also provided weapons and transport, training assistance, shared personnel, and carried out joint operations with para units.[112] The model massacre was at Mapiripán on July 12, 1997. Two chartered flights carrying paramilitary combatants flew from Urabá to a military-controlled airport at San José de Guaviare, where army soldiers helped transport their weapons and gear and waved them through army checkpoints. After joining one hundred eighty local paras, they spent five days in Mapiripán, hunting specific "subversives" they had earlier identified as guerrilla supporters. These people were taken to the local slaughterhouse and murdered. The army later denied any responsibility, claiming they simply had no troops available to counter this attack. These denials are belied, however, by the fact that the army's Third Brigade in Cali, Fifth Brigade in Librija, Santander, and Naval Intelligence Unit No. 7 in Barrancabermeja also supported paras and have been linked to murders. The army's 24th Brigade in Putumayo even coordinated operations with paras. The military has been known to cordon off areas before para attacks. One instance was the attack at El Salado, Bolívar, in 2001. For two days, three hundred paras killed, tortured, raped, decapitated victims, drank, and danced, while the Navy's First Brigade manned roadblocks. On other occasions military units abandoned regular roadblocks right before a para attack, as they did before the La Granja Massacre in Antioquia in 1996.

Regarding the question of why the military would give up its "monopoly over the legitimate use of violence," it seems clear that letting paramilitaries do the dirty work gives the regular forces plausible deniability. Though "unofficial," the paras are integral to the antisubversion fight. As many officers in Colombia have argued, "the paramilitaries were simply brothers-in-arms, able to carry out those missions that the military itself could not."[113] Yet at times the military dispenses with any pretense of separation and simply works with the paras, as when they have coordinated efforts to weed out leftist political candidates.[114] Paras have also done the bidding of local police departments. Carlos Castaño told journalist Salud Hernández-Mora that police would often point out individuals they believed to be guerrillas. There was no proof, they said, but the implication remained that there was something Castaño could do. The autodefensas took the hint and would execute the subversives.[115]

Yet close ties to Colombia's security forces did not translate into consistent relations with the national government. These have been driven by other players in the elite and the military and are not always as close as paramilitary/military relations imply. National policy has been erratic, whipsawing through a series of course changes. In 1982, President Belisario Betancur tried to curb military and police brutality while negotiating with guerrillas and oversaw the creation of the Union Patriotica. His actions led to several reactions. In its own struggle with the executive branch over these issues, the army looked to the regional elites for alliances. Both felt betrayed by Bentancur's negotiations with the guerrillas and consistently blocked any talk of reform beyond simple surrender and demobilization of the guerrillas, with no political reform or wealth redistribution.[116] Carlos Castaño became the poster boy for the no-peace-negotiation crowd and the defenders of threatened rural property interests. As a master of political murder, Castaño made lots of friends, including rural property owners who would lose out in a peace deal; urban elites afraid of kidnapping; the army; political bosses; and narcos.[117] In 1989, the Colombian Supreme Court declared armed civilian paramilitary bands unconstitutional and banned them. But this was a long-practiced tradition, and local elites were ready to fight their own dirty war when their legal status was revoked. And of course they were still supported by portions of the military.[118] Under the Gaviria administration, paramilitaries were relegalized yet again with the CONVIVIR movement after 1994, which was particularly embraced by Alvaro Uribe as governor of Antioquia, and ushered in the ACCU and its brethren. There were some subsequent efforts by the state to control the paras, in particular when President Andrés Pastrana created a special unit to arrest paramilitary leaders, and indeed called them "paras" and not "autodefensas."[119] Yet Uribe, as president, reversed Pastrana's policies and definitively ended twenty years of attempts at peace and guerrilla inclusion into politics, doing a 180-degree turn in 2002.[120]

Paramilitary groups in Latin America represent contradictory trends. They can exhibit clear national state involvement, as well as uncontrolled adventures by powerful regional elites. Yet they are not the most problematic incarnation of "wet work" practice.

Freelancers and Rogues

At the chaotic end of the death squad spectrum, political murder professionals can easily come untethered from centers of authority and operate in freer forms. Such groups have much in common with paramilitaries but are less organized. (In fact, the grand paramilitary federations of the Colombian experience are a fragile anomaly.) Off the leash, these bands can run wild like a hound too long confined, not necessarily restricting themselves to direct "state" interests. They represent the ragged edge of the paramilitary impulse, never enjoying even short moments of legality, and not really needing them.

Scholars often reject the very idea of an "out of control" death squad. Governments evoke them to deflect blame, seeking plausible deniability and even sympathy (that is, when they are not categorically denying death squads' very existence). The Reagan administration and the U.S. State Department, for instance, insisted that in El Salvador the "violence came from fringe elements on the left and right" and that the government was innocent. The various state agencies there appreciated this "death squad cover."[121] Pushing back against such deliberate nonsense, many interpretations stress state supremacy and insist that "out of control" arguments are just part of the denial game. Piero Gleijeses argued that by the late 1960s in Guatemala, "civilian" death squads acted increasingly "under the orders of the military" and noted that in 1981 Amnesty International doubted claims that death squad abuses were the fault of "independent groups." Martha Huggins dismissed the "outdated" idea that death squads in Brazil were random and disconnected from one another and from the state. And Patrice McSherry, alluding to military states in particular, has pointed out that to bolster their legitimacy and cover up their unsavory operations, they "created shadow systems to carry out illegal acts that were, on the one hand, visible—part of the strategy of terror—but on the other, deniable." Murder, mayhem, and assassinations, cynical governments argue, are the fault of such death squads and, lamentably, beyond their reach.[122] Such claims are clearly phony much if not most of the time.

Yet occasionally death squads really do get out of hand. As noted at various times in this study, nonstate elites have their own interests, while Latin American central states often lack the wherewithal to impose the classic Weberian monopoly on the use of violence. Bruce Campbell noted that it is "easy to see why states" (and/or other backers) "lose control over death squads; their irregular, informal organization and the demands of covert action make the exercise of control very difficult. Moreover, death squads exist to act outside the law: by definition their 'job' is to commit extrajudicial murder."[123] Even police states have their problems with control. McSherry acknowledged that the intelligence communities of various countries had structures that operated "outside normal military chains of command." In Brazil, for example, the 1964 junta created a covert intelligence organization called the Serviço Nacional de Informaçoes (National Information Service), or SNI. The SNI and its paramilitary squads "became semi-autonomous and occasionally acted to derail the political program of the military government itself."[124] And when the military government in Brazil placed police power under military control in 1969, they caused increased tension between civilian and military authorities and police hierarchies. Their attempts at control fostered the creation of additional police death squads that could evade military control, resulting in overlap and conflict between units.[125]

Death squads can have their own agendas, compete with other death squads, and at times answer only to themselves, becoming powers in their own right. Indeed, police "extensions" were often influenced but not "commanded" by police or other arms of government, such as the army. They could have "a life of their own," with their own structures, traditions, intelligence, and funding.[126] The death squads of the Salvadoran military employed, in the words of CIA analysts, "both active-duty and retired military personnel" and were not necessarily controlled by the military establishment. Squads were led by junior officers as well as noncoms, often without consent of their superiors. These officers shared Roberto D'Aubuisson's attitudes toward leftists, and though he had been kicked out of the military, did his bidding.[127] In Brazil, as death squad violence became "institutionalized," Huggins has argued, "it eventually began turning against itself. The combination of pressure on security forces to make arrests, get confessions, collect intelligence, and eliminate dangerous elements—all carried out in a climate of total war—exacerbated competition among them." The system of social and political control became diffuse and hard to manage; many police units, and their semiofficial offshoots, operated as autonomous death squads. Indeed, even as Brazil's last two military presidents attempted to scale back state violence, the number of unofficial death squads expanded.[128] In Colombia, El Vampiro, one of El Condor's lieutenants during the Violencia, insisted on his autonomy of action—he was on a mission. He claimed to have worked alone, arriving at a town and putting together a Conservative team of five to ten people in a cantina or in a neighborhood to do a "little job." The party elite made him a police inspector, but "nobody gave me orders." He understood how to "defend Conservative interests."[129] Even Guatemalan military governments, known for their high level of coordination among death squads by Army Intelligence, could manage only varying levels of direct state control over its wide variety of groups.[130]

Not uncommonly, death squads and paramilitaries will feel the entrepreneurial spirit and "go rogue" for their own benefit, morphing and blending into and out of petty criminality. Sergeant Ibañez of the Argentine army noted that most GTs "self-financed" their activities with victim loot and cash, often driving victim-owned vehicles. There were also bitter rivalries between GTs. Some were unofficial and operated with no written orders; these groups were particularly "interested in money." As a result, "no one trusted anyone." It was "a very dirty atmosphere," in which GT members would get drunk and head out on their own initiative for their own benefit. Ibañez asserted that "the situation had slipped out of the leaders' hands; they had lost control."[131] Argentine task forces would ransack a target's home, stealing cash, art works, jewelry, televisions, refrigerators and other appliances, alcohol, cars, oriental rugs, books, basically anything not nailed down—even the victim's children.[132] In Colombia, in 1951, Governor Braulio Henao Mejía of Antioquia noted that violence was getting out of hand and moving beyond politics. Death squad groups (and even some guerrillas) were more intent on pillaging and used murder, burning, and rape to facilitate their economic activities. These groups in eastern Antioquia became largely independent actors.[133]

Death squads can likewise work directly for business interests. Local Conservative authorities during the Colombian Violencia used Contrachusmas for robbery, extortion, and land seizures.[134] And Colombian pájaros moonlighted beyond the political for a whole host of groups that benefited directly from their work, particularly large coffee farmers and sellers. Later, more "professional" versions of pájaros sold their services to rural Conservative groups in western Colombia.[135] In more recent decades, freelancing paras in Colombia practiced "limpieza social" ("social cleansing") against people who threatened the interests of small-business owners (and sometimes bigger firms). They targeted, "petty thieves, beggars, the homeless, poor mentally ill people, garbage and recycle collectors, informal street vendors, street prostitutes . . . drug addicts, and homosexuals." As a store owner at the Valledupar bus terminal put it, "the station used to be invaded by guerrillas and bums. . . . Then someone called the self-defense groups to help us bring about order."[136]

In Brazil, Milton Le Cocq, one of the founders of the modern police death squad impulse there, also created an eight-member semiofficial group known as the "Turma de pesada" ("hard duty group") that received extra compensation from business owners. This group represented a breed of privatized death squads (well before military rule) that emerged to serve the interests of business owners, who "subcontracted service" from them. Policeman Ademar Agosto de Olivera (known as "o fininho"—the sly one) led such an eight-member death squad in São Paulo, as did the former police officer Silas Pereira de Andrade, "Sergeant Bob," in Rio de Janeiro, which was funded by a supermarket chain. And, in July 1969, the OBAN program for the São Paulo region, created to eliminate subversive groups, spawned a privatized offshoot, funded by local business and multinationals (purportedly including Ford and GM) that eventually expanded to other parts of Brazil after 1970.[137] Brazilian "policing extensions" readily demonstrated their more "commercial" inclinations with a mixture of "organized crime and private security companies as co-organizers of death squads and death squad activity." These squads, comprised of former and moonlighting police, were well paid and worked on a contract basis.[138]

And, finally, regional elites can have their own ideas. In Mexico, in the decades after the revolution, the power and activity of the local caciques waxed and waned. They employed "a kind of hardball politics" that "involved recurrent use of force and intimidation; murders, ambushes, and 'punitive expeditions.'" Over time the central government came to exercise more control over these players, but it was never complete.[139] During the Violencia in Colombia, the national police in Bogotá did not universally approve of the use of Conservative faux police to harass public employees and blue-collar workers who happened to be Liberals. In January 1950, for example, the Director of the National Police in Bogotá complained to the governor of Antioquia about such practices. But local bosses and mayors often ignored Bogotá's wishes.[140] And, of course, one of the most famous "rogue" death squads in Colombia was Los PEPES. On the one hand, this squad seemed to work in very closely coordinated fashion with government assets. Los PEPES was the classic intersection of U.S. elements (DEA, CIA, the Army's Centra Spike and Delta Force) with a homegrown base. Los PEPES was the most specific death squad in Colombian, and perhaps Latin American, history, devoted to taking out Pablo Escobar's organization and Pablo himself. While the U.S. element was rogue by definition, there were plenty of suspects and conspirators, besides the Gringos, who were not under state supervision, including disgruntled members of the Medellín cartel, leaders of the rival Cali cartel, and especially the brothers Castaño.

Los PEPES certainly did not seem to be tightly controlled by the Gaviria administration.

The enormous array of organizational methods employed to murder advocates of change in Latin America can bewilder and befuddle. They are very messy and convoluted in practice; overlap is the norm. To say that not all death squads are alike is an understatement. They have demonstrated both overt and covert connections to the state, or other elites. Death squads and paramilitaries served powerful people, but not always the state. Indeed, as the case of Colombia showed, attempts at political reform, decentralization, democratization, and increasing political competition had the effect of increasing political violence and polarization. The national state was trying one thing, and some elites were trying another.[141] Paramilitarism is an old, old proclivity in Latin America and a fundamental expression of the political culture of murder. Paramilitarism embodies the expectation on the part of the elite, or part of it, that official security forces should kill threats to the status quo, and reflects their anger when government does not take up the job.

Chapter 3

Bodies of the Slain

In 1982 Joan Didion traveled to El Salvador. She went there to witness firsthand the murderous rampage being perpetrated by that country's ruling elites. Her writer's eye quickly focused on the practice of body dumping. She noted that bodies, often mutilated, appeared on the shoulders of roads. Their faces might be destroyed with acid, or pummeled beyond all recognition, or have crosses carved into them. She learned, as did all visitors to San Salvador in those years, that vultures start on the eye balls and genitalia, if they are exposed, and on the mouth. She discovered that mouths could be stuffed with things, like the victim's penis, or dirt. Bodies or parts of bodies could turn up anywhere, any day, often heralded by a murder of crows or a group of curious children. They appeared in vacant lots, garbage dumps, public restrooms, bus stations, lakes, and rivers. Some dumpsites even became de facto tourist destinations. Sometimes people were killed elsewhere and moved in for viewing; other times they were killed on location and left where they dropped. Particular spots were supplied with a constant stream of precisely placed corpses. Locals would argue about how many there had been, when they appeared, and whether the supply was waxing or waning.[1]

As Didion illustrated, killing thousands of people has many implications, both physical and political. The corpses literally begin to pile up and start to rot. How each national or regional elite has dealt with this issue is instructive: some saw it as a problem to be solved; others viewed it as an opportunity to communicate. The absence of bodies, that is, to be disappeared, is perhaps the quintessential image associated with Latin American political murder, but it was not the most common outcome. Bodies usually turned up, sometimes sooner, sometimes later. In some cases they were buried in mass graves. In others they were thrown into bodies of water. And sometimes, as the example of El Salvador makes clear, they were purposefully left where they fell or dumped in meaningful places for public view.

Transformed into symbols, bodies served as fantastically expressive canvasses in a macabre form of art created to send powerful political messages. They demonstrate what can happen to pesky irritants to elite programs. Their significance can be blunt, of course, but also surprisingly subtle. There are, for instance, signs of torture that were clearly inflicted while the victims lived. And then there is the fanciful mutilation of corpses. Both are intended to communicate different impressions. Ultimately, however, the bodies of political murder victims have a clear relationship to ideas and to political practice. They are especially connected to collective ideas, which they are meant to discourage, or even quash. They give a new twist to the concept of "embodiment" by turning ideas themselves into corpses. Throughout Latin America, bodies, their conditions, and their final resting places have long been an important symbolic element in the practice of political murder.

In recent decades scholars have focused a great deal on "the body" and have produced an enormous quantity of works relating the state of human bodies to questions of gender, state control, economic development, and sexuality, among other themes. The body has been something of a boom industry, in which investigators have examined "embodiment, embodied experiences, body regulation, bodywork, representations of bodies, and cultural exposures of bodies." There are, however, holes in the literature. There has been, for instance, limited consideration of "the visibility of bodies."[2] And even more pronounced is the paucity of work on the meaning and uses (political or otherwise) of corpses.[3] Most studies (perhaps not surprisingly) have focused on living bodies.[4] But there is one recent work that takes up the challenge: Katherine Verdery's *The Political Lives of Dead Bodies* (1999).

Verdery explores how human remains can inflame emotion and embody political ideas. She points out that dead bodies "have enjoyed political life the world over and since far back in time."[5] She views politics as a struggle over meaning and finds "dead bodies a particularly good vehicle" for the distribution of political messages. Dead bodies "offer us some purchase on the cultural dimension" of politics, specifically "meanings, feelings, the sacred, ideas of morality, the nonrational." Verdery insists, however that there is "no uniform interpretation of the political lives of dead bodies" and stresses their local context. Portraying dead bodies "as unusually ambiguous, protean symbols," she points to "multiple possibilities lodged in a given corpse." While noting that bodies are "material objects" that are "indisputably *there*," and that a cadaver "can be moved around, displayed, and strategically located in specific places," she still insists that "the significance of corpses has less to do with their concreteness than with how people think about them." The meanings of these "symbolic vehicles" are set by "culturally established relations to death."[6]

In the specific case of Latin America, Lyman Johnson and a group of collaborators have recently addressed the question of "body politics" by focusing on "martyred heroes" and investigating "the political meanings associated with bodies, or body parts," some of which were "reclaimed symbolically by later generations who found enduring meaning in the sufferings of these martyrs."[7] Johnson argued that the "human remains of these heroes, and the locations associated with their sacrifices and martyrdoms, retain powerful emotional content that can be used to mobilize mass action on behalf of a nation, an ethnic group, or a class." His group believed that "these highly political dead bodies . . . have the potential to illuminate Latin American political culture." They tie the use of bodies to the "Western tradition" of political reverence and remembrance that relies "on a symbolic language uniquely informed by the enduring importance of catholic Christianity," on the region's "experience of conquest and colonization," and on the "complexity" of its "cultural practices." Most important for the current study, Johnson asserted that given "the persistence of economic and social injustice" throughout the region, it is clear that "dead bodies in Latin America are likely to speak the language of social protest or to urge resistance to foreign exploiters as to celebrate national greatness."[8]

But even these important exceptions to the dearth of literature on dead bodies do not address the masses of dirty war dead. In their explorations of the political uses of corpses in Latin America, Johnson and company touched on two important victims of political murder (or at least extrajudicial execution): Emiliano Zapata and Che Guevara. They did not, however, address the wider issue of how the hundreds of thousands of bodies of lesser-known dirty war dead were used. And with due respect to Verdery's wise insistence on the importance of local historical context and astute observation that corpses can have many meanings, it can be argued that all dirty war dead are "politicized" corpses and that they "say" similar things and repeat certain themes, even if some speak louder than others. That is, historical context influences how the sight of a body will affect witnesses. Yet even in dirty war times and places, when one might think that their ubiquitous presence would become mundane, dead bodies continue to jar and disturb. The sight of them never becomes ordinary.

Dead bodies in Latin America, as we shall see, have been put to many political uses, and indeed, are themselves contested territory. The fight "over" bodies exists in two senses: they lie underfoot (as it were) while political battles rage, and they become objectives in themselves. In a horrifically literal interpretation of an old cliché, many of the perpetrators actually prefer to enforce their will "over" the dead bodies of anyone who might object. Elaine Scarry speaks of "injuries and deaths" as a "by-product" of war that is "usually preceded by an adjective," and lists "terrible," "necessary," "acceptable," "inevitable," and "unacceptable." She leaves out some obvious qualifiers, however, with regard to political murder in Latin American. Many elites consider the bodies generated by political murder to be useful and desired byproducts.[9] On the other hand, survivors and resisters seek and use bodies as evidence for indictments, as historical documents, as reminders to assure that such crimes never happen again ("nunca más"), and finally, as sacred relics of struggle and mobilization. Oftentimes the witnesses and victims of violence become traumatized and unable to see political murder as part of a larger phenomenon. The political purpose of murder is lost on them, and they come to regard it as a "mindless" act. Scholars can lose sight of the bloody and disturbing nature of what they are abstracting and generalizing. Balance can be hard. Yet the bodies are reminders. The mutilation and display of corpses showcases the human capacity for brutality, savagery, and slaughter for political purposes. Bodies tell the tale of the long history of vicious struggles for domination, even as their ultimate political meaning remains ambiguous. Nevertheless, elites clearly believe that savagery works to cow people into submission, and there is unfortunately ample evidence to support their view.

Dust to Dust

In recounting his experiences as an officer in the Royal Welsh Fusiliers during an offensive against the German position at La Bassée in the fall of 1915, the poet and classicist Robert Graves provided a powerful image of human decay. "After the first day or two the corpses swelled and stank. . . . Those we could not get in from the German wire continued to swell until the wall of the stomach collapsed, either naturally or when punctured by a bullet; a disgusting smell would float across. The colour of the dead faces changed from white to yellow-grey, to red, to purple, to green, to black, to slimy."[10] Vivid and haunting, this is also a highly accurate portrait of the progress of decomposition.

Autolysis, literally "self-digestion," is known as the "fresh stage" of decay. In a moderate environment, a dead body loses about one and a half degrees Fahrenheit an hour until it cools to the temperature of its environs. Even while there are no obvious signs of decay, the body's cells have begun to break down, as tissues fall prey to enzymes that normally deconstruct compounds for the body's use. As cell walls disintegrate, fluids seep out. These fluids are a rich food source for the body's resident bacteria, whose populations consequently explode. This exponential increase in bacteriological metabolic activity produces acids and gas, which a dead body cannot readily expel, so its cavities and more elastic tissues begin to bloat, especially the abdomen, lips, and tongue. As putrefaction progresses, gas in the abdominal cavity forces feces and other liquids out of the corpse. Pressure will eventually cause a rupture, usually in the intestines, and gas will escape after about a week. Flies will lay their eggs in any and all of the body's openings, and maggots will soon begin to attack the body's fat stores, and as they grow larger and stronger, all the soft tissues. Indeed, hungry and energetic maggots can make the tongue and facial features jerk and twitch, seemingly reanimating a dead face.[11] Beetles will also move in to attack muscle mass.

Bacteriological breakdown of hemoglobin causes the body's color to turn green. As the lips and tongue swell, they distort the face. Blisters develop and ooze serous fluids, and the whole skin becomes loose and prone to slipping off if the body is moved. Body hair starts to fall off, though hair will remain on the skull long after the soft tissue is gone. The body's color will change from green to brown to black. Typically, decay will result in the liquefaction of all the body's soft tissues. Bones will start to become visible ten days to two weeks after death, depending on the temperature, even if the remains dry out and begin to mummify. The smell of death will pass, and what is left might become covered with grave wax, a white flakey, soap-like substance that builds up wherever the body's fat deposits break down into fatty acids, on the cheeks, chest or breasts, and the buttocks. Under the right conditions, and allowed enough time, the cadaver will decompose completely to its skeletal structure. Finally, along with insects, scavengers and larger carnivores will naturally attack an unattended body and disarticulate its parts; the bones might end up widely scattered.[12]

Such a graphic description of decay reminds us that political murder is not a historical abstraction but causes the death of real, physical people. It underscores our mortality, our shared and universal fate. To quote Genesis, 3:19, "In the sweat of thy face shalt thou eat bread, till thou return unto the ground; for out of it wast thou taken: for dust thou art, and unto dust shalt thou return." As Verdery argues, dead bodies "evoke the awe, uncertainty, and fear associated with 'cosmic' concerns, such as the meaning of life and death." They bring onlookers "face to face with ultimate questions about what it means to be—and stop being—human." Human remains are "heavy symbols" because they once belonged to individuals who had lived among those left behind, people who cared about them.[13]

Decaying bodies are thus physically repulsive and emotionally disturbing. Respected people and loved ones have become disgusting heaps of rotting flesh and bones. This fact has political uses.

Ancient Traditions

Political manipulation of corpses was hardly unique to twentieth-century Latin America. It reflected a broader historical framework of social engineering through body disfigurement and display. While now reclassified as "extrajudicial," these traditions long represented legitimate and overt mechanisms of control. This was savagery as legal and political theater, the symbolic utilization of publically displayed corpses (often mutilated) by conquerors, by elites, by the state, and even by organizations such as the Italian mafia and other organized crime groups that aspired to political dominance. This was not just a sadistic game but rather the product of genuine political rationale. Rulers in the Western tradition have long used bodies to make the point that they are in charge, and that they will prove it on the person of anyone who doubts it. In fact, such displays have been widespread in the history of human civilizations. Jean Elshtain noted that human history "is a story of deportations, banishments, bodily wrenching and torments of every kind." It is the very omnipresent nature of such practices that invite "sober meditation on how much politics, from its very inception, has had to do with the disposition of human bodies." And Timothy Cloyd agrees that human history "is dotted with the invention and application of ingenious ways of inflicting pain on the bodies of our fellow human beings."[14] In this sense, participating Latin American elites are unabashedly old school.

Before the late eighteenth-century, European states routinely indulged in what Michel Foucault called the "gloomy festival of punishment," involving torture, dismemberment, amputation, symbolic branding, and public displays of maimed corpses. These practices displayed the power of the sovereign in a graphic way.[15] And these are very old traditions. Crucifixion, generally associated with the Roman state, but also used by the Persians, Greeks, Macedonians, and Carthaginians, among others, always involved display of the corpse. The point of crucifixion, whether tied to a tree or nailed to a post or a cross, was to cause death in a slow, horribly painful and very public way. It was, indeed, designed for maximum humiliation. The condemned were invariably naked, and since the process could take days, they had to urinate and defecate for all to see (and on themselves). And of course, the body was left to rot, disintegrate, and be picked apart by vultures and crows. In the Roman world, such a fate was reserved for rebellious slaves, pirates, and anyone declared enemies of the Republic (or Empire). At the end of the Third Servile War in 71 BCE, Marcus Licinius Crassus famously crucified the remnants of Spartacus's defeated army of rebellious slaves, numbering over 6,000, and exhibited them along the Appian Way stretching from Capua to Rome. While certainly a large mass crucifixion, it was hardly out of the ordinary. The Romans regularly crucified hundreds of condemned at a time. Crucifixion, and the accompanying exhibition of the cadaver, was meant to bring dishonor on those killed. In most traditions, certainly in the West, bodies were supposed to be buried or burned; if not, there had to be a good reason. Constantine the Great, as a recent convert to Christianity, discontinued crucifixion as a Roman method of execution in the early fourth century, given the associations with his new God. Yet the general concept survived, and even thrived, as Vlad III, known as "Vlad the Impaler," prince of Wallechia (part of modern Romania), would later demonstrate in the fifteenth century. Though death came much quicker with impalement, it was a close cousin of crucifixion, given its equally gruesome and long-lasting displays.

Competing legal methods for showing elite displeasure with popular behavior ranged from grotesque (yet nonlethal) torture to fiendish butchery: whipping, ripping out teeth, blinding, branding with irons, castration, breaking bones (in "breaking on the wheel," the victim was tied on and spun as heavy blows were dealt with large hammers—the breaking was literal), boiling in oil, scalding with water, roasting, burning at the stake, flaying, choking, sawing, and finally, dismemberment, usually with axes or swords, though sometimes horses were used to pull bodies apart. Dismemberment reflected the widespread Christian belief that bodies needed to be buried intact and facing east in order to rise and meet God on Judgment Day. Many people believed that dismemberment could prevent resurrection of an individual at the Second Coming, thus ensuring the most eternal punishment. When victims were "drawn and quartered," parts of the body were typically sent to all points of the realm, and of course the head invariably ended up on a stake.

By the late middle ages, however, hanging by the neck had become the most common form of execution in the West. In villages, towns, cities, and on great estates, the gibbet, the traditional gallows configuration of an upright post holding a crossbeam that formed a T or an upside-down L, generally stood as a permanent feature in the local architecture, invariably in a prominent place. The elaborate triangular gallows at Tyburn, outside London, could accommodate up to twenty-four individuals at once. "Gibbets with human corpses," Roger Ekirch noted, "littered the early modern countryside," though sometimes "trees provided handy substitutes."[16] Gallows and cages were also routinely placed at crossroads, as crosses were in Roman times. Bodies, as a rule, were left hanging until they disintegrated. Thus fresh corpses or skeletal remains were usually on constant display. Captain William Kidd, for instance, was hanged for piracy in 1701, and his remains were suspended in an iron cage at Tilbury Point over the River Thames for the next twenty years. His body served as a not-so-subtle reminder to outward-bound mariners of the dangers involved in the path he purportedly followed. Such demonstrations were especially useful in the political realm, and even today, "political transformation is often symbolized through manipulating bodies."[17] A famous example occurred after the Restoration of the monarchy in England in 1660. The newly installed Charles II went out of his way to make a political point about his old adversary in the English Civil War, Oliver Cromwell, and to clear up any ambiguity about the return of royal sovereignty. Charles had Cromwell's body exhumed from its exalted resting place at Westminster Abbey. It was first hanged in chains for a spell at the famous gallows at Tyburn, and then drawn and quartered. The decapitated bulk of his corpse was thrown into a common grave, and his head was displayed on a pole outside Westminster Hall for the next twenty-five years (until a storm blew it down.) The same "punishment" was dealt out to two of the other most high-profile, yet deceased, signatories to Charles I's death warrant. A fourth regicide was too decomposed to castigate.

Yet by the early nineteenth century, as Foucault noted, most European states had begun a process whereby "the great spectacle of physical punishment disappeared; the tortured body was avoided; the theatrical representation of pain was excluded from punishment." He argued that "disciplinary power, focused on individuals" came to operate "through institutions and discourses to make docile subjects and productive bodies," and went on to explore the many "subtle mechanisms" of coercion that lead people to police themselves.[18] This move away from the bloody legal displays of earlier ages, an evolution evident on both sides of the Atlantic, came to obscure the more obvious and red-toothed relations of power. Executioners carrying out official state killings began to seek more "humane" methods, a process begun with the invention of the guillotine. (Executions with axes seldom occurred with a single blow. The condemned were often still alive after repeated blows.) The bloody "mess" of killing was thus minimized. States practicing official, judicially sanctioned executions, such as the United

States, now aspired to a "clean death" and hoped to avoid earlier images of "murder" by the state. "Execution" is a term that "denotes a higher level of ceremony and efficiency than murder, as well as carrying the weight of law." And some states even prefer the more "neutral" and "ambiguous" phrase "put to death."[19]

Interestingly enough, many states in Africa and Asia that still practice execution do not aspire to the modern "clinical" and "clockwork" ideal of killing. They revel in messy executions, what are referred to as "dirty deaths." These "ancient, pre-modern methods of execution" are "decidedly bloody." They include stoning (in which the victim is buried up to the neck in sand and bombarded with stones) and beheading (usually with a sword, though axes are not unheard of).[20] These practices demonstrate that one can still find bloody-minded elites who believe in the old ways. The murderous Latin American elites, it can be argued, might be an anomaly in the West, but not in the broader global context.

PURPOSEFUL DISPLAYS

In most of the Western world one thus seldom encounters rotting bodies on display. But various Latin American states, or at least some of their elites, remained decidedly out of step with current trends throughout the twentieth century. They continued to look back to older traditions that did not hide the connection between killing and power, and in fact aimed to make the relationship unmistakably clear. Death was supposed to be a messy, gory, and horrifyingly visible display of supremacy. Many of the region's murderous elites looked beyond the subtleties; some still do.

Such body display has had a long history across Latin America. Its authors have consistently used fear to make points about power. In Argentina, in the 1830s and early 1840s, during the height of Juan Manuel de Rosas's terror, "headless bodies were found in Buenos Aires every morning." For the Mazorca, "the demonstration was as important as the deed." Of course the heads themselves were not allowed to go to waste. The "common practice" was to jam them "on long poles and display them in public squares." In 1920s Nicaragua, the Conservative party gang leader Anastacio Hernández also favored decapitation. He would pull the heads of his victims out of his saddlebags and place them on the tables of other potential victims "in order to induce a sense of terror." During Fulgencio Batista's repression of the opposition during the Cuban revolution, "hundreds of mangled bodies were left hanging from lamp posts or dumped in the streets in a grotesque variation of the Spanish colonial practice of public executions." In the early 1970s, in Paraguay, "the bodies of many prisoners who allegedly had died while in the hands of the police turned up on the shores of Uruguay and Argentina. The practice of throwing them into the Paraná and Paraguay rivers was meant to have a 'demonstration effect' on the entire population." Torturers in Guatemala and El Salvador regularly tossed the "raped and mutilated bodies" of their victims into "shantytowns and busy streets as warnings to spread fear."[21] Indeed, in El Salvador in the early 1980s, it was common for victims to be killed elsewhere and dumped at famous body dumpsites such as El Playón, or killed on the spot at Puerta del Diablo, another well-known and aptly named dumpsite, where bodies were either purposefully left where they fell or thrown over the cliff. Often a different body would appear at the exact same spot day after day, and locals felt that it would be dangerous for anyone to move them, as the killers seemed to want them to remain in plain sight. During the early years of the Brazilian police Esquadrão da Morte (in its many variations), the "bullet ridden corpses" of people sought by the police, and even of individuals who had already been arrested, "began to be noticed on the sides of roads or bobbing down outlying rivers." There was also a man "who called himself 'Rosa Vermelha' (Red Rose)," who called press outlets to alert them to the locations of "fresh presuntos" or "hams," as victim's bodies were called. (R.S. Rose suggests that Brazilians used "ham as slang for cadaver" because they "invariably eat ham cold.") And to make sure no one missed their point, bodies typically had notes pinned on them, with messages such as, "I was a thief," or "I was a criminal," and signed "EM." They often showed signs of torture.[22]

In the most high-profile instances of threats to power, pains are taken to ensure that statements made with bodies are official and clear. In the case of Emiliano Zapata, his killers "displayed his body, like a hunter's trophy, to convince his followers and partisans that his revolution had ended."[23] After Constitutionalist soldiers lured Zapata into a trap and ambushed him, they took his corpse, "threw it over the back of a horse and rode north to Cuautla." There the body was identified before a judge and photographed. It was then publically displayed at the police station for roughly twenty-four hours. Thousands of people came to gawk or mourn. While some parties, especially newspaper men, wanted the body displayed in the capital, President Carranza thought differently. To avoid honoring Zapata's memory, the body was buried locally in a simple pine box, very deep in the ground. The Constitutionalist camp hoped that would put an end to Zapatismo.[24] The same was true for Che Guevara. After his surrender, the Bolivian rangers who had captured him could, of course, have executed him "on the spot and dumped his corpse on the side of the road." But political considerations prevailed. After they had interrogated him, President Barrientos decided to execute Guevara (despite the objections of Félix Rodríguez, the Cuban-born CIA operative working with the Bolivians, who had been ordered to bring Guevara back alive). The Bolivians wanted him dead, but they had to prove that they had captured and killed the world's most famous guerrilla leader. Indeed, "they could not have buried him in an unmarked grave without first displaying his body, because nobody would have believed that they had killed Che." Such proof would, they believed, serve to make Guevara's death a warning to all would-be revolutionaries. And since they had already reported that he had died in combat, an exit wound in his head would not do. The final image was thus an intentional creation. They injected the body with formaldehyde and had nuns clean it up. They propped up his head and generally treated his body with respect, partly because Félix Rodríguez admired the courage with which Guevara died. That respect, and the necessities imposed by the cover story and identification, prohibited the mutilation of his body. Finally, to reassure the nonbelievers, they made sure the corpse was photographed with its eyes open.[25]

During their Violencia, the Guatemalan government and armed forces developed a bureaucracy of violence that strove not only to eliminate the guerrilla movements but also to employ the byproduct of murder—the bodies—as tools for controlling the general population through terror. One element of this effort was "a repetitive and orchestrated display of fear-inducing images and texts." In particular, the Guatemala establishment published politically charged images and descriptions of the bodies of murder victims. At the peak years of killing, these "cadaver reports" (just the existence of such reports is a red flag) appeared in daily newspapers, on average about twenty times a month. They were "patterned" by "an organized system" and "intended to create a sense of generalized fear."[26] In effect, just in case people did not see the dead, the state stepped in to describe them. One famous case of body use in Guatemala was that of Nobel laureate Rigoberta Menchú's mother, who worked to organize villages and traveled through many provinces. She refused to go abroad to seek asylum, and eventually the army kidnapped her. Soldiers raped her, tortured her for days, and cut off her ears. They fed her enough to revive her, and raped and tortured her anew. Finally they put her under a tree in plain view, and left her there exposed. She lasted for days in the sun and rain, covered with worms. When she finally died, the army stationed a small detachment to guard her body. They ate near her, and made sure she could not be moved. Her body was eaten by buzzards and dogs, and finally disintegrated. In the end, even the bones disappeared.[27]

Sometimes members of the murderous elite have used bodies to make more personal statements about power. Between 1978 and 1980, the poet Carolyn Forché traveled to El Salvador to work as a human rights activist. Early in her time there she went to dinner at the house of a high-ranking officer in the military regime, and based on that singular experience she wrote her famous poem, "The Colonel." She later told Bill Moyers in an interview that "I was just trying to capture details so that I would remember. I didn't even think it was a poem. I thought it was a piece of memoir that got mixed up with my poetry book." In the poem, the Colonel spoke of "how difficult it had become to govern," and then left the table. He "returned with a sack used to bring groceries home. He spilled many human ears on the table. They were like dried peach halves. . . . He took one of them in his hands, shook it in our faces. . . . I am tired of fooling around he said. As for the rights of anyone, tell your people they can go fuck themselves."[28] Forché later marveled that audiences in the United States had so much trouble accepting that her poem depicted an actual event. Some people just said that it could not have happened. What is more, many commentators could not believe that a Salvadoran officer would keep a bag of ears. One postulated that she stole the image from one of Ernest Hemingway's novels about bull fighting (since bulls' ears are often severed and given as awards). And a spokesman for the U.S. State Department asserted that Forché was "delusional" about "fictitious" death squads.[29]

Such denials seem laughable in retrospect, as the region-wide history of dirty war has made clear. Throughout the 1980s and 1990s, Colombian paramilitaries carried on the tradition. One such case was that of Jesuit Fr. Sergio Restrepo, a poet and parish priest in Tierra Alta, Córdoba, who, in response to paramilitary activity, painted a mural on the inside and outside of his church depicting justice and peace. Paras killed him and left his body in front of his church on June 1, 1989. Another example was that of independent gold miner Juan Camacho (whose breed is said to be in the way of multinational mining firms). In April 1997, paras in Rio Viejo killed and decapitated Camacho. After playing soccer with his head, they mounted it on a stake.[30] Michael Taussig described what he called the "classic scenario of paramilitary terror" and body display in Colombia. Armed and uniformed men "would scrutinize a list of victims, sometimes on a laptop computer, round them up, torture and kill them, often with machetes or the peasants' own chainsaws, and leave the bodies suspended in public view before they drove off."[31]

TORTURE, MUTILATION, AND IDEAS

A fundamental aspect of body display as it relates to politics and ideas involves torture and the mistreatment of corpses. The public torture of individuals (or even whole communities) that elites have identified as would-be agents of change, and the accompanying mutilation of their bodies, involves a type of political theater. This grotesque performance art seeks to manipulate and violate cultural attitudes with the conscious goal of sending unsettling but powerful messages about who is in charge.

Without a doubt, such displays violate deeply felt human values that are both local and universal in nature, beginning with the fact that human societies generally treat dead bodies with respect. Verdery reminds us that most human communities "have ideas and practices concerning what constitutes a 'good death,' how dead people should be treated, and what will happen if they are not properly cared for."[32] Families of the disappeared in Argentina invoked "cultural patterns going back to the stone age, Sophocles' *Antigone*, and domestic and international law" when they called on the Argentine judiciary "to declare a right to truth and to mourning and an obligation to respect the human body." They argued that since the Neanderthals began to bury their dead, the importance of burial rituals have been central to human culture, along with use of fire and tools. And they insisted that denying people the right to bury their dead is to deny their humanity.[33] Anthropologists recognize that "no society anywhere at any time, so far as we know, has been disinterested in death and the fate of the human body." "Bodily identity is one essential dimension of the human person. To harm a dead body/person, is to assault the fabric of the human community." Across cultures, "abuse of the dead body is repulsive."[34] But it is also politically useful, as is clear in the case of torture, which over its long history has of course had the general goal of producing a "confession (true or false)," but perhaps more important, has also sought to "inscribe in the memory" of the victim, or anyone else paying attention, an incentive to avoid repeating certain actions.[35]

Certainly much widespread body mutilation left little to the imagination. Mistreatment of the bodies aimed to injure the ideas associated with them. In nineteenth-century Argentine warfare, defeat and death often meant mutilation for the body of the commander, particularly decapitation and display of the head. It was meant to humiliate and dishonor the leader, his family, and his cause and faction, and symbolized its "political dismemberment." There were clearly racist overtones—this is how defeated Indians were treated.[36] Killers also used curses and insults to degrade, dehumanize, and objectify all their victims. Objectification—the process of thinking about corpses as objects—is a useful coping mechanism for medical students and professionals and for undertakers. It is also common for butchers and shoppers for the main course, who speak of pork instead of pig and beef instead of cow. But cadavers look like people, and until the eighteenth century human dissection was largely frowned upon.[37] In Latin America, the victims of political murder found themselves objectified even before death, as demonstrated by their treatment in Argentine detention camps, where they were "transferred."

During its Violencia, Colombia, land of the ubiquitous machete, became infamous for ritualized mutilation of the dead. This mutilation, in fact, evolved into a form of generalized communication. Bodies were transformed with *cuchillos* and *puñales* (knifes and daggers) and machetes. Eyes were pulled out and exhibited, ears cut off, and decapitation and castration were common. Fetuses were cut out, breasts cut off, and intestines pulled out. An elaborate style of "cuts" evolved, with descriptive names. There was the *corte de corbata*, the "necktie" (now often known as the "Colombian necktie"), in which a slit was cut under the jaw, through which the tongue was pulled to lay like a necktie on the victim's chest. In the *corte franela* (the "flannel"), the muscles holding the head upright were sliced, allowing the head to fall backward, resembling a sailor's collar. In the *corte de florero* ("flower vase"), the dismembered limbs and head of the victim were stuffed into the body cavity in a bunch. The *corte de mica* (the "monkey") was a cut that harkened back to the time when a killer placed the severed head of the victim's pet monkey in his lap. It was imitated thereafter by killers who placed the decapitated heads of their victims in the victims' own laps. The still-living victims of the *corte Frances* (the "French cut") had the skin on their heads peeled back, while the *corte picar para tamal* meant the body was literally minced, as if being prepared for inclusion in a tamale. Finally, in a practice known as *bocachiquiar*, assassins cut groves in the victim's back, imitating the handling of the spiny-backed "bocachico" fish, which fishermen score with knifes.[38] Such cuts were used by both Liberals and Conservatives, though Conservative "police" and *pájaros* had the wherewithal for more involved and brutal displays. At the October 23, 1949, Massacre of San Rafael, Conservative police near Tuluá on the Rio Bugalagrande took more than forty Liberals from their homes and meeting places and slaughtered them. Their tongues and eyes were cut out and thrown in the river.[39]

The victims of torture have regularly been deployed as bloody props in Latin America's political murder theater. In Nicaragua over thirty Conservative gangs worked to quash Liberal electoral participation in 1928.

The gangs "made every effort to ensure that their actions would become publically known and collectively remembered." They grabbed people out of their homes, tortured them, and paraded them, bleeding, in noisy processions "through adjacent hamlets or villages" to a public execution site "where they performed various rituals of death and dismemberment—all to the raucous sounds of gunfire, shouts, music, songs, laughter, dancing, and drinking, punctuated by the anguished cries of the victims." Invariably, their "mutilated corpses" were left at the most traveled crossroads.[40] Rigoberta Menchú provided one of the most famous examples of torture as ghoulish performance art in the story of her younger brother's murder in 1979. Kidnapped by the army for his organizing work in various communities, he was brutally tortured "for more than sixteen days." He was thrown naked into a well, with other torture victims, to spend the night on a pile of rotting corpses. "They cut off his fingernails, they cut off his fingers, they cut off his skin, they burned parts of his skin. Many of the wounds, the first ones, welled and were infected." On September 23rd villagers were informed that the military was planning a spectacle to showcase the punishment of "guerrillas." They "handed out bulletins" announcing the time and place and insisted that the people come and watch. Indeed, "any who didn't go to witness the punishment were themselves accomplices of the guerrillas."

Members of Menchú's family and community made the arduous mountain journey to the village of Chajul. The army was there in force, with machine guns, armored cars, jeeps, and helicopters. An officer harangued the assemble campesinos, and was eager to show a group of "guerrillas" (her brother among them) that the army had been entertaining with "a little punishment." Such punishment was appropriate for "communists," "Cubans," and "subversives." The officer's tirade stressed that the Indians should be "satisfied with eating bread and chile" and should not "be led astray with communist ideas." Said Menchú, "he must have repeated the word 'communist' a hundred times." The prisoners arrived in an army truck, and were herded before the witnesses. All had obviously been badly tortured. "They were monstrous . . . they were all swollen up, all wounded . . . their clothes were damp . . . from the moisture oozing out of their bodies." The officer had soldiers cut the clothes off the victims "so that everyone could see for themselves what their punishment had been." Their bodies displayed the marks of different torture methods, and the officer "devoted himself to explaining" each one to his captive audience. One had been perforated with needles. Another had been burned by heated wires. Three people had been grotesquely inflated with liquid "like bladders." Her brother had been cut in various places; he had no finger nails, no skin on the soles of his feet. One woman had been shaved; one nipple had been cut off, while the other breast was missing altogether. She had bite marks all over her body. "She had no ears." The officer went on with his oration, and stressed that "subversives brought foreign ideas, exotic ideas" that would only make trouble. He pointed to the bodies of his prisoners to drive home the point. The soldiers then dragged the victims to a spot where they could finish the "punishment." They poured gasoline over them, lit it, and withdrew. (Far from being cowed, Menchú recounted, the Indians were so enraged by this inhumane display that they almost made a suicidal charge at the heavily armed troops.) Some of the victims leapt about; others, who still had tongues, screamed. When the fire went out, "the bodies kept twitching."[41]

The Contras in Nicaragua were also masters of savage display and mutilation. In March 1982, a union member in Rama, Zelaya, was murdered and his tongue cut out. In Rio Blanco, an education administrator named Maria Martinez Alvarez had her throat slit and her breasts cut off. The Contras killed two workers in Rubén Dario, cut out their hearts and fed them to dogs. In April 1984, a major Contra attack on the village of Waslala left thirty-seven killed. Hundreds more were kidnapped. When one family was found hiding in a ditch, the father had his fingertips cut off, then his whole right hand, then was beheaded and had a cross carved into his back. In June, Contras sought out schoolteacher Pedro Sambola Adkinson. In front of his wife and children they cut off his ears and tongue, forced them down his throat, cut off his penis, and killed him. In July 1984, during a national drive to register voters, the Contras murdered seven would-be suffragists in Tapasle. Victims were castrated, throats were slit, bodies were dismembered and their parts were scattered. One victim had the skin scraped off his face.[42] Such sadistic mastery also appeared during Chulavita massacres in Colombia. In Tolima, victims were generally dispatched with a shot to the head, and usually decapitated. The killers would then move on to the postmortem carving. After a massacre, the scene was often carefully prepared for those who would encounter it later. The vista could range from a totally chaotic landscape of sprawling cadavers and scattered body parts, to a meticulously staged panorama of neatly arranged bodies in lines, or seated, with their heads placed nearby.[43] Later paramilitaries updated the old Colombian practice of dismemberment with "practice." Para testimony has confirmed that the AUC designed methods for quartering their victims for terror purposes, and gave classes in their chainsaw technique, using living victims. According to para commander Francisco Villalba, they used fifteen elderly people, in groups of five. The participants in the training session were instructed to take off the victims' arms and heads.[44] One famous example was Holy Week of 2001, when paras massacred a good part of the indigenous population of Alto Naya on a bridge over the Rio Cauca. Around one hundred thirty were slaughtered, some with chainsaws, their bodies thrown in the river.[45] When Colombian drug dealers in the movie *Scarface* deploy chainsaws, it is not a mere Hollywood embellishment.

The point of all this savagery, beyond sadism or information extraction, is that "torture is education" for activists, and has an observable multiplier effect beyond the specific individuals tortured. Corpses that show evidence of long torture "are reminders that death could be long in coming."[46] In Latin America, murderous elites have frequently attempted to carry out this education on a broad, collective level. In Guatemala, mutilated bodies found on roads had often clearly been tortured. The bodies of vocal and outspoken NGO leaders, Héctor Gómez and María Rosario Godoy de Cuevas, for example, told the tale of their treatment after their abductions in 1985. Dumped at the side of the road, Gómez's tongue had been cut out, and there were blowtorch burns on his body; the back of his head had been crushed. Godoy de Cuevas had been taken with her two-year-old son, and their bodies were found together. The toddler's fingernails had been ripped out.[47] Indeed, the mutilated bodies of more prominent victims were typically deposited in public places, with notes and signs, to make sure no one missed their significance. Yet, a "body's symbolic effectiveness does not depend on its standing for one particular thing." One of a body's key properties in this regard is its "ambiguity." Human remains "do not have a single meaning but are open to many different readings."[48] This disconcerting ambiguity is good for such murderous projects, as it encourages peoples' imaginations to run wild.

One of the main reasons torture and mutilation are seen as effective is that dead bodies "come with a curriculum vitae," in fact, with "several possible résumés." This background helps make the connection to why people were killed. Seeing their bodies makes one think of one's own death, and "enables one's identification with one's own body, thereby tapping into one's reservoirs of feeling."[49] The message the murderers want to send is that what this person did in life got him or her killed, and can get the onlooker killed as well. They strive to waken universal human reactions to dead bodies, thereby generating fear, dread, and political paralysis. Gabriela Torres has shown that during their Violencia, state authorities in Guatemala used bodies proactively to tie ideas and actions to consequences. Their published reports on dead bodies might have been "a coded type of fear-mongering" that sought to instill "fear by example." Since the cadaver reports most often lacked a clear explanation of the causes of the death, they created "a diffuse, almost intangible sense of insecurity." People could (and were undoubtedly encouraged to) identify with the victims and imagine the consequences of certain behaviors and associations. Not surprisingly, "Guatemalans during the period of la Violencia considered any type of political activity as potentially lethal." Thus the "code" was not difficult for the politically active to break. In fact, Guatemalans living in exile read the reports for clues as to who had done the killing. The various agencies and death squads left telltale signs of their participation; marks of torture were read as signatures, or "inscriptions." The mood created by violence, and reinforced by publication of cadaver reports, helped discourage "even the possibility" of "anti-elite or antigovernment action."[50]

The flip side of obvious display was the absence of bodies, and this could also be used to great effect in spreading fear. In this field, too, that of "disappearances," the Guatemalans were quite accomplished. Piero Gleijeses recalls a particularly evocative Mayan legend to illustrate this point. In Mayan mythology, the spirit Win abducts people who are never seen again. Gleijeses went on to point out that over forty thousand Guatemalans were disappeared between 1954 and the late 1980s.[51] But it was the Argentine military, of course, that was most well known in this regard. Antonious Robben argued that the military purposefully exploited "the central importance of human remains and reburial in Argentine political culture"—especially "the belief in the influence of the dead on the world of the living" and "the emotional need for mourning." Robben stressed that the Argentine military was drawn to the practice of disappearing for specific cultural reasons. In particular, he says, the military manipulated how "Argentine culture has conceived of the spirit of deceased political opponents." The idea was that the "fate of the body is a model for the fate of the soul." General Catholic belief "that the soul survives after death, that human remains carried a spiritual power that could affect the world of the living" was put to use. This power became "a metaphor for the ideas associated with the remains of the deceased."[52] And there was good reason to be concerned about the fate of the disappeared in Argentina. It was widely known from grim experience that since the early twentieth century the "Special Section" of the Argentine Federal Police could boast considerable expertise in the methods of torture used during the Proceso. These included squeezing testicles, crushing fingers, beatings, mock execution, water blasted at tender parts of the body, and of course their specialty, the "picana eléctrica," the electric cattle prod.[53]

But as useful as corpses could be, they could also present problems for the murderers.

QUESTIONS OF DISPOSAL

In 1984 famed forensic anthropologist Clyde Snow spoke of the murder of Spanish poet Federico García Lorca. During the Spanish Civil War, Francoistas "branded him undesirable." And, "like the gypsies of his poetry, García Lorca's ideas had apparently wandered too freely." On August 19, 1936, he was shot in an Andalusian olive grove and buried in a clandestine grave.[54] As the case of García Lorca illustrates, sometimes murderers in power just want to make the body of their victim go away. Argentine military leaders during the Proceso, for instance, clearly operated under the theory of no body, no crime. They believed that historical condemnation, and legal unpleasantries, could be avoided "if there was no body to mourn, dead to commemorate, or epitaph to read." Antonious Robben argues that the junta leaders knew that eventually they would have to turn power back over to civilians, and they were banking on the belief that "without a corpus delicti future criminal prosecution would be impossible."[55] With individuals, this is usually a fairly straightforward exercise. But when the number of victims grows, creativity is called for.

Some considerations are strictly practical and logistical. During the Salvadoran Matanza of 1932, groups were slaughtered in such numbers that their bodies could not be disposed of quickly enough to prevent a general reek of decomposition from permeating the countryside. Immediately after the killings, for lack of adequate disposal methods, bodies were simply scattered widely. Many were merely dumped into ditches where hogs and vultures feasted on them.[56] In the case of Argentina, given that one of the most widespread practices by police and military teams was to drop their corpses off at municipal morgues, where they would be registered as "N.N." (*ningún nombre,* or no name), bodies sometimes just piled up. In fact, in June 1980, General Videla received a demand for better working conditions from the workers at the city morgue of Córdoba. A large number of bodies had been left for more than thirty days, unrefrigerated, and were covered by clouds of flies.[57] These bodies would eventually be dealt with in the most obvious way, by being buried in mass unmarked graves. This method of disposal was especially favored in Guatemala. During Operation Ashes the army often moved so far and so fast that there was no practical alternative to burying the victims of their massacres all together where they were killed. There is strong evidence that massacres took place in at least 626 villages, with a correspondingly large number of mass graves.[58] Guatemala was hardly alone in this regard; mass graves can be found all over Latin America. It will take decades just to identify their locations.

Another widespread practice was to throw corpses into bodies of water. In many countries rivers are large, handy, and plentiful. In the Colombian departments of Cauca and Valle de Cauca, the Cauca River (Colombia's second largest) has long been the preferred depository for the bodies of labor organizers, suspected guerrilla sympathizers, or anyone foolish enough to want to hold on to his or her family farm. Over several decades, bloated and ghostly white cadavers (often with their faces and fingers burned off) have floated down the river, providing a continuous feast for voracious flocks of condors and vultures.[59] Colombian paramilitaries, infamous for their prowess with chainsaws, typically have not used them for workaday, utilitarian dismemberment because they tend to get clogged with clothing. They instead have relied on the trusted and traditional methods that call for machetes. Dismembered bodies are easier to bury, of course, because they can be put in shallower graves, but disposal in rivers also works best if the bodies are first cut up—the parts scatter in the current and sink. AUC leader Salvatore Mancuso admitted that he had his men dig up indigenous leader Kimi Pernía's remains and throw them in the Sinú River. The Aguilas Negras (Black Eagles), a new postdemobilization para group, has dug up clandestine graves and thrown the remains into rivers. In a practical take on the old "flower vase" cut, one para leader in the Llanos said that it was typical to gouge a hole in the victim's torso and stuff it with the limbs.[60] In the graveyard of Puerto Berrío on the Magdalena, corpses or pieces thereof that float down the river are buried in tombs marked N.N. Townsfolk often adopt these bodies and care for their graves.[61]

Rivers are used well beyond Colombia. Tensions between the government of President Alán García and indigenous groups over the development of the Amazon region by mining, petroleum, logging, and agribusiness companies led to deadly clashes between protesters manning roadblocks and police and Peruvian special forces sent to open the roads. Witnesses say that the government underreported the numbers of protestors killed, and claim that police put bodies in bags and threw them in the river from a helicopter.[62] There have been lots of bodies in Brazil, but their political significance was generally, perhaps purposefully, obscured. Rose used bodies sighted in the Guandu River and other places (noted in popular newspapers and tabloids) to produce body counts for the numbers of death squad victims. For the years 1951–1999, this produced 14,770 for Rio; and for 1963–1999, 17,905 for São Paulo.[63]

Bodies were, of course, also thrown into the ocean. The classic case was in Argentina during the Proceso, though in actuality, the prisoners thrown from Argentine military aircraft were not yet dead. The details first came to light with the "confession" that Lt. Commander (Ret.) Adolfo Francisco Scilingo of the Argentine Navy made to Argentine journalist Horacio Verbitsky. Scilingo was ordered to participate in two flights, one made on a Coast Guard Skyvan carrying thirteen prisoners, and another on a Navy Electra carrying seventeen prisoners. Prisoners were told they were being transferred to the south and had to receive a vaccination; instead they got an initial dose of anesthetic, with a bigger dose once the flight took off. "In their unconscious state, the prisoners were stripped, and when the commander of the airplane gave the order, which happened according to where the plane was, the hatch was opened and they were thrown out, naked, one by one" into the South Atlantic.[64] In Argentina, "the joke among the military was that they were dumping 'fish food.' "[65] Several countries experimented with this method of body disposal, but the Argentines (who wanted their victims to literally disappear), carried it to its most brutal extremes.[66] The Argentine practice combined execution and disposal. People falling from high altitude into water, undergoing an "extreme water impact," suffer massive internal trauma. It takes only five hundred feet to reach terminal velocity, or one hundred twenty miles per hour; anything over seventy mph is usually fatal. As the body decelerates (when it hits the surface of the water), its organs are still in motion and slam into the rebounding body wall. The blood vessels tear from their moorings in the body cavity, and the ribs break. Their sharp edges cut into the heart and lungs.[67] Water, like concrete, does not compress on impact. So, unless the "diver" can manage a vertical entry, hitting one is much like hitting the other.

Perpetrators have also showed a good degree of flexibility and a willingness to experiment. In Argentina, bodies were sometimes burned in small, shallow pits with gasoline, though this method was not really practical. Some bodies were likewise burned in Guatemala.[68] Those with bodies to dispose of were also ready to change their procedures as circumstances evolved. In Guatemala, changes in procedure occurred as the dirty war there progressed. Under General Efraín Rios Montt, a process of professionalization of the paras, police, death squads, and military units "meant that bodies would no longer be dumped on the streets." Rios Montt promised as much in a television address. A former G-2 wet-work *especialista* recalled to anthropologist Jennifer Schirmer that "the High Command gave us the order to no longer assassinate people in plain view, or leave their bodies on the streets." Before, they would "leave four here, and another four there." It was not uncommon for travelers to encounter up to twenty cadavers on an eight-mile stretch between towns. Now they were instructed to do the actual killing on the military base "without alarming people" and to "bury the bodies precisely without people taking notice." This more subdued mode of murder was carried out "in clandestine cells on military bases, in basements and sub-basements of the National Police headquarters, and when these were sealed off, in private houses." Now bodies of victims were "thrown from helicopters into lakes or the sea, or buried in mass graves."[69]

Body disposal could even be innovative and entrepreneurial, and the bodies themselves could become valuable commodities in the political murder economy. In Colombia in the early 2000s, a practice known as "legalization" developed whereby paramilitary units would murder guerrilla "supporters" and then turn their bodies over to the army. The army then tallied them as guerrillas killed in combat (body counts benefit units). The paras were paid in weapons and material.[70] And, in 1992, people in Barranquilla were being murdered so that their bodies could be sold to the anatomy lab of the Universidad Libre. It was rumored that the police were also selling bodies of political murder and social-cleansing victims. A well-known case was that of a garbage picker named Oscar Rafael Hernández, who survived.[71] In Argentina, the military attempted to blackmail the families of the victims by "using the fate of the disappeared as a bargaining chip." The perpetrators made it clear that if a deal could be cut that would eliminate the threat of prosecution, "then they would be willing to reveal the makeshift resting places of the disappeared."[72]

Not surprisingly, disposal could pose problems, especially if the victims were famous in life. The primary danger for murderous elites was that the bodies of some victims could be turned into icons and fetish objects. Zapata's killers did not anticipate "the complex ways these witnesses would understand the meaning of the display,"[73] or that something of a cult would grow up around Zapata's body. Some people believed he was alive, or risen as a Christ figure (the "hidden King.") There were also fights over his body between Tlaltizpán and Cuautla and Chinameca, the hacienda where he was killed. Other elites have seen the potential for trouble and literally and symbolically buried the dead. On April 10, 1948, the day after his assassination, Jorge Eliécer Gaitán's widow, Doña Amparo, took his body home from the Clínica Central. There she and a group of loyalists protected it and controlled its destiny. Political leaders fretted over where to bury Gaitán. Putting him in an unmarked grave would "have promoted his inevitable martyrdom" and allowed his image to escape their manipulative control. But too public a place could become a popular, and dangerous, rallying point for political mobilizations. Ultimately, Doña Amparo agreed to the transformation of their house into a national monument and museum so that Gaitán could be buried there. This suited the political elites perfectly, since "Gaitán would not have to be moved at all; he would be buried on the outskirts of the city, and in a private building." He would not be visible in the city center nor in any other politically significant space. And his followers "would find little room to congregate in the narrow residential streets outside the house."[74] Gaitán's body was literally too hot to handle, a volatile element best buried and forgotten, and Colombian political elites hoped that with its burial his legacy would wither.

But easily the most famous case concerned the body of Che Guevara, around which many unintended messages were sent. After his execution, the photographs of his corpse were "printed in every major newspaper around the world," and unfortunately for his killers "conveyed the image of Che as a fallen martyr, hero, or saint, a perfect, noble ending to a legendary and remarkable career." This was the result of the fact that "they washed his hair, cleaned his body, and displayed his corpse in a manner that left an indelible impression on all those who saw him then and those who see the photos today, a Christ-like figure, martyred for a revolutionary cause." Certainly "the message they intended to send was quite unlike the message that people received," mainly because the "famous photograph taken by Freddy Alborta confirmed the value of Che's life, giving Che the glorious death that he anticipated in his writings." The famous photo was compared to classical paintings by Mantegna and Holbein the younger of the body of Christ after it was taken down from the cross. "In both images, the corpse is emaciated, wounded, and covered from the waist down; the eyes are wide open and staring into eternity. The long hair and scraggly beard are strikingly similar." Everyone saw the Christ imagery, which was even clear to Freddy Alborta, who had never seen the paintings. After the body was displayed in the laundry shed behind the Vallegrande hospital, it was buried in an unmarked grave near one of the airport's runways. But the lavadería (laundry shed) became a shrine. Che's body was finally moved to Cuba in 1997.[75]

Tellingly, disposal was a "collective" problem for the Argentine military, a duty shared by all naval personnel ("the whole navy was involved"). Every Wednesday for at least two years "the flight" that would dispose of between 15 and 20 people took off. Scilingo called participation in these missions "a kind of communion." They did it "all by rotation," and "everyone in the navy knew." On the flights there were "special guests," that is, "Upper echelon navy officers who didn't participate . . . captains, high-ranking officers who were posted elsewhere." They were there as "a way of lending their moral support to the task we were doing."[76] The Argentine military instinctively understood that they needed to hang together because, in the long run, bodies tend to turn up.

Bodies as Witnesses

As Katherine Verdery argues, bodies are "protean" and "ambiguous" objects. They can also be rather dangerous, as many dirty warriors have understood. They are seldom forgotten, and they do not always stay buried. Even those consigned to the deep have been known to return and bear witness. Bodies thrown out of early flights during the Proceso, for example, washed ashore in Uruguay fully clothed (normally they were stripped naked first.) Francisco Scilingo characterized the incident as "really fucked up, the worst atrocity." He noted that the officer in charge of the flight "went crazy," did not take off the victims' clothes, and dumped them as they were—"He couldn't take it, and asked to be discharged."[77] Later, bodies sealed in eight oil drums were found in the San Fernando River. Most were shot in the head. One of them was Marcelo Gelman, son of Juan Gelman, a noted poet who joined the Montoneros in 1975, before going into exile in 1976.[78]

Mass graves are especially problematic. They bespeak the means of slaughter and the kinds of people killed; they have stories to tell. As Clyde Snow has pointed out many times, "bones don't lie." While murderers often make bodies speak through mutilations, and even with their mere presence, investigators like Snow (who worked in both Argentina and Guatemala) can also make them speak. Likewise, after seeing "hundreds of bodies on two continents telling a single story," forensic anthropologist Clea Koff identified "a common denominator." She repeatedly encountered "straightforward government level decisions to gather and kill selected people."[79] Koff, and others like her, who are ready to dig up the thousands of mass graves, represent a long-term threat to elite programs of political murder. Their goal is to gather evidence against the perpetrators of human rights atrocities by examining the bones and bodies of their victims. This way, she insists, the victims can still accuse their murderers. They are not silenced forever.[80] Like Clyde Snow, Koff has worked to make bones talk—to fight oppression, and to uncover the truth about political murder in the face of official disinformation. When the victims' "own government, military, or police" (who are in all likelihood behind their murders) scoff at witness testimony as unbelievable, they can be confronted with the "physical evidence of facts most indisputable: human bodies in a grave." Based on her experiences with mass graves in Africa and the Balkans, Koff rejects talk of "spontaneous" violence. This political violence, she insists, displayed clear evidence of "methodical preparation for mass murder." Bodies of noncombatant murder victims told a "common story" of government decisions "to gather and kill selected people and expel the rest, either actively or through the spreading of fear."[81]

There are many mass graves in Latin America, which will keep anthropologists busy for many years to come. Decades after the slaughter of 1932, for instance, rural people in El Salvador remembered well where the burial pits were located, from Turín in the north to Acajutla in the south, and from Tacuba in the west to Ilpango in the east.[82] Along with the clandestine gravesites in Argentina and Guatemala already mentioned, thousands more are waiting to be discovered. Common graves for murder victims in Colombia, for example, remain an ongoing phenomenon, and one year after the government began excavating graves, the Attorney General (Fiscalía) had received tips on more than thirty-seven hundred possible sites for clandestine graves.[83] As anthropologist Victoria Sanford noted, "mass graves of massacre victims are referred to as clandestine cemeteries," yet, survivors, other witnesses, and indeed, the broader community know where they are. "Thus, they are truly clandestine only in the official negation of their existence and the silence imposed on communities."[84]

Not surprisingly, the first line of defense on the part of perpetrators is intimidation and more murder. In response to local efforts to exhume mass graves in Guatemala, the subcommander of the local army base in Rabinal summoned all the men of the surrounding villages, several thousand in all, to lecture them. He wanted the exhumations in the village of Plan de Sánchez to cease, and asserted that the anthropologists, foreign observers, and journalists "were all guerrilla." Then he added that "you know what happens when you help the guerrilla," and alluded to the massacres of 1982. He finished with "an order" and told them to "leave the dead in peace." The exhumations continued, however, and official complaints were made and noted in the press. The army disavowed the officer's threats and transferred him. Yet as late as 2002, eight years later, threats to forensic anthropologists were commonplace.[85] And people understood that death threats to forensic anthropologists were not empty, as the case of Myrna Mack made clear.

Yet bodies in mass and clandestine graves have turned up as damning witnesses. Police surgeons in Argentina argued with Snow about a body with a bullet hole in the head. He thought it looked like "an execution style wound." They argued that it showed that the desaparecido had been killed, as the story always went, in a gun fight with the authorities. Snow countered that shootout causalities tend to be hit all over their bodies, not just once in the head. An examination of the number of N.N. graves in the cemeteries of the province of Buenos Aires, comparing the years before and after 1976, indicates that the historical norm before that year was four or five per one hundred thousand of population per year. From 1976 to 1978, in parts of the province, the rate jumped to fourteen "N.N.s per one hundred thousand. During the same period, reported political disappearances also increased. The percentage of women jumped from twelve to twenty. Age shifted down, as the huge majority before 1976 were over thirty-five years old at death, with only 15 percent between twenty-one and thirty-five. From 1976 to 1978 the percentage of those aged twenty-one to thirty-five at death rose to 56. (This was the same age range as that of most of the desaparecidos). And there were also dramatic changes in cause of death. Normally, few indigents die from gun shots, and even fewer from head shots. In the key parts of the province of Buenos Aires for the years between 1976 and 1978, the percentage of N.N.s killed by gun wounds rose from 5.5 percent to over 50 percent, and most were wounded in the head.[86]

In Guatemala, despite the dangers, significant work has already been carried out by the Fundación de Antropología Forense de Guatemala, or FAFG. In 1994, Victoria Sanford worked with the FAFG on the clandestine cemetery in Plan de Sánchez.[87] Survivors and relatives sought the exhumations and reburials. They did it together, without acknowledged leaders, because local military commissioners kept asking who was in charge and what organizations were behind it. Sanford recalled that "sometimes when we opened a new grave or if it was a damp day, a light smell of life lingered. It wasn't a putrid smell; the earth had long since absorbed the rot of death." The odor that remained was a "light murky smell . . . not a noxious aroma" that evoked a "movement or transformation" in sync with nature. Graves belie the official story. One grave contained a woman's skeleton that still had a shawl wrapped around it; inside the shawl was the skeleton of an infant. A customs police officer guarding the site (and who had wanted to remain aloof) came and looked at the grave and called his fellow officers to see. He said, "Look at this. It is a woman with a baby on her back. They told us these were pure guerrillas. These aren't guerrillas. That's a mother and a baby. That's a crime." Sanford pointed out that the army "claimed that there had been a battle with the guerrilla in Plan de Sánchez." Yet the evidence provided by the exhumation "clearly showed that the vast majority of victims were women, children, and the elderly." In fact, "the forensic evidence unquestionably demonstrated that the skeletons in the grave were victims of a massacre, not an armed confrontation with guerrillas and not civilians caught in crossfire, as the army had asserted about mass graves throughout the country."[88]

One of the most famous graves exhumed was that of the murdered nuns from the United States (Donavan, Kazel, Clarke, and Ford) in El Salvador. After their murder, local people were told by a judge and military personnel to bury the bodies together in a nearby field. A local priest was told. He informed his bishop and the U.S. ambassador to El Salvador, Robert White. On December 4, 1980, two days after the murder, the graves were exhumed in the presence of reporters, assorted church leaders and missionaries, and Ambassador White. Lots of people were being killed in Latin America in those years, but these were American nuns. The incident caused uncharacteristic public anger in the United States. The Carter Administration, which temporarily suspended military aid, forced the Salvadoran regime to investigate. After several attempts and the creation of a United Nations–appointed truth commission, a handful of low-ranking National Guardsmen were convicted.

Ironically, bodies can even be unwelcome reality checks for survivors and victims' relatives. In Argentina, some human rights groups, especially Las Madres de Plaza de Mayo, and a number of victims' families, often fought exhumation early on because they wanted the desaparecidos "returned alive."[89] Bodies could also complicate the wider political struggle. In 1984, some of the Madres, especially followers of Hebe de Bonafini, began to oppose exhumations. Part of the opposition stemmed from ignorance of forensic science and was based on the belief that only the cause of death could be determined (the political value of which was ignored), and not identities. Also, since many of the Madres had become radicalized, they argued that they had to "socialize their maternity" and pick up the political causes of their children. They feared what would happen to the movement if the desaparecidos were properly buried. Closure, they anticipated, might cause the struggle to fade with the pain.[90]

Latin American elites believe in the power of bodies, literally, as demonstrated by a creepy and darkly amusing story. In Madrid, where Perón was in exile, the coffin containing the embalmed corpse of Evita was illuminated with candles, and José López Rega (whose nickname was "El Brujo"—the wizard) recited spooky incantations while Isabel (Perón's third wife) lay on top of the casket to receive Evita's "spiritual energy."[91] It is thus no surprise that murderous elites use bodies to send messages about power. Yet such brutal communication is also dangerous because it can just as likely anger and mobilize those it was meant to intimidate. The double-edged nature of political murder (and the body manipulation associated with it) is typically ignored, however, both by those who condemn it and by those who use it. The lesson many activists might draw from history is that repressive regimes will inevitably be swamped in a flood of martyr's blood, that in the long run, those who rely on cruel and barbaric violence will be overthrown. Murder-prone elites in Latin America (and perhaps worldwide) might respond that, in the long run, as John Maynard Keynes famously pointed out, we are all dead. Many continue to trust in the utility of their demonstrations of power. These days it is more common to hear of savage attacks (by political radicals or religious militants) against "civilized society." But many of those in power, or with power—or who aspire to have power—have made and continue to make influential and bloody-minded statements with human bodies.

PART II

Justifications, Associations, and Consequences

CHAPTER 4

DIRTY WARRIORS ON DIRTY WAR

General Ibérico Saint-Jean, the military governor of Buenos Aires during the opening rounds of the Proceso, infamously characterized the practice of political murder in Argentina in astonishingly blunt (and often quoted) terms. "First we'll kill all the subversives," he explained, "then we'll kill all the collaborators; then the sympathizers; then those who remain indifferent; and finally, we'll kill the undecided." His words echoed through the region in the following decades as other dirty warriors warmed to the theme. In 1981, a month before he founded the ARENA party in El Salvador, Roberto D'Aubuisson spoke of the necessity of killing 200,000 to 300,000 people there to "restore peace." The following year in Guatemala, the ever-colorful General Efraín Rios Montt told Gringo reporters, "We have no scorched-earth policy. We have a policy of scorched communists." Of course, his definition of "communist" was notoriously inclusive. And almost two decades later, Colombian paramilitary leader Carlos Castaño would insist that, while normally crimes, the "extrajudicial executions" he had carried out throughout the 1980s and 1990s against "guerrillas" (also generously defined) were justified in the Colombian context as a "legitimate defense" of the patria.[1] As these quotations demonstrate, the practitioners of political murder believe in their work. Dirty warriors are not shy, and they like to speak for themselves. They tend to be proud of their accomplishments, but even when they are not, they have not proven reluctant to talk about them.

In this chapter we examine the various justifications for political murder and dirty war, as well as thoughts about its practice, as expressed by generals, regional elites, paramilitary commanders, and other theorists, apologists, beneficiaries, and bankrollers. Our goal is to listen in on their echo chamber and follow their conversations. The chapter is guided by the assumption, amply illustrated by the honest General Saint-Jean and company, that dirty warriors are simply more frank in expressing ideas widely accepted in the more murderously inclined circles of the Latin American elite. What is more, we discover that these beliefs are not limited to the psychotically violent, low-class, and tacky *narco* upstarts (as portrayed in Hollywood movies about Colombia or Mexico) but shared by many in the most rarefied, Ivy-League, Ox-Bridge, or Sorbonne-educated sectors of the *oligarquia*. This raises the question: how do we recognize the *violentos* of the murderous elite? American anthropologist Leslie Gill summed up the stereotypical image of a dirty warrior with "dark aviator glasses, a pencil-thin mustache, a permanent scowl, an arrogant swagger, and a protruding gut." However, on meeting retired Colombian General Luis Bernardo Urbina Sánchez (who had been head of DAS, served in various intelligence units in areas of guerrilla influence, and was linked personally by human rights groups through the confessions of trigger men to several disappearances and murders), she noted that he seemed more like a middle-aged academic.[2] Dutch anthropologist Antonius Robben as well stressed that dirty warriors are not "monsters." The military men he interviewed "exuded great civility and displayed a considerable knowledge of literature, art, and classical music." Many were quite cultured and charming (as were many Nazis), and in fact, were affable and chivalrous.[3] While the proponents of political murder do not necessarily look like their stand-ins from central casting, what they have to say can nevertheless be quite clear.

Dirty warriors' arguments and explanations for their actions underscore another historically justified working assumption—namely, that Latin American societies are more alike on the elite level. Members of the elites have similar concerns, interests, experiences, suppositions, and reactions. What they offer when they address the theory and practice of political murder is an amalgamation of apology, justification, and dialogue on practical considerations. This study posits a "culture" of murder, the often unspoken agreements and assumptions that perpetrators generally take for granted. Yet sometimes protagonists speak directly and clearly. In this chapter, dirty warriors explain their intellectual framework and even smugly gloat about their effectiveness. Justifications morph and evolve, shifting from the religious to the political and beyond, and theorists draw on many sources to legitimize their use of political murder. They can reach into a big tub of concepts from across history and around the world, a hairy mess of ideas they sample promiscuously and with great aplomb. Some ideas and techniques were imports, but more were homegrown "ideas criollas" developed in the region with attendant local practices. It is, therefore, important to note that these ideas and practices were hardly forced down their throats by outside forces. The murderous elite's belief in the utility of political murder is an expression of Realpolitik with teeth that has a long history in the region, where widespread slaughter of dissenters, and their real, potential, and alleged supporters, is a very old tactic. The murderous elite can be found in many parts of a country's power structure. Of course one usually finds adherents in the military, but not to the same degree in every country. Elites are fractured; some are more sophisticated and cagey about the implications of their actions, while others are more candid and forthcoming, arguing in elegant terms that their use of murder as a tool is reasonable, given the dire circumstances. But all of the murderous elites, military and civilian, are prepared to go all out, to do what they see as necessary to protect their hold on power. Their willingness to kill should not be underestimated. This is a war; they are clear about that.

BLOODY CLASS STRUGGLE (AND FROM THE TOP DOWN)

As recognized at the beginning of this study, the murderous elites do not form a "class" in the Marxian sense. Yet despite a fair measure of heterogeneity, they do exhibit a significant degree of solidarity and consciousness of their shared interests regarding threats from below. As even Marx might agree, the murderous elites definitely act collectively as a "class for itself," and have traditionally demonstrated a strong and coherent sense of "class consciousness" regarding their enemies. Certainly the depth of their hatred for the forces of change cannot be doubted. Across the region, the "pueblo" is regarded as *la chusma* (scum) and worthy of repression. There is at any rate a complicated lattice of local and international interests, political, ideological, and economic, in support of dirty war. These ideas and assumptions form the very core of the political culture of murder. Elites are united by a belief in the utility of political murder and their broad faith that it is the proper response to protect elite interests.[4]

It bears repeating that there are also divisions among elites. Not all of them buy into the idea of political murder. Some sectors of the elite see the use of political murder as bad for business. The downsides of violent repression have become clear to those parts of the economic elite tied to international conglomerates.[5] Colombia has seen repeated attempts at reform: the 1968 land reform, Betancur's efforts in 1982, and the Constitution of 1991. Even in El Salvador "neither the oligarchy nor the military was a monolithic entity, and both had factions advocating moderate reform while others were committed to severe repression."[6] By the same token, the militaries of the region are by no means ideologically unified regarding the use of political murder. The Argentine military in the 1970s ranged from liberals to Peronist populists to Catholic elitists. But, tellingly, they did see themselves as a special cast, as "guardians of the nation." And as a group they were sworn enemies of "Marxists and radicals" and generally unsympathetic to the messiness of democracy. Finally, in their "smug pride," they were convinced of their own qualifications to run the country.[7]

Yet despite its uneven distribution, the mindset of class conflict was deeply embedded and broadly spread in the region's elite political culture, and that legitimized the use of murder to protect a status quo. Elite participants in this culture considered their political order not only legitimate but natural, even sacrosanct. Regarding the elites in Mexico, Colombia, and El Salvador, Julie Mazzei has pointed to a "collective identity" and a "shared sense of grievance." In El Salvador, in particular, a system emerged that defined any threat to elite interests as a threat to the nation's interests (and elites actually exhibited outright anger at popular mobilizations). Death squad backers in El Salvador were "linked by their determination" to stop the left. People funding them, as one of Mazzei's interviewees told her, "wanted to preserve the system. They wanted to stop any reform, protect their control over the land, money."[8] In fact, for many elites in Latin America, diversity has often been condemned as disorder, a close cousin to communism, subversion, and chaos.[9] In Colombia, regional elites and their allies on the national level have historically refused to recognize other perspectives and ideas as legitimate. This absence of recognition is not limited to the political realm but extends to the social and cultural as well. They are antagonistic toward any ideas and modes of behavior they do not accept as "normal."[10]

This worldview was an old and enduring one. In El Salvador the "continuity" of an elite political culture of murder resided "in the minds and ideologies" of the perpetrators of the 1932 repression, as well as those who came later. Elites developed "a language, and a confirmed justification for what was perceived as the necessary solution to the problems of social and political mobilization from below." These were powerful ideological constructs, in which "the mere act of organizing activities with a popular ideology of liberation was perceived as a threat and repressed."[11] As Thomas Anderson mused, "what was going on in El Salvador after the crushing of the rebellion?" The state, after all, quickly moved beyond putting down a rather inept uprising to carrying out one of Latin America's most savage repressions. One can argue that it was an overreaction of epic proportions, though a rather telling one. In probing "the mood of the bourgeoisie and the army," Anderson perceived their foreboding about the "dark rumblings" of the Salvadoran people. The rebellion realized "their worst fears" about the insidious influence of international communism on the rural population, which (like most elites in Latin America) they instinctively characterized as violent, emotional, and unpredictably dangerous.[12] Such views of the pueblo are widespread among Latin American elites. According to Paul Lewis, Argentina's "entrenched elites, the so-called oligarchy" never accepted mass democracy. They were "used to running" the country and its political system. A member of the elite typically "viewed the classes below him with fear, contempt, and loathing." The "people" were characterized as "el populacho, la chusma, los guarangos—the rude dirty riffraff."[13]

This class struggle has to be won at all costs, and murderous elites have long been on constant guard. In 1974, Augusto Pinochet asserted that plebian minds clouded with "envy, rancor, and in the irreconcilable struggle of classes" were more dangerous than actual weapons. He was representative of military rulers in Latin America who, "in terms reminiscent of those used by the Nazis in Germany," openly declared their goal of eliminating "subversives from the body politic." Such struggles "quickly become wars against the social forces and organizations from which . . . subversion might emerge."[14] According to an M-19 leader, the Colombian oligarchy believed that the key to holding onto their power and economic control was crushing and silencing not only insurgent movements but also democratic groups and "the new forces that want a different life."[15] General Ramón Genaro Díaz Bessone in Argentina, for one, feared wider networks on the left—especially the many connections between both Argentine communists and left-wing Peronists and the Soviet Union and revolutionary Cuba (in particular, the influence of Che Guevara).[16] Díaz Bessone reminds one of General Jack D. Ripper, Stanley Kubricks's paranoid and suicidal Air Force Base Commander in *Dr. Strangelove,* who obsessed about "your postwar Commie conspiracy," and fluoridation. As we shall see, Latin American generals had a habit of channeling General Ripper.

The sense of class struggle could play out as a broader ideological war, as the case of Colombia demonstrated. Since the National Front era, elites had consistently worked to thwart land reform and democratic impulses. This was evident after national government attempts at agrarian reform in 1968. The departments of Córdoba and Sucre became the "epicenters" of campesino resistance in the early 1970s, as even the attempt at a tepid (and ultimately failed) reform had the effect of opening up the local political system for a short spell. Local elites consequently felt fear and loathing as the popular classes (once again) forgot their place. At the same time, the central government seemed unable to cope with, or was believed to be too sympathetic to, the popular cause. This experience led directly to the local reemergence of paramilitarism. Likewise, Colombian political decentralization, initiated in 1988 (especially the devolution of power to elected mayors), generated a "blood bath." Many in the local elite feared the horrible possibility of the election of "leftist mayors." Driven by the well-founded Liberal and Conservative establishment fears that political monopolies in different municipios might be lost, and landowners' fears of land reform, local elites embraced paramilitary groups as "extreme defenders of the status quo" and elite power. At first glance it seems odd that large parts of the elite would sign off on the paras' bloody tactics, but this "self-defense" struggle had developed over time as paras became identified with, and perceived as defenders of, elite interests. Kidnapping elites by guerrilla groups was of course a big motivation, but it was not the only one. Elites also hated the very ideas of social justice and equality that the demobilized guerrillas included in their public discourse; even in peace, the ex-guerrillas wanted land reform and spoke of "class struggle." It is not surprising that demands for social justice were met with counter demands for "order" and "security."[17]

Elite hatred of change came to focus with laser intensity on the guerrillas, the most obvious emissaries of change in the political landscape. This obsession, and the sense of class struggle and war that drives it, has had a tendency to color elite views of movements on the Left. Pablo Emilio Guarín, one of the intellectual fathers of the Colombian "autodefensa" movement (especially in its early manifestation in Puerto Boyacá) exemplified this tendency when he had a sign put up that read: "Welcome to Puerto Boyacá, Land of Peace and Progress, Anti-subversive Capital of Colombia." As a congressman in the national congress, Guarín confronted Carlos Enrique Cardona of the UP in "a real fist fight," and laid out the perennial paramilitary refrain, insisting that he was really "a guerrilla dressed as a civilian." In the legislature, Guarín insisted, Cardona enjoyed the protections afforded by democracy, and he comported as the "peaceful Carlos Enrique Cardona, defender of human rights." Yet when Cardona left he became "the terrible Braulio Herrera," (his guerrilla nom de guerre) who, Guarín insisted, had gunned down defenseless women and campesinos.[18] The key idea is that guerrillas never change; once a guerrilla, always a guerrilla (and always a target of political murder).

This fight against subversion was directed, according to Carlos Castaño, by individuals like the "Group of Six," an elite cabal of superpowerful über Colombians whom he described as men from the highest levels of Colombian society, "la crema y nata," who for decades had moved behind the scenes—"true patriots, committed to Colombia." These men, "without being in power," endeavored to "pull the strings" of the nation. They advised him about which subversives "to execute," such as Bernardo Jaramillo Ossa of the UP. And, he argued, in some cases (like Jaramillo's) "in all the spheres of power, from those affected to the beneficiaries to even the mere spectators, everyone knew where the orders came from." That is, from "the Colombian ruling class."[19] Alma Guillermoprieto recognized that "although Castaño tells a sordid story . . . he appears to do so straight forwardly." She notes his personal involvement in the murders of hundreds of "military objectives," and his indirect responsibility for thousands of others. While voicing skepticism about his tale and pointing to his "self-aggrandizing and twisted moral vision," she credits the image he creates as believable enough. Throughout the "secret history of Colombia" (or, one might add, most of Latin America) operators like Castaños have served the interests of "the country's most prominent businessmen and politicians" who, while "engaging in drinking bouts," drew up lists of "left-wing activists or impoverished peasant supporters of the guerrillas" to be eliminated[20]

The guerrilla movement in El Salvador also drove elite fears and bloody-minded resolve. D'Aubuisson "was dogmatic in his determination to eliminate all leftists from El Salvador." Though extreme, he was not really an anomaly, and he was a useful tool of the elite, in whose circles he was loved. Journalist Tina Rosenberg noted that "upper-class" women and teenage girls "screamed" as they might have "at rock stars" when he looked their way at a rally.[21] And, as in Colombia, elites in El Salvador believed that the taint of the guerrillas was widely spread. CIA analysts writing of D'Aubuisson and his moneyed patrons in power noted that "Rightwing extremists have viewed government reformers as national security threats equal to those posed by the guerrilla movement." Former U.S. Ambassador to El Salvador Robert White linked D'Aubuisson to Operación Piña—the murder of Archbishop Romero—and noted that embassy informants stated that he "presided over the drawing of lots for the 'privilege' of killing the Archbishop." In El Salvador, the backers of the various death squads "in the military and security forces and the civilian sector" were united by a shared belief that "measures taken by the government to contain the insurgency, "however repressive," were "insufficient." In their view, "only extreme terror would suffice to eliminate subversives and the threat they posed to the political and socioeconomic order."[22]

JUSTIFICATIONS

Dirty war practitioners and apologists have offered a number of justifications, ranging from patriotic duty and national defense to Christian holy war and vengeance, and in most cases their arguments have been presented forcefully and unrepentantly. Yet beyond any single justification, the culture of political murder lives in the minds of various elites—political, military, economic—whether in or out of power or control of the state. Elite belief in the legitimacy and utility of using murder to protect the status quo is deeply embedded in Latin America's history of repression. Some practitioners are not only unrepentant but have eagerly made the case for their actions.

There have been, of course, denials and obfuscations by individuals, and by states, that have reached for some plausible, and not so plausible, deniability. This was especially the case for leaders in Argentina, who feared they could eventually become targets of prosecution. Some of these denials were laughable. One Argentine commander, when asked about desaparecidos, answered, "On this topic, what can I say? At the time I was only a lieutenant colonel, and my mission in the war against subversion was to control one area through patrols." He made a point of stating, clearly for the record, that his unit followed regulations, checked cars, people, and houses, in broad daylight, wearing official uniforms. He, seemingly alone among Argentines, only learned of disappearances "after 1983, when the famous book *Nunca Más* appeared," but even then thought that the stories could just have been "propaganda."[23] In this public statement, he was following the official line. During the Proceso, military officials "angrily denied that anyone was being held in unofficial custody and charged that the so-called disappeared were all guerrillas or their sympathizers who had broken with their families and gone underground, or else had fled to Europe where they were living it up in Paris or Madrid."[24] And after the fact many important participants in Argentina tried to spin the struggle. Miguel O. Etchecolatz, the head of the investigative unit of the Buenos Aires Provincial Police from 1976 to 1979 (the worst years of the dirty war), was charged, tried, convicted, jailed, amnestied, and released. He was recharged in 2006, tried, and returned to prison. During his years of freedom, he published a book entitled, *La Otra Campana Del Nunca Más*, one of the most important book-length defenses of political murder by a practitioner. Etchecolatz believed that the military won the war but lost the political struggle for peace. He also downplayed the numbers of dirty war dead, even as he justified his actions.[25]

Even more slippery was the performance of Admiral Emilio Eduardo Massera, who had been part of the original Junta as Commander in Chief of the navy. In 1976, he defined the struggle as being between "those who are on the side of death and we who are on the side of life," and assured Argentines (in strangely Orwellian language) that "we will not have death roaming freely." The Argentine military was "not going to fight to the death;" rather, it would "fight to victory, whether it lies before or beyond death." Massera later attempted to cover up his role. When questioned in a military court about whether he had information concerning "kidnappings, secret detention centers, torture, assassinations, or violations of decency and sexual freedom," Massera "replied unhesitatingly: 'at no time.' " He had the shameless gall to add that he visited each unit and warned their commanders "to act with prudence" because "yesterday's heroes" would be "tomorrow's enemies," and that "any excesses" would have "to be analyzed." Massera "denied the very existence of the clandestine concentration camps." To the question of whether "annihilation of subversion" justified the use of "extreme measures such as torture, illegal imprisonment, [and] homicide," he answered, "obviously not." Massera understood that the practice of dirty war would be judged as a crime. He admitted, somewhat awkwardly, that "some mistakes may have been made" but rejected the idea that "excesses" were committed. He asserted that the military did not "exceed the limits of the lawful principles of warfare." He emphatically denied that any "operative plan" caused thousands of people to be kidnapped, tortured, and murdered. These denials came from a man already sitting in jail for taking Fernando Branca, "the husband of one of his mistresses," on a one-way trip out to sea on the yacht reserved for the use of the navy commander. The Argentine military as a whole also tried to cover itself on the way out of power. In September 1983, the chiefs of staff of the three armed forces signed the optimistically named "Final Document of the Military Junta on the War Against Subversion and Terrorism." Within the "almost apocalyptic context" of this just war, "mistakes were made that, as happens in all wartime conflict, could cross the limits of respect for fundamental rights." According to Horacio Verbitsky, the military insisted that "such errors should remain subject to the judgment of God and the compassion of mankind."[26]

As a general rule, however, many individual theorists and practitioners have recognized the absurdity, or at least the probable futility, of lying about the use of political murder and other dirty war practices. On the contrary, they are proud and inclined to brag. Unlike his commanding officers in the Argentine ruling Junta, Rear Admiral (Rt.) Horacio Mayorga spoke freely in 1985 of "the Astiz affair." He insisted that Astiz (who had infiltrated the Madres de la Plaza de Mayo) was not an anomaly; in the navy alone there were hundreds like him who fought and killed for the patria. They "were men who bet everything on what they were doing. Did they kill people? Of course. Everyone knows we eliminated them," meaning the "subversives." As far as Mayorga was concerned, the real tragedy was "what those men have to go through now"—that is, under democratic government. Mayorga would have made dirty war manifest, and felt contempt for the Juntas' dissembling "in the shadows." Speaking for the record, he let the world know that "in my opinion, they should have put the prisoners in front of firing squads in a soccer stadium, offered free Coca-Cola, and broadcast the whole thing on television." Mayorga was no backbencher in the dirty war. He had been chief of the naval base in Trelew in 1972, when one of the first massacres took place. Sixteen political prisoners were shot "attempting to escape."[27]

Admiral Mayorga demonstrated two dominant themes of dirty war defense—pride and patriotic duty, concepts also addressed by one of the most loquacious practitioners of political murder, Carlos Castaño. And while Castaño's "confession" (dictated to journalist Mauricio Aranguren Molina in 2001) is obviously political, misleading, and self-serving (when it appeared, he was worried about avoiding extradition for drug trafficking, or less likely, for human rights violations and war crimes), one can argue that his intent was sincere. Castaño was a true believer in the "antisubversive" fight (though he was also clearly in it to avenge his father's murder by the FARC). First and foremost, as noted at the beginning of the chapter, Castaño justified his extensive use of political murder as a legitimate defense of the fatherland. Carlos Pizarro, the M-19 guerrilla leader and later presidential candidate "had to die." By way of explanation, Castaño asked, "How many assassinations have states committed to benefit the national interest?" He and his followers "had to do it." Pizarro was the creature of Pablo Escobar, he claimed, who dreamed of real power through control of the presidency. He insisted that Pizarro's "extrajudicial execution . . . had to be done to protect the country." Pizarro's killing was "a truly patriotic action." Castaño never quite explains how Pizarro could ever actually have won the presidency; Antonio Navarro Wolf, the M-19 candidate after Pizarro's murder, received 12 percent of the vote. Yet Pizarro was the leading leftist candidate, which for Castaño seemed a pretty good reason to assassinate him.[28] (In an editorial on the AUC website, Castaño proclaimed that the paramilitary movement's "achievements in political and military matters against the guerrillas cannot be denied." His pride at paramilitary effectiveness was certainly supported by its record against leftist political movements.) Finally, Castaño clearly demonstrated how the fixation on pride and patriotism ultimately leads to preoccupations with the judgment of history. Castaño clearly wanted "to dictate the terms in which he will go down in Colombian history books."[29] Dirty warriors realized that their actions were open to various interpretations, as the most-conflicted Lt. Commander Scilingo made clear when he admitted that "we did worse things than the Nazis."[30] Antonius Robben notes that for dirty warriors, "the question of historical interpretation is of great importance." In his experience, "they will do their best to convince us of their rightness."[31]

Another dominant trope, not surprisingly, is the relationship between guerrillas, their terrorism, and the necessary measures to combat them. Murderous elites have a strong tendency to equate leftist and popular politics with terror and terrorism, particularly when guerrilla movements are somehow involved. By this logic, leftist movements can be justifiably attacked with violent repression. Such attacks are simply legitimate acts of war against internal enemies. Murderous elites have no objection to being on a perpetual war footing. Not to blame the victims,[32] but it is true that in many places with pronounced and prolonged dirty wars there were also significant guerrilla insurgencies, though not all were serious threats. This says a couple of things: one, fighting "insurgents" is a good excuse to initiate a wider use of political murder to smash all forms of opposition; and, two, in general, guerrilla war and armed struggle is often a bad idea for popular movements. It should be the very last resort because it is extremely dangerous. Security forces, even mediocre ones, are likely to win.[33] It is clearly not the best option, or even a viable one, in most cases. And, even in places where guerrilla movements survive (e.g. Colombia), they often do not seem to offer a good path to a better society. But it is important to remember that dirty warriors do not need actual guerrillas to fight—any subversives will do.

Argentine General Ramón Díaz Bessone's treatise, *Guerra Revolucionaria,* is one of the classic works of dirty war "apology"—unrepentant and serenely confident in the truths it offers about the need for political murder. The work clearly represents the Argentine military's perspective on "revolutionary" war and what it necessitated. In Díaz Bessone's view, such struggles succeeded in Cuba and Nicaragua but were defeated in Argentina only because the military took appropriate measures. The threat was real, the enemy ruthless and committed, and it had significant help from outside. He argued that both the Montoneros and the ERP saw their struggle as a revolutionary war, a violent struggle that looked to attack the armed forces and overturn the existing power structures. Díaz Bessone concluded that there was no room to doubt that this was "war."[34] Miguel Etchecolatz likewise engaged the theme of necessary measures. As he attacked the conclusions of *Nunca Más,* he conversely presented a series of justifications for the dirty war. In particular he insisted that the forces of subversion represented a grave threat to the Argentine state and society at large. The military and its allies in the various police forces were at war and did what they had to do to prevail. (Along the way he also insisted that the accepted numbers of people killed by the state were hugely inflated.) The armed forces and police,

Etchecolatz maintained, had to contend with a true "subversive war." The enemies of the nation did not present a clear battle front, where combatants and civilians were plainly defined; they preferred the shadows, wore no uniforms, and were known "to fight ferociously down to their last bullet." Argentina in those years suffered from a "general climate of insecurity" brought on by the terrorists' arms and explosives, their killing and their kidnapping. In essence, the guerrillas did not fight fair, so neither could the military. Etchecolatz insisted that *Nunca Más* was not written "to inform" but rather for "vengeance" against the honorable men who had answered the call of the fatherland for the "sacred mission" of its defense. He just could not abide the "lies," so his work was written to tell "the truth" and give "the facts" about the "terrorist war." His chief sources, he insisted, were the ideas, opinions, and writings of the guerrillas, "the words of the terrorist."[35] Finally, Sergeant Ibañez was on the same Argentine page of stressing the necessity of dirty war tactics. Like his superiors, he insisted that "it was war." The military had to "finish with the bad people." Since the subversives "wanted to destroy the family, impose totalitarian government under the red banner . . . [and] do away with our traditions, our nation, the Church, and our institutions," the military had to combat the enemy to the point "of total extermination," with all the necessary "death" and "blood."[36]

Even the guilt-consumed Lt. Commander Scilingo referred to necessary actions. Regarding the death flights, he told Verbitsky that "we were convinced it was the most humanitarian thing to do." And he insisted that "the armed forces weren't the only ones responsible. A large part of the country consented to the barbarities that were being committed. . . . It was accepted. Very few voices were raised against it. If the majority of the population had demonstrated against it, things would have been different." Seemingly arguing with himself, he somewhat unsurely contended that "today I'm telling you that it was a barbaric thing. At the time we were totally convinced of what we were doing . . . it would be a total lie if I told you that I wouldn't do it again under the same conditions. I would be a hypocrite. . . . I was convinced they were subversives."[37] Perhaps the favorite rationalization and proof of necessity is the "ticking time bomb" scenario. Vicente Massot, an ultra right-wing Argentine Catholic intellectual "who had written essays justifying Hitler and Franco," and who was also a close chum of Admiral Rubén Jacinto Chamorro, commander of ESMA, gave a literal time bomb scenario justification. "What we have to ask ourselves, in Machiavellian terms, is up to what point, on certain occasions does the end justify the means. A prisoner knows the location of a bomb about to explode that will kill hundreds of people. You could end up responsible for a bombing in an elementary school, for the death of hundreds of kids, because you refused to use torture." Yet as Verbitsky pointed out, the Argentine guerrillas never attacked schools. The military tortured them to get "their next appointment with their comrades," or just for fun.[38]

Finally, dirty war is widely defended as holy war. During the Violencia in Colombia, pájaros were tied to the most stridently right wing of the Conservative party, the portion most desirous of a violent struggle, a "hot war" of "sangre y fuego" (blood and fire). Theirs was a "saintly crusade" against masons, communists, and the "forces of evil."[39] This perspective continued to thrive in the 1980s and 1990s. Ernesto Báez spoke of one Father Ciro, who "from the pulpit and in the confessional, in the street, and at community get-togethers" condemned the "guerrillas" (any leftist, one assumes) as "atheists." He assured anyone who would listen that "a communist is an ally of the devil, of Satan himself."[40] (This was a holdover from the hereditary hatreds. A popular Conservative refrain held that the traditional blue of the Conservative party stood for God's Heaven, and the traditional red of the Liberal party stood for the Devil in Hell.)[41] In fact, many dirty warriors identified their acts with a long-term Christian struggle against subversion. Argentine Colonel E. Querol asserted in 1961 that "the modern world's troubles began with the Protestant Reformation." What is more, the splintering of "God's Truth," as embodied in the Roman Catholic Church, was exacerbated by the French Revolution. It severed individuals from their religious duty and seduced them with "rights." Thus, for Querol, the "ideology of liberalism," as Paul Lewis argues, became "a querulous, carping doctrine that holds everything traditional and sacred up to criticism and finally ends by spreading cynicism, atheism, and nihilism." Thus, not surprisingly, the leader of the first ruling junta in Argentina, Army General Jorge Rafael Videla, saw himself and his associates as the defenders of "Western Christian Civilization" and spoke of "categories of guilt," in which leftists and intellectuals figured prominently. Argentine generals "were charmed by the thought that they were part of a grand crusade to save the Christian West from communism."[42] In Chile as well, General Augusto Pinochet, and others, often spoke of their "holy war" against the "Marxist cancer" afflicting society. What is more, the clergy were known to give across-the-board religious absolution. Troubled by his role in his first flight, Francisco Scilingo sought out a chaplain "who found a Christian explanation for it." The priest argued that "it was a Christian death, because they didn't suffer, because it wasn't traumatic, that they had to be eliminated, that war was war and that even the Bible provided for eliminating the weeds from the wheat field."[43] And of course not everyone felt guilt like Scilingo. As one Argentine general told Antonious Robben, "I am a very religious man. And I know deep in my heart that my conscience before God is clear."[44] Likewise, in the prologue of *La otra campana*, one of Etchecolatz's former police colleagues insisted that he had acted in the name of Christ and the patria.[45]

Subversion as Disease

General definitions of subversion usually encompass unwelcome, sometimes "illegal," even "immoral," always insidious attempts to transform, undermine, overthrow, or erode the existing, sanctioned, established power structures of society, especially in the economic and political realms. For many Latin American dirty warriors, subversion was really no different from "sedition," and other more direct attacks on norms and institutions. Ideas of change were equated with words or actions that led to insurrections and open violent rebellions. As General Rafael Videla in Argentina put it, a "terrorist" was "not just a person with a gun or a bomb" but could be anyone likely to disseminate "ideas that are contrary to Western and Christian civilization."[46] There was also a tendency to see any kind of popular mobilization or activism as subversive in its most "immoral" sense. Dirty warriors felt an urgent need to fight all forms of subversion, especially ideas. It was surprisingly easy for ideas, as well as intellectuals who thought them, to be included in the subversive column. Intellectuals were identified as guerrillas—guerrillas dressed as (and hiding among) civilians. But, most important, subversion, especially Communism, was seen as a "cancer" and "infection," and intellectuals as infectious agents.

The Argentine dirty warriors spelled out their understanding of the need to fight subversion. On March 24, 1976, the first ruling junta issued a manifesto that vowed to "restore the 'basic values'—such as morality, competence, and efficiency—on which the state must rest." They aimed to "uproot subversion and promote economic development." The generals and admirals pledged Argentina to "adopt a clear commitment to the western and Christian camp in the Cold War." They also promised (their emphasis) to "*definitively eradicate the vices affecting our country*." The united armed forces of Argentina would give battle to "subversive criminality, whether overt or covert," and would "suppress all demagoguery."[47] Argentine General Roberto Eduardo Viola, along with other generals, explained their war on ideas, their offensive against the "ideological enemy," at a press conference on Subversion in Argentina in April 1977 (as quoted in the prestigious Buenos Aires newspaper *La Nación*). Subversion, they argued, is any action, open or clandestine, that seeks to alter or destroy a people's "moral criteria and way of life," and replace them with new values and ways of living.[48] That is, any forces of societal change were declared the enemy. Martin Gras, a lawyer who was held at ESMA for two years, engaged his captors and later pieced together the rational for disappearing subversives that was consistent with the regime's public statements. Their goal was to eliminate "anybody with a project for social change" that ran counter to the armed forces' "conception of a natural social order." This was "total war" that had to be taken to "those institutions and ideologies that nourished and sustained subversion."[49] Their ideas were echoed by their contemporaries in other Latin American countries. In Colombia, while Liberal president Alfonso López Michelson (1974–1978) sought reform, the head of his armed forces, General Luis Camacho Leyva, believed in eradicating subversion on the Left by directly attacking "delitos de opinion" (crimes of opinion), especially by targeting intellectuals, labor leaders, and activist academics. Camacho publicly condemned Nobel Prize winner Gabriel García Márquez for his supposed ties to the guerrillas. He was also responsible for the brutal suppression of a large strike in 1977. Then, under Liberal President César Turbay Ayala (1978–1982), Camacho was the logical choice to lead an offensive against thousands of "subversives" singled out by the armed forces and police, especially militants of the M-19. General Camacho consistently pushed a "hard war" strategy and wanted to criminalize the dreams of change advocated by the political left—that is, "subversives." People with these ideas were the "unarmed wing" of the guerrillas.[50]

Thus, to eradicate subversion, one must attack both ideas and intellectuals. Dirty warriors denied any real difference between violent and nonviolent actors, as "Colonel Lorenzo" of Argentina would later explain. He had served in an infantry regiment in Buenos Aires "during the epoch of the subversion" and argued that "the subversive phenomenon" had deep roots in the early 1960s.[51] He claimed that, beyond the armed fighters of the ERP and the Montoneros, the tens of thousands of people who provided those groups with logistical and intellectual support were legitimate targets. Ideas were what made them dangerous. Seemingly stepping back from his claims' more radical implications, however, Lorenzo stressed that the fight was not against leftist ideas per se, "because the left can be peaceful or terrorist." It was only "when the left wants to impose its ideas through the use of arms and terror" that there is a problem. Yet his nod to a reasonable middle ground was quickly forgotten when he also asserted that "ideas associated with violence" are out of bounds. Such an idea "is a dirty thing" and "associated with death." This argument opens the door to repression of anyone with alternative ideas, whether they advocate violence or not. As he argued, a "guerrilla leader who attacks people" and a person "who, with ideas, argues in favour of the one who has committed the attack," are, in fact, "the same thing." That is, he makes no distinction between "the one who thinks and the one who does."[52] One suspects that it did not take much to be considered an advocate of such dangerous ideas, and thus every bit as worthy of elimination as a violent revolutionary. Without coming out and saying that torture is justified, Lorenzo argued that it is "a desperate method that is used to try and win when there are no other ways of doing so." In fact, he presented justifications for a wide definition of legitimate dirty war targets. The "subversive" and "terrorist" war "has very different faces" from those of traditional war. And "in this war, young people, pregnant mothers, and sometimes even children have to die." The responsibility for their deaths lies not with their killers but with those who poisoned their minds and convinced them to participate in the war. He asked, "Who is responsible for taking a child, a youth, or a mother to war?" This question demonstrates the huge assumption that drove the dirty war: that all the people, "chupado," actually were participating. Since a friend of the daughter of General Cesareo Cardozo, head of the Federal Police, had placed a bomb under his bed, children, seemingly lots of them, could reasonably be considered combatants. Finally, Colonel Lorenzo asserted that it cannot be known how many of the desaparecidos were innocent. Probably there were a few but not enough to bother him much. It was war.[53]

Similarly, Carlos Castaño in Colombia dedicated himself to attacking the "brains," that is, the "subversives in the city." He was always looking for "the brains of the guerrillas." He carried out the struggle as "a war of high intensity" against the "secret allies of the guerrilla." The ELN, he claimed, liked to infiltrate union leadership; the FARC liked to worm their way into union support positions, especially in medical associations, always staying close to the money. Castaño killed union leaders, such as Jaime Angel from Valle, Jesús Agudelo of Medellín, and Jorge Gneco and Luis Felip Vélez. They died, he claimed, not for being union leaders but for being guerrillas "hiding in a union." This was his primary theme—that all sorts of people were really guerrillas, and thus fair game. Another case was that of Pedro Luis Valencia, a professor at the Universidad de Antioquia, and a national senator for the UP. Castaño went to three of his lectures and declared him to be "an impressive leftist theorist." According to Castaño, it "was clear" that Valencia aided the cause of the guerrillas with his class analysis, which blamed the rich for all of society's problems, and that he "was a great disseminator of hatred." Valencia was thus captured and executed. Castaño insisted that guerrilla intellectuals who had penetrated government institutions were "military objectives." They were "guerrillas hidden in the legal realm." This included civil servants and bureaucrats, such as Carlos Lozano and Iván Orozco, who worked as human rights advisors to Vice President Gustavo Bell. For most if not all dirty warriors, human rights worker equals guerrilla equals legitimate target. One of Castaño's biggest contentions was that Colombia's "peace communities" were infiltrated by guerrillas, where they sought support and "hid among the civilian population." When a book was being published about paramilitary activity at the Universidad de Antioquia ("based on lies"), Castaño threatened the participants, especially Hernan Henao, whom the paras executed in May 1999.[54]

Castaño described subversion as a kind of infection and prescribed a surgical approach to its eradication. Others were even more direct in making the disease analogy. For the Argentine generals, Donald Hodges noted, subversion "was likened to a highly contagious social disease that had to be eradicated." Anyone infected by this sickness, unfortunately, was lost and irredeemable. Thus, "the carriers of the germ and those directly exposed to it as well as those already infected" had to be exterminated,[55] like so many zombies. In an interview in August 2001 former Argentine Colonel Mohamed Seineldín (of "Carapintada" attempted-coup fame) viewed the murderous policing of the dirty war as combat against "internal diseases" in the body politic, or "microorganisms that rot from the inside." Subversives were "filth" and "contamination" and, of course, "evil." He "defended irregular methods" and taught them enthusiastically in Argentina and Central America.[56] Argentine Rear Admiral César Guzzetti portrayed political murder as the normal action of the nation's immune system: "the body of the country is contaminated by an illness that corrodes its entrails and forms antibodies that should not be thought of as germs." The appearance of these "antibodies" (that is, death squads and dirty war theorists) was only natural and, indeed, beneficial in "a sick body."[57] "Beneficial," one should clarify, in a body politic that shows signs of skipping from its "natural" hierarchical, elite-dominated ways. And, in Guatemala, dirty war was likened to a public health measure. General Alvaro Valencia Tobar argued in 1981 that international communism, operating out of its safe havens in Fidel Castro's Cuba and the Sandinista's Nicaragua, threatened the entire Caribbean basin with contamination. "Like the single tropical amoeba, he said, leftist guerrillas were parasites that would continue to multiply unless appropriate measures were taken to eradicate them completely."[58]

THE LAW: CO-OPTED, CIRCUMVENTED, AND IGNORED

In her study of Guatemala's military, Jennifer Schirmer described the law as a belief system about "the proper order of things." These beliefs prescribe what should and should not be and set boundaries of what is inside and outside the law. Yet these codes of conduct can be manipulated, and are often used to create institutions to oppress and restrict. Dirty warriors are quick to commandeer the law and bend it to their purposes.

Schirmer noted the old Spanish saying, "El que hace la ley, hace la trampa" (He who makes the law, crafts the ways to thwart it), and argued that the Guatemalan military men who were adept at manipulating their nation's "legal apparatus" did not "view themselves as bound by the system of regulations."[59] Dirty warriors, in fact, sometimes look to the law and hide in it, or behind it. Other times they look beyond it, float above it, or flow around it, like water around a boulder in a stream. In this, the Latin Americans are hardly alone. French attitudes about counterinsurgency, which emerged during their bloody conflicts with insurgents battling to end the French colonial adventures in Africa and Southeast Asia, showed considerable flexibility regarding matters of strict legality. Though ultimately unsuccessful, French military thinkers provided influential theories about the kinds of struggles Latin American militaries were facing. In particular, the French strategists stressed the political and ideological aspects of these conflicts. They thus recommended targeting anyone with ideas about societal change and advocated a wide range of offensive measures. They recognized that not all of these were legal, nor were they very pretty. In his widely read work, *Counterinsurgency Warfare: Theory and Practice*, David Galula echoed other French military theorists in advising that anyone serious about carrying out successful counterinsurgency operations in a timely fashion must be prepared to jettison many normal legal standards.[60]

Thus the key to dirty war constitutional theory is the dirty warrior's core belief that he should not let the constitution get in the way, and cannot allow it to give aid and comfort to the enemy. Generally oblivious to the irony of their approach, dirty warriors refuse to let the law be an obstacle to their defense of the patria and the constitution. General Díaz Bessone laid out the classic argument. The problem in Argentina, he insisted, was that the guerrillas, and their many collaborators, could hide behind legal protections and constitutional guarantees. They numbered, he claimed, in the tens of thousands, and were organized and well equipped. They could not be dealt with through police action, as leftist guerrillas in Europe had been. In Argentina, stronger measures were called for to facilitate the necessary "annihilation" of the guerrilla threat.[61] In essence, to save society, soldiers had to ignore the constitution. It was a dirty job, but someone had to do it.

It is important to remember, however, that the first strategy dirty warriors generally employ involves manipulation of the law. General Héctor Alejandro Gramajo Morales, Guatemalan Defense Minister from 1987 to1990, argued repeatedly that the Guatemalan constitution mandates that the army "maintain all military action as a basis for national stability." And Colonel Homero García Carillo, who had been Director of Civil Affairs, claimed that "we [the army] are what give laws their force." Or, perhaps, take it away. As Schirmer pointed out, the "salience of law here is what one can *do* with it, how it can be used to carry out 'operations' against opponents and how power can be consolidated in its name." Dirty warriors emphasize "the law as a sanction rather than a system of rules."[62] In fact, double standards and arbitrary definitions can be wonderfully useful. Law and legality are what the dirty warriors say they are. All the officers Schirmer interviewed insisted on the distinction between "legitimate" state violence and the "illegitimate" violence employed by their enemies. As Colonel Luis Arturo Isaacs Palacios argued, "the subversives are outside the law . . . and we are within the constitution." General Gramajo, who was "proud of having pacified Guatemala," overtly "equated law with institutionality." As long as the military acted within its institutional mandate, it was lawful, regardless of the laws it temporarily (or even habitually) ignored. For Schirmer, such an "us-versus-them attitude reinforces the idea that unjustifiable violence only occurs outside state structures; violence by the state to defend itself is mandated, and thus justifiable. Defensive, preventive measures are collapsed into offensive, strategic ones."[63]

Dirty war theorists are also inclined to define people out of their constitutional rights. Groups engaged "in denouncing human rights abuses" were typically denounced by the Guatemalan army as "outside the boundaries of 'lawful dissent.'"[64] This practice of lumping human rights organizations in with guerrillas was an old one, as Argentine and Paraguayan security reports from the early 1970s demonstrated.[65] Peruvian General Luis Cisneros Vizquerra argued to Americas Watch that a Peruvian NGO, the Asociación de Abogados Democráticos (Association of Democratic Lawyers) AAD, was "an integral part" of Sendero Luminoso's structure, and that these lawyers were therefore legitimate targets.[66] This spurious association of human rights advocates with guerrillas has also long been common practice in Colombia. In his retirement, General Urbina Sánchez argued that Colombian human rights organizations were in cahoots with guerrillas and other criminals.[67] The purported connection between the struggle for human rights and guerrilla warfare was later a recurring theme of the Alvaro Uribe administrations between 2002 and 2010.

Yet dirty warriors all over Latin America were most likely to simply ignore any constraints imposed by the rule of law, to "temporarily" step outside the dictates of the constitution. Carlos Castaño related that an Israeli trainer told him and others in Colombia: "Don't be afraid that I'll call you mercenaries . . . you have to defend the state both within the confines of the constitution and outside the constitution."[68] (The Mossad, after all, knew how to organize death squads.)[69] São Paulo state officials told Sergio Paranhos Fleury of the Departamento de Ordem Político e Social (DOPS; Social and Political Police) that "society needed cleaning up because the courts were very slow about deciding things; the law was tying the hands" of the police. He thus put together an informal, though semiofficial death squad.[70] This attitude toward "crime" easily translates to the political. The Brazilian experience of political murder in particular grows out of its practices of social, class, and racial control through violent repression. Carlos Castaño, moonlighting as a constitutional theorist, also demonstrated this phenomenon. "States protect themselves within the Constitution, and outside it," he noted, "when they are threatened by monsters like Pablo Escobar." For Castaño, this justification was obvious, essential, and good. And, thus, within the confines of his self-serving "confession," he always asked himself: "Why yes against Pablo, and no against the guerrillas?"[71]

Though Guatemalan field military commanders had no legal training, and never had legal advisors in their units, they deemed themselves, and only themselves, "capable of recognizing illegal subversion and dissent." In fact, the military considered itself (and still considers itself) "to be within, above, and sometimes outside the law," depending on the circumstances and the needs of security. Military needs and objectives trumped law, and if the law got in the way, it could be ignored. As noted, this is the old idea of suspending the constitution in order to protect it. Guatemalan officers admitted that they "must occasionally go outside the law 'temporarily' to combat subversion." (Once again, laws are general suggestions, not strict guidelines.) Discussing the "limits of the law" in military operations, Guatemalan Navy Captain Jorge Arturo Mazariegos Aquirre argued that while the military tried "as much as possible for all our actions to be within the law," they had to respond to military contingencies and could not "aspire to 100 percent respect for human rights." When asked to clarify "that in order to maintain security, the military must, from time to time, go outside the law to maintain the law?" he responded, "That's it exactly. We might go outside the law *unconsciously* to maintain security, but we do not break the law."[72]

In El Salvador, General Medrano, founder of ANSENAL, was more direct. He dismissed legal concerns as silly, holding that the dangers of subversion, and their necessary countermeasures, were obvious. He "was unapologetic" about the use of extralegal executions by Guardia Nacional and ANSENAL units. He insisted that all the guerrillas (and their supporters) were "traitors to the Fatherland." And since "the law" calls for "the death penalty," his men had simply "applied the law against them." Regarding the *Major Bob Show* (as the U.S. Embassy staff called it) on Salvadoran television, in which Roberto D'Aubuisson singled out traitors for elimination, Medrano characterized it "simply and straightforwardly." His old protégé was merely "pointing out the communists so the troops could kill them."[73] In a more sophisticated vein, Antonius Robben's anonymous Argentine general expressed his belief that all's fair (and legal) in love and war. Regarding licit and illicit rules of engagement as defined by international law, he asked: "What is licit and what is illicit, when war presupposes that I am going to kill my enemy?" Pointing to Von Clausewitz, he noted approvingly that he "talks about the tendency to go to extremes." Von Clausewitz recognized that the combatant who will use violence "without any consideration" will have a clear advantage over one "who has considerations." (This is a version of the "psychopaths make better soldiers" argument.) After pointing, once again approvingly, to Harry Truman's use of the atomic bomb at Hiroshima and Nagasaki, the general declared that "the distinction between the licit and illicit in warfare is absurd to me." Using Clausewitz as his guide, he insisted that "war presupposes from the start the use of violence" and this violence will be used "without restraint till the objective is attained."[74]

Finally, even Gringos could sound quite a bit like dirty warriors, with similar ideas about the selective application of the law. Mark Bowden noted that the "official forces arrayed against Pablo [Escobar] were not always at pains to disguise their preference for killing him rather than taking him alive," and specified General William F. Garrison, head of the Joint Special Operations Command, and Ambassador Morris D. Busby. Garrison, who had worked in the Phoenix program in Vietnam, observed from experience that "death squads were horrible, but nothing equaled them for striking fear into the hearts and minds of would-be Marxists." Busby had been the State Department's "ambassador-at-large for counterterrorism." He "believed that virtuous goals sometimes demanded hard methods, and he had seen the advantages of playing ugly. It was always a temptation. There would always be powerful, well-intentioned men who believed that protecting civilization sometimes required forays into lawlessness."[75] Yet he neglects to mention that "civilization" was often used as a direct synonym for "elite privilege."

NATIONAL SECURITY DOCTRINES

From Stanley Kubrick's film *Dr. Stangelove:*

> General Jack D. Ripper: Mandrake, do you recall what Clemenceau once said about war?
>
> Group Capt. Lionel Mandrake: No, I don't think I do, sir, no.
>
> General Jack D. Ripper: He said war was too important to be left to the generals. When he said that, 50 years ago, he might have been right. But today, war is too important to be left to politicians. They have neither the time, the training, nor the inclination for strategic thought. I can no longer sit back and allow Communist infiltration, Communist indoctrination, Communist subversion and the international Communist conspiracy to sap and impurify all of our precious bodily fluids.[76]

Many Latin American generals over the decades would have agreed with General Ripper's 1963 musings, given the international context. The success of insurgent, socialist, and anticolonial struggles in China, Indochina, Algeria, and Cuba, as well as Che Guevara's call for "many Vietnams," had decidedly focused their fears by the early 1960s. These fears in turn drove military intellectual engagement throughout the region with a corpus of ideas known generally as National Security Doctrine, or NSD. The NSD way of conceptualizing the world precipitated the eclipse of traditional notions about "national defense" against external threats (especially those represented by rivals in the region), and their displacement by ideas of "national security" against internal threats (namely ideological ones).

Many scholars have attempted to characterize NSD. Margaret Crahan argued that this mindset places "national security above personal security; the needs of the state before individual rights; and judgment of a governing elite over the rule of law." In NSD, the military often sees itself as the only neutral force, unencumbered by economic or political interests, and able to act in the interests of the fatherland. Most important, the military tends to believe that it is the only entity equipped to combat subversion with the needed force. Under NSD, military leaders believe that the state is under attack by internal, leftist enemies, and the military has the right and obligation to take over from incompetent, weak, and corrupt democratic governments; they (the military) are the last line of defense against Marxist threats.[77] Luis Roniger maintained that Latin American militaries instinctively "saw themselves as guardians of the nation's values and traditions, especially in times of crisis." It was thus no surprise that versions of the doctrine of national security floating about provided a shared framework that all drew upon to varying degrees. Military leaders naturally considered themselves the most qualified guardians of national defense and "perhaps the only capable institutional actor" to do what had to be done. Seeing the nation's "basic values" firmly anchored within Western Civilization and Christianity, they stressed the defense of private property and opposition to communist and Marxist ideas. They tended to view the world in binary terms that made elimination of the perceived enemy the only option. Invariably, Latin American military interpretations of NSD "stressed the primacy of national well-being over individual rights." It followed that "the most basic human rights" had to be "subordinated to national aims and goals whenever necessary."[78]

At the heart of NSD in the Latin American context was a focus on counterinsurgency. Patrice McSherry has insisted that "U.S. national security doctrine, especially after the 1959 Cuban revolution, increasingly encouraged a concept of unconventional war subject to no rules or ethics, a 'dirty war' to be won at all costs." For some U.S. "policymakers," communist subversion, emanating from Moscow, was behind all social and political unrest in the third world.[79] Michael McClintock has also argued that in the early 1960s U.S. military strategists were already advocating that counterinsurgent operations be carried out by mixed forces employing both regular military and paramilitary elements. These forces would rely on the brutal methods of terror (an approach especially evident in Vietnam). In particular McClintock focused on U.S. government publications, such as the classified 1960 U.S. Army Special Forces manual entitled *Counter-Insurgency Operations,* which advocated and justified the use of "terror operations." Other works encouraged, under certain circumstances, kidnapping and assassination in "political warfare." In a 1962 article for *Foreign* Affairs, Franklin Lindsay (who trained partisans in Yugoslavia and Ukraine for the OSS—forerunner of the CIA—during World War II) commented, "When two forces are contending for the loyalty of, and control over, the civilian population, the side which uses violent reprisals most aggressively will dominate most of the people, even though their sympathy may lie in the other direction."[80] For McSherry, counterinsurgency is "conducted in the shadows, using paramilitary forces and secret armies operating outside lawful state action." She argued that it generally targeted civilians rather than combatants. In general "counterinsurgency doctrine advocated" use of irregular units, informants, and other "civilian auxiliaries," combined with expanded state intelligence operations that could provide ideological filters to separate out dangerous elements. Counterinsurgency was devoted to the use of psychological warfare and "black propaganda," which was intended to work with "counterterror" operations.[81] In fact, U.S. military strategists have recycled the idea of low-intensity warfare several times over the decades, and carried numerous proxy wars: in Guatemala in 1954, in Cuba (Bay of Pigs) in 1961, in Bolivia in 1964, in the Dominican Republic in 1965, and especially via the Contras in Nicaragua during the 1980s, to name but a few. Where the proxy wars were successful, political murder was always abundant.[82]

But U.S. military thinkers were certainly not the only ones turning their attention to these matters. Paul Lewis noted that while the Argentine military "was drawn into the Cold War, became part of the Western Hemisphere's defense system, accepted the U.S. concept of a bipolar struggle, and began to focus its attention on internal enemies," they also developed "a broader vision of a titanic world struggle in which Argentina was an important battle ground." Their understanding of the struggle against subversion led to "a more or less coherent nationalist ideology justifying a new kind of military intervention that would be both broader in scope and more intensive in its methods."[83] Nor, as noted concerning legal questions, was the United States the only font of ideas. Argentines are a theoretical bunch (witness the number of psychoanalysts per capita in Buenos Aires) and given to Francophilia. Thus when theorizing about dirty war, the Argentines looked to the French. According to Lewis, the influence of the United States' military and intelligence community on the motivations for and practice of dirty war "was much less than the contribution of French counterinsurgency doctrine or even of Argentina's own military thinkers." General Osiris Villegas "acknowledged the importance of the United States as a source of equipment but not of strategic doctrine." General José T. Goyret argued that even though U.S. strategists published quite a bit on counterinsurgency after 1961, "they emphasized the military aspects while mostly ignoring the political side of revolutionary warfare." He was seconded by General Ramón Camps, who believed that "the French approach was better than the North American. It pointed to an all-around conception of the problem of subversion."[84]

Based on their experiences in Vietnam and Algeria, French ideas evolved in the 1950s, exploring what they called the "new revolutionary war" and developing the concept of "total war." As French Colonel Charles Lacheroy argued, it "not only takes possession of people physically . . . it also takes possession of their souls." This theme was expanded by one of the French military's principal thinkers, General Andre Beaufre, in his book, *La Guerra Revolutionaria*. Beaufre's book became essential reading in the Argentine military. In particular, he stressed the problem of revolutionary ideology. Subversive ideas could quickly spread from country to country, creating sympathy for insurgents, as well as direct support for their cause. Paul Lewis points out that Beaufre did not propose specific solutions, "but his brief discussion of Israel's dealings with its Palestinian population suggested that counter terror and real full-scale repression might be the most effective response." Other French soldiers were concrete in their recommendations. In his book *La Guerre Moderne,* Colonel Roger Trinquier, a veteran of World War II, Vietnam, and Algeria, focused on anti-guerrilla operations. Experienced in both irregular rural warfare and the suppression of urban insurgents, Trinquier argued that "terrorists" draw from two types of people: "idealists and criminals." Yet Trinquier's "terrorist" considered himself "a soldier engaged in a war." And "he should be treated as an enemy soldier whose army has to be destroyed so that it will be unable to continue fighting." To this end, Trinquier stressed the importance of torture in counterrevolutionary struggles. Because of the rapid pace of irregular warfare, and the mobility of insurgents, captives had to be forced to give intelligence quickly. He also advised the establishment of "secret detention centers." This conception of total war, with its emphasis on the danger of revolutionary ideas, called for extreme measures. In the modern Latin American context, it also had to focus on civilians. "It was a struggle for civilian minds and souls."[85] It was thus no accident that Argentine General Ibérico Saint-Jean (whom we met at the beginning of the chapter) took such a broad view of who to kill.

Counterinsurgency and National Security Doctrines thus made the rounds in Latin America from the 1950s through the 1980s from a variety of origins. Dirty war practitioners could pick and choose among them, adopting those that best suited their traditions and proclivities. John Waghelstein, a U.S. army colonel who supervised the training of Salvadoran soldiers in the early 1980s, argued that "real counterinsurgency techniques are a step toward the primitive." As Greg Grandin has pointed out, Waghelstein was actually advocating a step back from overreliance on high-tech weaponry and systems in favor of a refocus on nontraditional low-intensity conflict. But, as Grandin argues, Latin American militaries took up the low tech methods of slaughter with gusto. So, while Waghelstein's "call for a return to primitivism" did not openly call for such close-in and simple terror, this type of brutality "was a constitutive element of low-intensity warfare, as many of its practitioners would come to admit,"[86] or, at least as it was practiced in Latin America, where such things had deep roots. And though, given U.S. involvement, it was nauseatingly hypocritical and self-serving for Jeane Kirkpatrick to stress the local origins of political murder in her 1981 article "The Hobbes Problem," she was correct when she pointed out that "traditional death squads" have profound roots in El Salvador's history.[87]

Many commentators have looked at NSD as a deep explanation of when and why the use of political murder originated in Latin America. Michael McClintock argues that the key impact of counterinsurgency doctrine was that it legitimized state terror in the fight against dissent and subversion.[88] And Kruijt and Koonings insist that "without the supporting doctrines of low-intensity warfare against the internal enemies of the state," Latin American societies would not have experienced such high levels of political violence.[89] Certainly, Latin American dirty warriors were eager to find justifications and a clear set of ideological underpinnings for their use of violence, but the big question about the role of such ideas concerned how they influenced actors in Latin America to use political murder. Tellingly, Jeffrey Ryan argues that Uruguayan military leaders "cobbled together their own particular version of the National Security Doctrine." They "took the basic elements of preexisting doctrine and adapted them to suit their needs."[90] Though Uruguay was a country where the North American influence was supposed to have been of pivotal importance in the decision to jettison a long-established democracy, its leaders clearly had an agenda of their own. In a parallel argument, Carina Perelli suggests that many students of National Security Doctrine have overstated its causative powers in regard to the repressive actions of Latin American regimes. She argues that it was less a "trigger" for military coups and dirty wars, and more of an after-the-fact justification for actions they were already inclined to take. It provided intellectual cover and allowed them to point to other regimes that had reacted in similar fashion to similar threats.[91] Thus National Security Doctrine might have helped push some regimes over the edge, but more likely gave them leave to employ the terror they were already utilizing. Latin Americans seized onto these doctrines to justify long-held routines and practices. Gringos and others offered nice Cold War repackaging of the idea of political murder. Though they provided new terminology for old practices, along with some new techniques, they did not, in general, drive its practice. Murderous elites took what they wanted from counterinsurgency theory and added to it their own traditions.

More Practice than Theory

Some historians and social scientists do not see murder as a viable, long-term, and sustainable strategy of politics, insisting that the world is too complex to be manipulated so easily. Yet through the ages, political murder has exerted a powerful attraction. It reflects a mindset that yearns for the simplicity of a quick, blunt "solution." In the main, one can argue, Latin American power elites are not philosophers. They look to what they believe works to maintain their control, and are not overly concerned with the implications. Some, as noted, are more thoughtful and seek justifications for the status quo, as well as for the methods employed to police it, but many take a practical view. Soldiers, in particular, are nothing if not goal oriented. Their questions focus more on the nuts and bolts of political murder, the tactical and strategic aspects of its use, such as when to use death squads, regular army units, or paramilitaries; how to manipulate connections between the state and death squads (whatever their form), and the perceptions thereof; whether or when to employ bigger massacres or smaller ones, or individual murders; and when is the season to be covert rather than overt.

Regarding these nuts and bolts, Colombia has produced several hands-on, how-to discussants of the practice of political murder. General Alberto Ruiz Novoa, who was one of the commanders of the Colombian battalion sent to fight in the Korean War, advocated the recruitment of armed civilians to provide local intelligence and fight alongside the army in the Violencia. (It must noted, however, that during the Violencia local Conservatives were already doing this on their own, organically and automatically; pájaros, working alongside chulavita "police" units, were used by Conservative party elites to "homogenize towns" and to "change consciousnesses."[92]) Drawing on ideas produced by U.S. military strategists, General Ruiz advocated "hunter-killer" units to attack guerrilla supporters, though he also believed in a "hearts and minds" component of the struggle against subversion, underlining a classic theory versus practice problem. In his *Counterinsurgency Warfare* (1964), David Galula also stressed that operations doing the killing should remain apart from those equally important efforts to win hearts and minds.[93] This was commonsense advice, though it was not generally followed, and anyway, Latin American dirty warriors of this bent were not really concerned with hearts and minds—those were the concerns of the old manipulative populists of an earlier age. Certainly General Ruiz's replacements were more inclined to stress force, and to resolve any theoretical problems in favor of murderous practice.

Another classic problem that dirty warriors did not seem to lose much sleep over was the question of collateral damage. In "asymmetrical conflicts" it is often difficult or even impossible to distinguish between armed insurgents, their noncombatant supporters, and innocent bystanders. As a consequence, counterinsurgency operations have been known to employ arbitrary and inconsistent distinctions between combatants and noncombatants. In fact, dirty warriors often doubt that there is a distinction (who says they are innocent?) or do not worry about it, nonchalantly accepting the necessity of killing noncombatants. They espouse their own version of the unofficial philosophy often attributed to the U.S. Marine Corps, Army Airborne, and other special forces: "Kill 'em all, and let God sort 'em out." General Rafael Videla of Argentina, for one, was quite chatty on this point. The newpaper *Clarín* reported in October 1975 that Videla had discussed the fight against subversion (and the military's resolve) with foreign reporters, promising that "as many people as necessary will be killed to assure the country's security." And talking to a meeting of Latin American military leaders in Montevideo, soon after the coup, Videla insisted that "if needed, in Argentina as many people will have to die as are necessary to achieve peace in the country." Subversives, according to the general, were not worthy of Argentine citizenship. By definition, they were outsiders, dangerous aliens, and fair game, even if bystanders got hurt.[94] Peruvian General Luis Cisneros Vizquerra echoed these sentiments in a January 1983 interview on combating guerrillas, and on the necessity of killing a lot of people to get at them: "In order for the police forces to succeed, they would have to kill members and nonmembers of Sendero, because this is the only way to ensure success. The police kill sixty people and maybe three are Senderistas."[95] Then there was Argentine General Ramón J. Camps, whom Donald Hodges believed was possibly "the most vocal defender of political genocide." General Camps saw the struggle against Marxism in global and even apocalyptic terms. For him, military defeat of the subversives was not enough. Their capacity to wage ideological war also had to be crushed, and the methods available were, admittedly, not pretty. Anyone willing to fight a successful war against ideological subversion, and to really do what it takes to win, he argued, must be prepared to "cover himself in mud." Echoing Galula, he argued that traditional rules of civilized warfare had to be discarded.[96]

In fact, many Latin American military men strategically embraced the killing of noncombatants (and definitely jettisoned all civilized conduct of war) in their obsession with "draining the sea." This was in reference to Mao Zedong's famous dictum regarding the nature of guerrilla warfare, that the people "are like the water" and the revolutionaries "are like the fish" that swim through it. Soldiers fixated on this image in Guatemala, El Salvador, Colombia, Argentina, and other countries. In Guatemala, the army was not inclined to agonize over the question of how to "differentiate the tame and the rebellious among the Indians in the highlands." The guerrillas, one army officer wrote, "have penetrated entire populations which now support them unconditionally." The army believed that "selective repression no longer cowed them." Now it was necessary to slaughter entire communities to "dry the river in which the fish swam."[97] General Ríos Montt, for one, was a big supporter of turning Mao's famous dictum on its head and "draining the sea" through massacring Mayan peasants. And this policy worked its way through the ranks. During a massacre at the community of Sacuchum in January of 1982, an army captain harangued the assembled villagers about their "punishment" for giving support to the guerrillas. He observed that "fish only live where there is water," and you, he assured them, "are the water." He added that "when the pond dries up, the fish die."[98] In El Salvador, as well, the army strove to "quitarle el agua al pez"—that is, "as the officers put it: to take away the water from the fish."[99] In Colombia, the ACCU terrorized the "guerrilleros de civil" and sought "to dry up the water the fish swims in" to neutralize guerilla support. In this they were simply echoing arguments made by General Ruíz Novoa decades earlier.[100] Finally, in Argentina, the fight against "subversion" led to the death of thousands of people, "most of whom would be considered innocent by any standards other than those of the military assassins in power." As more and more guerrillas were disappeared in Argentina, those left "suffered a sense of impotence and insecurity because they were no longer able to move about 'like fish in water.' "[101]

Thus the method for defeating guerrillas was clear. As an analyst for the RAND corporation (the Defense Department's most beloved think tank), Benjamin Schwarz spent two years assessing U.S. policy in El Salvador. He recognized the obvious—that victory in the struggle against guerrillas in El Salvador "was built on a foundation of corpses." Schwarz argued in a RAND report that what defeated the guerrillas there, or at least kept held them in check, was "lavish brutality." A U.S. military officer who had served as the military attaché to El Salvador related to Schwarz how the upper echelons of the Salvadoran military responded to the idea that they should control death squad activity; "a high-ranking officer retorted in a dismissive tone that talk about respect for human rights was a luxury the United States could afford only because of the cold efficiency of the death squads of the early 1980s: 'We cleaned up San Salvador for you.' "[102] This conclusion, that political murder on the grand scale can stymie a popular movement or a guerrilla insurgency, was well known to Latin American murderous elites.

Yet sometimes practitioners have seen the necessity of scaling back their efforts, or covering them up. There is no contradiction in being one moment heavy-handedly brutal and visible, and another being more selective, sophisticated, and covert. Such was the evolution in Chile from the oppressive DINA to its later more-discerning incarnation, the CNI.[103] In his war with the UP in Colombia, Carlos Castaño freely admitted to "executing" many of its members, but was a bit cagy about exactly how many; he only confessed to "thirty four guerrillas outside of combat, hidden in the Unión Patriótica." He claimed to differentiate between "a man of the left in the UP, and a member of the FARC in the UP," and insisted on his professionalism and precision. Speaking of his urban death squad operations, Castaño described how, "after identifying guerrillas and important collaborators of subversion," his group often carried out simultaneous operations in various cities, though he claimed that "the operations were clean . . . with no innocent victims."[104] In December 1984, members of the supreme court of the armed forces of Argentina provided similar insight into their choice of tactics when they explained to anthropologist Antonius Robben why disappearances of subversives (which they clearly believed were justified) were employed rather than public executions. A brigadier general explained, as other judges concurred, that "there would have been immediate revenge, not only on the executioner or those who presided over the trial but also on their families."[105] It was important to protect the innocent soldiers from the wrath of "terrorists." Finally, Alan Knight explained why the Mexican style of state-sponsored political murder has been more hushed in recent decades, dealt out in smaller, more demure doses. Since the practice was "at odds with the public transcript" of the postrevolutionary state, which trumpeted popular mobilization and democracy, its use "is not shouted from the political rooftops." Rather, it was "officially denied, decried, evaded, or overlooked." While many Argentine dirty warriors have been all too eager to "publically justify" their use of political murder, "Mexican generals keep their mouths shut."[106]

The practice of political murder in Latin America was not an import, nor was it just a Cold War ideological construct. Latin Americans have their own complex understanding of what constitutes subversion, which emerged well before the Cold War and lingers after it. Such ideas were hardly a revelation; the value of killing internal enemies was not news to Latin American murderous elites, who understood the nature of the bloody struggle. The United States military's version of NSD, along with French theories, tied into older traditions in the region; it was not the grafting of an alien weed but rather a new sprout from old, deep roots. Nor was this a case of ideological "software" being "downloaded" into U.S.–directed military automatons. NSD at times provided a trendy ideological makeover for Latin

American practices, picking up on the latest terminology and fashions, but this was a fraternity, and the brothers knew how to throw murderous keggers long before the Gringos showed up. And just as Marxist revolutionary ideology was not monolithic across the region, military use of NSD also varied. Connections to the Cold War were clear, but the obvious question is, What was all this paranoia, violent rage, and fear based on? The reason these concepts found such a ready and receptive audience was that they meshed with existing proclivities.

Chapter 5

International Collaborations and the Conflicted Roles of the United States

The South American military men were proud of their bold initiative. In his book *The Condor Years,* John Dinges described the November 1975 meeting in Santiago, Chile, at which *Operación Condor* was officially launched. A journalist who covered the dirty wars of the Southern Cone for the *Washington Post* and *Time,* Dinges depicted how the government of General Augusto Pinochet invited military intelligence officers from Argentina, Uruguay, Bolivia, Paraguay, and Brazil to attend the "First Inter-American Meeting of National Intelligence." Once there, Colonel Manuel Contreras (Pinochet's trusted underling and the Chief of Chile's Gestapo-like security agency DINA) told them of his vision of a grand regional alliance against the communist specters haunting the modern world. He reminded the assembled officers that subversives do not "recognize borders," and assured them that insidious subversive influences were "penetrating every level of national life" in each of their respective countries. To combat the threat, Contreras proposed a program of international collaboration that would unfold in three phases. The first phase would entail the creation of a central depository of information and seat of coordination based in Chile, "similar" to Interpol but aimed exclusively at eradicating "subversion." It would be high tech, state of the art, and aided (he implied) by the CIA, the FBI, and the U.S. defense establishment. Yet the real show would begin with the operational efforts, the "pinnacle" of which, in the intelligence realm, Dinges insists, is "wet work." To this end, the second, and key, phase would involve the internationally coordinated capture and (almost inevitable) extrajudicial execution of subversives in all the member countries. Finally, the third phase would broaden the struggle against targets outside the region.[1]

In this chapter we examine the networks of regional cooperation that emerged to facilitate the efficient employment of state-sponsored political homicide. Latin American militaries (which had historically viewed each other with suspicion and hostility) began to work closely together in the 1970s and 1980s. Such arrangements do not necessarily imply an organized conspiracy of Latin American elites meeting in some stylish, subterranean lair a lá James Bond's evil-doing enemies at SPECTER (or, as in the Austin Powers version, coordinating their activities while they stroke white cats and practice their maniacal laughs). Over its long history, the political culture of murder in Latin America has never been so centralized or institutionalized. It has been, rather, organic, spontaneous, pragmatic, individualistic, and ad hoc. At times it was decidedly entrepreneurial. On the other hand, as Operation Condor demonstrates, these images of sinister coordination might, in some instances, not be too far off the mark. The networks of cooperation occasionally created by Latin American governments or regional power establishments demonstrate that there has long been an influential plurality of Latin Americans who agree on the general usefulness of political murder. Perhaps (returning to Austin Powers) there has never been one Dr. Evil directing the show. A better image would be of several loosely connected evil cabals, presided over by a series of Mini-Mes.

In this chapter we will also consider the varied roles played by the United States. The chapter's perspective is anchored in the observation, made in the book's introduction, that the elites of Latin America do not need the Gringos (or Yankees, depending on how far south one goes) to show them how to kill and disappear their "subversives." Many studies begin with the assumption, implicitly or explicitly, that U.S. government and North American corporate interests are the driving force behind the practice of political murder in the region.[2] It is a seductive argument because with one handy variable, the Gringo connection, one can explain the widespread use of political murder across time and in very different countries. Unquestionably, U.S. imperial activity on the periphery has done a great deal to drive the phenomenon of political murder. There are plenty of cases in which the United States organized and bankrolled the killing, and generally called the shots (as with the Contras), and many more in which its involvement was secondary but significant. Yet there are a variety of problems with this mechanistic and simplistic interpretation, beginning with that fact that it leaves out a great deal of political murder that had no connection to U.S. influence. Another complicating factor is that the United States has not followed a consistent policy in the region, emphasizing first the fight against subversion and later that against drugs, advocating human rights, democracy, and the rule of law, or U.S. economic interests, in alternating fashion, or all at once. Also, the tendency to privilege U.S. contributions creates an ever more awkward dilemma in that it shifts the focus away from the Latin American murderous elites, downplays their roles and degrees of responsibility, and generates a strangely condescending outlook that ignores Latin America's long history of repressive government and elite domination. Finally, such an interpretation gives the United States too much manipulative credit. The Gringos are often as much naïve bumblers as evil masterminds, with little understanding of how their interventions will play out. Guatemala in 1954 was a prime example. Many observers would agree with Dirk Kruijt that given "the sad series of military dictatorships, fraudulent 'constitutional' general-presidents, and the bitter guerrilla warfare" that resulted from Jacabo Arbenz's ouster, " 'Operation Success' should have been renamed 'Operation Disaster.' "[3] Ultimately, an overemphasis on the U.S. role just does not explain enough. The practice of political murder is too old, spread too broadly, and has been too varied to be explained primarily in terms of Gringo/Yankee influence, desires, and commands.

But even if the United States is not the root of all political evil in Latin America, it hardly follows that the United States can be absolved of its share of guilt. The record of the United States is a deeply troubling one for a country that sees itself as a paragon of democratic virtue and an example to the rest of the world. The United States has proven to be an essential enabler, especially during the early 1980s, acting as the perfect codependent in Latin America's political murder habit, bringing out and allowing to flourish some of the region's worst tendencies. So while the United States did not create the use of political murder, it did readily facilitate it. Far from being exonerated, parts of the U.S. government and many U.S. corporations have been and continue to be active participants in political murder endeavors, highlighting the fact that many Gringos partake of the elite political culture of murder, and hold the same assumptions. It is a shared collaboration, a partnership, in which the United States is one of many players. The United States is an enabler, and more—it is one who sits down and joins in. So rather than a puppet master pulling Latin American strings, Uncle Sam is a crony and travel companion, a fully paid-up member of the collaborative effort through which the united hemispheric murderous elites act to protect a broader status quo.

Thus Latin American elites were hardly dwelling in some primordial garden, blissfully ignorant of the knowledge of good and evil of political murder, waiting for the serpent of U.S. imperial interests to slither up to tempt them with its use. What is more, the Gringos did not force those elites into a reliance on wet work. Just because certain ideas were suggested (such as killing the troublemakers), it did not necessarily follow that Latin Americans would automatically employ them on demand. But they did often embrace the practice of political murder in the second half of the twentieth century, as they long had done, and they often did it working together and with the Gringos.

The American Empire

Certainly one can talk of something like an "American Empire" in Latin America, even while acknowledging that it has waxed and waned. After the Spanish-American War of 1898, especially, and through the "gunboat years" of the first decades of the twentieth century, the United States pursued objectives in Latin America that struck both its neighbors and its rivals as decidedly imperial. Of course, Latin America enjoyed a respite from U.S. attention under the "Good Neighbor" policies of the 1930s and during the upheavals of World War II. The United States nevertheless returned to its old ways in the 1950s, when Latin America became a battlefield of the Cold War, and especially after the Cuban Revolution of 1959, when the United States once again overtly moved to dominate the hemisphere throughout the 1960s and 1970s. Yet it was after the Sandinista Revolution of 1979 in Nicaragua that the United States exhibited its most intense preoccupation with the region, particularly in Central America. During the 1980s it was deeply implicated there in counterinsurgency operations and dirty war. This high degree of involvement gave way to the Neoliberal attitudes of the 1990s, and a focus on the War on Drugs. Finally, after the September 11, 2001, attacks on New York City and Washington D.C., and the U.S. government's resulting fixation on Islamic terrorism (as well as two shooting-wars in Iraq and Afghanistan), Latin America once again became something of a side show.[4]

One can argue, however, that this kind of empire is a wobbly shadow of its more traditional and muscular incarnations. There is, we should remember, no Colonial Office in the State Department. But whether or not one completely accepts the paradigm of an "empire," U.S. foreign policy in Latin America has generally been aggressively nationalistic, and has often employed and encouraged political murder. The United States also has a sector of elites that is clearly involved in the political murder business, with expertise that evolved outside Latin America, especially with the Phoenix program in Vietnam. It is useful to note, however, that the conflict between interpretations, particularly between those that focus on external influences (e.g., the Gringos are to blame) and those that focus on internal dynamics and trajectories, is an old one. There is, to be sure, no zero-sum game at work in the case of political murder, since both external and internal influences are clearly involved. Yet interpretations do tend to lean one way or the other, and often fall along predictable lines. Students of 'international" or "U.S.–Latin American" relations are primed to see the external. Country specialists are perhaps given to privileging internal developments (though students of Central America and the Caribbean have more reason to look to U.S. influences). In all these interpretations there is a different calculus of external (especially United States) influence and the degree of autonomy and agency awarded to country elites. The U.S. footprint is huge, but it varies from country to country and across time.[5]

Latin America surely has, in the words of Greg Grandin, "long served as a workshop of empire." In general it has not proven to be Thomas Jefferson's "empire of liberty," a fellowship of "equal, sovereign democratic American republics . . . led but not dominated by the United States." Instead, throughout the nineteenth and twentieth centuries, the United States followed its own expansionist and self-centered destiny. After conquering and annexing the northern half of Mexico in the 1840s, it went on over the ensuing 170 years to dominate large parts of the hemisphere militarily and economically. Alternating between the use of "hard" power (gunboats, invasions, occupations) and "soft" power (ideas, trade, cultural interactions), the United States has consistently viewed the region, so the saying goes, as its own backyard. What is more, according to Grandin, "by the early 1950s, Washington found that it was increasingly difficult merely to support dictators from the sidelines." In the 1960s, European empires were imploding or being abandoned, often in ugly anticolonial struggles. Cold warriors (in the United States and in other places) feared the rise of Soviet influence. As a consequence, the Kennedy administration "committed the United States to strengthening the internal security capabilities of Latin American nations to protect against subversion, turning the region into a counterinsurgency laboratory." Trainers and advisors from the Defense department and the CIA helped militaries and security services improve interrogation techniques, develop better counterguerrilla tactics, and upgrade their equipment. The United States "fortified and in some cases, created" the various intelligence agencies that would "transform themselves into the command centers of the region's death squad system."[6] The United States also benefited from its private fiefdom in the Panama Canal Zone "and other sites in Panama" that became arenas "for testing ideas and technology that had applications elsewhere." In the Canal Zone, "the U.S. military had the reputation and lack of accountability of royalty." Its power was "daunting" and Americans were "looked upon as untouchable." U.S. military personnel there acted with "privilege" and "imperial impunity."[7] Even though the Canal Zone was "returned" to Panama in the 1970s, the 1989 invasion was seen by the military establishment as a legitimate U.S. prerogative.

The United States thus developed a wide range of tools and attitudes to pursue its imperial adventures in different parts of the globe. Some of these facilitated political murder. In particular, there was a clear transfer of U.S. expertise from the Vietnam era Phoenix Program, with its "hunter/killer teams," which carried out "snatch and snuff" operations, to Latin American militaries via the School of the Americas (SOA) at Fort Benning, near Columbus, Georgia. Patrice McSherry points out that "torture manuals" used at the SOA drew on materials developed out of the counterinsurgency efforts of the Vietnam War, particularly the Army's "Project X." Project X manuals reflected the know-how gained through the Phoenix program, which employed assassination, extortion, kidnapping, and torture. It also clearly targeted civilians as well as Viet cong.[8] And this "educational" influence did not begin in the 1960s. The United States has a long history, stretching back to the early twentieth century, of training Latin American police forces, though the stated goals of "professionalizing" them and "democratizing and humanizing their practices," Martha Huggins argues, "seem to have backfired." In fact, many scholars believe that an alternative goal was actually being sought, "that U.S. training of Latin American police was never meant to make them more democratic or more responsive to civilian government." Rather, many believe that such training was "deliberately" calibrated to "increase U.S. control over recipient countries and those governments' undemocratic control over their populations."[9] In other words, were U.S. trainers incompetent, or was their real goal more nefarious? Grandin argues that after the failure of direct U.S. military intervention in Vietnam, its theorists and practitioners followed a new path in confronting guerrilla insurgencies. In places like Guatemala and El Salvador, the United States decided "to farm out its imperial violence."[10]

Leslie Gill has investigated how the United States constructed "a repressive military apparatus" in the Americas. Though her focus was on the School of the Americas, she insisted that it was only a small piece of the mosaic, given the "myriad of venues" for training. The forerunner of the SOA was the Latin American Ground School, established in Panama Canal Zone in 1946, which became the SOA in 1963. The institution was moved to Fort Benning in 1984, and since 1996 has been known as the Western Hemispheric Institute for Security Cooperation (WHINSEC), though most activists still refer to it with the more graceful (and easier to remember) "SOA."[11] The SOA curriculum covered "techniques for waging small-scale strikes, counterterrorism activities, psychological operations, foreign internal defense (i.e., organizing training and advising military and paramilitary forces) [and] 'unconventional' warfare (i.e., support of military and paramilitary operations against a standing government)." This military training was in turn fueled by the U.S. arms industry. Though the SOA pushed both "hearts and minds" approaches and "coercive counterinsurgency" techniques, the latter tended to win out. This was especially clear in the "combat-oriented" courses, which are still the biggest draws among Latin American trainees. Before its PR-driven makeover in 1996, the SOA used the so-called "torture manuals" that "advocated the use of fear, beatings, the payments of bounties for enemy dead, false imprisonment, executions . . . or 'neutralization' of enemies." The SOA has always touted its mission as "sustaining democracy" by "engaging" Latin American militaries and "exposing Latin American soldiers to 'American values.'" (Gill points out that, in purporting to offer the "civilized" benefits of the "American way of life" to "benighted" Latin Americans, the SOA reaffirmed U.S. imperialist aims and attitudes). Yet the concerns of the Cold War were clearly the driving factor. After the Cuban Revolution, the newly renamed SOA was energized, and "training the militaries of the Americas to fight communism became its raison d'etre, and counterinsurgency instruction evolved as a major new focus of its activities."[12]

U.S. "imperial" adventures south of the border were naturally facilitated by Gringo members of the murderous elite, who were just as quick to advocate murder to thwart serious threats to the status quo as were their Latin American counterparts. U.S. Secretary of State Henry Kissinger, to cite a famous example, gave repeated words of support and good will to the Argentine and Chilean militaries. In fact, Kissinger served as enabler in chief. Former U.S. ambassador to Argentina Robert Hill later asserted that, at the 1976 Organization of American States meeting in Santiago, "Kissinger had specifically given the Argentine generals a green light for continued repression." And as declassified State Department documents would show, Kissinger took the opportunity to assure General Pinochet that his soon-to-be-given speech on human rights was "not aimed at Chile," and that the U.S. government rather "welcomed the overthrow of the Allende government."[13] Likewise, Kissinger told Argentine Admiral César Guzzetti that "our basic attitude is that we would like you to succeed."[14] Finally, as John Dinges argued, Kissinger was a strong supporter of Pinochet, since he "had done an enormous service . . . by stopping the advance of Allende's democratic but pro-communist movement before it could become a showcase for non-capitalist solutions to social problems in the region."[15]

Kissinger, however, merely played the role of a blood-spattered John the Baptist to Ronald Reagan's murderous Messiah. By 1980, as William LeoGrande has reminded us, "Central America had been a backwater of U.S. foreign relations" for decades. But that changed with the arrival of Reagan's administration in 1981. Reagan was obsessed with reversing what he and many right-leaning Americans saw as the decline of U.S. power after the Vietnam War. He was personally determined to lead a Cold War counteroffensive, and his most obvious opportunity presented itself in Central America. The region was brimming with revolutionary movements, especially in El Salvador, Nicaragua, and Guatemala, all of which Reagan blamed on outside subversive, communist influence, rather than on decades of inequality and oppression. "Reagan declared Central America the place to draw the line against the expansion of Soviet influence in the Third World." For Reagan and company, this was a "struggle between good and evil" (thus his description of the Soviet Union as the "Evil Empire.") And while his administration included both ideological "hard-liners" and "pragmatists," the former tended to prevail since Reagan himself "was the premier hard-liner." LeoGrande noted "a slightly conspiratorial mentality" and a "touch of the paranoid style" exhibited by many U.S. conservatives, many of whom "became convinced that domestic opposition was being fueled clandestinely by America's global enemies." In their eyes, many people in the United States had clearly joined with the evil forces of the Soviet Union. This conclusion led to "the corrosion of civility in the foreign policy debate," as well as a good deal of Republican "red-baiting." In the wake of the lies and illegalities of the Iran-Contra Scandal, "neither Reagan nor most of the responsible officials were contrite. On the contrary, they defended their actions as necessary to defeat communism." What is more, "most Republicans endorsed this rationale, praising the inauguration of the new Imperial Presidency."[16]

Greg Grandin has pointed as well to a U.S. branch of the murderous elite, but noted its protracted evolution. After the Good Neighbor era, "America's corporate and political leaders" came more and more to advocate "counterrevolution." Washington "threw in with the forces of order, sponsoring coups, championing death-squad states, and embracing dictators." U.S. corporations with big investments in the region were known to work with the CIA to encourage coups that would produce more friendly governments. And some of these companies—Ford, Coca-Cola, and Del Monte, to name a few—"have been accused in recent years of working closely with Latin

American death squads." In the 1970s, Grandin argued, the "praetorian wing of the Republican party" was focusing more on international issues, just as other economic and policy elites "were turning mean." Yet Grandin also focused on the "New Right" that emerged in the Reagan years of the 1980s, a large part of which was obsessed with Central America. His rogues' gallery included Elliott Abrams, John Negroponte, Otto Reich, John Poindexter, John Bolton, and Oliver North. This faction wanted to erase the stain of defeat from the Vietnam era, and was intent on finding routes around breaks on presidential power, especially regarding waging war and deploying covert operations, both foreign and domestic. This elite was a "coalition made up of neoconservatives, Christian evangelicals, free marketers, and nationalists." Grandin also defined them as "New Right militarists," "militarists, idealists, and religionists," and "economic internationalists joined with militarists and Christian capitalists."[17]

What is more, murderous elites north and south tend to mesh rather nicely in an organic relationship, overlapping and comingling. Latin American soldiers who train at Fort Benning usually benefit professionally, socially, and economically as a result, especially those "upwardly mobile officers" who take the "flagship Command and General Staff Office course." These are the "future leaders of their respective militaries."[18] And U.S. representatives in the region often work and play well with their Latin American counterparts. In the 1990s, U.S. ambassador to Colombia Morris D. Busby, CIA station chief Bill Wagner, Joe Toft (the DEA country attaché), and assorted military and intelligence agents, "were not displeased" with the appearance of Los PEPES, a group that could take on Pablo Escobar using his own rules (or lack of them.) Los PEPES, they hoped, could provide the much needed "extralegal muscle." In this the Gringos were demonstrating strains of reasoning very familiar to Latin American dirty warriors. Wagner had cut his teeth with the CIA in Chile in the late 1960s and early 1970s and, not surprisingly, one of his main objectives for Colombia "was to establish a link between cocaine trafficking and the FARC and ELN, links that would justify pushing anti-narcotics work from the realm of law enforcement into the realm of war."[19]

Yet political murder across the region does not track perfectly with the Cold War and National Security doctrine. It is difficult to give even big patterns of Gringo influence credit for regional causality. While the bloodiest periods in Guatemala, El Salvador, and Nicaragua coincide with the early 1980s and with the first Reagan administration, the cases of Argentina, the rest of the southern cone, and Colombia are not such a close fit. And more important than Gringo influence was the critical mass effect in the

1970s and 1980s. Lots of governments were doing lots of political murder in a big way at the same time. The sheer volume created considerable cover in itself. If everyone breaks the law at once, enforcement becomes impossible. The United States' role does help explain the huge bulge of political murder in the 1980s, but there was much before and plenty after, enough to argue that Latin Americans would have killed even without the Gringo contribution. Clearly, they had a long history of doing so. The United States did, however, supercharge the political carnage, and drove the timing, especially in Central America. As noted earlier, Latin American generals could be paranoid about subversion, and undoubtedly went further in repressive efforts because of the ideological atmosphere created in no small part by U.S. influence. Yet, while there were plenty of paranoid, commie-hating Gringo generals as well, the fact remains that political murder and massive repression were not employed in the United States itself. Ideas alone do not automatically jump-start mass political murder—the relationship is not mechanistically causal. Nevertheless, it must be acknowledged that the U.S. role was not just a case of "a few bad apples." Clearly the U.S. government has been deeply involved in political murder. But neither is it the case that all the apples are rotten.

A Split Personality

The first big problem with what can be called the "all power to the Gringo Empire thesis" regarding the use of political murder in Latin America is that U.S. policy in the region is not particularly coherent. In fact, U.S. involvement in Latin America seems to suffer from dissociative identity disorder, or DID—also called multiple personality disorder. Over the past forty years in particular, U.S. behavior has shown signs of DID, as evidenced by its fairly wild policy swings. On rare occasions the contradictions have even been embodied in individuals. John F. Kennedy set the standard with his dual preoccupations with fighting the Cold War and encouraging development and "progress." Latin American elites, for their part, understood all too well that certain kinds of progress could lead directly to unwelcome changes to the existing order. JFK was "a committed militarist" and cold warrior who began his presidency with a powerful faith in "counterinsurgency and covert operations." Yet Kennedy also believed in winning hearts and minds, and that desire led to the foundation of his Alliance for Progress. "But," Grandin noted, "while Kennedy's revolutionary rhetoric encouraged those who sought change, his actions empowered those who opposed it."[20] Such contradictions live on. For example, in light of its obsession with the War on Drugs, the U.S. government's support of the Colombian army and its narco-paramilitary allies is truly bizarre. At the same time, sincere commitments to both encouraging human rights and fighting "subversion" are impossible to reconcile. These contradictions make the point that the United States is a big, powerful, and influential player, but one with confused and contradictory polices. The United States seldom "wants" a single, coherent thing, nor can we really talk about the United States as an integrated actor. There are divisions among U.S. government elites, as in Latin America. This is the fundamental problem with seeing "states" as individual protagonists. While one can question the DID diagnosis in individuals, most states suffer from it to some extent; they are legion.

Even with regard to such revered U.S. values as freedom and democracy, problematic contradictions arise. David Schmitz noted that during the twentieth century U.S. support for right-wing dictatorships was often justified "in the name of stability, trade, and anticommunism." The United States hoped that authoritarian allies would provide order and forestall revolutions, ensuring the safety of U.S. interests and investments. Third world societies were assumed to be too "weak and unstable" for self-governing democracy and prone to radical ideas and unrealistic solutions. But support for dictatorships in the name of freedom became untenable. All along there had been a clear disconnect between U.S. values and U.S. policy abroad, but after the political struggles engendered by the Vietnam War, an alternative framework emerged for the interpretation of U.S. foreign policy. Now actions had to be judged in light of their impact on human rights and democracy (especially during the Carter administration). Ronald Reagan, of course, tried to dismiss the issue of human rights as detrimental to U.S. interests, while still insisting on the morality of his support for selected "freedom fighters." This strategy largely collapsed under growing "accusations of hypocrisy." Knowledgeable observers also pointed out that "the United States was often responsible for the very existence of many of the most odious rulers in the world."[21] This was especially clear in Central America.

The United States can certainly be fickle. LeoGrande showed that even in Central America, where the strongest case can be made for U.S. domination, the U.S. role regarding political murder is hard to characterize as consistent. On the one hand, U.S. support for the Contras led to the death of more than thirty thousand Nicaraguans (given Contra brutality and blood-thirsty strategies) and turned over one hundred thousand more into Internally Displaced Persons (IDPs). Reagan was willing to destroy Nicaragua in order to save it. But, on the other hand, the Reagan administration moved the Salvadoran regime to lessen its reliance on such violence—"U.S. pressure produced significant reductions in the number of political murders." And, as Kathryn Sikkink has argued, when the George H. W. Bush administration "finally sent a clear cue to El Salvador that it supported a negotiated resolution," it demonstrated that the U.S. government could opt for human rights and the rule of law.[22] There is no master plan. There are multiple agendas and plenty of contradictions. State Department reports on human rights are often critical of U.S. clients, showing that different parts of the government are not on the same page, that the state is hardly monolithic; the fact is that U.S. policy can be deeply ambiguous. And it continues to be so. As Schmitz pointed out, even after the end of the Cold War (and its usefulness in justifying support for authoritarian governments), "the conflict between American efforts to promote democracy in other nations and the need to protect other national interests remains." He insisted that the United States "remains divided on these issues, and decisions most often have been made on a case-by-case basis rather than following a coherent policy."[23]

Different approaches led to back-and-forth swings between administrations. Undoubtedly U.S. polices have long aimed to control "access to resources deemed strategic" for U.S. investments in the hemisphere.[24] From 1900 through the 1930s, the United States carried, and wielded, Teddy Roosevelt's Big Stick, especially in Panama, Cuba, Nicaragua, Haiti, and the Dominican Republic; it also tried similar polices in Mexico under Woodrow Wilson, though less successfully. The Good Neighbor policy, instituted by Herbert Hoover in the 1930s and continued by Franklin Roosevelt in the 1940s scaled back U.S. interference, but after World War II, under Dwight D. Eisenhower, the United States fixated on military and police training (and the Cold War), only to break step and encourage democracy and economic development in the early 1960s under John F. Kennedy. But, in 1963, JFK started to move away from his Alliance for Progress and related reformist programs. Lyndon Johnson, for his part, began backing dictators even more (Brazil in April 1964; Bolivia in November 1964). Grandin shows that while JFK's Washington "continued to support Latin America's 'democratic left,' " many of democracy's most ardent proponents were likely to be "singled out for execution by Washington's allies." Unfortunately, most of the money JFK sent to Latin America ended up bolstering the mechanisms of repression. And, of course, "Johnson and then Richard M. Nixon kept Kennedy's commitment to counterinsurgency funding," but "tossed out his revolutionary ambitions."[25] Henry Kissinger made the stance of the Nixon and Gerald Ford administrations clear enough. Then there was a zig with Jimmy Carter toward human rights, and a zag with Ronald Reagan back away from them and toward suppressing communism. There was also variation across the region. "While the issue of direct [U.S.] influence is rather clear for the case of Central America under the Reagan administration, the picture is more complex when assessing the U.S. impact on the genocidal practices carried out in the Southern Cone." The United States under Carter tried to pressure Chile and Argentina but was largely unsuccessful.[26]

Perhaps the most abrupt shift between administrations occurred in 1981. The Carter-appointed U.S. ambassador to Honduras, Jack Binns, for instance, wanted to pressure Col. Gustavo Álvarez Martínez to stop disappearing people. In late 1981, the Reagan administration replaced Binns with John Negroponte, who had served in the U.S. embassy in Saigon during the Vietnam War. Negroponte, an avid anticommunist crusader, was pleased when Álvarez was named head of the Honduran armed forces in January 1982. Senior U.S. officials pooh-poohed assertions by former Honduran army colonel Leónidas Torres Aries that Álvarez (now a general) was disappearing leftists, calling the allegations "preposterous." They continually denied Honduran military death squad activity. In October 1982, Negroponte told *The Economist* that reports of death squads there were "simply untrue," though years later a State Department officer admitted the real U.S. policy in Honduras: "The green light was kill a commie. Everybody was winking and nodding." The United States denied that political murder was policy, but Hondurans understood that as far as the United States was concerned, they "could get away with it."[27]

Transitions between administrations could be rather messy, opening space for independent action further down the chain of command by forces that could work against the wishes of a particular administration. As Los PEPES in Colombia eliminated "the secret white-collar infrastructure of Pablo (Escobar)'s organization," they seemed to be using the detailed information on its composition and interconnections that U.S. agents had put together over the preceding months. It was not just a matter of who they murdered, "but who they did not." Many people closest to Pablo were left untouched. That is, those people were under constant surveillance, and thus, "anyone paying them a visit, threatening them, or killing them would likely show up in the American monitoring." Yet, as Mark Bowden noted, "no one in Washington was watching too closely." This was because, as administrations traded off, "there came a window of opportunity for the covert ops community" while new staffers and appointees learned their way. In fact, experienced operatives "were aware of this interruption in oversight and had been known to take advantage of it." It was hardly a coincidence "that Los PEPES went public just days after Clinton moved into the White House." It was not until August that "the new Clinton administration overseers had noticed how neatly the dirty work of Los PEPES dovetailed with the U.S. mission."[28]

Beyond the confusion of administration change, different agents of the U.S. government often work at cross-purposes. The CIA, the State Department, the DEA, and the FBI each seem at times to have their own takes on foreign policy. A prime example was the Iran/Contra scandal, which showed just how dysfunctional U.S. policy could be. Gung-ho operatives directed personal campaigns, and covert organizations ran amok in inter-agency and interdepartment turf wars. Iran/Contra represented the pinnacle of Cold War–driven multiple personality disorder, especially regarding drugs, since "the CIA employed Latin American cocaine and marijuana dealers as middlemen, using their planes to ship arms to the Contras in exchange for easy access to American markets."[29]

Just as disturbing was the 1976 assassination of Chilean diplomat Orlando Letelier in downtown Washington D.C., about which many questions remain unanswered. Did the State Department know about and fail to stop the assassination? Was the CIA part of it? Clearly not in the loop, the FBI and Justice Department broke the case by focusing on Paraguayan passport photos of Pinochet's DINA agents, Townley and Fernández, who did the deed. John Dinges argued that the CIA knew about planned phase III Condor hits outside the region, and clearly considered whacking communists and subversives in Latin America to be fine. But were U.S. government officials sanctioning assassinations inside the United States? Dinges had his doubts and thought that it "would be a mistake to assume there was a nefarious plot in the State Department to encourage the dictatorships to violate human rights, and that the plethora of cables to the contrary was some sort of elaborate fabrication." Yet Dinges also pointed out that the U.S. was sending both "green light" and "red light" messages.[30] Even within the State Department itself there have conflicting agendas and messages regarding Latin America. Kathryn Sikkink established that many people in the U.S. government have long been very pro–human rights, and insists that "the U.S. government has given mixed signals about its commitment to promoting human rights and the rule of law as part of foreign policy." She also noted a clear split among U.S. Foreign Service officers regarding their attitudes toward human rights and U.S. policy. Not surprisingly, those with contacts and connections to the Latin American military and intelligence communities have been more sympathetic to struggles against subversion, while those who advocate human rights are generally aghast at U.S. support for antidemocratic repression.[31]

At different junctures, representatives of the U.S. government have declared mea culpa regarding murderous policies. In 1999, Bill Clinton famously said that U.S. tolerance of and support for repressive governments was "wrong" and a "mistake" and should not be repeated as U.S. policy. But these moments are not consistent or even predictable. Less well known is the fact that Jimmy Carter's administration, not happy with the likelihood of a Sandinista victory in Nicaragua, wanted to find Guardia Nacional "moderates" to deal with. The failure of this pipedream pushed Carter to redirect aid in an attempt to lessen Cuban and Soviet influences. It is often overlooked that the covert actions that led to the organization of the Contras were originally authorized by Carter.[32]

This uneven process can be disorienting and exasperating to Latin Americans. At the end of the 1980s, U.S. interest in Central America evaporated (along with aid and military assistance), leaving its residents at a loss. LeoGrande quoted a Honduran businessman who likened U.S. involvement in the region to a "hurricane" that had passed through, "and all that is left is the bad aftermath." Sikkink has also noted that the contradictory, two-faced nature and "ambiguity" of U.S. policy can be rather confusing to Latin Americans. She argues that these contractions "grew from an identity conflict at the heart of U.S. policy toward Latin America." There simply "was no one U.S. policy, no single vision of who or what the United States was and what it stood for." And Schmitz maintains that, tellingly, the problems generated by ideological inconsistency are recognized inside the U.S. government itself. "What is clear from an examination of American support for right-wing dictatorships is the policy's failure." While it "often provided short-term stability," it also led to "long-term problems." In fact, the CIA even coined the term widely used for the negative reactions, confusion, and hostility around the world toward U.S. policies: "blowback."[33]

Many students of U.S.–Latin American relations have mentioned the various "green lights" and "red lights" flashed from Washington D.C. to ruling elites down south, and noted the confusion this has created. Yet the murderous elites understand that in the contradictions of U.S. policy there is opportunity and profit. And anyone who has driven in Latin America knows that drivers there are not given to strict compliance with traffic signals. Just as obviously, Latin American dirty warriors were not waiting around for green lights from the Gringos, and did not always stop at the red ones.

THE AGENCY PROBLEM

There is a second, and more important, difficulty with the "all power to the Gringo Empire thesis"—that Latin American elites can think and act for themselves. This observation points to a conundrum, or as Malcom Gladwell might call it if he were writing this book, the "agency problem." Clearly, not all political and social reaction has been in defense of the "American Empire." Latin American elites have their own reasons to kill, they follow their own well-established traditions of repression, and they can be decidedly autonomous actors.

For decades, historians and social scientists have rightly studied "agency" for the popular classes in Latin America (otherwise known as "subalterns"), but, strangely, many studies that focus on U.S. involvement with political murder in the region seem to deny it to Latin American elites. They give all the initiative to Gringos and relegate elites there to secondary, passive, and merely supporting roles. In *Empire's Workshop*, Greg Grandin seems at times to assign Latin American elites to the role of local auxiliaries, or even puppets. He argues that Latin America has long been the place "where the United States studied how to execute imperial violence through proxies." Working "through the actions of local allies," the United States "executed or encouraged coups" and turned the region into "the laboratory for counterinsurgency." Lesley Gill, who wrote of the United States and its "local allies in the dominant classes," drew the same conclusion. She called members of the Latin American militaries "foot soldiers of the U.S. Empire."[34]

Interpretations that award most or all agency to outsiders reflect an assumption about the ultimate seat of power. In many analyses, the great (and evil) power dominating Latin America is generally located at the CIA. As portrayed in too many movies to count, "they" are behind it all. Many Latin Americans buy into this idea. Argentine journalist Stella Calloni insisted that behind political murder and repression throughout the region, "in all cases" one finds "the hand of Washington and the framework of the National Security Doctrine," and of course, the CIA.[35] And it would seem that a number of U.S. academics agree, judging by the extreme statements that some have made. Patrice McSherry maintained that the "CIA basically coordinated all counterinsurgency in Latin America throughout the Cold War, an era that began in Latin America in the early 1950s." She went on to claim that the agency brought everything together when "CIA officers secretly laid the groundwork for Operation Condor by stitching together the Latin American intelligence organizations."[36] And alongside the CIA, of course, is the School of the Americas. Lesley Gill, whose stated goal was to study "the involvement of the United States in training terrorists," made clear her view of the commanding role played by the United States when she wrote of "the Third World security forces that do its bidding." The SOA, in her view, is dedicated "to training new cohorts of officers ready to defend the ramparts of the American empire."[37] Various accounts of political murder typically include the obligatory qualifier: "killed by [blank], trained by the United States." The fact that some individual attended classes at the SOA is presented as a self-evident and deeply explanatory element, trumping all else.

The language used to describe events in the region often betrays the single-minded intensity of this outlook. McSherry stated that "in the Americas, the United States acted;" "Washington took the lead;" "Latin American armies" functioned "under U.S. tutelage;" "U.S. personnel played a key role;" "U.S. personal played a central role." In fact, "Washington" and the "U.S. government" get all the action verbs. They do things. They "strengthened," "trained," "urged," and "encouraged." The CIA "introduced." Latin Americans, on the other hand, are passive recipients of U.S. actions. When they do get action verbs, and appear to be acting under their own power, they still always seem to need U.S. help: "The Brazilian and Argentine militaries—the most powerful in the Southern Cone region—intervened in Uruguay, Bolivia, and Chile to assist counterrevolutionary forces and undermine democratic systems, aided indirectly by the U.S. national security apparatus."[38] Even more telling is a statement (or Freudian slip) by Gill that the "key feature of U.S. imperialism" is that the United States "uses its power to penetrate and transform other states for its own purposes."[39] In other words, the United States is El Macho, dominant and phallic, while Latin America is La Hembra, the female, the submissive, who is "penetrated."[40]

At the core of the "American Empire" position, Gringos call the shots, are in control, and seem to dispense all knowledge of repressive techniques. For Michel McClintock, since the 1950s, the U.S. combined its anticommunist ideology and programs with its technical, training, and material support to become the driving force in the Salvadoran government's campaigns of terror, providing both the philosophical underpinning and physical wherewithal to act.[41] Political murder becomes U.S. violence. Grandin argued that after the failure of direct U.S. military intervention in Vietnam, its theorists and practitioners followed a new path in dealing with guerrilla insurgencies. This trajectory in U.S. policy found its true fulfillment in Central America where, after 1980, "not just murder but mass slaughter" played an outsized role. Grandin insists that there "was not even a whiff of rural insurrection" in El Salvador in the early 1960s, when Green Berets, CIA agents, and other operatives "organized two paramilitary groups that would become the backbone of that country's death-squad system," namely ANSESAL and ORDEN. (Overlooking El Salvador's earlier history, Grandin ignored the Matanza and earlier political murder activities, clearly this idea not novel to Salvadorans. Also, if there was no danger of popular mobilization, why organize death squads?) Grandin also stressed that U.S. training of the various Latin American intelligence agencies "directly led to the emergence of a dense, Central American–wide network of death-squad paramilitaries." He further claimed that these death squad groups "were essentially appendages of the very intelligence systems that Washington either helped create or fortified," and that "the first sustained campaign of death-squad-executed 'disappearances' of political dissidents occurred in Guatemala in 1966," perpetuated by a unit that, of course, was "created and directly supervised" by Gringos.[42] For McSherry as well, the game was directed from the north: "U.S. national security strategists and their Latin American counterparts began to regard large sectors of these societies as potentially or actually subversive," and, as a result, "Condor specifically grew out of Western hemisphere relationships and programs forged in the School of the Americas and elsewhere, a product of inter-American doctrine and strategy disseminated through the continental military system."[43] Even in Colombia, it has been argued, the "destruction of the U.P. during the last years of the Cold War was possible due to the anti-communist geopolitical indoctrination of Colombian militaries trained at the School of the Americas," even though the Unión Patriótica was mainly wiped out by paramilitary units, who hardly needed Gringo training.[44]

Such overreaching does lead at times to qualifications. McSherry opened the door to a bigger picture when she admitted that "Condor death squads were created as an integral part of a broader counterinsurgency or 'counterterror' campaign condoned by elite groups as well as their key foreign ally the United States." South American militaries, "encouraged and assisted by their U.S. partners," had begun their collaborations "to repress leftists and even oust leftist governments long before Condor was officially instituted." She thus pointed to older, regional traditions of repression. While she acknowledged that the evidence is "still incomplete," she insisted that it "allows us to state quite conclusively that Washington not only collaborated with Operation Condor and took advantage of the Condor system to advance perceived U.S. interests, but also played an indispensable role in its genesis and functioning." Not only was the U.S. role "indispensable," the CIA and U.S. military were "instrumental" to Condor's organization and "crucial" to infrastructure. They also "sanctioned, encouraged, and at times actively collaborated." But did they run the show? She could not quite call it. Also, it is unclear if she was arguing that the Latin Americans could not, or would not, have done all this without the Gringos.[45] Grandin too made a nod to Latin American elites as actors in their own right. Reformers and democrats in Latin American found their initiatives "thwarted by their respective nation's ruling classes, made up of military officers, Catholic conservatives, and economic elites." These groups "embraced terror as the only way" to stave off "revolution."[46] Certainly the U.S. goal was to create good *clientes*. As Paul Gorman, retired General and former commander of the U.S. Southern Command put it: "an officer who has gone to the School of the Americas is 100 percent easier to do business with than somebody who has not." Yet even Gill admitted that "the union of U.S. and Latin American military power did not happen the same way everywhere." And there were "continuous threats to U.S. hegemony."[47]

Yet attempts at balance often fall short when the ultimate objective is keeping the United States at the center of things. Jasmin Hristov accurately recognized elite interests in Colombia, and identified political murder a as tool of class struggle, arguing that the "last fifty years of Colombia's history have witnessed a war of violence and repression against the poor, in order to protect and advance the interests of the upper classes and foreign enterprises." She faltered, however, when she insisted that this was "largely made possible through generous U.S. support."[48] Plan Colombia certainly funded the Colombian military, but the murderous Narco elites kicked in cash to fund political murder in amounts that dwarfed U.S. aid.

At other times, observers have recognized the agency problem, as well as old traditions of repression, but attempted to slide out from under them. Cecilia Menjívar and Nestor Rodríguez did not credit Latin America's "brutal" heritage of colonialism as the root of its "state-directed" political violence, but rather stressed "a regional political structure in which U.S. political interests have weighed heavily." Back-peddling a bit, they admitted that while "Latin American state terror" is "derivative" of U.S. domination, they did not mean to "reduce all explanations of Latin American political violence to a one-dimensional causality of U.S. involvement." They saw "a clear and persistent pattern of U.S. influence over the political violence conducted by Latin American states," but allowed that cases vary. Sometimes "governments enthusiastically received U.S. support for their campaign of terror," and at other times, "weaker" states were pressured by the United States "to undertake such campaigns." They recognized that "the United States did not unilaterally implement a system of terror across the continent but was able to do so with the cooperation and, to a large extent, due to a coincidence of interests and objectives with the local military, and with political and economic elites."[49] Yet they still credited the United States with the implementation of "a system of terror." Gringos were still at the wheel. While Latin American elites were credited with a role, once again it seemed to be a subordinate one.

Clearly, the role of the "American Empire" and the U.S.–based murderous elites is significant. But was Gringo participation the *causal* driving force? Influences can be murky. Delving into the U.S. role in state terror in Latin America and the world, and considering big external influences in general, Jeffrey Sluka noted the various accusers who rightly point to the United States as an active provider of technical and material support, or as an enabler and encourager. Noam Chomsky and Edward Herman have asserted in multiple works "that the global rise in state terror was concentrated among Third World states in the U.S. 'sphere of influence,' " especially in Latin America. Herman was blunt: "the death squad is a manifestation of U.S. influence. Torture and the death squad are as U.S.-related as apple pie."[50] The Chomsky/Herman thesis, according to Sluka, "is that the global rise in state terror has been mainly or fundamentally a result of U.S. foreign policy." This theme was picked up by McClintock in *The American Connection*. But with the publication of *Western State Terrorism* in 1991, many of same authors allowed that it was "not just 'the U.S. connection,' but the wider context of Western state-sponsored terrorism which underpins the 'New World Order.' " (Even Chomsky agreed.) For Sluka, the spread of state terror was clearly the product of wider "diffusion."[51]

Problems also exist with the timeline for causality of political murder. Many countries (Mexico, El Salvador, Colombia, Argentina, and others) were using it on a large scale before the United States arrived with its ideological and military bag of tricks. The Gringos just improved technique and adjusted the scale (away from big-unit massacres to small-unit death squads). Yet in most places, most victims were still killed by big units of regular military. And as the old saying goes about leading horses to water, it is true that you "can't make 'em drink." Quoting Ernesto López, Paul Lewis pointed out that the Argentine military could not be dismissed as simple "instruments of the Pentagon." U.S. military training, material, and funding "could not have had an effect unless it had corresponded to local military demands." Such aid "accentuated an already existing predilection on the part of the Argentine military" to take a forceful role.[52] The same might be said of other Latin American militaries. SOA commandant Col. Glen Weider pushed the "few bad apples" defense of the school. These "rogue actors" might have attended, but their "crimes" represented "unconscionable acts" not taught there. He also insisted on the "redemptive" influence of SOA on Latin American soldiers, and its ability to "impart democratic values." Yes, this is largely self-serving blather, given the abundance of evidence regarding what was taught at SOA (and, for that matter, by the CIA and military MTT—mobile training teams—outside the United States), not to mention the long history of U.S. soldiers murdering and torturing pre- and post-9/11. Nonetheless, Weider was right to question whether the SOA caused Latin Americans to commit political murder.[53] It is also important to remember that not all the horses drank. Venezuelan intelligence officer Orlando García remembered Colonel Contreras's pitch. Contreras wanted the Venezuelans to round up Chilean exiles there and put them on a plane to Chile. García recounted how Contreras insisted that "we have to eliminate the enemies," and perceived that the colonel meant only one thing—that anyone sent back would be tortured and killed. The Venezuelans declined.[54]

The most important point is that Latin American dirty warriors knew what they were doing. They were clever and inventive in this regard, and long experienced in the art of political murder and attendant practices. Elites in Brazil, Colombia, Mexico, Guatemala, Argentina, El Salvador, and other countries had developed their own versions of police death squads in the 1950s and before. As argued in earlier chapters, the idea of killing troublemakers for the status quo, as well as the basic techniques for doing so, were well established in the nineteenth century. As the case of Mexico in the 1920s makes clear, political murder was not something they learned from the Gringos. CIA and U.S. military input was certainly important in the diffusion of refined political murder techniques from country to country. Latin Americans often took to these with gusto and added them to their traditions, making them their own. Yet even in this process, native Latin American expertise was a crucial element in the equation, and something to be shared. One Salvadoran officer at the SOA "explained how he blindfolded captives, took them up in a helicopter to disorient them, and then, with the helicopter hovering just above the ground, threw them out." And a Nicaraguan known as "Moisés," who had served as an officer in Somoza's Guardia Nacional and later joined the Contras, was trained in Chile and Argentina. Yet he "didn't bother with their manual" because he "already knew how to kidnap a person." And, finally, Argentine Sergeant Ibañez asserted that the practice of torture "is not learned." He reasoned that "if you enjoy making a guy suffer, what is there to learn?" He allowed that individuals could "perfect" their skills "in the course taught in the Intel Battalion," but insisted repeatedly that the capacity for torture "isn't learned."[55]

Finally, Latin Americans have not always been good, obedient U.S. *clientes*. In fact, Latin Americans have old traditions of flouting imperial power in the spirit of "obedezo pero no cumplo" (I obey but do not comply). There is a large literature on local resistance to Spanish and Portuguese imperial projects. Historians have long shown that Latin America has never been an easy region to control if its leaders were not onboard. The metropole really only gets its way if its wishes correspond with those of the local elites, and that can change, as the wars for independence demonstrated. Periodic lack of control (as evidenced by rogue death squads) was clear all the way down the supposedly tight chain of command, with regional notables defying national governments, and local elites defying regional leaders. And beyond the country level, Latin American governments across the region were known to thwart their U.S. "imperial" masters. Latin American militaries themselves could become "out of control" death squads, thwarting both government and Gringo control. As Carolyn Forché explained to Bill Moyers regarding the Colonel in her poem about El Salvador (who told the Gringos to go fuck themselves): "He got a little intoxicated and angry, and he wanted to send a message to the Carter administration. He wanted me to go back to Washington and tell President Carter, 'We've had enough of this human rights policy,' and his actions [with his bag of ears] were his way of demonstrating his contempt."[56] This sense of free agency was even apparent with the Somozas of Nicaragua, who were deeply involved with the SOA and seemingly the definition of U.S. clientele.[57] Anastasio Somoza Debayle spoke English perfectly and was a West Point graduate, but he was no mere U.S. surrogate. The Somozas were not doing what they did (that is, repression) for the Gringos as their *clientes*, but for themselves, and their own *clientes*. Even Gill pointed to a broader impact of the SOA, especially for fostering connections between Latin American military establishments. Yes, it was good, she concluded, to study there, since it brought prestige, and it is not a surprise that it would be sought after, and that the most ambitious future leaders would end up there. But what made it good was not becoming a Gringo *cliente*. As Colombian General González Herrera argued, "I don't believe that what the boys learn or don't learn is particularly important. . . . They learn many things but that is really of secondary importance. The relations they establish with others are at bottom the most important."[58] These relationships were both with Gringos and with other Latin Americans. And, ultimately, if Latin American militaries were so clearly linked into a U.S.–dominated system, how could the Argentine military get it so wrong and believe that the United States would back or even tolerate an invasion of the British-held Falklands/Malvinas? There were also the problems involved in the Letelier assassination, not to mention those of Manuel Noriega of Panama, who, although he was a U.S. client, had to be taken out with a massive invasion.

Thus the murderous elites of Latin America were not mere Gringo stooges. Although in most periods the United States was there to encourage and enable political murder, there were plenty of times when Latin American states and elites went further, and were more savage, than the Gringos had the stomach for. Often the numbers of those they killed went way beyond the U.S. comfort zone. This is not just a point of contention between academics. Interpretations of the U.S. role are important because if it is true that the Gringos have not been the prime movers behind the practice of political murder, it follows that just ending or curtailing the U.S. role will not end the practice. Political murder is a phenomenon that goes deeper, and is more insidious, than a simplistic "blame the Gringos" account can explain. While such an interpretation might be emotionally satisfying for some observers, it simultaneously gives Gringos too much credit (whether intended or not) and lets many other culpable actors off the hook. Edward Herman might have a point that death squads are as (North) American as apple pie, but they are also as Latin American as tacos, arepas, and mate. In the end, the local elites of Latin America have been the biggest beneficiaries of political murder.

FLIGHT OF THE CONDOR

The most famous example of cooperation among countries in the hemisphere was, of course, Operation Condor, the top-secret system established by the various South American military dictatorships (in conjunction with the United States) during the 1970s and 1980s. Condor shared intelligence on leftist political opponents, and coordinated their extermination. Practicing what they referred to as "hemispheric defense," they targeted not only would-be guerrilla fighters but also any "subversives" that trafficked in dangerous ideas. Originally organized by the Pinochet regime in Chile, the militaries of Argentina, Brazil, Paraguay, Uruguay, Peru, and Bolivia all participated, but the Chileans, Argentines, and Uruguayans were the most enthusiastic. Condor specialized in cross-border operations against exiled dissidents, and necessitated a large degree of international cooperation. It also enjoyed significant U.S. backing.

The poles of interpretation for the U.S. role in Condor are predictably consistent. Some place the blame squarely with the United States and the CIA. Patrice McSherry, who has produced the most in-depth study to date, argued that it was "inspired by a continental security doctrine." She emphasized that it was "a secret component of a larger, U.S.-led counter insurgency strategy to preempt or reverse social movements demanding political or socioeconomic change." For McSherry, "transnational collaboration" always seemed to mean U.S. organized and administered. Certainly there is little doubt as to U.S. ideological, financial, and technical assistance. As she noted, the "diffusion of the new security doctrine and organizational model was accompanied by massive U.S. expenditures to reshape the hemispheric security architecture and mobilize its military partners in a U.S.-led anti-communist crusade." This function was especially important regarding technological knowhow. U.S. operatives "played a central role in setting up Latin American intelligence bodies that used computers to upgrade their lethal capabilities, agencies such as DINA in Chile, La Técnica in Paraguay, the intelligence apparatus in Guatemala known as the Archivo, Department 5 in El Salvador, and later Battalion 3-16 in Honduras."[59] Likewise, Stella Calloni's view of Condor also stressed NSD and the central role of the United States. Latin Americans were victims of "the politics of state terror" that were largely "designed in Washington." The United States "inspired, financed, assisted" the repression, and the CIA of course, was the main player during assassinations, disappearances, and torture.[60] Others are not so sure. John Dinges believed that the Gringos knew a lot about Condor, and knew early. At best, they did nothing to stop it, but in all likelihood were also involved, though this falls short of seeing them in charge. And some Latin American interpretations have stressed that regional elites and military governments were the real forces behind the mutual creation.[61] Gringos certainly had a big hand in Condor, but was it really theirs? Even in this instance, where U.S. participation was intense, it is still the case that Latin American elites did not need outsiders to show them how to kill popular threats. But, aside from the question of the degree of U.S. involvement, Condor made it very clear that these Latin American military governments and state elites were all on the same page. Put in the context of the long, varied, and very widespread history of political murder, Condor seems more like a native variety than an invasive transplanted weed.

It is important to remember that Condor found its immediate origins locally, in Chile, where Pinochet had his own reasons for its implementation. Condor was very much an outgrowth of his struggles against opponents there. It also reflected the evolution of dirty war in other countries. After the 1973 coup, many of Pinochet's high-profile enemies escaped abroad to lead the resistance. His government thus began preparations for international operations soon after securing power. Brazil and the United States were quick to help. Pinochet and his advisors viewed "subversion and terrorism" from abroad "as their gravest threat." At the Academia de Guerra (the War Academy), a postcoup "think tank" emerged. The officer Pinochet placed in charge was Col. Manuel Contreras Sepúlueda, who used it as a base to create DINA. Leftists fled Chile to Perón's Argentina in large numbers (along with Bolivians, Uruguayans, Paraguayans, and Brazilians). Many of them were welcomed by Argentine revolutionary groups, especially the ERP. Some intellectuals continued to call for revolutionary armed struggle.[62] There were also democratically inclined or leftist military officers to be dealt with.

It is true that Condor "was not a rogue or ad hoc operation, but a well-organized, sophisticated, and well-equipped network with systematized planning and training, operations and communication centers, and a chain of command in each country."[63] Yet, despite this degree of international coordination, the fight against subversion inside each country was still focused on local concerns. As Dinges noted, "each country's apparatus of death had its peculiar characteristics."[64] These were the Triple A years in Argentina. Condor grew out of the various countries' specific dirty wars, evolving separately, but as a logical extension. Early operations (which McSherry called the "Condor prototype"—before the program's official beginning in November 1975) were up and running in late 1973 in the form of surveillance agreements between Argentine and Chilean military intelligence. CIA documents from February 1974 confirm that an early meeting in Buenos Aires united civilian and military police from five Condor countries: Argentina, Chile, Uruguay, Paraguay, and Bolivia. It was called the "First Police Seminar on the Antisubversive Struggle in the Southern Cone," and was intended "to prepare coordinated actions against subversive targets." In the early 1970s, the idea of international cooperation was obviously bumping around. Separate agreements were worked out among Chileans, Uruguayans, and Argentines; Chileans and Bolivians; Argentines and Brazilians; Brazilians and Paraguayans. Thus the Condor pattern was emerging as early as September 1973, when Bolivian Jorge Rios Dalenz, leader of the Bolivian MIR, disappeared from his Santiago home. Another prominent Bolivian was abducted in Santiago in November; Jorge Gallardo Losada had been interior minister in Juan José Torres's leftist government, and had written a book on the international forces behind the Torres government's fall. And of course Carlos Prats (and his wife) were killed by a car bomb on September 30, 1974, in Buenos Aires.[65] Prats was the very symbol of military subordination to democratic and constitutional government, and was writing a memoir on that theme when he was killed. Torres himself was organizing both a democratic political return to Bolivia, as well as an armed uprising of miners and campesinos. He ended up under a bridge on a back road seventy-five miles from Buenos Aires, shot in the head and neck, and left blindfolded, in June 1976.[66] Thus throughout 1974 and 1975, exiles all over the southern cone disappeared in ever-increasing numbers. By November 1975, the process that was christened Operation Condor was coming into full swing.

Perhaps Condor's "defining" feature was that it deployed units composed of mixed nationality that specialized in "cross-border and foreign operations against exiles." Yet beyond their high degree of transnational cooperation, Condor death squads were fairly conventional in their composition and range of action. Condor personnel were drawn from military, intelligence, and police organizations, as well as from paramilitary groups, of the various countries. Mixed teams moved between countries and outside the region. Their actions, of course, were denied, as when exiled Uruguayan legislators Zelmar Michelini and Héctor Gutiérrez Ruíz were disappeared and killed in Argentina. Though involved in the operations, the Argentine military government cynically called for an investigation. Condor units were quite specific in their selection of targets, which were most often leaders of leftist, labor, and political organizations. They employed the latest technology and mobilized "criminal" networks to lend a hand. In both its targets and its goals Condor fit comfortably into the general practice of political murder in the region. It targeted "persons who espoused political, economic, and social programs at odds with the ideologies and plans of the military dictatorships, their elite allies, and their sponsors in Washington." Its goal was "to extinguish the aspirations for social justice and deeper democracy held by millions of people."[67]

Another significant thing to remember is that Condor's most active years were from 1976 through 1980, and that it acted largely against the wishes of the Carter Administration in Washington. Edgardo Enriguez of the Chilean MIR was abducted in Buenos Aires and sent to Chile; Orletti Víctor Lubian, an Argentine who had been active in Uruguayan student organizations, was abducted from his home in Argentina and sent to Montevideo. In July and September of 1976, combined units of Argentine and Uruguayan military grabbed sixty Uruguayans of the leftist but nonviolent Partido por la Victoria del Pueblo movement in Buenos Aires and sent them to Montevideo.[68]

Gringos spent a lot of money and bought the Latin American militaries lots of toys. The Latin Americans took what they wanted to use, along with plenty of aid, and improved their capabilities. As McSherry noted, Condor was created to target "ideological enemies." But as such it was part of an older, larger political culture of murder that was not "U.S.-led." There is abundant evidence of Gringo involvement, but not of Gringo control. The CIA participated, but was not the driving force. Colonel Contreras in Chile was seen as a CIA "asset," though to what degree the CIA "controlled" him is far from clear. The Latin American militaries had their own agendas, which sometimes meshed with those of the United States but sometimes did not.

Exporting the Counter Revolution

Though it was the most elaborate system of international cooperation, Condor was hardly an anomaly. South American military advisors were also dispatched to Central America, particularly from Argentina. There they assisted the brutal regimes in Guatemala and El Salvador, with side trips to Nicaragua and Honduras. Plenty of elites in Central America and parts of South America (both military and civilian) were keen to import the Argentine experience. This helps explain how the slaughter correlated in countries across the region during certain key periods, especially the early 1980s. Argentina, Colombia, Guatemala, El Salvador, and others demonstrated similarities that indicated that this coordination was not all the Gringos' doing. Ariel Armony has addressed the question of whether or to what degree the practice of political murder can "travel from one country to another." Stressing both internal and external influences, he argued that "the knowhow associated with state terror can be circulated as a particular type of commodity, thus exported and deployed in different settings."[69] Argentina, it turns out, was both an independent exporter and a U.S. proxy. Yet the Argentines saw themselves as the real experts, and they shared their dirty war expertise in Bolivia, El Salvador, Guatemala, Honduras, Uruguay, and Nicaragua.

Argentines were proud of their accomplishments, and indeed were widely respected. Honduran General Gustavo Álvarez Martínez, who wanted to pursue his own vigorous war on subversion, told U.S. Ambassador Jack Binns that he "admired how the Argentine military . . . had dealt with subversives," and vowed to use similar methods. Álvarez believed that Western democracies were soft and not really up to resisting subversives. He insisted that the "Argentine Method" was the only way to deal with them, "tough, vigorous, and extra-legal."[70] Regional cooperation was clear to observers in 1982, as the "Argentine Method" was obviously being exported to Honduras. The Argentine modus operandi was apparent in new use of "disappearance" tactics, which precipitated a drop in the number of legally arrested individuals. Units of military and police personnel were mixed with criminal elements functioning as death squads, and the efforts of all these were directed at "political dissidents." Death squads were operating with impunity in public and in homes of victims; agents never identified themselves and used unmarked cars.[71] Argentine expertise was also appreciated by the Gringos. While "a number of Argentine officers were trained at the School of the Americas," it is more telling that Argentines "also excelled as counterinsurgency instructors." Once Argentina's own insurgency had been contained, the Argentine military looked to the wider threats of subversion in the hemisphere. They felt a sense of urgency because they believed that the United States under President Carter, who stressed human rights, was letting the side down. At the same time, important players in the Argentine military "perceived the interest of the CIA in the Argentine operations as an endorsement of the counterinsurgency methodology implemented in the 1970s."[72] Evidence suggests that Argentine trainers remained in Central America even after the United States and Argentina fell out over the Malvinas war. Ultimately, Armony's work described "how perpetrators of the infamous 'dirty war' in Argentina transferred their model of mass repression to Central America and how the United States supported this effort."[73] The Argentines wanted to export their counterrevolution, and U.S. support was very enthusiastic, but the United States was not mandating, originating, or directing the effort.

Another case was that of Uruguay, where the Gringos were very decisively involved. McSherry pointed to the work of Jeffrey Ryan, which demonstrated how "external influences"—that is, the United States—distorted "the Switzerland of South America" into a military regime. Uruguay's police were transformed "from a neighborhood law enforcement force that served its citizens to one that terrorized them." These outside forces "converted a constitutional military into hardened shock troops that imprisoned and tortured large numbers" of their countrymen and women.[74] Yet, once again, it was not just the Gringos. Altering Uruguay was a regional project, as Ryan showed. Uruguay, whose total population was smaller than the number of inhabitants of most Latin American capitals, was considered by its military government, those of its neighbors, and by the United States as the weak link in the region's defenses against subversion. In the three years running up to the 1973 coup, the United States earmarked almost 10 percent of its Latin American military aid budget to tiny Uruguay, especially cash and equipment for the training of its police and military. While the "vast majority of this training was carried out by the United States," it is also true that "Brazilian and Argentine personnel were thought to have provided some of the more nefarious instruction, particularly in torture techniques." The U.S. role in training Latin Americans in torture techniques is widely assumed (as in the case of police instructor Dan Mitrione), but the United States was primarily interested in facilitating training by Brazilians and Argentines—"U.S. officials eventually preferred to play matchmaker in Uruguay." The Argentines were ready to step up, and in fact were already involved in the training of Uruguayans. The U.S. embassy reported in 1971 that the "Argentine authorities have long been distressed over Uruguayan ineffectiveness in combating subversion."[75] Thus, even in the case of Uruguay, the chain of causality does not lead clearly to the United States, as the Brazilians and Argentines were enthusiastic trainers in their own right.

The Argentines also worked in Bolivia. The Argentine army and navy were active in the July 1980 coup of General Luís García Meza (against U.S. President Carter's wishes). Their efforts were brutal and precise. Argentine Junta leader General Videla insisted that Argentine involvement was necessary "to prevent the emergence of 'a Cuba in South America.' " In a side deal, García Meza and his associate Col. Luis Arce Gómez were deeply involved in cocaine trafficking (thus its name, "The Cocaine Coup"). Argentine army General Guillermo Suárez Mason used Bolivian drug money to fund anticommunist paramilitary groups in Argentina. Argentines, including former officers who served at ESMA, held training sessions for the Bolivian SES.[76]

Finally, there was the case of the Contras. The standard narrative has some generally recognized elements, most important that this was a CIA operation run by Oliver North (and the National Security Council) from his office in the White House, and by William Casey, head of the CIA. The Contras were certainly dependent on their Gringo protectors after 1982, when the Argentines backed out. As Greg Grandin noted, "Casey and North presided over the construction of an elaborate transnational support network designed to bypass congressional and public scrutiny." And "most infamously, North created an elaborate circuit of exchange that, with the help of Israeli arms traders, sold U.S. missiles to Iran at inflated prices, with the profits from the deal used to supply the Contras."[77] Yet the often unknown or overlooked fact is that the operation was taken over from the Argentines. The Argentines had worked closely with (former) CIA deputy director, Lt. General (Rt.) Vernon Walters, who had consulted them on setting up the Contras in 1980, but William Casey found it already in place when he became CIA director. The key is that the Argentines had already been on the ground in Central America working to create a counterrevolutionary army. Casey thus "instructed the CIA station Chief in Buenos Aires to advance a proposal to the army commander in Chief, General Galtieri, indicating U.S. interest in the Argentine military program in Central America." Soon thereafter the U.S. relieved the Argentines of paying for it, so Galtieri signed off. Argentina began working with the CIA.[78]

The important theme here is that the Argentines worked hard in Central America where they were especially busy, but they worked alongside U.S. operatives, not under them. Argentine officers taught interrogation and torture techniques, and dirty war tactics, to units in Guatemala, El Salvador, and Honduras (especially Battalion 3-16), as well as the original Contra unit, the "Legión 15 de Septiembre."[79] Of course there were dense CIA and Argentine Contra connections. There were "two strategies initiated by the CIA for the Contras: Plan C of 1982–83 . . . and its successor, Operation M83, which grew out of the Argentine efforts. The first had FDN troops attack Nicaragua from Honduras to create "liberated" zones and destroy the coffee harvest. The second was focused on creating political havoc for the Sandinistas and demoralizing the populations with terrorist attacks.

A final illustration lies in the case of Jorge Ramírez Zalaya. Ramírez, a graduate of the Nicaraguan Military Academy and later trained in counter-insurgency in Argentina, had been a lieutenant Colonel under Somoza. He was ordered to assassinate Father D'Escoto (Nicaraguan Foreign Minister), Deputy Foreign Minister Nora Astorga, as well as Father Ernesto Cardenal.[80] In February 1981, Argentine military instructors in Buenos Aires were still teaching Nicaraguans interrogation (and related) techniques. (Question: what is done with a person "allied with the enemy" who has been captured but who nevertheless has no useful information? Answer: "elimination.") Obviously, many of their trainees were old hands, with little need of training. Most of the Nicaraguans were former members of the Guardia who were already well versed in the "techniques of torture," interrogation, and use of explosives. They thus found "little new in the lessons the Argentines were giving." But, as a Spanish journalist noted, they could appreciate a job well done, and applauded Argentine efforts in other more benighted countries (without such a rich indigenous tradition of political repression). The most experienced members of the Nicaraguan cohort in Buenos Aires "spoke proudly . . . of the fine job the Argentines were doing in El Salvador, Guatemala, and Honduras" in their struggle against "international communism."[81]

Thus it is clear that Argentine actions belie the generally recognized timelines and interpretations. As Armony has argued: "Argentina acted alone in becoming involved in the organization and training of a contra army." Only later, after the arrival of the Reagan administration and its anti-Sandinista obsession, did Argentina become "a U.S. surrogate in Central America." But the original Argentine/Contra affair was an "independent venture" that predated Reagan by years. Argentina supported Somoza in Nicaragua, and provided training and aid to El Salvador, Guatemala, Honduras, and finally, the Contras. Armony's analysis shows that Argentina was more a partner than a proxy. He has also demonstrated that the "counterrevolutionary venture" in Central America (and one can argue throughout Latin America) was the fruit of "collaboration between states and transnational non-state organizations" (the murderous elites) that shared "ideological-based coalitions" (the political culture of murder). In fact, "the prestige achieved by the Argentine security forces within key military circles in the hemisphere was a function of the effectiveness of their unconventional counterinsurgency methodology," while the ideological influences on Argentine NSD were diverse, including "German geopolitical thought, the Roman Catholic Church canon, and principally, French counterrevolutionary doctrine and U.S. cold war security policies." Armony also stresses that Condor was a Latin American initiative.[82] Finally, Latin American militaries were more militant anticommunist fighters than their U.S. counterparts, an interpretation echoed by John Dinges. In 1975, military men of the Southern Cone saw it as their job "to defeat what they variously referred to as subversion, terrorism, or international Communism." They recognized the United States as the natural leader of the West in the Cold War, but were shaken by the fact that it abandoned the government of South Vietnam and allowed it to fall to the forces of Marxism. Despite his extrajudicial execution in 1967, the words of Che Guevara echoed in their ears about creating "many Vietnams" in Latin America and the rest of the Third World. Latin Americans were not always happy with the degree of the Gringo commitment to the fight against subversion. The reality was that the Latin American murderous elites could be even more bloodthirsty than the CIA wanted them to be.[83]

Interpretations that credit the United States with all the power miss the fact that, far from seeing themselves as U.S. apprentices or proxies, Latin American dirty warriors could feel quite superior to their Gringo overlords and recognize their shortcomings. In an interview with Armony in 1993, Argentine Naval Captain Carlos H. Raimondi argued that the U.S. military and intelligence community in Central America did not believe they could do what Argentine, Chilean, and Uruguayan armed forces had already done at home: "The United States was losing the war in Central America. It was a war that the Americans could not win by themselves. Had they remained alone, there would have been another Vietnam."[84]

The murderous elites of Latin America were active agents in the deployment of political murder around the region and did not act under U.S. tutelage or orders. But they certainly acted with plenty of U.S. aid and encouragement. Across the spectrum of U.S. involvement (from Central America, with the Marines in Nicaragua and later the CIA running the Contras, to Chile, where Kissinger did not come up with the idea of Condor but signed off on it, and, most famously, to the CIA in Guatemala in

1954, where the United States repressed "leftist" ideas and activism in the form of the Arbenz government), the United States enabled, encouraged, and empowered the murderously inclined. This dynamic was also clear in Colombia, where the United States did not create Los PEPES, but worked with them; it was a Colombian initiative, but embraced and encouraged by the Gringos (or some of them anyway.) Certainly the United States often moved in the spirit of the Latin American political culture of murder and repression. The United States was always close to the state security forces that "according to numerous truth commission reports from the 1980s and 1990s" were the ones responsible "for the vast majority of massacres, murders, disappearances, and extrajudicial executions that characterized the twentieth-century Latin American 'dirty wars.'"[85] Even though the United States was not the main source of political murder in Latin America, it has some explaining to do.

CHAPTER 6

THE ENDURING APPEAL AND CONTINUING CHALLENGE OF POLITICAL MURDER IN LATIN AMERICA AND BEYOND

The Cold War is over. The military governments are gone. U.S. geopolitical thinkers have long since returned Central America to backwater status. Yet the dance of death continues. The age of political murder persists, blurring past and present. The habit of silencing voices of change through murder in Latin America has yet to fade into the realm of history. The 1996 murder of investigative journalist José Cabezas in Argentina was reminiscent of a Triple A hit, and various other journalists have been killed in the years since. In 2002, La Masacre de Avellaneda saw the murder of Darío Santillán and Maximiliano Kosteki ("Darío y Max"), activist leaders of the "piqueteros," the street protesters and activists who specialize in paralyzing Buenos Aires traffic in the name of the unemployed. And, in September 2006, Julio López, a star witness in the case against Miguel Etchecolatz, was "disappeared."[1] The 2007 Guatemalan elections were marred by violence and intimidation, Colombia paramilitaries in the "post-demobilization" phase have continued their murderous work unabated, and there were plenty of assassinations around the "election" of Porfirio "Pepe" Lobo in Honduras in November 2009, with more journalists killed since. And of course the lists of murdered journalists in El Salvador and Mexico are long.

Thus it is impossible to wrap this study up nice and neat. The practice of political murder continues to lurch along, its edges still jagged and raw. Admittedly, the long-term impact of political murder varies throughout the region, and in most countries there have been fewer murders in recent years than in earlier decades. The evolution of political murder is a moving target and there has been no single outcome. Yet even if political murder is not as overt now, one can still find its effects everywhere. The patterns persist, and the political usefulness of killing certain kinds of people remains attractive to the murderous elites, who still want to crush even symbolic threats. So while conditions now are less favorable to widespread overt use of political murder (compared to the 1970s through the 1990s), elites and militaries in the post–Cold War, post–transition-to-democracy world still make use of the tradition from time to time. Most countries had some kind of dirty war (often more than one), usually in reaction to some kind of popular mobilization, and elites are reluctant to give up what has been an effective strategy. This continued inclination to rely on violence has the potential to pervert, disrupt, and negate democratic processes across the region. The numbers of people murdered, relative and absolute, are not the key factor in assessing the long-term impact of political murder. How many killings does it take to influence society, to dampen democracy? That, of course, depends. There is little doubt, however, that the legacy of political murder hangs over the region like a lingering radioactive cloud. There might be "progress" on the national levels, as perpetrators are prosecuted, while political murder continues at the local level in several countries to varying degrees. The practice of *limpieza social* (social cleansing), for example, is now deeply embedded in Latin American societies. And the extent of the U.S. role in these efforts remains unresolved. Documents remain classified, and there are copious amounts of denial and impunity. For all these reasons, political murder still haunts Latin America.

Yet it is no less important that the people of Latin American continue to resist such forms of domination and successfully mobilize. Indeed there are now left-leaning governments (on both national and local levels) scattered throughout the region. So while this is a work of history focused on a clearly defined part of the world, its concluding chapter must also pivot toward the future and make some global observations.

A Living Tradition of Death

The Latin American murderous elites still agree with the maxim widely attributed to Joseph Stalin: "Death solves all problems. No man no problem." Stalin had a point. Murder finally dealt with his arch rival Leon Trotsky, who had found refuge in Mexico City only to have an ice axe smashed into his head. This proclivity has staying power. There continue to be significant examples of political murder beyond the classic era of dirty war. As with populist politicos and governments that continue to pop up decades after the age of populism, these dirty war phenomena hang on, morph, and reappear, sending loud echoes of murder through the broader society. The political culture of murder is like a tenacious virus. Several Latin American societies are trying to shake it; several still have a low-grade fever. Political murders have had an obvious and ongoing effect on Latin American societies, particularly on their political institutions and civil society.

In his encyclopedic exploration of political murder from ancient times to the late twentieth century, Franklin Ford argued against its long-term effectiveness. To the question "does assassination work?" he contended that the "history of countless assassinations, examined with an eye to comparing apparent motive with actual outcomes, contains almost none that produced results consonant with the aims of the doer." Ford, we should remember, was most interested in "the intentional killing of a specified victim or group of victims, perpetrated for reasons related to his (her, their) public prominence and undertaken with a political purpose in view." Ford made a convincing case that killing a leader in power seldom has the desired effect.[2]

Yet the evidence from Latin America strongly suggests that political murder can be quite successful in thwarting social, economic, and political change.[3] The Salvadoran Matanza of 1932 not only smashed the political left, it "decapitated and dismembered it." In fact, "what remained of civil society organizations disintegrated under the weight of fear that became part of the very political system in El Salvador."[4] In Colombia, Gaitanismo was definitively eradicated as a cohesive political movement after 1948. Studies of the Violencia sometimes get caught up in the Liberal/Conservative divide, and too quickly forget its origin as an attack on the Gaitanistas and the Liberal left.[5] In later decades, Colombian murderous elites recognized the need to revisit the use of political genocide in order to destroy the Unión Patriótica. They were happy with the results. In 2001, defense analyst David Spencer noted that it would be "highly unlikely" that paramilitaries in Colombia would voluntarily demobilize, even if and when the guerrillas were defeated. In his judgment, "they would be loathe to lay down their weapons" and give total control to the Colombian state. The continued existence of guerrilla movements give paramilitaries a wonderful excuse to persist, and practically ensures that paras will continue to assert their will through the "threat" (and one might add, practice) of violence. Spencer asked, "Why does this unsavory movement that commits human rights abuses and profits from drug trafficking continue to grow?" Most obviously, he answered himself, "because they are successful." Their brutal tactics pay off.[6] The former RAND analyst Benjamin Schwarz noted that some people in the U.S. government believed that the Salvadoran guerrilla offensive of 1981 failed because of U.S.–sponsored land reform efforts. Schwarz thought this interpretation "was nonsense." He argued that "the dirty little secret" among those in the know in the Salvadoran military, U.S. armed forces, and the U.S. State Department, was that "the death squads worked."[7] This, of course, is the conclusion most dirty warriors have also drawn. General Alejandro Fretes Dávalos, a former chief of the Paraguayan general staff, mused openly to journalist John Dinges that political murder, in the form of Operation Condor, worked, and could only be termed a success. "It made short work of the international subversion. Otherwise we might have had communist governments in all our countries."[8]

There are undeniable problems and dangers involved in relying on political murder. For example, it often generates violent resistance. James Henderson noted that many observers in Colombia understood the futility and counterproductivity of brutal suppression early in their decades-long odyssey into violence. By April 1952, "it had become almost a truism that violencia created bandits and guerrillas, and not vice versa."[9] Sometimes repression backfires or just plain fails. In Brazil, political blowback caused by the bungled assassination attempt on journalist Carlos Lacerda drove President Getúlio Vargas to commit suicide with a shotgun while lying in his hammock. In other places heavy-handed repression led to dictators' overthrow, as happened to Trujillo, Batista, and Somoza. Students of Salvadoran history recognize the assassination of Archbishop Romero as something of a "turning point" in the county's political story. Murder and repression alone cannot sustain a regime forever. They are most effective as part of a mix of strategies. Still, political control through murder can be stable and productive. Differing degrees of lingering impunity have created a continuum—from Guatemala and Colombia, where political murder is still actively applied, and Mexico and El Salvador, where much of the "drug" and "gang" violence is decidedly political, with no accountability, to Argentina (generally seen as a success story, but leaving some observers apprehensive about whether dirty war could return).[10]

Regarding the economic benefits of political murder, however, there is less uncertainty. Its impact in Latin America has been decidedly in elite favor. In many countries the heightened concentration of wealth made many elites feel like the winners. The vast neoliberal transfer of wealth to the rich in the 1980s, 1990s, and later was greatly facilitated by political murder.[11] It is true, interestingly, that there is no necessary or automatic connection between political murder and economic structures. The same neoliberal transfer of wealth toward the top happened in United States as well, but without the murder. (The intriguing question of whether such murder could play a role there as well, if forces of political change show signs of success in their drive to redistribute wealth, is an open one.) Also, countries with the historically worst income distributions are not necessarily the ones most prone to political murder, as the case of Brazil demonstrates. Finally, neoliberal policy did not always walk hand in hand with political murder. Pinochet's Chile was neoliberal, but only to a degree and after the fact; the same is true of Colombia. Argentina under the Juntas did not pursue much "free market fundamentalism" at all. That came after the return of democratic government. The basic fact is that neoliberal economic policy did not cause political murder in Latin America.[12] Yet there was plenty of interaction, especially where elite economic priorities met a complementary and reinforcing long-term practice and set of attitudes (the political culture of murder). It is more probable that neoliberals learned some useful tricks from the murderous elites. But to return to the point, political murder often proved itself to be of economic value to elites in Latin America; in some countries, the economic uses of cowing people have long been well understood. Students of Guatemala have wondered why it was necessary to kill so many Maya: "Why . . . commit genocide against a population that has ostensibly constituted the country's prime source of wealth since the sixteenth century?" To intimidate and control them, of course, to destroy their will and ability to mobilize, especially in the face of waves of popular mobilization by community cooperatives, labor unions, and even insurgent groups in the 1980s. "Thinking ahead to brighter economic times, it was undoubtedly important to teach the Indians a lesson once and for all."[13]

Perhaps the best evidence that the political culture of murder remains a vibrant living force is that in many places the murderous elite remain firmly in control. Guatemala, once again, is a prime example. In the postviolence year of 1989, Vice President Roberto Carpio Nicolle admitted to the still uncontrolled nature of political violence there. Civilian leaders had to "share power with a lot of players, some of them invisible." Military and paramilitary death squads, the criminals and drug lords, "are present and absent at the same time. They are nowhere and everywhere."[14] In Guatemala, with the peace accords of 1996, military and police death squad units were supposed to have been disbanded, but considerable evidence suggests that "this process is still unfinished." Old habits die slowly, if at all. "In the armed forces, the police, and right-wing political circles, the philosophy, tactics, and habit of repressive policing, with secret operations using death-squad-like units and hired gunmen, persist. They live on in the minds of some police personnel and former military personnel transferred to the police." Some secret units and networks remained intact; retired military, with ties to organized crime, "continued to have significant influence within the army, police, judiciary, and executive branch." In 2002, there were still "many plausible allegations of politically motivated killings by non-state actors," and of course, "only limited willingness" to investigate and prosecute. The old patterns still held. The targets were human rights activists, threats to impunity, and enemies of the establishment. Police death squads were still believed "to intimidate and kill persons of political relevance." They were part of "a hidden but clearly present set of problem-solving and power-executing arrangements that fit into a wider political and administrative structure and culture." Ultimately, peace in Guatemala "is still fragile and unstable." Elite economic and political interests, which benefited from and were responsible for political murder in the past, are still very much in the game, and encourage "the continuity of a violent and repressive regime."[15]

Other countries also reveal deferring degrees of the ongoing use of political murder. In Colombia, under President Uribe, there was no doubt whatsoever, despite paramilitary "demobilization." On the other hand, some observers have noted that the peace process in El Salvador "is generally seen as a relative success story in terms of ending civil war and political violence." But Salvadoran society suffers from high levels of generalized violence. The general claim is that state-institutionalized violence, controlled by elites throughout the twentieth century, was largely tamed, and "depoliticized" after 1992. But violence is still prevalent in daily life, especially in poor neighborhoods. "Gangs often treat their neighborhood as their empire."[16] One can postulate that gangs there are the violent new micro-elite, demonstrating an evolution of the tradition. There is also the murky case of Mexico. Raquel Sosa Elizaga has argued that in Mexico today "a national policy does exist regarding the use of public force," and that the implementation of that force often lies "outside every constitutional norm." The army moves in and involves itself in local economic and political life. In particular, military personnel intrude on independent political activity while carrying out arbitrary arrests. "Everything is done in accordance with the counterinsurgency program dating back to the 1970s that was used in various Latin American countries." These operations exhibit "a vast horizontal network of political assassinations." While most of these "have been concealed within intercommunity confrontations," they are still effective in producing "collective terror and paralysis." Deployment of "mixed operation brigades" (of state police, federal judicial police, and municipal police, under army jurisdiction), alongside paramilitary units, are still used against "high risk" communities.[17] Current "drug war" murders and violence are perhaps the extreme, out-of-control version of the murderous elite's logic, extended past its typical boundaries. It is now in many ways a generalized war among elites, and on society at large. The Mexican state might eventually pick a side to come out on top, and might already have, viewing the more violent cartels like the Zetas as the bigger liability. Murderous elites do best when they can ally themselves with or use part of the state; when they take it on directly, as Pablo Escobar found, they tend to lose. There is no denying that since 1994 the Mexican political elites "have been reacquainted with violence." Now, as Alan Knight noted, "politicos emerging from Mexico City hotels have to look over their shoulders. . . . And if their narco-paymasters are engaging in selective violence, removing actual threats, or discouraging potential ones, they are, in a sense, taking a leaf out of the dog-eared Mexican political manual."[18]

Even in Argentina, which has made some headway against the political culture of murder, there are holdovers. In the 1990s, police in Buenos Aires were still using routine and excessive deadly force, "summarily executing suspects" on a routine basis. These incidents were characterized, of course, as "shootouts."[19] An Argentine NGO, CORREPI, has documented over two thousand suspicious deaths by police and armed forces since the end of the military governments in 1983. In Argentina, "state violence has not ended but has become diffuse." CORREPI noted that, circa 2007, "too many individuals detained for identification or misdemeanors seem to feel the urge to commit suicide by hanging right after entering police stations in Argentina." Officers of the provincial police forces "are responsible for 66 percent of the deaths documented by CORREPI, a reminder of the role of provincial state apparatus as an authoritarian reservoir in Argentina."[20]

The tradition lives on in the United States as well. The fact that President Gerald Ford signed Executive Order 11905 in February 1976, banning political assassinations, and that no president has since countermanded it, is largely beside the point. Influences continue to run both ways between Latin America and the United States. The U.S. military gave useful insight into its mindset by openly discussing the use the "Salvador Option" in Iraq (that is, running death squads there), providing strong evidence that many people in power still believe in the utility of political murder. U.S. special operations units such as the Intelligence Support Activity of the U.S. Army, SEAL Team Six (that took out Osama bin Laden), and CIA paramilitary squads all ply the trade. There are also "contractors" and U.S. versions of the Latin American paramilitary entities, best represented by Xe Services, LLC, formerly known as BlackwaterUSA and Blackwater Worldwide, a "private military" company founded in 1997. Such companies, many observers believe, regularly act very much like their Latin American counterparts, often reportedly outside the confines of international law.[21]

Certainly in the Latin American mind Gringos seem perfectly attuned to death squad wet work. Perhaps the best representation of this belief can be found in the Argentine cartoon character, Boogie "El Aceitoso" (the Oily One), created by Roberto Fontanarrosa. In this comic, which ran from 1974 to 1995, Boogie is a "Yankee" formed in his profession of hit man, bodyguard, and mercenary during his tours fighting in Vietnam. (He was Rambo before Rambo.) Boogie is a coldblooded psychopath, for sure, but he is also supremely competent, controlled, and "principled." He is a firm believer in the American "free enterprise system." He hates communists, blacks, Asians, Latinos, Arabs, and he routinely slaps women around (when they need it). Though a fiercely independent freelancer, he will work as a violence contractor for anyone who will pay him. He is chummy with police (he believes in law and order, after all) and occasionally works for the CIA, in Africa, and later in Central America, when he provides his services to the Contras in Honduras and Nicaragua. He even serves in the First Gulf War.[22] His career parallels that of many of his real-life countrymen. Of course, not all Vietnam veterans were converted into sociopaths, but some do play to the mercenary stereotype in their memoirs. A case in point was Billy Waugh, the "special forces legend, seasoned CIA paramilitary, renowned assassin, covert operator, and the world's longest operating 'Green-Badger' or CIA contractor," (in addition to his days as a direct "company" employee, or "Blue-Badger"). His general counsel was "kill them . . . Flatten the place. You have to not mind killing innocents. Even the women and children."[23]

Clearly this mindset lives on among U.S. murderous elites, as the popular FOX television thriller "24" demonstrated. The brainchild of conservative writer Joel Surnow, it followed the adventures of Agent Jack Bauer (played by Kiefer Sutherland), who wrestled manfully with terrorist threats to the American way of life. Bauer killed a lot of bad guys and tortured "terrorists" (in myriad gruesome ways). He even disemboweled one evil doer to recover a cell phone SIM card, all for the most patriotic of reasons. His victims were always dangerous scumbags, and their information was always useful (and time sensitive). It was a reactionary fantasy akin to, but even more extreme, than those of Ayn Rand, and it had loud echoes in the broader political culture of the United States. Supreme court Justice Antonin Scalia, for example, cited the show's "ticking time bomb scenarios" as justification for repressive tactics.[24] (He was in good neofascist company. As noted earlier, Hitler-apologist Vicente Massot made similar arguments justifying the Argentine Dirty War.) Television evangelist Pat Robertson did Scalia one better, and openly called for the assassination of Venezuelan President Hugo Chávez, to prevent Venezuela from becoming "a launching pad for communist infiltration and Muslim extremism all over the continent."[25] Yet beyond television Realpolitik, right-wing politicians continue to embrace murderous polices in the United States. Sharron Angle, Republican candidate for the Senate from Nevada, made her position clear enough in a January 2010 interview: "You know if this Congress keeps going the way it is, people are really looking toward those Second Amendment remedies." That is, they will use guns to counter the kind of change represented by the Obama Administration. Later that year, Georgia State representative John Yates stressed that troops stationed on the border with Mexico "ought to be armed" and that Mexicans should understand that "we will shoot to kill if anybody crosses." And, most famously, in January 2011, Michele Bachmann, Republican congresswoman for Minnesota, leader of the House "Tea Party" Caucus, and candidate for the Republican presidential nomination, wanted people to be "armed and dangerous" to resist liberal legislation on the climate.[26]

The utility of political murder is also clear in its connections to conventional politics. In Colombia (and in Guatemala and El Salvador, for that matter), political murder undeniably has led to enduring strife that continues to affect every member of society. Yet it also severely weakened the unarmed political left, and created an atmosphere conducive to capital accumulation (especially as people abandon their land). There are, not surprisingly, right-wing political parties that defend dirty wars, and that look back on them fondly, such as the Unión Democrática Independiente (UDI) of Chile, an assembly of hardcore Pinochet defenders.[27] Other examples include Alvaro Uribe's Partido de la U (and the "parapolítica" struggles it generated), as well as his newer Centro Democrático, elements of the Mexican PAN and PRI parties, and of course, Roberto D'Aubuisson (Mr. Death Squad) is still revered by many in El Salvador. On January 20, 2007, Salvadoran President Antonio Saca commemorated the anniversary of D'Aubuisson's death and promised "to continue the ARENA party, based on his ideological legacy." The ARENA party even tried to have him named a "meritorious son of El Salvador."[28] And there have been echoes in Argentina, as when right-wing politician Carlos Ruckauf became governor of Buenos Aires province in 1999 "with the promise of 'filling criminals with bullets,' "[29]

In their cost-benefit analysis, as they weigh the pros and cons of employing political murder, some elites have recognized that the price can be quite high. This is especially clear in terms of what it does to society—increasing all forms of violence, severely damaging tourism and other industries, and undermining political legitimacy. And there are political and legal means to protect elite interests that may lessen paramilitary strength. Asking what changed in El Salvador, and why the broad use of political murder has fallen off, Julie Mazzei answered that "groups now compete to implant their agendas via electoral competitions and political institutions rather than with weapons." She argued that the demise of paras in El Salvador was the result of three changes: first, the international situation shifted—the USSR was gone, and U.S. funding "dried up"; second, the military was restructured, and its "internal focus" ended; and, third, right-wing political elites opted for politics. D'Aubuisson himself supported talks while "the business elite who had been willing to support the PMGs [paramilitary groups] found a new and less costly ally in ARENA, and they found their interests could be protected via political means rather than via PMGs."[30] Yet she is perhaps too optimistic. The murderous elites were happy to practice politics because they had first crippled the leftist opposition to the point of general paralysis. It is not outside the realm of possibility that if the FMLN government in El Salvador endures over several electoral cycles it could eventually face a resurgence of reactionary political murder.

Yes, it was time for a change, but did it mean a permanent shift away from the use of political murder? The murderous elite rode political murder as far as they needed to. They are walking the steed now, but they can remount and return to the use of such focused violence if right-wing politics cease to produce the control they desire. Even if Mexico and Colombia go this route, and forsake political murder to the degree that some observers claim El Salvador has, the political murder option will still be there. As the Colombia case shows, political murder (and not just overt paramilitary structures) is really useful. Post-para "demobilization" political murder proves that the practice can outlive any particular method or organizational structure, which can anyway reemerge when needed, as demonstrated by "new" paras in Mexico. Political murder remains an important part of a larger strategy of repression and hegemonic (political and economic) domination. Many in the Latin American elite believe it works. The possible downsides are just the cost of doing business, maybe even a bargain. The reason there are fewer murders these days (at least in most places) is that the elites have in good part accomplished their political goals; now it is a matter of maintenance. They kill fewer people, as needed. Their point is made; in many countries they are in control. They beat back the specters of populist mobilization and revolution. Now they can go back to trying to manage or co-opt popular movements; they can always kill more later. The practice of political murder has often moved those sectors of society prone to mobilization and activism away from work for social justice and democracy and toward a focus on survival. It keeps them on the permanent defensive. Julio Simón, "El Turco Julián" of the Argentine Federal Police (an ardent Nazi sympathizer) was convicted of various dirty war crimes in 2006. Before his conviction, he summed up the situation: "democracy is coming now, but do not forget: we will always be here."[31] It was a warning that left-leaning governments in Latin America would do well to remember.

FEAR AND RESISTANCE

Fear can rewire a political culture, dampening impulses for popular and democratic mobilization. The perpetrators strive to make it clear that there is indeed more to fear than fear itself. Pushing for change can get you killed. Rumors, conspiracy theories, speculations, gossip, and paranoia all play their roles. Fear makes people look over their political shoulder, drives self-censorship, and restrains popular mobilization. In many places threats are still heavy in the air. In Guatemala, forensic anthropologist Fernando Moscoso admitted that "when I am excavating, I am conscious that in a year, or two, or three, the skeleton in the ground might be me."[32] The practice of political murder evokes some big open questions: Does killing the leader of a popular social, religious, or political movement really quiet the forces of social change and resistance? If it does so, how long and to what degree will the effect last, and at what cost? Do groups that employ political murder believe in "great man" theories of history? That is, do leaders call forth these movements from out of the ether so that once leaders are killed, movements die? Or are they replaceable representatives of deeper social forces, not so easily put down? Whatever the answer to these questions, it is important to recognize the limits of repression. People in Latin America have continued to resist. There was no universal, across-the-board response to fear. Every country in Latin America had its own somewhat unique experience, and even that depended on the period. In Guatemala, fear was more pervasive and debilitating; Argentines went to therapy; Mexicans and Colombians have tended to write gangster ballads and "aguantar" (suffer, abide, and endure). And, as Robben has pointed out, the disappearances in Argentina also spurred the rise of human rights organizations across the region.[33] After a while, fear ceases to paralyze action. Like an antibiotic overused, it can have diminishing returns. New generations have to be terrorized all over again, and even parts of the older generations get tired of being afraid. The real question is what form resistance, class struggle, and popular political mobilization will take: conventional politics, armed revolution, or human rights activism? Victims of repression found multiple ways to face and mitigate their fears. They continued to fight for human rights and civil liberties, to accuse their oppressors and to mobilize against murder, torture, and disappearances. One student has observed that "history seems to reveal that fear scares individuals and affects their behavior, but that societies have a great capacity to absorb traumatic experiences and to look ahead to the future without making direct reference to memory."[34]

In different parts of Latin America, observers have identified what they call a "culture," "climate," or "society" of fear.[35] Anthropologists Michael Taussig and Linda Green explored the concept, noting that "cultures of terror" develop where social and economic order is maintained by violence and intimidation: "In such a system, there is an ever present threat of repression, torture, and ultimately, death for anyone who is actively critical of the politicoeconomic status quo."[36] Or even critics who are not so active. The Guatemalan military's anti-guerrilla maneuvers of the 1960s helped in "the creation of a 'society of fear.' " Using anticommunist campaigns as a pretext, "the military institutions began to monopolize their institutional strength against all other organized segments of the civil society," such as political parties and social movements. The machinery of repression was "expanded towards all segments of civil society that, maybe, one day, would or could support the guerrillas."[37] This was true in other countries as well. The enormous security apparatus created by the military government in the late 1960s and early 1970s was "largely uncontrolled and arbitrary." It gave birth to "a climate of fear."[38] Southern Cone military regimes "combined fear of the known . . . with fear of the unknown." The known was up front and personal: repression, threats, and the unavoidable presence of the state. The unknown came with disinformation and the unpredictable patterns of physical intimidation and murder.[39] In the "culture of fear," fear is "ultimately connected" to the "question of order." Fear is felt on both sides, driving behavior of both the suppressed population and the authoritarian regime,[40] and/or elites.

Fear of actual physical harm, Norbert Lechner argued, is but "the tip of an iceberg" of generalized anxiety, the "diffuse, apparently objectless fear that eats away at everything, crumbles hope, flattens emotions, and saps vitality—a cold that invades and paralyzes."[41] Effects of fear are felt throughout society. For Kruijt and Koonings, fear creates a "generalized climate of individual weakness, of permanent alertness without the possibility of escape, of collective powerlessness, of lack of control" where "all news is threatening" and "self-blame is followed by self-censorship" in a "culture of silence" that leads to "an avoidance of discussion." This generalized fear "surfaces in dreams and chronic illness. Whisperings, innuendos and rumours of death lists circulate. Ambiguity becomes institutionalized."[42] In Guatemala, Piero Gleijeses saw cultural cohesion through fear (making a broad argument that explains all of Guatemalan history, beginning with the conquest). The "culture of fear" is "the taproot of Guatemalan history." He insisted that "violence, torture, and death are the final arbiters of Guatemalan society, the gods that determine behavior." The Arévalo/Arbenz years loosened its grip a bit, but then it returned to crush all popular impulses and "over the next three decades, intransigent opposition to social reform" characterized Guatemalan elites. Repression and fear generated silence, which "permeates the political realm."[43] Daniel Wilkinson found evidence for this view as a young postcollege wanderer and eventual human rights activist when he tried to get coffee workers from a Guatemalan coffee plantation called La Patria, and their descendents, to talk about their experiences during the Violencia, beginning with the burning of the coffee farm's main house. Wilkinson ran into a generalized wall of silence and fear. He was usually told that "nothing happened." A local historian "forgot" what happened while he was mayor. Wilkinson finally got some people to open up about the 1982 massacre at the mountain village of Sacuchum, where 44 were killed.[44] They were not just paranoid to think that it could happen again and to remain silent.

Fear clearly provides political control. In postcoup Chile, "the new authorities consciously generated fear and insecurity." The military largely institutionalized a permanent state of emergency. They insisted that "the enemy" could attack again at any time. The country moved through years of varying degrees of vigilance, from "state of war" to "state of alert" to "state of national commotion."[45] They employed a varied strategy to keep the populace off balance, switching from covert repressive operations and veiled state-sponsored homicide to overt and dramatic actions missed by no one. The key and purpose "of state terror in Latin America," Patricia Fagen has argued, beyond "removing leftists and identifying genuine subversion, was to discourage people from organizing for any politically related motive."[46] Torture centers in Uruguay were especially for intellectuals, the resultant culture of fear not an accident. Information was allowed to escape via military personnel and friends and relatives of the victims; "these communications conveyed knowledge of what could happen to those who opposed the regime. They were intended to convince potential opponents that terror has no limits and that for them there was a fate in store that could be worse than death."[47] Robben asserted that Argentine disappearances "had their greatest effect within the homes of the victims." Fear often permeated private life of the victim's families and friends, and had "lasting political and psychological effects." The drive for social and political activism could be "dwarfed in comparison to the disappearance of a loved one."[48] Exile and IDPs—the great Latin American political murder-driven Diaspora—has kept the region churning for decades. Torres-Rivas stressed that political violence in the years of military dictatorship was "without parallel" in Latin American history and that "the search for order via the use of violence left society even more disorganized than before, paralyzed cultural life for a significant period . . . and left entire societies in a continuing state of fear."[49] Finally, John Dinges noted that "state sponsored terror had eviscerated the nonviolent political opposition, creating an entire generation of political exiles forced to look over their shoulder wherever they were in the world, haunted by the specter of the assassination attempts against leaders like Letelier, Michelini, Gutiérrez, Torres, Prats, and Leighton, and even Paraguay's Goiburú."[50]

Latin American resistance traditions, however, have pushed back. Patrice McSherry recognized "some hope" and noted "political and social forces" that struggled against the traditions of repression. She pointed to the efforts of "relatives of the victims, citizen organizations, human rights groups, nongovernmental organizations, international lawyers and judges, and networks of activists and truth-seekers."[51] Impulses for popular mobilization have endured, waiting to spring back. Kathryn Sikkink asserts that we have learned that the "only long-term solution to the problem of terrorism is one that that promotes democracy, human rights, and the rule of law."[52] This "liberal" solution, of course, rests on a belief in the transformative and healing power of democracy. While Rummel rightly observed that democratic governments can be guilty of terror, he argued that authoritarian governments are the more likely to use it. His hope, and prescription for the way to end state political murder, was to restrict power and foster democracy.[53]

One of the key axes of this resistance was the emergence of human rights activism in Latin America, beginning with Las Madres and Abuelas de Plaza de Mayo in Buenos Aires, which spread a way of understanding the fight against political repression to other countries. Winifred Tate has argued that "the stated intention of much human rights activism . . . has been to reveal the secrets of hidden violence, connecting observers to violent abuses and inspiring their action to prevent it." This is the "paradigm of transformative witnessing." She identified "several important generalizations" about human rights practice in Latin America in the decades after it was first inspired by military dictatorships in the Southern Cone (and later emulated in other parts of the region). For one, "authoritarian states were the target of activism focusing on the state as the central actor in political violence." Another is that "the practice of human rights activism involves more than simply counting the dead; it is also making the dead count." The "real work of human rights activists" involves "giving deaths meaning, making them socially legible, and filling out the narrative arc that explains why people died and how to prevent such violence in the future."[54]

Tate also considered the connection between human rights activism and the political left, and the problematic relationship between human rights struggles and leftist politics. They are certainly fellow travelers. Tate showed how these activist groups "emerged from complex oppositional political cultures." In fact, many early human rights activists throughout Latin America saw their efforts as a "radical vocation." In Colombia, of course, many activists grew up during the Violencia, but activists in most countries were also responding to some form of homegrown repression. In Colombia, activists "learned about human rights, and how to use them, from other activists, many from the Southern Cone." Yet their activism moved beyond a more generic understanding of human rights because it "was not simply a response to political violence but was profoundly shaped by the political culture" of leftist radical activism, and they tended to interpret political killings as "violence perpetrated by the state against the left." These pioneer human rights activists "also largely viewed violence as employed by the Colombian guerrillas as the legitimate expression of the 'right to rebellion' and collective defense." These activists "shared a commitment to radical social transformation, shaped by their participation in consciousness-raising groups organized through the Catholic church, universities, and unions."[55] There are also clear parallels with human rights movements in other countries, with the same early mindset. As human rights activism became professionalized in Colombia in the 1990s, it became "centered on objective reporting that depoliticized human rights knowledge, adhering to legal standards and using a dispassionate tone rather than explicitly expressing alliance with leftist programs." But, she insisted, "activists did not abandon their participation in the Colombian left," even as they had to deal with the rise of new victim populations in Colombia: women, indigenous groups, Afro-Colombians, and gays and lesbians.[56]

It is thus not surprising that some resistance has naturally been, and will probably continue to be, violent. Not everyone on the Latin American left has faith in the inevitability of a "liberal" democratic victory. Thus it is not just cooptation and marketing that keeps Che's face on t-shirts. Many Latin Americans still believe in the efficacy of armed struggle, and that belief is widespread, despite the failure of most guerrilla movements. The examples of Cuba in 1959 and Nicaragua in 1979, or the many insurgent groups of Colombia, Guatemala, El Salvador, or even Mexico after 1910, for that matter, are still alive in the minds of Latin American youth, who often grow weary of ineffectual politics. This belief helps explain the longevity of the FARC in Colombia, and the periodic emergence of new guerrilla groups in other countries. Certainly one of the side-effects of the continued armed struggle is that human rights activism will continue to have a "criminal" and "guerrilla" taint in some elite circles.

Finally, there has even been a U.S. role in aiding resistance. Sikkink noted that U.S. human rights policy has periodically offered a framework that can successfully compete with traditional U.S. support for anticommunist and murderous regimes; "when it was consistently implemented, the United States switched from contributing to authoritarianism to joining coalitions in favor of democracy." Of course, this movement toward human rights "wasn't predestined or obvious." Nor, one can add, permanent. There is often some backsliding. This occasional nod to human rights "was the result of a struggle over the heart of U.S. policy that took place in the 1970s through the early 1990s." This struggle, to the degree that it has succeeded, did so "against considerable odds."[57] And it is still true that many inside, and others outside but close to, U.S. government, intelligence, military, and big business circles have not renounced their support for (or perhaps their own involvement with) regimes that use political murder.

Practical Issues: Peace, Justice, and Impunity

Since the 1980s, resistance to political murder has manifested itself around the questions of how to end the practice and how to bring the perpetrators to justice. Many countries have struggled to face the legacy of political murder, and to seek justice for both victims and the broader society. There have been winners and losers, both economic and political, and varying outcomes, but no clear or easy path. There are only painful choices and tradeoffs. There is no indication of what the impact of human rights campaigns will be, or where the evolution of international law will ultimately take Latin America. What, for instance, are the true implications of the so-called "Pinochet effect" (observed since the 1998 arrest of Augusto Pinochet in London on a Spanish warrant for human rights violations)? Some predictions have been guardedly optimistic, while others are more fearful and pessimistic. Certainly there are some difficult issues to resolve, especially the question of whether or to what degree Latin American societies can have both peace and justice. Is short-term sacrifice of justice necessary to build a new, long-term societal model in which political murder cannot function? There are also many conflicting views about acceptable levels of impunity, and whether the prosecution of perpetrators is necessary as a deterrent to future murderous elites. But it is clear to all that bringing perpetrators to justice while ending the practice of political murder will be devilishly hard.

So far, "post" murder experiences vary, with different outcomes regarding peace and justice. There are a few partial success stories, with Argentina at the head of the class. After the *Nunca Más* report, President Raúl Alfonsín identified some officers for prosecution. A number of former Junta leaders were tried and convicted in June 1985, but the military in general resisted further prosecutions, and rebelled repeatedly in the "carapintadas" (painted face) uprisings of 1987, 1988, and 1990. This resistance led to the 1986 Ley de Punto Final (Full-Stop Law), short deadlines for prosecutions, and the 1987 Ley de Obediencia Debida (Due Obedience Law), which ruled that most soldiers were "just following orders." Soon thereafter, President Carlos Menem pardoned many convicted officers, though the courts ruled in 1998 that pardons could not cover the kidnappings of children of victims, and several were reconvicted. Finally, in 2001, the Full Stop and Due Obedience laws were declared unconstitutional. Prosecutions have continued (in Argentina and Spain), and Etchecolatz, Scilingo, Astiz, and military Chaplin Christian von Wernich were among the defendants. While "Argentina originally preferred to pursue truth-telling and reparations, the past several years have witnessed a return to prosecutions of major offenders."[58]

The case of Chile has been another slow-motion success story. The transition to civilian rule was very slow and controlled by the military. Round one included the 1978 amnesty and a new constitution giving the military dramatic powers, especially in the Senate. After the referendum he called went against him, Pinochet gave up the presidency, but not command of the military. In 1990, President Patricio Aylwin established the Truth and Reconciliation Commission, whose final report, in February 1991, held state security forces responsible for 95 percent of violations and procured some reparations for survivors and families. But the issue gained little traction until October of 1998. Pinochet was in London for medical treatment when he was detained on a warrant by a Spanish judge. (If nothing else, this episode demonstrated that as the perpetrators get old, they sometimes become weak and vulnerable.) Pinochet was kept in detention for almost a year and a half before the British (who were uncomfortable with setting such a precedent) released him on the questionable grounds of health. Yet, after his return to Chile, it soon became obvious that he and his comrades were clearly exposed to further attempts at prosecution. Pinochet was eventually charged with torture in 2006, shortly before he died. His detention greatly boosted efforts to pursue prosecutions under universal jurisdiction internationally, and weakened Chile's amnesty law. By the time Pinochet was charged, more than one hundred police and military personnel had been convicted of murder, torture, and abduction, while over thirty generals faced further prosecution. It is important to remember, however, that many Chileans (as well as other Latin Americans) still praise Pinochet's war.[59] And despite the existence of socialist governments, Pinochet's constitution still hampers democracy in Chile.

In 2001, a decision by the Inter-American Court of Human Rights ruled that the 1995 Peruvian amnesty violated international law. Peru's Truth and Reconciliation commission, the CVR, was the first in Latin America to hold public hearings in which victims spoke out about their travails, with upward of seventeen thousand testimonies. The participants identified forty-six hundred mass graves, and twenty-two hundred of them were inspected. The final report, in 2003, documented political murders, massacres, disappearances, rapes, and torture. It was unique in that guerrillas of the Sendero were responsible for a large portion of the mayhem, but the military and police were also deeply implicated. Since many of the guerrillas had already been tried, most of the free perpetrators were in the security forces. Among those convicted were members of the Grupo Colina, as well as Fugimori and his security chief.[60] These cases represent the most successful outcomes, such as they are.

In Guatemala, the prognosis has not been so good. Peace accords led to a United Nations–sponsored Truth Commission, the Historical Clarification Commission, or the CEH, whose final report in 1999 gave a "nuanced account" and "detailed massive human rights abuses by state security forces." It recommended "reparations for victims and institutional reforms of the judiciary and state security agencies." Also, the Catholic Church's human rights office did its own investigation, the Recovery of Historical Memory (REMHI). Its final report, *Nunca Más*, backed up CEH. Its driving force, Bishop Juan José Gerardi, was, as noted earlier, murdered. Justice has since moved slowly, if at all, in Guatemala. Its constitutional court refused to extradite General Efraín Rios Montt to Spain, and he remained a powerful political player in Guatemala until he was finally arrested (at the age of 85) in January 2012. There have been no reparations of note to the Mayas. Political murder remains in play, while the military and police are still unaccountable, and democracy remains weak.[61] To the Guatemala case we must add Colombia, with its evolving paramilitary structures, and El Salvador, which switched to elite-dominated politics, and has prosecuted no one of note. In May 2012, the Salvadoran Supreme Court denied Spanish requests for the extradition of thirteen former military personnel who are accused of planning and overseeing the murder of the six Jesuit priests in 1989, five of whom were Spanish. Now El Salvador also has a violent gang problem. Finally, there is the case of Mexico, with its "drug war," which has many political murder overtones. The key point is that success in bringing justice varies a good deal.

Nevertheless, many observers believe there is reason for hope, beginning with the original trial of the nine generals and admirals of the Argentine juntas. Their lawyers argued that "wars have no laws." Since Isabel Perón's constitutionally elected government had declared a state of siege in 1974, the military was just doing its job, and could not be condemned. They had to defeat the terrorist threat. The lead prosecutor, Julio C. Strassera, countered that "it is senseless for a man to destroy all the china in his house in order to catch a fly." He also asked, "Is it an act of war to occupy houses and keep relatives of those being looked for as hostages? To keep babies? Are those military objectives? Can you explain the systematic plundering as a necessary measure?"[62] Justifications such as those made by the Argentine military have been roundly rejected. John Dinges argued that "Condor's success turned out to be ephemeral." Military governments are gone, and campaigns to prosecute the offenders have emerged. Even though Condor's international operations were a small part of the overall dirty wars, it had symbolic significance. The "high-profile public figures, especially military leaders and democratic politicians" who were Condor's targets added publicity and clout to the storm of international human rights protest that arose in its wake. And the "international nature of the crimes" opened the door to multiple avenues of prosecution. Though military leaders such as Pinochet in Chile and the various members of the Argentine juntas tried to amnesty themselves with laws and constitutional amendments, many eventually faced arrest and conviction. Laws were overturned, and they discovered that it was impossible to inoculate themselves against international law. Despite efforts to cover tracks, Condor generated a huge paper trail, throughout Latin America and the United States, that has led to prosecutions.[63] Continuing in this spirit of the pursuit of justice, Virginia Bouvier's recent collection, *Colombia: Building Peace in a Time of War*, reflects the many continuing and dogged efforts to end Colombia's dark odyssey of political violence, at both the national and local levels.[64]

High-profile "perps" have been convicted, beyond Argentina, Chile, and Peru. Luis García Meza was tried in absentia by the Bolivians for human rights crimes and eventually extradited to Bolivia from Brazil in 1995, and sentenced to thirty years. Brazil may be outgrowing the political culture of murder, as its society becomes richer and more democratic. And even in Guatemala, Frank Afflitto has argued, "the effects of state-sponsored death squad terror have served as an impetus for bringing together Guatemalans" in movements of popular resistance. This "pluralistic national unity," through "community identification as survivors of state-sponsored violence" works to "undermine" the ideology and practice of terror.[65]

Most of the efforts to date have been driven by liberal beliefs and assumptions about democracy, the power of truth, and the value of prosecuting those guilty of political murder. The attitude of many activists is "do the right thing." Winifred Tate believes that governments in Latin America "should fortify the rule of law, not repressive security forces," but also insists that "the best way to reduce violence and end impunity" is for said governments "to bring perpetrators of abuses to trial."[66] One could argue, however, that this assertion still falls into the realm of faith. It is far from clear that both of these objectives are possible. More skeptical observers might argue that a fundamental conflict between "justice" and "peace" remains. Experience has shown that it is very difficult to both end violence and at the same time end impunity, and prosecute perpetrators, many of whom remain in their deeply entrenched and well-defended positions of power. At times there seems to be an insurmountable divide between these objectives.

Greg Grandin and Thomas Klubock have explored how these ideas played out during some of the earliest attempts to find a way to justice through Truth Commissions (TCs). Grandin and Klubock linked TCs to the so-called Latin American "transition to democracy." The first effort was Bolivia's Comisión Nacional de Desaparecidos in 1982, followed by the more influential Argentine Comisión Nacional sobre la Desaparición de Personas (Nunca Más) in 1983. Over twenty countries had TCs, in Latin America, Asia, Africa, and Eastern Europe.[67] In the main, TCs' primary task has been to seek out and record the testimony of both the victims of and the witnesses to political violence perpetrated by states and their nonstate proxies. In most cases, TCs were not created with the legal ability to carry out actual prosecutions, but they still "usually conducted their investigations within a framework supplied by national or international human rights law, making individual decisions on each case presented to them, similar to a panel of judges." When their work was finished, TCs invariably produced a final report. But beyond their legalistic functions, the TCs' ultimate duty lay in clearing the decks for a new, more legitimate, constitutional regime. Some of the original designers of TCs in Latin America "understood the function of such commission to be, first, the healing of the psychic damage caused by repression and, second, the deterrence of similar repression in the future." One, José Zalaquett in Chile, argued that "the truth in itself is both reparation and prevention." Uncovering the truth can "lay the groundwork for a shared understanding of the recent crisis and how to overcome it."[68] The original TC architects did not intend for their creations to preclude real criminal proceedings against perpetrators; national reconciliation did not, by their lights, require the sacrifice of justice for victims of terror. But as Grandin and Klubock argued, "finding a proper balance between prosecutions and reconciliation . . . proved to be impossible." The military and the political right retain considerable power (and, one can add, weapons) and have largely avoided prosecution. The practice of many TCs "prioritized catharsis and forgiveness over punishment, and tended to gloss over the de jure or de facto amnesties" that occurred. Another reason Grandin and Klubock are hostile to such "truth-for-amnesty swaps," as in the South Africa example, is that TC-generated "forgiveness" and political reconciliation were sought to facilitate a new age of market-oriented Neoliberal hegemony.[69] For Grandin and Klubock, TCs represented a moment that has passed. In their opinion, TCs have "exhausted their potential as instruments, however limited, of consolidating the norms and institutions of liberal jurisprudence."[70]

The big problem is that Latin Americans have had to confront questions about human rights violators and continuing impunity "in the context of highly constrained democratic transitions." In post-political-violence societies, people want many worthy things, especially truth telling, accountability, rule of law, and reconciliation. Unfortunately, as Ernesto Verdeja acknowledged with understated calm, "they do not always work together." And how these goals are pursued depends on a number of variables: the state of institutions (political and judicial); the health of civil society (and degree of freedom of expression); limits on elite power, especially repressive forces, and depending on the nature of the transition, the degree of negotiation needed, and how much power elites retain; the role of outside actors; and, finally, the nature and degree of political violence.[71] The point is, justice is very hard to get. Pursuit of justice might stand in the way of bringing peace and ending the use of political murder, creating a conflict between the present and the future. Manuel Garretón laid out the essential steps for overcoming the "legacy of fear," but they are not easy steps. First, the perpetrators (armed forces, paras, etc.) "must be subjected to strict controls by society and the political regime." Second, institutions must be strengthened, especially the judiciary.[72] These requirements are easy to recognize and prescribe but hard to implement

Impunity is still a dilemma in many countries. In Guatemala, a doctor described to anthropologist Victoria Sanford how a death squad broke into the surgery where he was treating a young man who had been beaten, shot, and stabbed. "There were three of them. They had machine guns. One of them shoved me away from my patient . . . as he said, 'with your permission, doctor.' Then the three of them lined up in front of me laughing as they opened fire. . . . They were still laughing as they left. The same man said to me, 'It looks like there's nothing you can do here. This time he's really dead.' " The doctor went on to marvel at "the impunity of the act." He explained that they were local men and had not bothered to wear disguises. Indeed, one of them was his neighbor and lived on the same street. "Each time he greets me, I relive those moments."[73] Not surprisingly, in 2009, there were still "no conditions for prosecuting perpetrators of genocide in Guatemala." The country suffered from "an embedded impunity supported by fear and a failed judicial system."[74] Such impunity plainly increases repressive activity; paramilitaries, police, and death squads could not do their work "without the open complicity of a section of civil society" such as judiciaries, regime-friendly media, and business organizations, all of which provide a "common repressive front." Edelberto Torres-Rivas has argued that "political order, in this atrociously authoritarian culture, can be guaranteed only through recourse to violence"[75] At least, the murderous elites think so. They thus hardwire impunity into their legal structures whenever they can. In Colombia, "the 1980 Penal Code lowered the recommended sentence for political murders, as compared with ordinary homicides, to between three and six years."[76] Gill has noted that "despite ample evidence of the involvement of security forces in human rights violations and a few victories for human rights activists, widespread impunity remains the norm throughout Latin America." Various amnesty laws "continue to shield the guilty." Many victims, survivors, and activists insist that "justice and accountability must take place for societies to come to terms with brutal, authoritarian pasts [and presents?]." Impunity of course "refers to the lack of accountability enjoyed by militaries, police forces, and paramilitary organization" but also can be seen to benefit "civilian elites" and "oppressive economic policies." In fact, as Grandin and Klubock noted, political murder and its generally accompanying impunity facilitated the free market and neoliberal "reforms" of the 1980s and 1990s. Many people, beyond victims and survivors, continue "to live in a state of fear" because so many known perpetrators of torture and murder live unmolested around them.[77]

Survivors of political violence often must "confront the physical reminders of terror that haunt their communities—massacre sites, trees from which victims were hung, places where loved ones were murdered, and unmarked graves." In Colombia, millions of small-town and country folk have simply fled to Ecuador and Venezuela, and to the outer reaches of major cities (current estimates place the number of IDPs in Colombia at over three million). Often times, squatter communities are composed of displaced families headed by widows suffering from varying degrees of PTSD. Many such settlements are dominated by paramilitaries, where "the impunity-generated fear and insecurity that pervades the rural communities and urban settlements of displaced peoples is amplified by informers."[78] As Argentine Minister of the Interior, General Albano Harguindeguy, arrogantly "boasted," Argentina "confesses its sins only before God, and triumphant armies are not put on trial or asked to account for their actions after the war." Many Latin American dirty warriors still believe this, and perhaps with good reason.[79]

Pessimists about the likelihood of lawful and liberal solutions, Kruijt and Koonings have taken the long view, arguing that it is "by no means certain that stable, civic forms of rule and social integration will prevail or endure in Latin America." They noted that "violence has historically been a central feature in the evolution of Latin America," and that "repression was essential" to maintain order. In Latin America, "the use of political and military violence to achieve or conserve power has been characteristic of a great variety of political systems, regimes and movements," some of which were democratic. To make matters worse, "the repressive instincts of the traditional elites and the security forces" must now face off against a "wide variety of actors who also have recourse to violence."[80] But the forces of the status quo still have the upper hand in the use of political murder. An undeniable fact on the ground is the attitude of an ardently unrepentant murderous elite in Latin American militaries. In spite of various "democratic transitions" in Latin America over the last two and a half decades, military leaders in the region are conscious "heirs to a long-standing tradition of political involvement, and still claim a kind of God-given right to intervene in times of crisis." Kruijt and Koonings thus doubt that Latin America's "political armies" are "a thing of the past," and instead point to "the fragility of democracy." The various militaries only relinquished power after complicated negotiations and after receiving numerous guarantees about their "permanent national objectives" and their "just" wars against subversion. Despite world opinion, a goodly percentage of Latin American militaries have demanded, and received, varying degrees of amnesty. Behind the scenes they retain virtually compulsory "advisory" roles, as well as hardwired constitutional prerogatives. The military remains the primary source of intelligence, and in most countries has a hand in police power; in several countries they are the sole government presence in remote areas. The military deployed amnesty and "full-stop" legislation with varying degrees of success, and "democratic governments have been unable to create (or quite slow in creating) conditions of accountability towards human rights violators." The military (and one should add, other elites) can still defend themselves and their interests. The list of countries that continue to award perpetrators "relative immunity" is long: Brazil, Colombia, El Salvador, Guatemala, Honduras, Peru (one can add Mexico, and even Chile and Argentina). Latin America's military establishments retain both political power and "strong elements of national guardianship." They also exhibit impressive post–Cold War ideological flexibility, which allows them to continue their self-appointed mission. "The internal enemy of 'Marxist subversion' has been traded in for more diffuse, socially and morally defined threats to national values and objectives."[81] While many elites still worry about leftist subversion, "the global war on terrorism" allows for continued struggle against "internal" enemies using "asymmetric warfare."

Jasmin Hirstov observed that "in many Latin American nations, after transitions from military dictatorships to formally democratic governments, substantial parts of the state terror apparatus remained untouched." Not only that, Torres-Rivas points out that in the midst of new efforts for democratization and human rights, "advances" have also been made in "new forms of political repression and violence."[82] Progress toward democracy has often been dubious since, as Hirstov argued, "the subordination of civil law enforcement to military security programs . . . permits the suspension of individual and collective rights while granting state forces more autonomy and immunity from ordinary justice. Moreover, such legal instruments enable state forces to violate human rights without consequence as long as such activities are claimed to be in response to a terrorist threat."[83]

These issues demonstrate why justice and peace can be elusive. Juan Corradi has argued that the "deconstruction of cultures of fear is a long, fragile, and incomplete process. For those who embark on such a journey there are no magic formulas nor a clearly charted course." Corradi speaks of "transitional justice" as a "trial by fiat of a previous regime." These trials drive home the dilemma that "the exercise of justice is at the same time indispensible and impossible," and the countries attempting to make such transitions face the various and perhaps incompatible agendas of "punishment and reconciliation, revenge and catharsis."[84]

Winifred Tate explored these problems through the "Trujillo Case," which, as "one of the most widely discussed human rights cases in Colombia in the 1990s," serves as both representative example and cautionary tale. The Trujillo Case entailed the murder of more than one hundred people, though it was unfortunately neither a unique nor a particularly noteworthy series of killings and massacres by Colombian standards. Trujillo, a small town to the west of Cali, hosted the typical mix of players: peasant small holders; an activist Catholic priest (Tiberio de Jesús Fernández Malfa, or just Father Tiberio); guerrillas (ELN and M-19); military and paramilitary allies; and narcos from the Cali cartel, merging with local landed-elites. In the late 1980s, rivalries and tensions came to a head, and by mid-1990 there was a significant body count. The army moved in and "militarized the area," a process which brought with it the usual complementary disappearances, assassinations, and bodies bobbing in the Cauca River. The murder of Father Tiberio topped things off.

What made the Trujillo case unusual was that human rights NGOs decided to use it to raise awareness on the international scene. A Catholic NGO, the Comisión Intercongregacional de Justicia y Paz, generally known as simply "Justice and Peace," first shed light on the collective Trujillo murders. Founded and led by activist Jesuit priest, Javier Giraldo, Justice and Peace specialized in documenting paramilitary massacres, which were growing in number in those years. It, and other NGOs, came to view the Trujillo killings as an "archetype" of political violence. Justice and Peace took the case before the InterAmerican Human Rights Commission in 1992, a move that helped bring the government onboard as an active participant, allowing it to avoid condemnation and public censure for its role. Both civilian and military representatives attended the Trujillo Commission, and thanks to changes in the 1991 Constitution, new institutions were now available to investigate. President Ernesto Samper admitted that the government had a human rights problem, but argued that it was victimized by right and left; he sought assistance, not criticism, for the broader community of nations. The Trujillo Commission's final report of 1995 was both an achievement and, ultimately, a frustrating disappointment. It was a "consensus document" that attempted to "clarify the events surrounding sixty-three brutal murders." The report stipulated that a "paramilitary death squad operated in coordination with the army's Palacé Artillery Battalion No. 3." As a consequence, the battalion's commander was relieved of command. Samper publically apologized. Yet NGOs quickly soured on the results. No military personnel were prosecuted, let alone convicted. Peace and Justice called the result "truth without justice." The army in its turn felt that it had been scapegoated. Even the new government human rights bodies were dissatisfied, since the Trujillo Commission's accomplishments were not repeated. On the other hand, paramilitary groups learned useful lessons on how to avoid human rights complications. Their commanders gave "lectures on how to escape the attention of human rights groups—by avoiding the publicity of a massacre by killing their victims individually or scattering their bodies."[85]

The conflict between peace and justice (or "accountability") again raises its head. Tate wrote that in "traditional NGO human rights activism, the central focus is on the perpetrator and on establishing accountability. For activists involved in other kinds of international interventions, such effort can seem frivolous (worrying about laws when people starve) or counterproductive (undermining efforts for negotiated settlements by insisting on trials for leaders.)"[86] And while the rise of state human rights agencies in Colombia (and other places) do change the rules of the game, they might actually contribute to impunity, Tate concluded. She focused on two examples: the Defensoría del Pueblo and Consegero Presidencial para los Derechos Humanos (Presidential Special Advisor for Human Rights). These agencies were entrusted with the protection of human rights in Colombia. In the past (the 1970s and 1980s), governments often just denied abuses, but now, with the rise of human rights agencies and international activism, violations could instead be buried under mounds of red tape: "Impunity is no longer a default resulting from simple denials but must be produced through government action. By channeling concern about human rights cases into an endless loop of bureaucratic programs, state human rights agencies often serve to minimize effective action." This "morass of governmental bureaucratic inaction" can be overcome by committed individual officials, but outside their generally heroic efforts, not much is accomplished. State human rights bureaucracies all too often "become another mechanism through which perpetrators of political violence evade public scrutiny and sanction." At the end of the 1990s, the Colombian military began to develop its own human rights policies (as did the School of the Americas). It started publishing reports and instituting human rights posts for officers at the battalion level. Yet Colombia's military and its career officers continue to see human rights activism "as part of a politically motivated war against them, an orchestrated campaign in favor of the guerrillas."[87]

Finally, even struggles over historical interpretation show how far Latin American societies have to go to tame the political murder tradition and reconcile questions of peace, justice, and impunity. This conundrum (demonstrating a conflict between hope and cynicism) is on display, for example, in the struggles between the Pinochetistas and the anti-Pinochetistas in Chile.[88] It is, in fact, apparent in the fight over the uses of history all over Latin America, over who gets to tell the story of what happened, who decides what is in the story, and of course, who gets to explain what it means. Such historical battles raged (and continue to rage) around the various Truth Commissions; this process is really just beginning. Some processes are country-specific and inward looking, while others are more regional in focus. And these arguments about history are not just academic exercises. Grandin and Klubock have suggested that there is a real danger in focusing too much on "individual" rights, and perpetrators, because it obscures the broader picture, and its messiness, especially its collective aspects, including struggles for social justice, democratic change, and the repression thereof. Or, one can add, the political rational for political murder. The problem with Truth Commissions was that they "presented history not as a conflict of interests and ideas within a context of unequal power, but as a parable of illiberal intolerance."[89]

CONCLUSIONS AND PROSPECTS

The practice of political murder endures in Latin America, seemingly hard-wired into the operating systems of Latin American societies or, to use a biological metaphor, written into the region's cultural-genetic code as a meme.

Yet this practice is plainly not a phenomenon unique to Latin America. Comparable cases abound all over the world today, and many clearly draw on the Latin American experience. The leader of Chechnya, Ramzan Kadyrov, repeatedly disappeared critics of his regime in the Argentinean fashion, complete with Condor-style agents who were sent to kill targets abroad. Umar S. Israilov was murdered while in hiding in Vienna after he accused Kadyrov of illegal executions and torture, and human rights activist Natalia Estemirova was killed in Ingushetia soon after Kadyrov made threatening remarks. Journalists and artists in Russia who dare to criticize the government have, of late, come in for decidedly rough handling. In Pakistan, there have been thousands of desaparecidos in recent years, most of them whisked off to secret prisons, where (according to human rights organizations) many have been killed. Though it has not gone to the same bloody extremes, China's government moved quickly to crush the "Jasmine Revolution" in early 2011, also disappearing potential troublemakers. And, finally, the United State provided an unsettling parallel with the killing of the U.S.–born Al Qaeda preacher and organizer Anwar al-Awlaki (a noisy voice of anti-American invective), silencing him with a drone missile attack in Yemen on September 30, 2011.[90] As the tools have gotten better, the practice has clearly prospered.

These parallels around the globe belie Daniel Pécaut's "banality of violence" argument for Colombia, though he had a point, in that, the world political murder has wrought is often wild, wooly, and chaotic. Michael Taussig also noted with acumen "the difficulty of fixing the meaning of violence," given that, "an inherent quality of terror is confusion."[91] Be that as it may, killing messengers of change in Latin America has been a method of defending the status quo long favored by the region's murderous elites, participants in the political culture of murder. Many of them still think it is effective, as do many of their quick-learning elite apprentices in other parts of the globe.

In fact, the goals and attractions of political murder are so clear to elites around the world that they suggest another fascinating question: Why have U.S. elites failed to utilize political murder in the Latin American vein inside the United States? An obvious explanation is that U.S. elites have always shown consummate skill at using nonlethal methods to quiet all forms of opposition and suppress popular movements.[92] They have been able to justify their hold on power with intellectual bait-and-switch maneuvers implemented with consummate skill. They are also adept at maintaining control through electoral manipulation. Their methods encompass the dubious social science of the likes of Charles Murray and the calculating political skill of Karl Rove. Yet, writing six years before the 9-11 attacks on New York and Washington D.C. (and the resulting wave of security paranoia), Timothy Cloyd argued that "reports of the barbarous treatment of human beings have not been restricted to 'renegade states' or to politics that have disintegrated into anarchy and civil war." We can point to "the use of excessive force by police officials in the United States and Western Europe."[93] And even more intriguing is the fact that a branch of the hemispheric murderous elite inhabits parts of the U.S. government, the U.S. political class, and the U.S. corporate world, and clearly supports political murder in Latin America. One might argue that they have a separate set of values to employ outside the United States' borders, though in the past, they did seem to flirt with a domestic version. During the social and political upheavals of the 1960s and 1970s, U.S. Army intelligence and the FBI carried out extensive spying operations on millions of U.S. citizens. They "infiltrated civil rights and antiwar organizations and conducted illegal surveillance of virtually every political protest group in the country." They had profiles, photos, and eventually produced "encyclopedia sized" blacklists of potential subversives. "Project Camelot" in particular was concerned with "assessing the potential for internal war."[94] Yet, so far, political murder of this sort seems only to happen in movies, such as Warren Beatty's 1998 film, *Bulworth*, or it (supposedly) follows the "deranged lone gunman" model, as in the cases of John and Robert Kennedy, Martin Luther King Jr., and even Harvey Milk. But given that elites in the United States seem content to watch their society slide into underdeveloped status in terms of economic, social, and industrial development, physical infrastructure, income distribution (say goodbye to the "middle-class"), rates of higher education, and general quality of life, it is reasonable to ask whether the use of political murder against critics is far behind. So far, at least, the vigor of U.S. democracy, with a less threatened media, independent police forces, and a comparatively truncated history of private armies and goon squads, has offered fewer opportunities for blanket impunity and held murderously inclined elites in check.

Though the last decade has seen progress in the curtailment of Latin American political murder, recent elections in Guatemala and Honduras demonstrate that even countries whose conflicts have been declared "over," and whose problems have been "solved," have a tendency to fall back into the practice of political murder. It is also an unpleasant fact that democratic traditions are not automatic shields against the employment of political murder. Its use in countries with weak traditions, such as El Salvador, Guatemala, Nicaragua, and Paraguay, was not surprising. But its repeated use in countries with stronger democratic traditions, such as Chile, Colombia, Argentina, and Uruguay, to name a few, is rather disquieting. Colombia has a long tradition of democratic political development, which was most evident in the 1930s and 1940s, a time when Colombia could claim to be one of the most democratic countries on Earth. It is true that Colombia's oligarquía dominated the two traditional parties, but the system also generated significant popular mobilizations. Unfortunately, Colombia is now well known for proving how the practice of political murder can fundamentally pervert a political culture. Today it has such an ingrained experience that its political system has become the poster child for political murder, automatically associated with the practices of assassination and massacre. The Mexicans, for instance, speak (unjustly given their own history) of the "Colombianization" of Mexican politics through political murder. (They also miss the extent to which political murder of the Latin American variety has evolved into a worldwide phenomenon.) Nevertheless, Colombia cannot really be said to have had "peace" at any time after 1946. Political murder is one of the key elements that continue to dump energy into the storm system that is Colombia's ongoing political dysfunction.

The tag-team interaction between hegemony and political murder in Latin America helps explain why some ruling elites routinely slip from the track of ideological policing in the realm of acceptable political ideas and behavior, and start killing people. These approaches often work together, pointing to the clear connections between political murder and mass politics in the twentieth century, even though outcomes vary. The practice of political murder can affect the legitimacy of a state, though states that suffer legitimacy problems are not the only ones to kill off threats. Death squads are generally de facto arms of the state, yet even when they are not, their actions are tacitly ignored, tolerated, or even encouraged by the state, or part of the state (such as the armed forces) or even a regional elite. International connections can be quite different, and there are also differences of strategy, attitude, and style among Latin American elites, both within and between countries, regarding political murder. Some elites, for instance, believe there is more political value when it is generally known who is behind killings, while others prefer obscurity.

It is thus important to return to the question of whether political murder is a truly effective long-term strategy for elite rule. Does political murder work? Does killing the leader of a popular social, religious, or political movement really quiet the forces of change and resistance? And, if so, for how long, to what degree, and at what cost? These questions can anger some observers. They insist that it does not, believe that it cannot, work. It has been argued in these pages that political murder does not function so well, is in fact counterproductive, when employed by popular mobilizations. The proper liberal stance thus would seem to be that "in the long run," it will not work for repressive regimes or elites, either, given resistance and general blowback. Murdered leaders, they would argue, are replaceable representatives of deeper social forces (history is a "boiling pot") that cannot be so easily put down. Yet, as this study has shown, some elites think that political murder does indeed work, and there is evidence to back them up, in the short run at least. Certainly dirty wars in Latin America have been effective from the repressor's point of view, smashing forces of change (the ideological left, organized labor, peasant movements, etc.), though it is clear that such outcomes have not proven to be permanent in most countries. And it remains unclear whether these earlier victories can be so easily repeated in the post–Cold War world, though many of the international conditions that encourage these "wars" (such as international capital's clear inclination to lend to repressive governments that can provide "order") are still in play.

In general, the degree to which political murder is used in the future will depend on how effective popular resistance will be. A cynic might note that, yes, cockroaches squirm when you step on them; resistance can be futile. Yet the effectiveness of stomping also depends on how many threats there are running around. Continued mobilizations pose an ongoing danger to hegemonic projects. There is no doubt that in Latin American today, after decades of repression, the spirit of popular mobilization—from both the "populist" and "revolutionary" periods—is clearly reasserting itself. There are left-leaning and populist governments from Central America to the Southern Cone, with plenty of leftist political mobilization in Mexico and Colombia to boot—countries that still suffer from demonstrable levels of political murder. But, in the long run, several questions remain. Will such mobilizations kick-start a new wave of political murder? Does popular mobilization in Latin America always breed political murder and repression? How effective can resistance movements be in reducing the use of political murder? In particular, will the existence of human rights organizations and leftist governments help forestall a return to the widespread use of political murder? Will they be viewed as the muscular and intimidating guard dogs of universal human dignity, or will they be seen by would-be perps as yapping annoyances that, however tenacious and indomitable, can still be kicked aside with a yelp? Civil society pushes back, but is it enough? Some elites might have learned a different lesson: that repression and political murder can (especially if used judiciously, and in some cases more sparingly—as an adjunct to more subtle forms of hegemony) be quite effective in protecting the status quo.

The long-term unknown is whether new generations of Latin American elites will be allowed to continue the political culture of murder. Or will Latin American societies be able to force a change in elite behavior? Unfortunately, most of the perpetrators of the past will not be brought to justice, but it might be possible to create conditions under which political murder is no longer a viable or attractive political strategy. Elites in other parts of the world would undoubtedly do the same if they could, but many do not, and it is not because they are less zealous in their self-interested and murderous resolve. But it remains a fact that political murder, whether manifested in the singular assassination of a popular leader or carried out wholesale as dirty war, continues to be one of the principal obstacles to peaceful political development and security in Latin America today. Understanding the dynamics of when and why people are murdered for political reasons, as this book attempts to do, is a necessary starting point in the quest for any likely solutions.

So the goal now should be finding ways for Latin America to put political murder behind it, to make it history and not current practice, something that is over and not a living tradition. Western Europe, for example, overcame its fascist past and evolved into a place where political murder aimed at voices of change is much less likely. And within the Latin American context there are, after all, other political cultures to cultivate, those of popular struggle for social justice and democracy, of political mobilization, and resistance. And there have been abundant hopeful developments. In Brazil there has been some progress in the area of wealth distribution, while in Colombia, the tree of democratic political culture—severely prune d by the last sixty plus years of violence (as have other such trees)—shows signs of springing back. It is a tough old perennial. Undoubtedly, the answer to the question of what to do about political murder is connected to democracy and the health of civil society, yet as pointed out at various points in this study, it is not a simple matter of merely increasing the amount of democracy. The "triumph" of democracy in the region has so far not brought the practice to an end. And while even "weak" or "false" democracy can help dampen the use of political murder, it is important to recognize that reform efforts that successfully increase democracy very often drive the use of political murder in the short run.

Political murder continues to be an unfortunate fact of Latin American life in a large number of countries. It is a phenomenon that deserves a great deal more attention. One can use the resources of the humanities (in this case, history) to help rebuild communities and institutions devastated by violence. The hope is that a better understanding of political murder will assist governments and NGOs in the development of policies that will redirect and strengthen the democratic elements of political culture in Latin America. And essential to this effort would be a decision by the United States to eliminate any tolerance for political murder in its own institutions, to stop enabling and encouraging its use, and to stop accepting it as natural or inevitable. This, unfortunately, is not likely to happen soon. The struggle will also undoubtedly continue, since there is a connection between mass dirty war and the existence of guerrilla movements (which also survive). Of course in many cases the use of political murder occurs independently of the operations of guerrilla movements, but their presence anywhere in the region fuels the feedback loop. Perhaps political murder will not happen again on the same scale without the Cold War to provide a context, but the murderous elites are always ready to pull it back out when they believe it is needed (and that they can get away with it). Clearly they are still using it. The problem of political murder is a generational problem, and its solution a long-term project. There are no quick or easy fixes.

APPENDIX

POLITICAL MURDER IN LATIN AMERICA

INDIVIDUAL COUNTRY NARRATIVES

Latin America is diverse. Mexico, Guatemala, Ecuador, Peru, Bolivia, and Paraguay formed the old Spanish colonial core where large populations of indigenous peoples survived the disease-driven demographic collapse of the sixteenth century. Each society had a European elite and a strong indigenous stamp, but over time developed an important mestizo (mixed European and indigenous) component. Cuba, Panama, and the Dominican Republic were also in the colonial core, but with a huge African imprint. El Salvador, Honduras, Nicaragua, and Colombia were on the old Spanish colonial periphery but were more clearly mestizo societies, though Colombia in particular also had important African elements. Chile, Argentina, and Uruguay, likewise on the mestizo colonial periphery, were the sites of huge late nineteenth- and early twentieth-century European immigrations. Brazil, part of the Portuguese colonial world, formed with an enormous African input, and also experienced influxes of later European immigration. Clearly, Latin American ethnic, cultural, political, social, economic, and labor structures vary; land-holding patterns vary; links to the world market vary; levels of industrialization, urbanization, literacy, and income distribution vary; relationships with the United States vary. But despite all their variations, all these countries have had intimate familiarity with political murder. As these narratives will demonstrate, some countries have (more or less) ended their use of political murder (for now at least), while in others the practice continues right up to the present.

While each country's ordeal has proceeded at its own pace, with its own eccentricities, parallels abound. This shared history makes clear that political murder and violent repression, ranging from notorious assassinations to obscure disappearances to bloody massacres, was sanctioned by states and/or power elites. Carried out by their agents, proxies, or surrogates, political murder evolved throughout the region into a remarkably consistent approach to dealing with popular threats. This series of narratives shows that even though experiences vary, one can identify broad parallels in the use of political murder across the region. The rest of this book is thus an attempt to unpack these various country histories.

Note: The Tontons Macoutes of the Duvalier regimes in Haiti, one can argue, fit the general patterns of political murder outlined here but are not included for somewhat arbitrary reasons of tradition and practicality. Venezuela has had scattered episodes, but no significant traditions, even under strongmen Juan Vicente Gómez and Marcos Pérez Jiménez.[1] And of course, Costa Rica is a true outlier in this regard, as a small, stable democracy completely unaccustomed to the practice of political murder.

ARGENTINA

Argentina, like Chile and Colombia, has enjoyed long periods of democratic development (much more than Central America) and pursued early and powerful experiments with mass democracy. Yet it also demonstrated a well-established penchant for political repression, which emerged long before the 1970s.[2]

The troubled decades after Argentina's de facto independence in 1810 were eventually dominated by the caudillo of Buenos Aires, Juan Manuel Rosas, between 1829 and 1854. These years saw the rise of one of Latin America's first death squads, Rosas's group of enforcers known as La Mazorca. Nonetheless, Argentina experienced massive change in the late nineteenth century, with a huge increase in the volume of European immigration, especially from Italy. There was also a flood of British investment capital injected into the economy. For some time the landed oligarchy retained control of politics and continued to exclude the lower-class urban and rural populations. Yet the early twentieth century saw the rise of mass politics, with growing participation of the middling classes, and the emergence of real democratic structures under President Hipólito Yirgoyen and the Unión Cívica Radical party. Yrigoyen and the Radicals also encouraged some working-class participation, especially from the nonsocialists, but they were always ready to use the hard hand. The most famous example of this was the "Semana Trágica," or Tragic Week of 1919, when the government allowed and even encouraged conservative vigilante groups to assist the army in crushing an urban labor uprising. Repression was even more savage in the countryside when, in 1921, striking rural workers were slaughtered in Patagonia.

From 1930 to 1976 Argentina followed an oscillating path between military and civilian government, between democratic impulses and violent repression. Amidst world economic turmoil, and after a military coup in 1930 (the first since 1861), elites returned to an older model of liberal institutions, tempered by electoral fraud. President Agustín Justo (1932–1938) maintained an anti-Radical coalition that attempted to revitalize the agriculture economy and encourage industrialization. Justo passed power to Roberto Ortiz, an anti-Yrigoyen Radical, by thwarting the opposition with intense amounts of violence at the polls. After Ortiz took office, the political elite lurched into a series of shoving matches over the amount of democracy that would be allowed, and over the question of neutrality regarding the European and Asian wars. Ortiz, ironically, allowed for more open elections on the national and provincial levels, but upon his sudden illness and death, his reactionary vice president Ramón Castillo displayed renewed authoritarianism and a pronounced sympathy for the Axis powers. Castillo, however, was replaced by another coup in 1943. In the new military government, a group of officers led by Colonel Juan Domingo Perón was set to reorient postwar Argentine politics.

Perón, as Vice President, Minister of War, and especially Secretary of Labor, laid the foundation for three decades of political dominance, which he maintained both in and out of power. After the war, Perón rode broad working-class support to the presidency in 1946, over the opposition of the traditional political elites and the military. As President, he employed state patronage to solidify a populist government and weld together a powerful coalition of support from the working-class and middle-class *pueblo*. Perón was able to quickly co-opt existing local political networks, to bring most existing labor unions under his control, and to double the size of the union movement, but he did so in a way that maximized his personal influence. His wife Eva (known as Evita) had a large devoted following of her own, who saw her as a sort of living saint who watched over the most humble members of society, a status intensified after her death from cancer in 1952 at the age of thirty-three. For a few years Perón could maintain urban support at the cost of undercutting rural producers, but this strategy failed as Argentine exports faltered. By the early 1950s, Perón attempted to make ends meet politically by increasing the authoritarian aspects of government. But in 1955 a group of Army officers overthrew Perón and sent him into a wandering exile, though he eventually settled in Madrid.

Over the next 18 years Argentina endured an accelerating round of civilian and military governments that attempted to eradicate or tame Peronismo. Their efforts, however, were always overshadowed by the caudillo from his perch in Spain. By the mid-1960s the Peronists had reassembled much of their former political coalition. In 1964, building on the labor unions, and led by Augusto Vandor, leader of the powerful metalworkers union, they began to push openly for Perón's return. Perón flew to São Paulo, but the moment proved too early, and he was sent back. Vandor subsequently set about rebuilding Peronismo sans Perón, and generally opening Argentina back up to democracy. Perón, nevertheless, had no trouble asserting his authority from afar, which he did via the provincial elections in Mendoza. His third wife, María Estela Martínez de Perón (known by her stage name, Isabel) was dispatched to plug Perón's choice for governor, who easily won. In response to Perón's continued influence, the military carried out another coup in 1966. This time the military government sought to contain the social and culture changes that had been at work since the Cuban Revolution of 1959, focusing on universities, urban artists, and intellectuals. They did not, however, come in with a concrete plan to carry out their objectives. Over the next two years, tensions mounted, finally erupting in May of 1969 in the city of Córdoba. University students, autoworkers, and a large part of the general population came together in a giant upheaval known as the Cordobazo. In its immediate aftermath, Augusto Vandor was assassinated, reportedly on Perón's orders. The uprising signaled a broad political breakdown that would pressure the military to relinquish power. The crisis also saw the emergence of new leftist insurgent groups, the most important being the Peronist youth group known as the Montoneros, and the ERP guerrilla army, or Ejército Revolucionario de Pueblo (the People's Revolutionary Army). The Montoneros marked their entrance on the political stage by abducting and assassinating General Pedro Eugenio Aramburu in 1970. Aramburu had led the coup that sent Perón into exile in 1955 and became the de facto president until 1958. The Montoneros, who carried out a number of high-profile kidnappings, claimed that Aramburu's execution (after a quick "trial") was to avenge the massacre of 27 Peronistas after an attempted coup in 1956. The military responded to such deeds in kind, with actions such as the Trelew Massacre of 1972, in which the navy slaughtered 16 leftist prisoners who had taken part in a theatrical mass escape attempt from the prison at Rawson in southern Argentina.

In the run-up to the 1973 presidential election, even the most anti-Peronist segment of the political establishment recognized the inevitability of Perón's return. Still in Spain, the caudillo cultivated the various factions of Peronismo. The first, of course, was that represented by the old-line labor unions. The second was the leftist Peronista youth movement. In fact, throughout the long years of exile, the left and right wings of Peronismo had been growing apart, and represented not just a political and ideological divide but also a generational one. Finally, there was a third group, led by José López Rega, a former policeman who had become Perón's private secretary, most trusted advisor, and accommodating crony during his exile. This Machiavellian game fell apart in a dramatic and violent way on June 20, 1973. That day Perón was scheduled to arrive at Ezeiza Airport in Buenos Aires, where the Peronista youth had hoped to welcome him home with a huge demonstration of support. Instead, while Perón landed at another airport, the Peronista youth were ambushed by union enforcers and right-wing gunmen of the old Peronist security apparatus, organized by López Rega. The Ezeiza Massacre was the end of big-tent Peronismo and marked the rise of the Peronista right.

Perón was elected president, with his wife as vice president, in October 1973. Though he carried a large majority, his triumphant return was short-lived—he died in office in July 1974. Though typically pegged to the years of military government by the various "juntas" that ruled Argentina between 1976 and 1983, Argentina's "dirty war" really began in earnest in 1973. With a wink and a nod, the governments of Juan Perón and later of his widow fostered paramilitary death squads. Isabel in particular followed the inclination of the Peronist right wing and instigated a violent full-frontal assault on the entire Argentine left. Groups such as the infamous Triple A declared war on "subversive elements." (Short for the Alianza Anticomunista Argentina, or Argentine Anticommunist Alliance, Triple A was created by López Rega, who embezzled resources from the ministry of social welfare to fund the group.) These groups killed at least two thousand "subversives" and enemies of the regime. In response, the various leftist groups united against Isabel's offensive, escalating their own violent activities. The ERP opened a Che Guevara–inspired "foco" style offensive in the mountainous and forest-covered province of Tucumán, but were quickly routed.

The heightened violence, combined with a disastrous economic situation, in which inflation approached 1,000 percent, encouraged the military to act once again. In March 1976, the united armed forces deposed Isabel Perón in a largely popular coup. Thanks to an offhand comment by Jorge Luis Borges, this became known as the Gentlemen's Coup. Calm, orderly, and articulate, the first ruling junta of president and army general Jorge Rafael Videla, air force brigadier general Orlando R. Agosti, and navy admiral Emilio E. Massera was welcomed by most Argentines, who blamed the unrest on Isabelita's misrule. The junta's reassuring public image inspired Borges, Argentina's most famous writer, to declare with relief that "now we are governed by gentlemen."

The military gentlemen, however, arrived with a less than genteel agenda. They intended to resume the work they had started with the coup of ten years before. Even though the repression carried out under the Peróns had largely neutralized the guerrilla threat, the military planned to carry on with more of the same, to fight what came to be known generally as "dirty war." The Argentine military referred to their task as the Process for National Reorganization, or El Proceso. It continued under various juntas from 1976 through 1983 and went on to claim another thirty thousand victims (though some students of the period believe that number is somewhat inflated). With a breathtaking blindness to irony, the military chose a name for their effort that overlapped with one of Franz Kafka's most well-known works. His last unfinished novel, *Der Process* (called *The Trial* in English) was translated into Spanish as *El Proceso*. It is the story of a bank clerk identified only as Josef K., who is arrested and prosecuted by a dark, mysterious government entity for a crime that is never explained (to him or to the reader). It was a text already much beloved by Latin American intellectuals. True to Kafka's work, the military intended to purge Argentine society of what they considered to be pernicious subversive influences that threatened "Western Christian Civilization." As in the Chilean case, they laid out "categories of guilt."

As reflected in the compositions of the various juntas, the different branches of the military adopted what they insisted was a unified front. This did not mean, however, that they carried out their war in a coordinated fashion. Bitter interservice rivalry meant that each branch carried out its own version of dirty war. Much of the lexicon of political murder in Latin America emerged from the Argentine experience. They coined the term dirty war, "guerra sucia," and created "desaparecer" as an active verb (though the term was used in Guatemala as well)—to "disappear" someone. "Los desaparecidos" were "the disappeared." The Argentine model of dirty war involved small groups of active-duty soldiers and sailors, often in plain clothes and driving green Ford Falcons, who would abduct individuals from their homes or off the street. The victims were taken to one of 340 detention centers and torture camps (planned before the coup), the most notorious of which was at ESMA, the naval mechanics school.

The years between 1976 and1978 were the most bloody, but the Proceso went on throughout the period. Argentine efforts to export their counterrevolution were notable in Uruguay, Bolivia, and Central America. The Proceso also spawned one of Latin America's most important human rights organizations, the Asociación Madres de Plaza de Mayo, or The Mothers of the Plaza de Mayo, which expanded with a sister organization, the Asociación Civil Abuelas de Plaza de Mayo, or Grandmothers of the Plaza de Mayo. The Argentine military's disastrous conduct of the Falklands War against the United Kingdom finally brought the military government and its project to an end in 1983. Echoes of the dirty war continue to reverberate in Argentine society, though Argentines have made significant strides in restoring and defending their democracy.

BOLIVIA

The Plurinational State of Bolivia, named for the liberator Simón Bolívar, was known for centuries as Alto Peru (Upper Peru). Comprised of high Andean peaks and eastern lowlands, it is now landlocked but rich in mineral wealth. Mining has always been central to the economy, though primitive levels of technology are often used in the smaller mines. Consequently, the economy has long been plagued by unstable boom and bust cycles around commodities, especially rubber, gold, tin, tungsten (and coca paste). Bolivia has traditionally had a very uneven distribution of wealth, with a history of coerced and controlled labor on large agricultural estates. A large percentage of the population is still made up of indigenous subsistence farmers. Bolivia has also had a churning political history, with certain actors giving repeat performances. During the nineteenth and early twentieth centuries, wars stripped Bolivia of over half of its original territory. Finally, Bolivia has a significant history of political murder.[3]

Defeat by Paraguay in the Chaco War (1932–1935) greatly weakened the hold of the old oligarchic elites. New movements emerged, leading to the Movimiento Nacionalista Revolucionario (Revolutionary Nationalist Movement), the MNR. Founded in 1941 by Víctor Paz Estenssoro, Hernán Siles, and others as a "reformist" yet "revolutionary" movement, it ultimately became a political party. Paz ran for president in 1947, came in third, and then ran again in 1951. Surprisingly, given property requirements to vote, the MNR won that contest. The old order annulled the election, but the following year the MNR rose up and ousted them in the Revolution of 1952. Paz served as president from 1952 to 1956 and enacted various transformations, including universal suffrage, nationalization of large mines, and broad land reform and redistribution. The MNR also reorganized the military under its own control, a move that would leave a legacy of leftist influence in the Bolivian armed forces. Hermán Siles was elected president for the 1956–1960 term, during which the MNR began to break into right and left wings.

Paz returned from a peaceful sojourn as ambassador in London to run for president again in 1960. His second term suffered from increasing violence, especially when he moved to amend the constitution so that he would be able to succeed himself, believing that only he could hold the country together. He came to rely more on the military, and chose General René Barrientos, Chief of the Bolivian Air Force, as his running mate. They took office together in August 1964, but in November, Barrientos, along with Army commander Alfredo Ovando, carried out a coup and sent Paz into exile. From that point, until 1982, Bolivia was for the most part ruled by military regimes. Barrientos was elected president in his own right in 1966, successfully defeating the guerrilla forces led by Che Guevara. As a white Argentine more interested in revolution in his native country than in Bolivia, Che was not popular. And despite its "Thermidorian" turn to the right, Bolivians believed they had already had a revolution. After Guevara's capture, Barrientos ordered his summary execution in October 1967. In April 1969, Barrientos died in a helicopter crash.

The slightly left-leaning Ovando led another coup in September 1969, this time in partnership with the even more left-leaning General Juan José Torres, who pushed Ovando to carry out more reforms. This prompted another coup in October 1970 by right-wing officers. The military split, with whole units choosing sides. Ovando sought asylum in a foreign embassy, but Torres rallied his supporters and defeated the rightist coup. Torres, a mestizo and "man of the people," called for an "Asamblea del Pueblo" and reinstated labor leader Juan Lechín as head of the Central Obrera Boliviana (COB; the Bolivian Labor Central). But while he was hated on the right, Torres was also not trusted on the left. Aided by the Nixon administration in Washington, a more violent coup erupted in August 1971. Despite strong resistance from the Torres government and many civilian supporters, the coup succeeded. Torres fled to Buenos Aires, where he was murdered in 1976 by an Operation Condor squad.

General Hugo Banzer ruled as dictator for the next seven years, until 1978, a period known as the Banzerato. The Banzer government originally had the backing of the two largest political parties in Bolivia—the now center-right strain of the MNR, led by Paz, and the conservative Falange

Socialista Boliviana of Mario Gutiérrez. Both currents were tired of turmoil and left-leaning governments. Banzer intended to end what he saw as the frustrating disorder and divisions of Bolivian political life in the 1950s and 1960s. Banzer was personally appalled by the idea of dissent, especially to his own authority, and was no proponent of free speech. He thus moved to suppress the COB, shut the doors of the country's universities, and eventually dispensed with his political allies. After first banning leftist parties, he then banned all political parties. His allies soon realized that he had no intention of calling elections. Paz Estenssoro was exiled, yet again, along with others, as Banzer's government became a more markedly military regime, and inclined to use violence. In fact, Banzer unleashed a small-scale dirty war. Thousands of Bolivians fled the country to seek asylum abroad. Over three thousand political opponents were detained, imprisoned, and tortured, and hundreds more were killed or disappeared. Like Pinochet in Chile, Banzer was jealous of his position. He eliminated close rivals within the military, such as his coup comrades from 1971, Colonel Andrés Selich and General Joaquin Zenteno Anaya.

Increasing pressure from the Carter Administration in the United States finally coerced Banzer to call for elections in 1978. Barred by the congress from succeeding himself, Banzer chose General Juan Pereda to serve as his stand-in. When it was clear that the left-wing coalition around Hernán Siles was so strong that even massive fraud could not deflect it, Banzer annulled the election (after first declaring Pereda the winner). Pereda, however, had ideas of his own. He led a coup against Banzer in July 1978, but was pushed out himself in November by more democratically inclined officers. The presidential election of 1979 was inconclusive. Congress could not agree on a compromise, so another election was held in 1980, and Bolivia seemed ready to re-install Hernán Siles.

In July 1980, General Luis García Meza, newly installed as Commander of the Army, carried out a bloody (because it was vigorously resisted) putsch, the so-called Cocaine Coup. His short rule, until August 1981, was a violent, supposedly pro-U.S. extension and culmination of Banzer's rule, with criminal overtones and even greater ambitions. García Meza had been promoted to General under Banzer. He became a leader among the right-wing officers, and eventually was given support by former Nazi Klaus Barbie and neofascist Stefano Delle Chiaie, among others. He and his followers were distressed at the thought of Bolivia returning to civilian rule, and angered by civilian attempts to prosecute members of the military for human rights abuses. García Meza and his cohort also believed (correctly) that the slipping influence of the Carter administration heralded the return of more aggressive cold warriors to control in Washington. García Meza was rabidly anticommunist. Using Chile's Pinochet and Paraguay's Stroessner as his role models, he hoped to set up a dictatorship that would last for decades. Not surprisingly, he banned, yet again, all political parties and unions, exiled the most high-profile opposition leaders, and harassed journalists and news outlets. He was even more brutally violent than Banzer. Bolivian security forces murdered at least one thousand people, the most famous victim being Marcelo Quiroga Santa Cruz, a congressman pushing to prosecute Banzer. García Meza's henchmen also attempted to murder Indigenous leader Genaro Flores, who was wounded by a shotgun blast. Colonel Luis Arce, García Meza's Minister of the Interior, famously advised Bolivians who were opposed to the new regime that they should carry their written wills around with them. Despite his anticommunist crusading, however, García Meza's overt connections to cocaine traffickers made him unpalatable even in Ronald Reagan's Washington. He was forced out of control in 1981.

In 1982 the Bolivian military finally returned the reins of power to the civilians. There followed a recycling of old Presidents, including Hernán Siles, Víctor Paz, and even Hugo Banzer. Evo Morales was elected president in 2005.

BRAZIL

Even in the Latin American context, Brazil stands out as one of the most polarized and unequal of countries. The social, economic, and political divide between the haves and have-nots is difficult to overstate. Historically, elites there have been hard pressed to even recognize the humanity of *o povo* (the people). Certainly many rich Brazilians in the late twentieth century, typically those of European ancestry, still did not see any reason to acknowledge political equality under the law for the poorest of Brazil's poor, who tend to be much darker skinned. Political violence, carried out by national and regional elites for social and political control, has long been a constant of Brazilian life. Since colonial times Brazilian elites have relied on violent repression to safeguard the status quo. Military governments expanded these practices in the twentieth century. The use of political murder in Brazil is both more subtle and more brutal than in many other countries. Its dirty war was not as overt, but the use of political murder has been pervasive nonetheless.[4]

In the Brazilian case it is important to differentiate the high rates of nonpolitical murder and violent crime from political murder. Brazil has, arguably, some of the worst rates of violent urban crime in Latin America, with a high murder rate. Between 1980 and 2000 there was a dramatic increase in homicide rates nationwide, especially firearm mortalities for young men. But Brazil is also famous for high degrees of "official" and "formal" violence. The Brazilian state's war on crime and criminals has often bled over to its war on "communists," "terrorists," and "subversives." These themes have played out in popular culture. The book and movie of 2002, *Cidade de Deus* (City of God), depicted gang violence in the favelas of Rio de Janeiro, where automatic weapons are everywhere, but this was already an old image. In the 1980 film *Pixote: O Lei do Mais Fraco*, a child from the favelas of São Paulo, Fernando Ramos da Silva, played a fictional street child named Pixote. Ramos da Silva could not outrun his life (or the police's image of him). He was killed by police in 1987. The role of the state and of the police have also been depicted in the hit movies *Tropa de Elite* (Elite Squad) from 2007 and *Tropa de Elite 2* from 2010. They are evocative of Brazil's "justiciero" tradition, in which vigilantes (often police officers) target criminals, vagrants, and street children. Often paid by merchants to "clean up" neighborhoods, police routinely torture and murder people taken into custody. Brazilian police generally shoot to kill, compared to other police forces, and their high lethality rates prove it. Social scientists have noted that violent acts by police are "products of a political culture" that divides people between those who "deserve" citizenship and those who are "unworthy" of it.[5] The dystopian future of the sci-fi thriller *Bladerunner* has in many ways been made concrete in Brazil's sprawling and chaotic mega cities, where elites fly from high-rise rooftops to skyscraper landing pads in private helicopters, and avoid actually going to the ground within city limits.

Brazil, like other Latin American countries, has a tradition of powerful elites fighting it out for local and regional power. The Coronéis (the Colonels) were regional elites with armed retainers whom they used in power struggles. Elite violent practices were of course also aimed at common folk for social and political control. But even more important was the long history of political involvement by the Brazilian military, starting in the nineteenth century, when it came to be known as a "quasi-party." In 1889, the army spearheaded the overthrow of Emperor Pedro II, after which the military assumed the emperor's traditional role of moderating power. Under the Old Republic (1889–1930), the military intervened in the interests of the national and regional elites.

This pattern was still generally in force under the varied rule of Getúlio Vargas between 1930 and 1954. Varga's career represented one of the most complicated political evolutions in Latin American history. Beginning with the coup of 1930, he led Brazil as head of a provisional government, and went on to rule as dictator of the Estado Novo (New State) between 1937 and 1945. Then he returned to power as a popularly elected president in 1951, remaining so until his death in 1954. Long able to balance popularity with the working classes (he was known as the "pai do povo," father of the poor, even before his so-called "populist gamble" in 1944–1945) and with continued support from the elites, Vargas was rightly known for his opportunistic political style. Yet he was also given to the intimidating use of the Brazilian state's coercive apparatus, especially its police forces. In his final years of power, however, his varied and contradictory networks of support began to fall apart. Groups on the left and center grew frustrated with what they considered his cynical "populist" maneuvering, and never really accepted his makeover as a man of the people. Meanwhile parts of the elite and military began to denounce him as a demagogue, or even a cryptosocialist. One particularly ardent critic was Carlos Lacerda, a young journalist with political ambitions who kept up a constant barrage of moralizing invective in newspapers and on the radio. Alarmed by the damage that Lacerda's campaign could inflict on Vargas's beleaguered administration, members of his inner circle, led by Gregório Fortunato, the commander of the president's personal security force, decided to use the political murder option. Unfortunately for the plotters, the assassin sent to silence Lacerda only wounded the journalist, who produced a weapon of his own and returned fire. But, more important, the assassin did manage to kill one of Lacerda's body guards, a moonlighting air force major named Rubens Florentino Vaz. Vaz's death produced a firestorm of protest that precipitated Varga's suicide on August 24, 1954.

The seeds of later military domination of the political realm were planted early in the Vargas era, with the inclusion of "national security" language in the 1934 Constitution. With the foundation of the Escola Superior de Guerra (Superior War College) in 1950, the military's approach to national security became more proactive. Leaders were inclined to fuse military objectives and political goals when confronting internal threats. Such "internal enemies" were now sought not just among opposition groups but also in the political realm. Essentially, any individual or group that opposed capitalist-style development and "modernization" became an enemy.

Most students of Brazilian political violence date the origins of the modern death squad there to 1958 in Rio de Janeiro, then the capital. Army General Amaury Kruel, Chief of the State Police, dispatched district police chief Cecil Borer to appease Rio's commercial association and address rampant crime. Borer tapped civil police inspector Milton Le Cocq de

Oliveira to create a special unit of "bandit" hunters, known as "homens corajosos" (courageous men). Le Cocq, nicknamed "o gringo" because of his blond hair, began as polícia military. He later joined the motorcycle section of the Polícia Especial (called the Tomato Heads because of their red berets), which reportedly served to protect Vargas's political interests. Borer and Kruel's creation, the Grupo de Diligencias Especiais, GDE (Special Diligence Group), was meant to exterminate delinquents. It was characterized by the way it took no prisoners, asked no questions, and left no paper trail. The GDE was part of a specialized motorized patrol, the Esquadrão Motorizada, or EM (also short for Esquadrão da Morte—death squad). They were given unambiguous instructions to kill dangerous criminals—indeed Kruel ordered them to kill without fail. In São Paulo, a similar evolution connected older informal groups to new formal death squads. The result was the Motorized Civil Police (Rondas Nocturnas Especiais da Polícia), or RONE, nocturnal police patrols devoted to the protection of elite interests and properties. They were independent yet had lots of legal cover for activities. In 1964, Le Cocq was shot by a notorious criminal known as Cara de Cavalo (Horse Face). Le Cocq's friends and followers created the Scuderie Detective Le Cocq (Shield of Detective Le Cocq), a so-called philanthropical club, to avenge his death. They pledged to kill ten "criminals" for every cop. The organization eventually became a nationwide network. The emblem of the Scuderie Detective Le Cocq was comprised of a skull and crossbones inside a circular border with the group's name. Below the circle were the block letters E.M. (supposedly from Esquadrão Montada but widely understood to stand for Esquadrão da Morte).

A 1964 coup driven by the military's obsession with supposed "radical" elements in the government of President João Goulart initiated a military government that lasted until 1985. From mid-1964 to late 1966, Operacão Limpeza (Operation Cleanup) sought to purge "subversives" (Goulart's people) from local, state, and federal systems. Ten thousand civil servants, over one hundred military officers, and close to four hundred politicians and public intellectuals were ousted, and thousands were arrested. But the military government went well beyond that. The repressive apparatus of antisubversive organizations and agencies it put together was huge, bureaucratically unwieldy, and ultimately impossible to control. The Serviço Nacional de Informaçoes, or SNI (National Intelligence Service), directly under the president and the Conselho Nacional de Segurança (National Security Council), had its own agents, though the three armed services all had independent intelligence and covert operation organizations as well. Especially important was the army's Centro de Informaçoes de Exército (Army

Information Center), the CIE. The armed opposition in Brazil was small (not more than a few hundred serious militants), weak, and fragmented. Yet, as in other cases (especially Argentina and Chile), the military response was massive overkill, quite out of proportion to the real size of the threat. Both legal structures and "unofficial" groups facilitated political repression and not insignificant amounts of political murder. Their policy was to treat urban leftist guerrillas as Brazilian police death squads had long treated common criminals. That is, they killed them.

In the 1960s and 1970s there was an overt military effort to exert total societal control. With the Second Institutional Act of October 1965, the military granted itself the right to rule without congressional consent or oversight. Increasing popular protests over the loss of civil and political rights led to increasingly massive repression. By March of 1967, Law 317, the Police Organic Law, put state and municipal police under military appointees. RONE night operations were usually led by a "delgado," a police officer with a law degree, who could quickly legitimize activities. (Although already enjoying total autonomy and impunity, the brutal RONE still spawned its own semiofficial death squad).

In 1969 the most stridently antileftist portions of the military pushed through the Fifth Institutional Act that allowed the military to close Congress and declare a state of siege, enforce extreme censorship, and suspend constitutional liberties for anyone found guilty of "political crimes." It was backed up by the National Security Law of March 1969, which forbade the publication of any news that incited public opinion against "the constituted authorities." Also, to beef up Law 317 of 1967, Law 667 of 1969 even more forcefully subordinated police to military control, while the National Security Law of 1969 greatly expanded the definition of what could be considered a crime against national security. In November of 1969, at the height of the military dictatorship, General Luiz Franca de Oliveira (Secretary of Security of State of Guanabara) formed Os Homens de Ouro (The Men of Gold), a group of twelve police officers designated to fight night robberies of taxis, trucks, supermarkets, and banks. (The unit eventually got into the drug trade for its own profit.) Thus "a picture emerges of Brazil's dirty war as a mix of superficial legality, visible violence, and willful illegality. National Security ideology . . . saw Brazil as fighting a special kind of war against internal subversion" in which police and military forces could not readily differentiate between subversives and civilians.[6] Nor were they much expected to. As Brazil came to the end of the 1970s, its military government had instituted a high degree of official and quasi-official torture and repressive murder. Much of it was employed to safeguard economic structures, but murder was also clearly used for political purposes. Official and unofficial political violence from the military, police, and various death squads had largely cowed the political opposition, especially in Rio, São Paulo, and Minas Gerais.

As Brazil returned to democracy in the 1980s, private enterprise death squads continued the tradition of political murder, with deniability. Members of Brazil's EMs were still fairly official in that they enjoyed high degrees of government tolerance and unacknowledged support. All along, "formal" and "informal" structures of political, economic, and social repression were clearly connected.

CHILE

Chile, by all rights, could have avoided inclusion in the current discussion. From early in the nineteenth century it enjoyed stable democratic development with few rivals in the region.[7]

Reformist presidents of the 1920s and 1930s, as well as some short and comparatively benign military governments, oversaw the enlargement of the government's role in the economy. And, after World War II, the Chilean inclination for constitutional democracy gained enough momentum to resurrect the country's prewar popular mobilization for social reform. By the mid-1950s the newly legalized Communist party joined forces with the Socialist party, now under the leadership of Salvador Allende, to create a powerful coalition of the Left. In the 1960s this coalition would emerge as the (barely) dominant force. Even conservative forces in the countryside acknowledged the need for social change and agrarian reform. Yet the parties of the right, led by the Christian Democrats, ultimately shrank from the progressive agenda, at the very moment that demands for reform gained momentum. The broad Left quickly moved to take the initiative. In 1970, after the death of Che Guevara in 1967, the moment for reform via conventional politics seemed at hand. Though still divided ideologically, Communists and Socialists got behind Allende as their candidate for president, and with a narrow electoral margin, began the experiment of the "Chilean Way to Socialism." Allende, however, did not receive a majority of votes, and his popular Unity Coalition did not control the Chilean congress. He thus insisted on strict adherence to the constitution, and remained acutely aware of the need to balance the demands of his followers with the fears of the opposition. Allende's early efforts, especially the nationalization of Chile's copper mines, unfortunately ensured that his government soon faced a massive wave of resistance from the well-to-do classes. Fearing expropriations and higher taxes, international companies ceased investing in Chile, while the United States threw up immediate and bitter opposition. And since they were inspired by the example of Cuba, Chilean Socialists overtly looked to the poor and the working class, which demanded rapid action on a broad range of issues. As a result, much of the middle class felt ignored, angered, and alarmed, and joined the elites in their vicious hostility. The resulting social and political antagonisms produced open class conflicts.

To better his chances of survival, Allende brought constitutionally minded military officers into his inner circle, particularly General Carlos Prats. There was a tradition in the Chilean military, embodied in the Schneider Doctrine of General René Schneider, that insisted on a strict military neutrality regarding politics. Schneider, who had served as the chief of the armed forces until his assassination in 1970 by members of the military, clearly had not convinced all of his comrades in arms. Prats had replaced Schneider, but he too broke with the idea of neutrality to serve in Allende's cabinet. Allende's foes, domestic and international, were not looking for compromise. The military thus eventually coerced the resignation of General Prats. His replacement, General Augusto Pinochet, came to lead one of Latin America's most shocking coups, which for a time blotted out one of the region's most successful democracies. On September 10, 1973, with overt sympathy from the United States, the armed forces moved against Allende's government. Pinochet did not originally lead the coup effort, but he took command and changed its objective from replacing the Allende government with another civilian government to a more ambitious and longer-term project of repression and personal rule. And to make their point, when President Allende refused to surrender on September 11, the military shelled, strafed, and bombed the presidential palace. Evidence suggests that rather than surrender, Allende committed suicide. His death marked the rise of a sustained Pinochet dictatorship, a regime that began with a rapid campaign of political murder.

The Chilean military met almost no armed resistance after the coup, but the "counterrevolution" was nevertheless decidedly violent. The army and police went hunting and killed thousands of "subversives," who were often identified by little more than their beards. Barricades and roadblocks were set up on the streets of the capital, complete with machine gun crews. Thousands of people were detained and sent to concentration camps (such as the famous camp at the soccer stadium). Many people were never seen again, having been summarily and extra-judicially executed. The military closed down the legislature and outlawed political groups that had supported Allende's government. They then began a campaign, dubbed a "holy war," against what they identified as a "Marxist cancer." They targeted leftist politicians, labor leaders, student activists, intellectuals, journalists, and academics, thousands of whom were killed in the first days after the coup. The victims even included U.S. citizens, such as journalist Charles Horman, whose fate was dramatized in the 1982 Costa-Gavras film *Missing*. Pinochet's government developed a special secret police organization known as the Dirección de Inteligencia Nacional (National Intelligence Directorate), or DINA. It was later replaced with the slightly less heavy-handed Central Nacional de Informacion (National Information Center), or CNI. His military also launched the infamous Operation Condor, in conjunction with the other military governments of the Southern Cone, and carried out the murders of Carlos Prats in Buenos Aires and Orlando Letelier (another of Allende's most high-profile underlings) in Washington D.C. Pinochet also eliminated many others who might have stood in his way, including serving members of the Chilean military.

Pinochet was in power until 1990, and remained in control of the military until 1998. He also saddled Chileans with a constitution that allowed him to retain significant leverage. Pinochet's coup against the government of Salvador Allende set the stage for the savage military regimes to the east.

COLOMBIA

Colombia enjoys pride of place given that it has the longest continuous tradition of political murder, and the largest kill tally, a history of nearly mythic proportions. Tellingly, Colombia also has a long and vibrant democratic political tradition. We should not forget that during the first half of the twentieth century Bogotá was known as the "Athens" of Latin America, a period during which Colombia spawned many powerfully leftist and populist impulses. Yet it is better known for its many civil wars of the nineteenth and twentieth centuries, especially for its partisan struggle between 1946 and 1966, the so-called Violencia, in which more than two hundred thousand Colombians were killed. Colombia is also significant in that its process endures undisturbed into the second decade of the twenty-first century. Especially since the rise of paramilitary armies linked to the illegal drug trade in the early 1980s, tens of thousands more Colombians have perished, a dynamic that continues to the present.[8]

After independence, wars pulsated through the nineteenth century, in 1831, 1839–1841, 1851, 1854, 1859–1862, 1867, 1876–1877, and

1884–1886, with smaller skirmishes interspersed. While these conflicts are called "civil wars," Colombian states were in some ways more like independent nations, given the republic's radically differentiated federal system until 1886. The War of a Thousand Days (1899–1901), the final and bloodiest war of the century, left about one hundred thousand dead, and cemented the so-called "hereditary hatreds" between the supporters of the Liberal and Conservative parties. But nothing was inevitable. Colombia enjoyed forty-five relatively peaceful years that witnessed the rise and evolution of populism on the Liberal left. This began with President Alfonso López Pumarejo and his reform program, known as the Revolución en Marcha, in the mid-1930s.

In the 1940s, the impulse reemerged around the person of Jorge Eliécer Gaitán, who had made his name championing the victims of the Banana Massacre of 1928. Gaitán inherited the mantel of López and the left-Liberal tradition of democracy, social justice, and popular mobilization after 1942. Apart from a short period (1933–1935), Gaitán stayed within the Liberal party, albeit on its far left, and he was never particularly friendly with the leadership of the Colombian Communists, with whom he competed for supporters. Though he was part of the establishment as a city councilman and Mayor of Bogotá, congressman, Senator, and cabinet minister, elites viewed Gaitán's mass movement as "radical." He was deeply hated and feared in elite circles, both Liberal and Conservative. Gaitán's run for the presidency in 1946 as a renegade Liberal candidate split the Liberal vote and allowed the minority Conservative party to regain control of the all-important executive branch. His campaign, and subsequent conquest of the leadership of the Liberal party in 1947, stimulated the resurgence of murder in Colombian politics. First, Gaitanistas were attacked by the official Liberals in power. Then Conservatives began their own violent political offensive against Liberals in general, and Gaitanistas in particular.

With Gaitán's assassination on April 9, 1948, in downtown Bogotá, the Violencia accelerated dramatically. The initial resurgence of political murders before and after the 1946 election was but a prelude to the political violence Gatián's murder generated. Popular urban uprisings (known collectively as the Nueve de Abril, or Ninth of April) exploded and were violently repressed. The best known was the so-called Bogotazo in the capital, where Liberal masses were joined by a large portion of the metropolitan police force (which had been stacked by Liberal governments with Liberals to counterbalance the more Conservative leaning military). After several chaotic days, it was crushed. Lesser-known uprisings occurred in Cali, Barrancabermeja, Barranquilla, and other cities, and these too were successfully repressed. In their aftermath, the Conservative-dominated national state began a long-term hunt for Gaitanistas in a vendetta that ultimately destroyed the movement in the first and largest political genocide in Colombian history.

A period of rural warfare followed, as Gaitanistas joined other Liberals in open rebellion in the countryside. This initiative, which lasted from mid-1948 until June 1953, was directed against the Conservative government of Mariano Ospina Pérez (1946–1950), and then against the even more repressive government of Laureano Gómez (1950–1953). In 1948–1949, the old elite-dominated "convivial" political culture fell apart, as the congress was shut down and conventional politics in general came to a halt. In 1949, the last Liberals of stature were kicked out of the ad hoc power-sharing arrangement put together in the wake of Gaitán's murder. Soon thereafter Gómez was elected in the 1950 presidential contest that Liberals would not, and mostly could not, participate in.

During the Ospina and Gómez years, two threads of a long-term pattern were established. The first was the practice of political murder by official and quasi-official units. In the 1940s and 1950s such groups tended to be identified as "police," called Chulavitas and Contrachusmas. The second was political murder by unofficial political death squads known as *pájaros* (birds.) This counterplay between official and unofficial violence carries on to the present day. This earlier history is often ignored by commentators who explore the period since the 1960s.

Elite divisions were short-lived. While such disunion had been a fundamental ingredient in the historical evolution of Colombia's political culture, after 1953 Colombia's elite became much more politically unified, and much less inclined to democratic give and take with the masses. That year the military government of General Gustavo Rojas Pinilla, which took power with widespread and bipartisan elite backing, ousted Gómez and offered a general amnesty. A ten-thousand-strong Liberal army on the eastern Llanos, or plains, accepted the offer, and under their leader, Guadalupe Salcedo, turned in their arms. Unfortunately, large numbers of the demobilized Liberal guerrillas would soon be murdered, including the politically ambitious Salcedo, who was assassinated in Bogotá in 1957. Despite his amnesty, Rojas Pinilla was closely linked to the ongoing Violencia, especially the notorious pájaros. Consequently, Liberal guerrillas in other regions fought on.

The united Liberal and Conservative elites ousted Rojas Pinilla in 1957 and created the Frente Nacional, or National Front (1958–1974), a sixteen-year power-sharing arrangement. Military governments have never been popular in Colombia, where civilian elites prefer to maintain their own (often fairly authoritarian) forms of rule. Under the National Front agreement, the Liberal and Conservative parties took turns filling the presidency. They equally divided other offices between them, and in the process excluded all other political currents. Significant fighting and practice of political murder lived on in the disjointed struggles under the National Front coalition, while state-sanctioned repression and semiofficial violence continued to be employed.

During the later stages of the Violencia, the military acquired a large measure of political autonomy in managing public order, and became more directly responsible for security issues. As many of the old ideological differences receded in importance, the political class operatives of the Liberal and Conservative parties, now safe in their exclusionary power-sharing structures, allowed the military to deal with social and popular political protests, even peaceful ones, and lump them in with the guerrilla movements. Concerns about "national defense" and external threats were slowly replaced with "national security" issues based on fear of internal enemies (a process at work throughout the region). The state of siege provision of the 1886 Constitution came to be used constantly and indiscriminately after the 1960s, especially in the repression of popular political movements. Given this independence, the military could follow its own interests, which clearly did not include peace. The strategies of low-intensity war and containment created an environment for the military that furthered its long-term institutional health. These tendencies were only strengthened by the Cold War, and especially by the reactions to the Cuban Revolution. For example, the early 1960s counterinsurgency initiative Plan Lazo featured bands of military personnel teamed with trusted civilians whose purpose was to hunt down and eliminate suspected supporters of Marxist sedition.

Paramilitary structures thus continued to evolve alongside the military. President Guillermo León Valencia issued Decree 3398 of 1965, which granted "self-defense" organizations the right to bear military style arms, basically allowing elites to organize their own "legal" versions of the pájaro death squads of the 1950s. Law 48 of 1968 allowed the existence of these organizations beyond state of siege expiration, giving them de facto permanence. Under President Misael Pastrana (1970–1974), counterrevolutionary repression continued in the countryside through an alliance between Liberal and Conservative landed elites. Landowners agreed to be more forthcoming in the payment of taxes, and in return were given free rein to repress those peasants seeking land reform in their regions.

The increasingly closed and repressive political system of the National Front and its successor political configurations saw, not surprisingly, the birth of evolved guerrilla movements that were now adapted for long-term armed struggle. Traditionally, historians have "ended" the Violencia in 1965 or 1966, the years in which Colombia's principal guerrilla bands reorganized themselves and changed their nomenclature, declaring themselves to be Marxist organizations. Curiously, the subsequent pace of political murder slackened somewhat in the late 1960s and early 1970s.

The Colombian military initiated a new phase with its launch, in 1964, of an offensive against the "independent" enclaves of the remote and mountainous Marquetalia region southwest of Bogotá. This area, peopled by the remnants of the Liberal, Gaitanista, and communist guerrilla groups, had not demobilized in the 1950s. During Operación Marquetalia, the army sent a large force to attack the mostly unarmed villagers. In 1966, the survivors formed the Fuerzas Armadas Revolucionarias de Colombia (the Revolutionary Armed Forces of Colombia), or FARC. In 1965, a group of Liberal guerrillas, middle-class Colombian students and radical petroleum workers in the department of Santander founded the Ejército de Liberación Nacional (the Army of National Liberation), or ELN, clearly beholden to the Cuban "foco" model popularized by Che Guevara. Yet, in both cases, the organization's roots were clearly anchored in the decades of the Violencia. In 1970, a splinter group of the FARC, along with other currents connected to Rojas Pinilla's populist movement, formed the M-19.

So while political violence receded in the 1970s, relative to the periods before and after, the practice of killing for political reasons, and indeed the struggle itself, continued. Guerrilla movements found it next to impossible to demobilize and to pursue political engagement because of the consistent murder (beginning in the 1950s) of any guerrilla who laid down his arms. Also, by protecting only strategically important regions, the military gave guerrilla groups relative freedom elsewhere. The guerrillas defended subsistence, smallholding peasants while providing services the government would not or could not provide. Even more than in the past, the government represented elite interests. Popular political movements were pushed to society's fringe and condemned as virtually illegal, certainly immoral, and downright subversive.

By the early 1980s important sectors of the elite in both traditional parties were frustrated with Colombia's stale and closed politics, continued repression, and the accompanying guerrilla insurgencies. This desire among parts of the elite to end guerrilla activity for good, and curtail the practice of political murder, led to the reforms offered by Conservative President Belisario Betancur (1982–1986). Betancur took peace seriously and initiated a peace process with the various guerrilla groups. In 1982 he declared an amnesty and freed more than one thousand guerrillas. Betancur's so-called "political opening" also aimed to better the economic lot of the pueblo. Though earlier reform impulses by President Carlos Lleras Restrepo (1966–1970) had come to naught, Betancur's efforts brought much of the Left back to electoral politics on a level not seen since the Gaitanista mobilizations of the 1930s and 1940s. In 1985, demobilized guerrillas and other leftists organized the Unión Patriótica (Patriotic Union Party), or UP. Though it had clear ties to the FARC and the Colombian Communist Party, many of its growing base of militants wanted it to be a broader party of the Left, and indeed, it did enjoy a significant following among a wider spectrum, especially in cities, as it advocated the old Gaitanista goals of social justice and expanded democracy. The UP benefited particularly from attempts by the central government to increase democratic participation on the regional level. In the historic 1988 local elections (since the Constitution of 1886, mayors had been appointed by governors, who in turn were appointed by the president), the UP won sixteen mayoral races and elected 256 individuals to local city councils.

Predictably, significant parts of the elite of both traditional parties were not in favor of reform and political opening. They remained united and intent (as during the National Front) on protecting the ever more exclusive political and economic system, and agreed on a sustained campaign of violent repression. In this project they were invigorated by fresh, and particularly able, reinforcements. In the late 1970s and early 1980s, successful "narcos" started to buy land, especially in the Magdalena River Valley. By then cocaine had surpassed coffee as Colombia's most profitable commodity. Pablo Escobar became first among many narco entrepreneurs. Ironically he saw himself as a populist (his mother was reported to have been a Gaitanista). He spent money on public projects and was even elected to congress in 1982 as an alternate Liberal diputado (but was eventually pushed from the Liberal party). At the same time, he was also instrumental in the murder of guerrillas and their supporters. Escobar, the Castaño Clan, and other drug lords either already owned land or were quickly acquiring it for social status and to launder drug profits. As landowners they became targets of kidnappings and "war tax" extortions levied by guerrilla groups, especially in the Magdalena Medio, as the valley is known. In response, the new drug elites teamed up in the early 1980s with older landed elites, such as the cattle ranchers association FEDEGAN, to start their own death squads, generically known as Muerte a Secuestradores (Death to Kidnappers), or MAS.

Thus the illegal drug trade was creating a new and particularly violent economic elite that buttressed the local landowning elites and the military with its new economic and social power. Indeed, the old and new elites began to merge. This new elite embraced the tradition of political murder with gusto, using "sicarios" of the drug trade to eliminate government officials who stood in their way. Fidel Castaño, also known as "Rambo," a drug business colleague of Escobar, became particularly devoted to the paramilitary cause and destruction of the guerrillas. He was, perhaps, motivated by the fact that his father was kidnapped and killed by the FARC. He also sent his little brother Carlos for training in paramilitary warfare by the Israelis in 1983. He created the paramilitary group known as Los Tangüeros, which later evolved into the Orwellian-named Autodefensas Campesinas de Córdoba y Urabá (Peasant Self Defense Forces of Córdoba and Urabá), the ACCU.

As a consequence, Betancur's opening was an unmitigated failure. In fact, the use of political murder erupted with new intensity after 1982 as the first of several recurring waves of newly created paramilitary organizations thwarted the beleaguered peace process. What is more, given the spirit of the age, the army would not back Betancur's initiative. Unfortunately for Betancur's good intentions, the timing of his efforts could not have been worse. At that moment in Central America, U.S. President Ronald Reagan was busy demonstrating his obsession with "Marxist" insurgencies. Soon thereafter, in 1984, the U.S. ambassador to Colombia, Lewis Tambs, coined the term "narcoguerrilla," tying U.S.–Colombia policy of the War on Drugs to the Reagan administration's Cold War concerns, while giving the green light for repression. In 1985, when the M-19 seized the Palace of Justice, over one hundred people were killed as the military, largely outside of civilian control, went all-out in its counterattack. At the same time, entire areas were cleansed of suspected guerrilla sympathizers, especially the Magdalena Medio. There General Farauk Yanine Díaz established "peace" by attacking actual and possible guerrilla supporters, and by increasing "civilian"/military alliances that showcased the emerging paramilitary movement. UP militants in particular, as the Gaitanistas before them, became targets, especially in rural areas and frontier zones where the group was characterized as nothing more than the FARC's unarmed wing of subversion. The military and paramilitary groups also targeted labor leaders and activists, indigenous leaders, teachers, academics, students, human rights advocates, and journalists, and were aided by Colombia's national security agency, Departamento Administrivo de Segurida (Administrative Department of Security), or DAS.

A clear cycle had now been established, in which attempts at reform were met and crushed by ever more brutal repression. In 1991, constitutional reform generated another attempt to open political structures to broader participation, and many smaller guerrilla movements (the EPL, M-19, Quintín

Lame, and PRT) demobilized to enter electoral politics. Unfortunately, this political opening was also doomed, as these reform attempts brought heightened violent repression from the expanding paramilitary movement. The conflict displaced millions of people, which brought recruits into both camps. While the army was responsible for many massacres, paramilitaries (in clear alliance with armed forces) were taking on most of the dirty work of political murder, like their pájaro and contrachusma forerunners. Mirroring the economy, political repression, in old Colombian practice, was privatized to independent subcontractors. It is also clear that the political decentralization generated by the 1991 Constitution strengthened regional elites and Liberal party bosses just as they moved wholeheartedly back to the use of violent repression. As in the late 1940s and early 50s, political violence and murder in the 1980s and early 1990s decimated the Left and drove it from conventional politics. After drug lord Fidel Castaño disappeared in 1994, purportedly killed in combat, he was replaced by younger brother Carlos, who merged the ACCU with other para groups to create the Autodefensas Unidas de Colombia (United Self-Defense Forces of Colombia), or AUC, in 1997. Driven by the new elite constellation of old landed wealth and the new narco money, the illegal drug trade was now firmly entrenched as the driving engine of the economy. Their paramilitary retainers were well paid.

By the same token, the remaining guerrillas of the ELN and especially the FARC were also flush with cash, not to mention recruits, as many survivors of paramilitary massacres joined the insurgents. By the 1990s coca was being produced on a large scale inside Colombia. In earlier decades most was grown in Bolivia and Peru, and processed in Colombia. Coca was now grown in frontier regions long controlled by the FARC. It was the only cash crop that was profitable, given the difficulty of transport. At the same time the FARC and ELN largely gave up on acquiring national power, and focused on local power. The traditional absence of state presence in many of their regions of influence, especially in the south and southwest, had long offered institutional space for the FARC to become the de facto local government, providing basic services, infrastructure, and law and order. And thanks to local cash in war taxes on the Narco trade, the guerrillas became increasingly potent military forces. By the mid-1990s the FARC in particular had become the largest guerrilla force, with "fronts" scattered throughout Colombia—growing from 17 fronts in 1978 to 105 fronts in 1994. The smaller ELN stayed out of the coca business and relied on kidnapping and oil "war" taxes. In 1996–1997, the FARC's capabilities had improved to the point that it could meet the Colombian army in pitched battle, and prevail, though it never could threaten the Colombian state. With units of three hundred to one thousand soldiers, they attacked a series of army bases. The outcome was army reform, but also paramilitary expansion. Paras made even more money from the drug trade than the guerrillas, and had the willing support of the landed elite, army, and elements of departmental and national governments.

A complicating factor for the new elite was the split personality of the U.S. government regarding drugs. In 1989, the threat of extradition motivated Pablo Escobar to have popular Liberal presidential candidate Luís Carlos Galán, who favored it, murdered. President César Gaviria (1990–1994), who had been Galán's "debate chief," and had subsequently been elected on Galán's popularity, pushed neoliberal economic reforms, and negotiated with the narcos, but still felt pressured enough to do something about Escobar, who was setting off car bombs in Bogotá in defiance of extradition. Escobar was finally coaxed into "surrendering" in 1991 into his own "prison" (he built it) known as La Catedral. It was staffed by his people, and he carried on his business as usual. But he "escaped" in September 1992, driven by the paranoia that had motivated him to murder several of his business partners (who were buried at La Catedral). In response, his competitors in Cali (more refined and socially savvy, and more tied into established elites) teamed up with the Castaño family, the Colombian police, military intelligence, and the DAS (Colombia's CIA/FBI/Customs) to hunt him down. This operation, known as the Search Bloc, was overtly aided by DEA, the U.S. Army, and the CIA. Pablo's many enemies also created a very specific death squad, known as Los PEPES (a rough acronym for Los Perseguidos por Pablo Escobar, or People Persecuted by Pablo Escobar) led by the Castaños. This organization hunted down and murdered people close to Pablo. The Search Bloc eventually cornered and killed Escobar.

Yet resolving the "Pablo problem," and taking some pressure off the paramilitary beneficiaries of the drug trade, did not solve the overall problem. In the 1990s, the old Medellín and Cali cartels were displaced and replaced by hundreds of small, decentralized networks of traffickers that continued to have significant political clout. In fact, Liberal President Ernesto Samper (1994–1998) was caught up in the question of his connections to them. The confused nature of United States policy was eventually embodied in Plan Colombia. Instituted in 1999, it was a U.S. program of aid aimed at combating both the drug trade and the guerrillas. It included highly controversial aerial spraying of coca fields, but largely ended up as a subsidy for the Colombian military and its drug-connected paramilitary allies. In this context, Conservative President Andrés Pastrana (1998–2002) represented another swing of the pendulum back toward efforts at peace negotiations.

He attempted to recognize the political legitimacy of the guerrillas, especially the FARC. Pastrana withdrew the army from an area of one hundred sixty-two thousand hectares (known unofficially as Farclandia) and promised serious land, political, socioeconomic reforms, but could not deliver. Regardless of whether the FARC was ever serious about demobilization, there was no doubt about the hostility of the army and the paras to the whole process, and the latter continued to carry out attacks. The FARC soon moved to use the area as a strategic zone, where they hid kidnap victims. The whole effort broke down in February 2002.

Into this drama stepped Alvaro Uribe Vélez. As governor of Antioquia (1995–1997), he oversaw paramilitary expansion in Urabá. Looking to the experience of 1940s and 1950s Antioquia, with its Contrachusmas, as well as to Plan Lazo in the 1960s, Uribe relegalized para groups there as "Convivirs," or Rural Vigilance Cooperatives. The Convivirs were enthusiastically supported by General Harold Bedoya, head of the Colombia armed forces. In their short period of legality (Convivirs were banned in 1999), they displaced over two hundred thousand campesinos from their land. Salvatore Mancuso (later a notorious and violent leader of the paramilitary umbrella group, the AUC) led a Convivir unit in Córdoba. Popular anger at the FARC's apparent duplicity, as well as FARC use of political murder, helped sweep Uribe into the presidency as a get-tough leader in 2002. He served as president in 2002–2006, and was reelected in 2006. Uribe was seen as the AUC candidate. Carlos Castaño, for one, believed that he was the candidate who most closely shared the AUC's "philosophy." Of all the Colombian murderous elites, Castaño was always the most frank about para goals and point of view. He claimed that two thirds of "guerrillas" were unarmed collaborators, a deeply ingrained belief in Colombia.

But Uribe was also quite popular with a large part of the urban middle and upper classes because he addressed their concerns about security. Uribe believed that he had been elected to end attempts at negotiation. He saw his election as a mandate to eradicate the guerrilla with a pure military strategy, and was supported in this belief by various interests, including cattle ranchers, flower exporters, emerald miners, narcos, and Liberal party bosses. Immediately after being elected, he declared a State of Emergency and changed legal structures to allow for political "negotiation" with the paras. Uribe pushed his idea of "democratic security," which aimed to increase cooperative ventures between military, police and civilians (Convivirs updated and writ large.) He set out to construct a first line of defense of so-called "peasant soldiers," meant to protect their regions, and encouraged people to spy on possible agents of subversion. Most important for his urban middle-class supporters, he worked to keep the roads free of guerrilla kidnap bands. After the murder of Carlos Castaño in 2004, Uribe began a process to "demobilize" paras in 2005 with the Justice and Peace Law. This, his critics have argued, gave them impunity, though Uribe had many extradited to the United States to face drug-trafficking charges. Para influences in politics led to an ongoing "parapolítica" scandal and caused observers to speak of "parauribismo."

The 2010 election of Juan Manuel Santos did not seem to mark a real change of direction. The AUC was replaced by a whole new slate of paramilitary organizations, including the Aguilas Negras, the Rastrojos, the Urabeños, the Paisas, the Machos, the Renacer, and the Nueva Generación, among others. Yet Santos shuttered Colombia's tainted security and counterinsurgency organization, the DAS, reorganizing and renaming it the National Directorate of Intelligence, or the DNI. He also eventually launched a new peace process with the FARC that resulted in ongoing negotiations in Havana, Cuba. Though students of Colombian history are given to speaking of its "exceptionalism," its experience with political murder was in no way unique. It has had several close competitors, especially in Central America and the Caribbean Basin, though these countries had special problems, particularly their proximity to the United States, with its long tradition of intervention.

CUBA

Perhaps the linchpin to the U.S. role in the region, Cuba had a long history of colonialism in which the place of Madrid was quickly filled by Washington D.C. From the Spanish American War to the fall of Fulgencio Batista, nationalistic revolution was long in coming, but was ultimately supercharged by extreme anti-Gringo feelings. Postrevolutionary "socialist" Cuba was in turn deeply hated by both the Latin American right and a continuing line of U.S. presidential administrations.[9]

When the majority of Latin American nations gained their independence in the early nineteenth century, Cuba maintained its ties to the Spanish crown, and was declared "La Siempre Fidelísima Isla" (the always faithful island). Yet the loyalty of the colony's elites was problematic, in that it was based in large part on fear of slave uprisings, and waned as the century progressed. After a series of rebellions, the final struggle for independence began in 1892 when poet and Cuban patriot José Martí helped found a revolutionary party in New York City and Florida. Though Martí was killed in battle soon after the fighting started in 1895, the Spanish took the small guerrilla army seriously, and sent more than two hundred thousand troops to crush it. The military governor of the island, Valeriano Weyler, then developed an inventive, brutal, and effective strategy. He forced Cuba's rural population into centralized locations, often compared to concentration camps—and called, in fact, reconcentrados. Once the population was thus accounted for, anyone else was shot on sight as a guerrilla. Spain's successes, however, were ultimately negated by a growing and intense U.S. interest in the conflict. When the battleship U.S.S. Maine exploded in Havana harbor in January 1898, the United States took the opportunity to pursue "a splendid little war" (as John Hay called it), which stripped Spain of not only Cuba but Puerto Rico, Guam, and the Philippines as well.

Though Cuba was granted independence in 1902, the United States remained a powerful, intrusive, and resented presence in its development for the next fifty-eight years and beyond. The United States attached the Platt Amendment to the Cuban constitution that allowed the United States to legally intervene in Cuban affairs (which it did repeatedly), and to maintain a naval base on Guantánamo Bay. Constitutional government endured until 1930, when President Gerardo Machado y Morales suspended the constitution. Though he claimed his goal was to turn Cuba into the "Switzerland of the Americas," he was rather authoritarian, and reportedly ordered the assassination of communist Julio Antonio Mella, who was exiled in Mexico. In 1933, he was forced into exile himself by a coalition of U.S. interests, Independence War veterans, military, students, and strikers. The ensuing collapse of government led to the so-called Revolt of the Sergeants coup later in the year. Though the presidency was filled by the collective Pentarchy of 1933, representing the various anti-Machado factions, the process really marked the rise of Fulgencio Batista.

Born illegitimate and of mixed race, Batista joined the army in 1921 at the age of twenty, and rose to the rank of sergeant while working as a stenographer. More important, he became a leader of Cuba's soldiers' union. He led the 1933 coup, and came to control the Cuban armed forces. The Pentarchy recognized this situation, awarded Batista the rank of colonel, and made him Army Chief of Staff. Batista quickly moved to purge the ranks of the commissioned officers, forcibly retiring most, and reportedly killing others. Batista also became de facto ruler of Cuba. For the next six years he manipulated a series of "puppet" presidents until he decided to occupy the president's chair himself for the 1940–1944 term. During this first period of power in the 1930s and 1940s, Batista pushed progressive labor laws, generally supported unions, and even had the backing of the small Communist party. In 1944, however, Batista's candidate was defeated by Ramón Grau San Martin. After draining the treasury and perpetrating other acts of political sabotage, Batista withdrew to the United States, moving between his house in Daytona Beach, Florida, and the Waldorf-Astoria Hotel in New York City. (He admitted that he felt "safer" in the United States.) But he remained engaged in Cuban politics.

In 1952, Batista ran for president again, but when it soon became clear that he would come in a distant third, he led another coup three months before the general elections could be held. Installing himself as "provisional President," he was quickly recognized by the United States. The somewhat progressive patina of his first stint in power now evaporated completely. Batista became the front man for a spectacular kleptocracy favoring U.S. big business, U.S. government interests, and even U.S. organized crime. Under Batista's benevolent (and well-compensated) gaze, Meyer Lansky, Charles "Lucky" Luciano, and other mobsters set out to control Havana's casinos, nightclubs, and racetracks and convert it into "the Latin Las Vegas." Just as galling to Cubans, private U.S. companies came to dominate the country's economy, while failing to provide for its people. The ITT Corporation, for instance, showed its gratitude for being allowed to charge exorbitant communication rates by presenting Batista with a gold-plated telephone.

A year after the second coup, on July 26, 1953, a small group of poorly armed would-be revolutionaries attacked the Moncada Army Barracks in Santiago. They were led by a young lawyer who had been a candidate for congress in the cancelled 1952 elections. His name was Fidel Castro. The attack was easily crushed, and Fidel and his brother Raul were taken prisoner. At their trial later that year, Fidel gave his famous "History Will Absolve Me" speech, making him an instant celebrity. Sentenced to fifteen years, he and others were released in a general amnesty in 1955. Rumored to be on a Batista hit list, the Castro brothers went to Mexico, where they founded the "26th of July Movement." They recruited other exiled Cubans, as well as a young Argentine medical doctor named Ernesto "Che" Guevara, who was a strong proponent of guerrilla warfare as the only path to social justice. On November 26, 1956, Castro's small band of eighty-one followers set out from Mexico on the yacht "Granma," and on December 2 landed in southeastern Cuba. Castro's force met immediate disaster, was rapidly shattered, and only about a quarter of the original group survived to escape into the Sierra Maestra Mountains.

In response to Castro's movement (and other challenges, especially the riotous university students, known for their violent demonstrations), Batista unleashed a savage campaign of repression, suspending constitutional guarantees. All young people, and university students in particular, became targets of Batista's military police. Popular leaders were thinned out, such as student leader José Antonio Echeverría, who was killed outside a radio station. The University of Havana was closed in November 1956, and remained closed until the end of Batista's regime. Frank País, urban leader of the 26th of July Movement, was killed by police in Santiago in July 1956. Police and army units killed thousands in the cities (twenty thousand by later estimates of the revolutionary government, though scholars put the number of people killed during the whole insurrectionary period somewhere between two and three thousand), but in the countryside the army, whose officer corps Batista had purged yet again after the attempted Conspiración de los Puros (Conspiracy of the Pure) in April 1956, made little headway. Corrupt, poorly led, with increasingly poor morale and high desertion rates, the Cuban army could not eliminate the initially small guerrilla movement. The guerrillas, known as "los barbudos" because of their beards, could boast some victories, but even more important, lots of good fortune. They narrowly escaped destruction several times. And perhaps most important of all, they displayed masterful skill at public relations, in manipulating foreign reporters (such as Herbert Matthews of the *New York Times*), and especially in operating their own clandestine radio station, Radio Rebelde. They came to enjoy growing urban middle-class support (as the Sandinistas would later) from people fed up with Batista, U.S. government and corporate domination, and preening gangsters. Batista, meanwhile, was losing U.S. backing as the Eisenhower administration cut military aid and other support. On December 31, 1958, Batista fled the country, reportedly taking hundreds of millions of dollars with him. What was left of his regime collapsed.

In January 1959, Castro's movement took control of Cuba and began an immediate series of purges. The victors moved to consolidate their position by sending hundreds, or even thousands, of Batista's police and military personnel before hastily assembled revolutionary tribunals for trial on charges of war crimes, human rights abuse, and murder. The large numbers convicted were executed forthwith by firing squads. Raul Castro shot seventy captured soldiers in Santiago, while Che Guevara, as the military commander of La Cabaña Fortress in Havana, shot many more. Scholars estimate that the new Cuban regime executed somewhere between three hundred and seven hundred individuals. By the latter part of 1960 the regime had expropriated billions of dollars of private property, with little real compensation, had nationalized public utilities, and shut down the mafia gaming industry. The Castro government closed opposition newspapers, television, and radio stations, purged the professions of supporters of the old establishment, and imprisoned tens of thousands of dissenters. Homosexuals, Catholic priests, and protestant ministers were sent to "re-education" camps. In the process, well over one hundred thousand Cubans fled the island, mostly landing in Florida. Thus in a short period the revolutionaries generated a multitude of enemies whose visceral hatred would last for generations. The early 1960s were particularly eventful, moving quickly from the failed Bay of Pigs invasion of U.S-trained Cuban exiles in 1961, to CIA-mafia assassination plots against Castro, to the Cuban-Soviet alliance and the 1963 Cuban Missile Crisis.

The Castro regime purportedly offered "revolution for export," ostensibly supporting seventeen leftist governments in Africa and pursuing revolutionary activity in Latin America. Much of this revolutionary reputation rested on the "foco" (focus) theory of revolutionary warfare, derived from Che Guevara's writings on guerrilla tactics and strategy, and further popularized by French intellectual Régis Debray. Foco theory, or *foquismo*, stressed the importance of a small revolutionary band (the foco), made up of committed revolutionaries, that would serve as the vanguard of and catalyst for a general insurrection. In reality, the Castro regime was rather cautious in its support of revolution (much to the consternation of Latin American leftists). Che was sent to Bolivia in1967, but Castro did not offer real support for the venture, with predictably disastrous results for the Cuban expedition.

Clearly undemocratic and overtly repressive, the Castro regime created an impressive coercive apparatus. Yet the dominant pattern of repression relied on two strategies that did not include wide use of political murder. The first was a massive regime of imprisonment. The second was the safety valve of immigration, which Castro employed with consummate ability. After the early waves of "counterrevolutionaries" abandoned the island, he periodically allowed other mass migrations, especially the 1980 exodus from the port city of Mariel, during which another one hundred twenty-five thousand Cubans left for the United States. Castro took that opportunity to empty some of his prisons and mental institutions. Castro's Cuba, however, was not a complete police state, and over the decades retained significant degrees of popular support after putting resources into education and universal health care.

Interestingly, Cuban exiles and dead-enders from the Batista regime took the political culture of murder with them. In Miami, as late as the 1970s and 1980s, hardline anti-Castro organizations Alpha 66 and Omega 7 threatened to murder anyone who voiced conciliatory views about relations with Cuba, or even traveled there. These threats were not idle. Businesses and homes of those who failed to comply were bombed.

DOMINICAN REPUBLIC

During the twentieth century, the Dominican Republic's penchant for political murder was associated with Rafael Trujillo and Joaquín Balaguer. The country also endured significant U.S. interference. Yet it already had a living tradition regarding both political murder and foreign involvement, a tradition with deep roots.[10] In the late eighteenth and early nineteenth centuries, the island of Hispaniola was traded back and forth between France and Spain, with the Spanish-speaking east ruled by both powers, and later by an independent Haiti. The Dominican Republic finally emerged in 1844, only to be returned to colonial status under Spain in 1861 by General Pedro Santana (known for executing and otherwise repressing his political opponents), but this unique experiment with "voluntary" colonialism was short-lived. By 1865 (with the end of the U.S. Civil War), the Spanish were forced to abandon the island following the War of the Restoration.

The Dominican Republic experienced endemic political and economic instability as caudillos jostled for power, until the rise of General Ulises "Lilís" Heureaux in the 1880s. Heureaux had been the power behind the presidential chair for some time. Adept at political and electoral manipulation, he was also inclined to assassinate any political operators he could not influence. Under his rule, sugar became the engine of the economy. He made efforts to modernize the country's infrastructure, but the nation became heavily indebted and more securely under the tutelage of the United States. Heureaux was assassinated in 1899 by President Ramón Cáceres, who was in turn assassinated in 1911, while presiding over a period of reinvigorated caudillo regionalism, political strife, and civil war. U.S. President Theodore Roosevelt (employing his "corollary" to the Monroe Doctrine, which authorized the United States to intervene in Central America and Caribbean nations to assure stability and the payment of their debt), moved to take over the Dominican Republic's customs collection for fifty years. Recurring political instability led first to U.S. President Woodrow Wilson's 1914 ultimatum that Dominicans must choose a president and behave themselves politically, and then to the 1916 invasion by U.S. Marines and an occupation that lasted until 1924. The U.S. presence brought economic revival, an expanded system of roads, and a degree of political calm, re-enforced by a new centralized Guardia Nacional that was able to tame the caudillos. Yet the occupation was widely hated, and few Dominicans of note would participate. Indeed, a guerrilla resistance arose that had to be brutally suppressed. Elections were finally held in 1924, and the victor, former President Horacio Vásquez, presided over six stable years of government. But when he ran for reelection in 1930, a coalition led by General Rafael Leonidas Trujillo (who commanded the new National Army that had replaced the Guardia Nacional) pushed Vásquez aside.

Trujillo went on to dominate the Dominican Republic for the next thirty years, beginning with the 1930 presidential campaign, marked as it was by the violent intimidation of his political opponents. Recent interpretations of the Trujillato have pointed out that Trujillo's long rule was based on significant support among the peasantry, given his land reform and redistribution efforts. His regime also oversaw improvements in popular health care, construction of hospitals and clinics, development of roads harbors, schools, and housing, and establishment of pensions. Yet Trujillo was decidedly buffoonish in his megalomania and greed. He renamed Santo Domingo (the oldest city of European origin in the hemisphere) after himself, (Ciudad Trujillo), as well as the Caribbean's highest mountain, Pico Duarte, which was rechristened Pico Trujillo. And through truly spectacular graft and corruption, he became one of the wealthiest men in Latin America. Finally, he was infamous for coercing women to serve his sexual appetite, and preyed upon women of all social classes.

The generous use of political murder, torture, and terrorism on the political opposition, however, was also an essential prop for the Trujillo regime. Early on, his government employed a death squad, known as "The 42" and led by Miguel Angel Paulino, that tooled around in a stylish red Packard called the Carro de la Muerte (Death Car). Trujillo later developed the Servicio de Inteligencia Militar (Military Intelligence Service) under Johnny Abbes García. But his most egregious act of repression was the 1937 massacre of more than twenty thousand ethnic Haitians. Anyone who thwarted his will could expect violent and likely fatal reaction. Over the decades his henchmen killed hundreds of critics and would-be political rivals. This treatment extended to anyone with familial or friendship ties to his recognized enemies. Indeed, Trujillo's agents hunted the perceived threats to his regime well beyond the country's borders, assassinating individuals in the mainland United States and Puerto Rico, Cuba, and Mexico. Trujillo even policed his own regime with political murder, executing officials who had fallen from grace. Famous late victims were the Mirabal sisters (critics of the regime known as Las Mariposas) Patricia Mercedes, Minerva, and Maria Teresa. (A fourth sister, Debé Mirabal, survived to tell her sisters' tale.) For years the United States (and even the Catholic Church) put up with Trujillo's excesses, viewing his regime as better than the possible alternatives. But in 1960, after a truly paranoid bid to assassinate Venezuelan president Rómulo Betancourt (who, for sure, was a Trujillo critic) the United States broke with his government. Trujillo was assassinated in May 1961, reportedly with CIA assistance.

Juan Bosch, intellectual, historian, writer, and leader of the exiled opposition, was elected president in 1963. The new president's leftist leanings set him on a course to restructure the economy and political system, and to break up many large land holdings. After seven months he was thrown out by the military. When less than two years later another military uprising removed the first junta and demanded Bosch's return, U.S. President Lyndon Johnson got involved. In April 1965 he sent forty-two thousand Marines and Army Airborne troops to the Dominican Republic to ensure that it would not become "a second Cuba" (this would be a recurring theme in Washington). With elections in 1966, Trujillo's last puppet ruler, Joaquín Balaguer, was elected president and served for twelve years, through 1978. While he embarked on ambitious building programs, his real mandate was to keep pro-Castro and procommunist elements at bay, and he used significant amounts of repression to do so. A paramilitary group calling itself the Frente Democrático Anticomunista y Antisubversiva (Anti-Communist, Anti-Subversive Democratic Front), also known as La Banda, was active in eliminating hundreds of leftist leaders and activists. Intriguingly, during the years since 1978, the Dominican Republic has known a significant degree of democratic stability.

ECUADOR

Though more Andean than Southern Cone, Ecuador should be grouped with many of its neighbors to the south in any discussion of political murder, if for no other reason than its brief participation in Operation Condor.[11]

Ecuadorian elites in the early twentieth century were not adverse to the use of murder against bottom-up threats. One such example was the November 15, 1922, massacre of striking cacao workers, who were protesting labor conditions in Guayaquil. Police killed upwards of two thousand strikers, and threw their bodies in the Guayas River. (See the novel by Joaquín Gallegos Lara, *Las Cruces Sobre el Agua*). Other incidents followed. In September 1923, the army killed thirty-seven Indians on the Leito Hacienda. In February 1928, the military killed fourteen Indians at Tisaleo, Tungurahua. In January 1929, military and police personnel are said to have killed hundreds of Indians at Colta, Chimborazo, and in September of the same year ten workers were killed at Tigua Hacienda. Echoes of this violence were heard in the Massacre of Salasaca Indians over water rights in

1962, and the murder of indigenous leaders Cristóbal Pajuña and Lázaro Cando, who were killed by landlords and police, respectively, in 1973 and 1974. In October 1977, hundreds of striking workers were killed at Aztra sugar mill, and in November of that same year police tortured and killed Indigenous leader Rafael Perugachí. Finally, President León Febres Cordero (1984–1988) culminated the tradition and brought Ecuador into line with the dominant spirit of the 1980s by pursuing a small dirty war against guerrilla groups, especially the Afaro Vive.

EL SALVADOR

El Salvador's elites have the dubious distinction of having killed, perhaps, the largest percentage of their own population in Latin America, in two periods separated by four decades. The first is known simply as the infamous Matanza (literally, the "slaughter") of 1932, which saw the murder of roughly twenty-five thousand people. During the bloody years between 1978 and 1991, another fifty thousand died at the hands of direct or indirect agents of the state.[12] El Salvador is famous for the small size and cohesiveness of its landed elite. The cream of the elite was known early on as Los Catorce, or the fourteen families. Even as the core of the oligarchy expanded, a remarkably small number of families owned the bulk of the nation's riches, especially after nineteenth-century land-grabs of indigenous communal property.

In 1932, the armed forces, led by General Maximiliano Hernández Martínez, butchered twenty-five thousand peasants and workers in answer to an uprising in late January in the western part of the country. The Communist Party was aware of the dangers involved in an armed struggle, given the dearth of weapons and military know-how, but peasant leaders and their followers were insistent. Wielding machetes and a few rifles, rebels gained control of a number of towns. They took over police installations and other symbolic targets, including municipal buildings, and houses belonging to the land-holding class. The insurgents and their popular movement posed a regional threat, grabbing some properties, burning others, and murdering individuals they saw as their oppressors. They killed thirty-five civilians and local police officers, and somewhere between twenty and forty soldiers. Yet the rebellion was doomed. The government had reliable informants and captured the insurrection's leadership days before the rebels could act. With little or no central coordination, the rebellion played out as unconnected local struggles. The army and Guardia Nacional counterattacked the western towns, and given their superior weaponry, quickly defeated the insurgents. Then the Guardia in particular went on to slaughter anyone they suspected of being a rebel, which amounted to killing anyone who looked like an Indian. This turned out to be most rural inhabitants. The Guardia actively duped their victims into turning themselves in to receive clemency, and then shot them forthwith. And while the killing was most intense in the rural western zones, the military government also took the opportunity to rid itself of large numbers of people in San Salvador and other towns who were believed to have leftist sympathies. The Matanza was an excellent example of the long-term usefulness of savage repression and political murder on the grand scale. Elite control was maintained, and popular mobilization was smashed for decades as fear spread over generations. Political and economic power in El Salvador remained heavily concentrated, even by Latin American standards, in the hands of a small and cohesive elite.

The slaughter of 1932 allowed for the installation of decades of military rule. The Hernández Martínez government, an old-style military caudillo regime, gave way to institutionalization. Military governments ruled the country more or less continuously until the 1990s, providing real stability that ensured the acquiescence of agrarian elites. Though the partnership between landowners and the military could be unpleasantly contentious, it was successful enough to allow for considerable independence for the armed forces, which alternated between various reform agendas. In the 1950s and 1960s, army units and the various police forces benefited from improved training and more modern military practices, especially in their intelligence capabilities. Yet continuity prevailed, represented in the centrality of the Guardia Nacional, the rural police force that from the 1920s to 1979 carried out most repressive violence in rural areas. Of key importance to the later period of slaughter was General José Alberto Medrano. From his perch in the Guardia, Medrano became known in the 1960s as the father of Salvadoran counterinsurgency by creating both ORDEN (a network of paramilitary groups) and the Salvadoran National Security Agency, ANSESAL. He bestrode both sides of the fight against those deemed subversive, the legal and the extra-legal, and connected them.

This regime, though it had dominated El Salvador for decades, began to face serious opposition in the 1970s, with the rise of the guerrilla movement, the Frente Farabundo Martí para la Liberación Nacional (Farabundo Martí National Liberation Front), or the FMLN. Events also demonstrated that even El Salvador could never muster a monolithically murderous elite. In 1972, the military and their oligarchic allies refused to accept the electoral victory of José Napoleón Duarte, candidate for the Christian Democratic

Party. Rather they arrested and tortured Duarte before finally sending him into exile. Yet in the later 1970s, even as El Salvador's rulers encountered an armed opposition with serious teeth, the Salvadoran military demonstrated that it had its own elements advocating for social transformation. In 1979, relatively progressive officers formed a junta to find a solution. They proposed a land reform program, and even invited Duarte to return and serve as president. But their efforts were quickly shattered by the more strident elements of the Salvadoran elites (both within and beyond the government), who launched an overt campaign of mass political murder against the opposition. The return to the overt and extended practice of political murder began in fits, with a series of massacres. A first one occurred in 1972, after the aborted election. Another took place in 1974 when guardsmen killed twenty organized peasants in the village of San Vicente. In 1975, government forces attacked over two thousand university students (who were protesting the Miss Universe Pageant being held in El Salvador) with machine guns, killing thirty-seven. In 1977, the government repeatedly attacked people protesting electoral fraud. This became something of a turning point toward out-and-out murderous brutality. Though the FMLN guerrilla "final offensive" of 1980 made some headway in rural zones, it largely collapsed when its urban component faltered. The Salvadoran security forces and their death squad allies crippled an essentially general strike of workers, peasants, and students in San Salvador with the murder of thousands of people.

This led to the bloodiest period, between 1980 and 1983. Thousands were killed, from the high profile to the unknown. Attorney General Mario Zamora Rivas, a representative of the left wing of the Christian Democratic Party, who had risen in influence after Duarte's exile, was killed in his home in February, 1980. The next month, the archbishop of El Salvador, Oscar Romero, was gunned down while he celebrated mass after he publicly and forcefully condemned the regime's massacres. For good measure, his killers also murdered dozens of mourners paying their respects at his funeral, using hidden bombs and gunmen. In November, the entire leadership of the nonviolent left was murdered, together, hours before they were to hold a joint news conference to discuss a plan for a negotiated end to the escalating civil war. In December, Catholic Church women from the United States, Maryknoll Sisters Maura Clarke and Ita Ford, a Ursuline Sister, Dorothy Kazel, and their lay missionary companion, Jean Donovan, were last seen when their car was stopped at an army checkpoint. They were subsequently raped and killed. Many rightwing Catholics alleged that the sisters were "assisting" the "Communist" insurgents, and thus had it coming. Even reformist army officers who spoke against the terror were eliminated. Close to twelve thousand people were murdered in 1980 alone, hunted down as individuals by urban death squads, or massacred wholesale in the countryside. In 1981, the number of people killed increased to over sixteen thousand, starting with the impudent murders of José Rodolfo Viera, head of the Salvadoran land reform effort, and Michael Hammer and Mark Pearlman, his American advisers, in the San Salvador Sheraton Hotel. Government forces, as well as more clandestine paramilitary groups, made up mostly of moonlighting military personnel, now overtly, and indiscriminately, targeted rural inhabitants of the regions where the FMLN guerrillas could count on the most support.

December 1981 saw the infamous massacre at El Mozote, demonstrating that even children were considered threats worthy of elimination. (It is worth noting that while government forces or their proxies killed over five thousand people each year in 1982 and 1983, the Reagan administration asked Congress in 1983 to send more aid to El Salvador.)

Central to the process was Roberto D'Aubuisson, a protégé of General Medrano and founder of the right-wing ARENA party. D'Aubuisson was known to his opponents (and the U.S. embassy staff) as Blowtorch, given his methods of interrogation. Often characterized as an energetic, heavy drinking, heavy smoking, agitated man who could not sit still, D'Aubuisson spoke rapidly and often about his hatred of communists. Officers who served with him called him a psychopath. A Salvadoran army officer, graduate of the School of the Americas, and specialist in military intelligence, D'Aubuisson was deputy director of ANSESAL before he was kicked out of the military for plotting in the attempted Coup of 1979, and because of his open connections to death squads. Indeed, he was the key figure in those circles, and was widely believed to have ordered the assassination of Archbishop Romero. He maintained close connections to hardliners in the military, and during his 1984 run for president he loved to hack open watermelons with a machete. These, he said, were symbols for the Christian Democrats—green on the outside (their party color), and red on the inside (thus sending a not so subtle message about their probable fate.) He also appeared regularly on Salvadoran television, known around the U.S. embassy as the "Major Bob Show," in spots paid for by moneyed Salvadorans living abroad. He used these segments to denounce "traitors" and "communists," many of whom were murdered in short order.

In 1984, peace talks were initiated, but they fell apart in 1986. In 1987, there were new attempts at peace talks, and, in 1988, the George H. W. Bush administration in Washington D.C. began to increase pressure on El Salvador to cut back on political murder. Yet in 1989 the military ratcheted up repression once again. The attorney general Roberto García Alvarado and the minister José Antonio Rodríguez Porth were both assassinated, neighborhoods of San Salvador suspected of FMLN sympathies were bombed, and the Jesuit leaders of the Universidad de Centro America were murdered. By the early 1990s military stalemate and increasing international pressure led to a "peace" process, but the political spectrum had been shifted definitively rightward. The Salvadoran elites were satisfied that political murder had done its job and were content to control the country through the ARENA party. The recent rise to national power by the FMLN, and its subsequent reelection, will offer evidence about the degree to which things might have changed in El Salvador.

GUATEMALA

After Colombia, the killing fields of Guatemala during the 1960s, 1970s, and 1980s rank second in absolute numbers of people butchered, though some would argue that it ranks first in sheer state-sponsored brutality. The process there (as in Colombia referred to as the Violencia) witnessed the murder of over two hundred thousand people, 83 percent of whom were Maya. Guatemala has a long history of extreme inequality, social injustice, elite privilege, and violence deployed to perpetuate the system. As late as the 1940s, land remained the principal font of riches and social position. The landed elite was small and exclusive. After World War II the economy began to diversify and the middle sectors grew, along with their political aspirations. But the bulk of the population remained Indian and Ladino (known in other Latin American countries as Mestizo), and by regional standards, poor. Subsistence farming was still the norm for a large percentage.[13]

Guatemala at the midpoint of the twentieth century, however, seemed to be on a different path. The period of 1944–1954 is known as the Guatemalan Revolution. A revolt of progressive young army officers in 1944 cleared the way for the election of Juan José Arévalo as president in 1945. An intellectual who had been exiled in Argentina, Arévalo's administration opened space for urban workers, peasant groups, and the Communist party to push more effectively for higher wages and enforcement of labor laws. In 1950, Guatemalans elected a reform-minded army colonel, Jacobo Arbenz, who quickly pressed forward to mobilize his government's popular supporters. These were easily the most democratic governments in Guatemalan history. Especially important was the fact that Arbenz greatly expanded efforts at land reform. To the horror of the Guatemalan landholding class, the not particularly radical agrarian reform law of 1952 sought to expropriate uncultivated territory. In particular, it threatened property owned by the Boston-based United Fruit Company. In response, U.S. secretary of state John Foster Dulles (who had close ties to United Fruit) encouraged the CIA, led by his younger brother Allen Dulles, to organize a counterrevolution and "liberate" Guatemala.

The 1954 invasion of mercenary forces was "led" by Col. Carlos Castillo Armas, but put together and financed by the CIA. In a rabidly anticommunist movement, Castillo and his followers set out to destroy all elements of the 1944–1954 period. Any protest, popular mobilization, or opposing view was labeled "communist." One could argue that the U.S.-led effort, known as Operation PBSUCCESS, was a rather pathetic and clownish affair, but what made it a success was the fact that most of the military and a large part of the civilian elites in Guatemala were determined that the counterrevolution should prevail. Indeed, Operation PBSUCCESS largely failed in its objectives, and in the end the U.S. military bluffed and threatened an invasion. This threat was enough to push the Guatemalan military into ousting the Arbenz government.

In the years that followed, a traditional Guatemalan military government sought to return the country to its pre-1944 parameters. This was not easy, given the high degree of popular mobilization achieved during the Arévalo-Arbenz years. In addition, the Cuban Revolution of 1959 created rising hopes, tensions, and fears, which only heightened the anticommunist obsessions of the Guatemalan military and parts of the elite throughout the region. Yet even as the Guatemalan government bowed to U.S. pressure regarding policy toward Cuba, more than 20 percent of the military rebelled. On November 13, 1960, Guatemalans witnessed a rare military coup attempt from the Left, carried out by four hundred officers who were tired of the corrupt government of General Miguel Ydígoras Fuentes. These men looked back favorably on the 1944–1954 period, and were also opposed to the training of Cuban exiles for the upcoming Bay of Pigs invasion. Though the initial movement was crushed, the revolt represented the beginning of almost four decades of guerrilla insurgency, as well as a massive buildup of the Guatemala army, which reached forty-eight thousand troops at the conflict's height. The survivors, especially Marco Antonio Yon Sosa and Luís Turcios Lima, escaped and organized a leftist guerrilla group called the Movimiento Revolucionario de Noviembre 13 (MR-13) in early 1961. The MR-13 soon joined the new guerrilla forces of the Guatemalan communist party (known as the Partido Guatemalteco del Trabajo, the PGT) and by 1963 had created the FAR Fuerzas Armandas Rebeldes (the

Rebel Armed Forces), which was influenced by the Cubans. In March 1963, Colonel Enrique Peralta Azurdia, Minister of Defense, deposed Ydígora, suspended the constitution, closed down the congress, and created a more overt and stridently anticommunist military regime. Now the military displaced other sectors of the elite, and started to spend a much larger percentage of the Guatemalan budget, and got into the habit of asserting its own agenda.

After 1963 the guerrillas became more active but were matched by a vigorous military response. Over the next twenty years, waves of popular mobilization and resistance were met by ever more brutal waves of repression. Since the military and its elite civilian backers faced a guerrilla opposition that included former Guatemalan army officers, and at times exhibited a high degree of competence, the Guatemalan government quickly moved toward outright repression. After 1966 the military's campaign of political murder against urban activists and peasant communities became a largely autonomous affair, uncontrollable by the occasional civilian president. This dynamic built pressure throughout the 1970s, and culminated in the mass slaughter of the early 1980s.

In 1965 Guatemala had a new constitution and in 1966 a civilian president, Julio César Méndez Montenegro. Méndez Montenegro, a lawyer and university professor, was backed by the Communist PGT and coalition of opposition groups. But the military retained its autonomy in the fight against guerrilla forces and other "subversive" groups. Indeed, in the week following the election, twenty-eight PGT activists were disappeared, as were law students who sought their release. The military, obviously, had no trouble intensifying their counterrevolutionary terror. In urban areas, death squads became a key element of their war. Mano Blanca, death squad of the right-wing Movimiento de Liberación Nacional (the Movement of National Liberation), or the MLN, employed military and police personnel. Leftist intellectuals, PGT leaders, and labor activists were murdered. The 1966–1968 years were a very bloody period, especially dangerous for anyone who had espoused any notion of reform, and not just on the Left. After 1968 the military aimed at popular leaders in particular. By 1970 the FAR was largely defeated, and in 1970, Colonel Carlos Arana Osorio, the leader of the Army's counterinsurgency effort, was "elected" president. From November 1970 to February 1972, Arana declared a state of siege and suspended the constitution. In rural areas police powers were stripped from elected civilians and given to military commissioners. There was open repression at the University of San Carlos.

Yet even as Arana's campaign was waning, civil society began to reassert itself. Labor disputes by railroad workers, teachers, and the countries' few industrial workers were on the rise, as were a growing number of militant student demonstrations. Campesino struggles over land issues increased as well. Old urges for popular mobilization, last manifested during the 1940s and 1950s, reemerged, built on peasant unions and literacy drives, and flowered into participation in municipal politics. President General Kjell Laugerud García allowed a small political opening, so that labor organization and political mobilizations expanded to a degree not known since 1954, accompanied by a lower degree of state violence. By 1976, more than five hundred rural cooperatives had a combined membership of one hundred thirty-two thousand, 60 percent of which was in the rural highlands. These co-ops and unions (the main collective tools to improve the lot of Indians) brought together Indian rural laborers, non-Indian merchants, and even some non-Indian landowners. This activity culminated in demonstrations of support for the strike of the Ixtahuacán miners and the workers at the Pantaleón plantation sugar refinery in 1977. In what came to be known as The Glorious March of the Miners of Ixtahuacán, one hundred thousand people marched to protest in front of the presidential palace. What is more, a new guerrilla movement emerged in 1972, the Ejército Guerrillero de los Pobres (Guerrilla Army of the Poor), or EGP, led by survivors of the defeated guerrilla movements of the 1960s. The EGP opened three named fronts: Ho Chi Minh; Augusto César Sandino; Ernesto Che Guevara. Though still obviously Marxist in ideology, the new movement was more *indigenista* in orientation, to appeal to a wider range of supporters. There was also a marked shift from the eastern highlands, since the successful counterinsurgencies of the 1960s had driven out popular movements there, to the more populated, and Mayan, western highlands. The EGP was joined a few years later by the Organización Revolucionario del Pueblo en Armas (Revolutionary Organization of the People in Arms), or the ORPA. Yet, as in Colombia, political opening seems to have led to repression. Death squads committed sixty-one murders in August 1977 alone.

It was thus no surprise that by the late 1970s the bloody counterrevolution had been kicked back into high gear. Even the February 4, 1976, earthquake, which left twenty-three thousand dead, seventy-five thousand injured, and one million homeless, was used for the army's purposes. As aid poured in, the army used relief efforts to extend its control over rural areas. By this time, Guatemala was in the grip of a brutal civil war, pitting an ever more bloodthirsty military against a determined guerrilla resistance based in Mayan territories. And thanks to the expanding productivity of Guatemalan agriculture, the increasing value of rural property compounded the conflict. Indian communal land itself thus became an added incentive for army attacks. Many offensives against "subversives" were also driven by the desire of military personnel to expropriate Mayan land. The mass slaughters of the May 1978 massacre in Panzós, Alta Verapaz, and the July 1982 massacre at Finca San Francisco in Nentón, Huehuetenango were both cases where campesinos did not have clear land titles.

This newly energized effort was the work of President General Romero Lucas García (1978–1982) who faced a more militant opposition, transit strikes, and talk of the "revolution" of 1978. He was also alarmed by the ongoing collapse of the Somoza regime in Nicaragua. He thus initiated an extremely bloody reaction, perhaps Guatemala's most intense period of political murder. This was made clear when on January 31, 1980, protesters occupied the Spanish embassy in Guatemala City to gain world attention for the violent repression of the Guatemalan opposition. The García government decided to use force, no matter what the cost. They threw incendiaries into the ambassador's office, where the protesters were holding their captives. State-sponsored killing rose steadily throughout 1978, 1979, and 1980. In 1978–1979, the death squads were especially active in Guatemala City, and other towns, with the killing of select leaders of the opposition, and intellectuals. In 1980, the effort broadened to the base of students and urban population still active in popular politics of opposition, and affiliated with the PGT and like-minded groups. People fled into exile, or hiding, or joined the guerrillas. But the killings really took off in 1981–1982. And though killing dropped in 1983, it remained significant for the rest of the decade.

At the end of 1981, killings shifted to the countryside of the Mayan western highlands. The EGP and other guerrilla groups expanded their operations. The surge of guerrilla war in the region encouraged the Guatemalan Left to intensify its struggle. In early 1981, the EGP launched their most ambitious offensive, and in 1982 the various guerrilla armies combined in the Unidad Revolucionaria Nacional Guatemalteca (the Guatemalan National Revolutionary Unity), or the URNG. Their strategy reaped the whirlwind and brought devastation because the guerrillas underestimated the likely counterrevolutionary response. Where the guerrillas went, the army followed, and since the guerrillas could not hold or defend territory, the inhabitants of the region suffered. The military reacted with massive force and stationed entire brigades in rebel territory, which in turn deployed smaller, more mobile units. Government forces, predictably, tended to accuse Mayan villagers of collaboration, making them valid military targets. The army set out to defeat the guerrillas by attacking their local base of support with a bloody campaign of terror. In mid-1981, the army attacked rebels in the coffee regions of the west coast and in the food-producing zones near the capital. The military's push intensified beginning in November 1981, spreading into 1982 with Operación Ceniza (Operation Ashes). As the name implies, this was clearly a scorched-earth strategy. The army used massacres and the destruction of entire villages to dominate the Pan-American Highway, and then push to the Mexican border.

In March 1982, a coup replaced Lucas García with the dictatorship of General Efraín Ríos Montt, who took the offensive to new heights of brutality. He suspended the constitution and set up secret courts to condemn whomever he identified as subversive. Ríos Montt combined repression with heavy-handed forms of aid, with multiple strings attached, creating "model villages" where food was handed out for work, and for information on suspected guerrilla supporters among the many refugees displaced by the war. Americas Watch, recalling Tacitus, argued that his government brought desolation to the countryside "and called it peace." Ríos Montt also maintained violent pressure on urban groups. Ríos Montt was replaced by General Oscar Humberto Mejía Víctores in yet another coup in August 1983, though Mejía Víctores too allowed the more traditional indiscretions and urban death squad activity, an offensive that he intensified even further. Though Mejía Víctores eventually allowed for a transition back to civilian rule under Marco Vinicio Cerezo (elected in 1986) under a new constitution, the military and its death squad proxies continued their work with clear impunity. The 1987 "Year-End Offensive" directed its fury against the handful of places that still offered a tepid resistance.

In the 1990s, political murder activity fell from thousands a year to hundreds. There was now a growing human rights movement with various groups, a United Nations mission, and a government ombudsman for human rights, though the military continued to link human rights activists to guerrilla groups. And significant practice of political murder continued. In April 1998, bishop Juan Gerardi was bludgeoned to death in his home after he released a report in four volumes about the Violencia entitled "Guatemala: Nunca Más." Elections in 2003 and 2007 were haunted by political murders and threats of more.

HONDURAS

Honduras is often seen, along with Costa Rica, as a Central American "exception," enjoying lower levels of political violence than those emanating from the repressive governments of its "reactionary" and "despotic" neighbors in Central America. But for a few years it conformed to the region's political murder norm, albeit on a small scale. Between 1980 and 1992 (especially during the 1980 and 1984 period), a policy of political murder produced 179 desaparecidos. Tutored by Argentine specialists in the brutal and aggressive "Argentine Method," which ignored the rule of law, the Honduran military began targeting dissidents, though its most effective instrument was a U.S.-trained unit known as Battalion 3-16.[14]

Ronald Reagan's obsession with the "spread" of communism in Central America faulted Cuban and Soviet influences, rather than poverty, inequality, or the lack of political rights. He saw Honduras as a "bulwark against communism," and used it as a base of operations and a staging area for the Contras. Referred to as a sort of fixed "aircraft carrier," the country was jokingly known as the "U.S.S. Honduras," and was one of the most obvious cases of negative U.S. influence regarding use of political murder. Observers stress that human rights violations there were the direct result of U.S.-driven militarization. The United States provided huge amounts of aid to the Honduran government. In particular, U.S. support strengthened hardline elements of the military, and helped them to dominate political affairs. With allies among Honduras' civilian elite, members of the military rode the wave of U.S. financial assistance to become a powerful economic elite in their own right. For a relatively short time, the Honduran military superimposed the practice of political murder in a country with little tradition of political violence.

Before the 1970s, Honduran elites were known to negotiate and compromise with the opposition. There was less concentration of land ownership there than in El Salvador or Guatemala, and local economic elites were not in league with foreign interests in the banana and mining sectors. Finally, the military (a series of regional militias really) was not traditionally involved in repressive operations, and not such a consistent tool of the elite. After 1946, U.S. trainers began reorganizing and professionalizing the militias, and after 1963, the military launched a number of coups. Beginning in the 1980s, the military made a deal with sympathetic elements of the civilian leadership for even more power. Their leader, General Gustavo Alvarez Martínez, who had served as chief of the Fuerzas de Seguridad Pública (FUSEP), the national police under military control, was intent on ridding Honduras of communist subversives. Trained in Argentina himself, he was a big fan of the Argentine way. After August 1980, the government permitted the military to actively target political dissidents for repressive measures. Honduran civilian leaders, president and congress, gave them the legal cover to pursue dirty war with measures such as Decree 33 of 1982, an antiterrorism law that reclassified the ubiquitous and essential machete as a "weapon." Battalion 3-16 (also known by various names) employed U.S. trainers known as "Mr.

Bill" and "Mr. Mike." In August 1980, twenty-five Hondurans were trained in Texas by the CIA and FBI. Back in Honduras, they received more training by Argentines in torture and disappearing techniques.

In April 1984, General Alvarez was deposed by younger and more nationalistic officers, who were angered over their diminished prospects for promotion and by Alvarez's subservient stance toward the United States. He was shoved, at gun point, onto a waiting flight for Miami. International pressure combined with the fact that U.S. aid was drying up to move the military back to less-activist roles. Honduras returned to something of its former "exceptionalism," though many veterans of Battalion 3-16 remained active-duty officers. And with the killings generated by the "election" of Porfirio "Pepe" Lobo in November of 2009, Hondurans saw what could be the beginning of a new phase of political murder.

MEXICO

Nominally democratic and comparatively stable, postrevolutionary Mexico was nevertheless no stranger to the practice of political murder. Like Colombia, Mexico has long been known as an "authoritarian democracy." And while Mexico's use of political murder during the 1970s and 1980s was of a lower magnitude than some other cases, the Mexican experience provides telling and significant parallels.

In the postrevolution years, elites used political murder consistently in Mexico, especially on the local level. The late 1960s and 1970s saw both national level turmoil and a localized dirty war in the state of Guerrero. More recently, massacres in Chiapas and Oaxaca have linked Mexico to the general rise of paramilitarism. The country also periodically experiences dramatic high-level political murders, such as those that rocked the country in 1993 and 1994. Mexico also allows a high degree of impunity for the perpetrators of political murder (begging comparisons with the more notorious cases of Colombia, Guatemala, and El Salvador). Also, many of the "drug" murders of late have political overtones, as in Colombia. It is certainly true that Mexico's admittedly "authoritarian" democracy has somewhat reined in the use of political murder. Mexico is also not given to military governments. Yet taken as a whole, Mexico's tradition is really no less bloody than that of its neighbors, and is certainly no less effective in silencing critics. It has a lengthy and complicated tradition of political murder.[15]

The "Porfiriato" of Profirio Díaz (1876–1911) was the veritable archetype for the Latin American model of strongman, personalistic rule—the granddaddy of them all, the Stronato, the Banzerato, the Trujillato, and many others. And like so many copies of Versailles, they all suffer in comparison. The Pax Porfirina was hardly a police state, given that it was based in good part on cooptation of competing interests and bribery. Yet Díaz selectively repressed dissidents of all stripes, from Yaquis and Maya Indians on the peripheries, to urban workers, to uppity local leaders. He deployed his band of thugs, his "bravi," in Mexico City, and a mounted police force known as the Rurales in the countryside. Nonetheless, the leap from the relative tranquility of the Pax Porfiriana into the inferno of revolutionary violence after 1910 was dramatic and lasting. The upheavals of the revolution remade Mexico, and political murder had its impact. Various agents of change, including Francisco Madero, Pancho Villa, and Emiliano Zapata, were among its victims.

After the Revolution and ensuing civil war among the winners, the central government slowly re-established political order and stability on the national level. Between 1917 and 1929, the central government oversaw a winnowing process through which revolts from within the revolutionary army were repeatedly put down. The postrevolutionary one-party state also began its evolution during the so called Maximato of Plutarco Eliás Calles between 1924 and 1934, first as the Partido Nacional Revolucionario (National Revolutionary Party), or PNR, and later renamed as the long-lived Partido Revolucionario Institutional (Institutional Revolutionary Party), or PRI. Calles served first as president, and then moved behind the scenes as the ruling caudillo. These years saw the development of two quasi-fascist death squads, known as the Camisas Rojas (the Red Shirts) and the Camisas Doradas (the Gold Shirts). Calles also oversaw the bloody elimination (by firing squad) of fourteen senior military officers who had conspired against him in 1927. Thus after 1929 politics on the national level were stable, if not particularly democratic, though the Mexican state's authoritarian nature was mitigated somewhat under President Lázaro Cárdenas (1934–1940). Cárdenas expropriated the foreign-owned petroleum companies and carried out significant land reforms, giving the national government considerable popular legitimacy.

Yet, at the local level, the practice of politics was less controlled, and political violence continued to play an important role. What is more, in the 1920s and 1930s the Federal Army did not drive local violence. This was the preview of local caciques, police enforcers, pistoleros, and paramilitary groups called "defensas sociales." Indeed, the revolution had primed the pump for the continued use of political murder. It provided plenty of arms and people skilled in their use who were inclined to employ violence for political purposes, some for progressive ends, some for repression. This continuation of an old tradition contributed to the period's general messiness, with plenty of struggles among factions.

Between the 1940s and the 1960s, Mexico's population doubled, becoming more urban and decidedly younger on average, with more than half the population under twenty years of age. By 1970, the Mexican economy was six times larger than in 1940. The postrevolutionary political stability was breaking down, however, as the children of the middle and upper classes were ready for a more open and democratic society. Many also railed against growing economic inequality. The Mexican political establishment responded by clamping down with more overt authoritarianism. (This was hardly unprecedented, as even during the relatively stable years of the Pax del PRI there had been unrest, resistance, strikes, protests, and repression). In December 1960, the army crushed a protest in Chilpancingo (the capital of Guerrero), leaving eighteen dead. And the government of Gustavo Díaz Ordaz (1964–1970) in particular brooked no political dissent. He led offensives against internal PRI efforts to democratize, and also annulled elections won by the opposition Partido Acción Nacional (National Action Party), or PAN, in northern Mexico.

In fact, Díaz Ordaz's government perpetuated one of Mexico's most infamous acts of repression. In 1968, on the eve of Mexico's first experience as host to the Olympic Games, university and secondary students expressed growing and widespread frustration with the political status quo by mobilizing massive protests in Mexico City. Ten days before the opening ceremony, police and army troops opened fire on protesting students in the Tlatelolco section of the city. Between three and four hundred people died in what came to be known as the Tlatelolco Massacre. Thousands more were wounded or arrested. Some observers claimed that thousands were killed, and while such estimates are not generally considered credible, they are no less absurd than the initial government estimates of "4 dead and 20 wounded." The later official toll of forty-nine was also contemptible.

Yet demands for change would not be forestalled. While order was restored in the streets, the slaughter of the sons and daughters of the political and economic elites was a measure that drove home the need for reform. And many of the young wanted more dramatic and immediate change. Also, there were larger numbers of desperate and landless people in the countryside than before the land reforms of the 1930s. These factors combined to produce a rural guerrilla movement in the state of Guerrero. Many young and educated Mexicans, like so many throughout Latin America, looked to the example of the Cuban Revolution. Though Che Guevara had been killed in Bolivia in 1967, his reputation as a guerrilla fighter continued to inspire imitation. The Partido de los Pobres (Party of the Poor), or PdlP, under Lucio Cabañas Barrientos, emerged in the 1970s in Guerrero. Like groups in Argentina, it financed its activities with bank robberies and kidnappings. Guerrero, a place of extremes, had a booming tourist industry (symbolized by Acapulco) in close proximity to crushing poverty, local government characterized by authoritarianism, and a vibrant resistance movement. Guerrero was also a focal point of radical teacher activism, with a tradition known as Guerrero bronco. Following the lead of the Movimiento Revolucionario del Magistradoa (Revolutionary Teachers Movement), or the MRM, a radical teachers' group that arose in Mexico City in the 1950s, teachers led the charge for improved economic well-being of the populace, as well as improved local- and state-level democratic institutions. In 1967, Cabañas was fired from his job as a rural teacher because of his organizing activism. When federal police shot and killed protesters demanding his rehire, Cabañas fled to the hills and started various guerrilla groups. He was killed in a shootout with police and army in July 1974.

In answer to such activity, the Mexican government fought a regional dirty war in Guerrero. The armed Mexican Left of the 1960s and early 1970s was fragmented and weak, with limited followings. Groups such as the Movimiento de Acción Revolucionaria, the Comandos Lacandones, the Liga Comunista 23 de Septiembre, and the Frente Urbana Zapatista were largely exterminated by the end of the term of President Luis Echeverría Alvarez (1970–1976). Echeverría had been the Interior Minister under Díaz Ordaz, and had a big hand in the Taltelolco massacre (indeed many held him directly responsible), but he played a double game. He made a show of opening the political system, for example, promising to make up with Mexico's students and recognize university independence, yet at the same time he was busily carrying out the bulk of Mexico's dirty war. As an example, on June 10, 1971, in an early Mexican paramilitary group, the Halcones (Falcons), attacked a student demonstration in Mexico City, killing twenty-five and wounding others. Echeverría's commitment to making peace with students, it seems, was somewhat less than heartfelt. The National Human Rights Commission of 1990 estimated that at least 350 people were disappeared between 1974 and 1978, but there were probably more, and at least 143 prisoners were killed.

But Mexico's experience with political murder did not end in the 1970s. The year 1994 saw multiple assassinations of presidential candidates and high-profile politicians, as well as the beginnings of a massive paramilitary counteroffensive against the Ejército Zapatista de Liberación

Nacional (Zapatista Army of National Liberation), or the EZLN. The so-called Zapatista movement carried out an uprising of sorts in Chiapas, resisting free trade and NAFTA, the North American Free Trade Agreement. The Zapatistas were not a particularly violent outfit, and more interested in generating international media exposure. Yet reaction to it was quite violent. At least twelve paramilitary groups emerged in response to the Zapatistas, groups that have committed more than fifteen thousand murders (and counting). And it is also clear that many of Mexico's current "drug" murders are also political in nature.

The postrevolutionary Mexican state and national elites, in contrast to the Southern Cone countries in the 1960s and 1970s, steered clear of military governments and their so-called "bureaucratic authoritarian" forms of governance. Rather, like Colombia, Mexico was known for civilian rule, and even welcomed political refugees fleeing other country's dirty wars. In broad terms, Mexico did commit itself to social reform and popular political participation. Alan Knight argues that its "official ideology was relatively progressive, enlightened, inclusionary and reformist." But it is also true that Mexico did not follow its neighbors into such overtly repressive measures "because it did not need to," given that "it already possessed a more discreetly authoritarian system." Knight notes that "Mexican political violence appears less extreme and significant, but that is partly because it is more discreet, anonymous, prolonged, and quotidian. It involves numerous small, often local, acts of violence, rather than massive, centralized campaigns of repression."[16] Often more freelance than official in its use of political murder, Mexico has long been good at using both carrots and sticks, and it continues to be so.

NICARAGUA

Nicaraguan history was marked between 1909 and 1932 by repeated and drawn out bouts of occupation by the U.S. Marine Corps. Under their tutelage, the Guardia Nacional evolved from a rural police force into a quasi-occupying army. The Somoza clan, making heavy use of political murder, controlled Nicaragua from the mid-1930s until the Sandinista Revolution of 1979. In the following years, elements of the old Guardia Nacional reemerged as a proxy army, the so-called Contras, originally trained by Argentine advisors, and ultimately funded and directed by the United States. The Contras were well known for their use of political murder.[17]

National politics in Nicaragua from 1911 to 1928 were dominated by Chamorrismo, the personal rule of Conservative Party caudillo and President Emiliano Chamorro, as well as by U.S. interests via the Marine Corps. Chamorrista Conservatives were generally obliging underlings for the United States through most of the period, but after his defeat in the 1923 election, Chamorro carried out a coup in October 1925. The Liberal Party revolted and waged a successful civil war from May 1926 to May 1927. The victorious Liberals then signed an accord that called for elections in November 1928, and for the establishment of the Guardia Nacional (to replace all the different caudillos' armed bands). Aware of their general unpopularity, and certain of electoral defeat, the Chamorristas pulled out all the stops in to scuttle the elections through the use of political murder. José María Moncada, the Liberal candidate, who was nevertheless elected president, also had close ties to the United States. The result was that the Liberals splintered as they simultaneously engaged in a popular struggle against Conservatives and a nationalist movement to repel foreign interlopers.

Thus, after 1927 the marines and the Guardia encountered a determined nationalistic guerrilla opposition led by dissident Liberal leader Augusto César Sandino. Counterinsurgency efforts against Sandino's followers were brutal, given that he and his cohorts were classified by the U.S. government as "bandits" and were pointedly not identified as legitimate combatants. Sandino's guerrillas thus did not receive the few considerations afforded by the recognized rules of war. What is more, people living in the regions where Sandino operated were also considered lawful targets for the marines and the Guardia. In these operations, political murder was viewed as a useful practice against the insurgents. Indiscriminate attacks on civilian men, women, and children, it was believed, would generate fear and undermine popular support. The Guardia and their tutors from the marines would also burn homes, destroy crops, and kill livestock. Ultimately, however, these tactics did not succeed in quelling the rebellion. Sandino and his fighters fought the government forces to a standstill (also using terror tactics), and continued to harass the marines and the Guardia until the U.S. withdrawal in 1933.

With the return of Nicaraguan sovereignty, Sandino called a ceasefire and switched his efforts to the political realm. Unfortunately, command of the Guardia was handed to the brutal, shrewd, and ambitious Anastasio Somoza García, who, after a period of maneuvering, ordered his men to arrest and then murder Sandino in 1934. Though unable to defeat them in the 1927–1933 war, Somoza was finally able to exterminate Sandino's now leaderless forces. With Sandino out of the way, Somoza could overthrow the elected government and make himself president. Somoza established a familial regime that endured until 1979. Never particularly popular with Nicaraguans, Somoza could rely on his control of the Guardia, and his slavish devotion to U.S. interests, to hold onto power. Even his assassination in 1956 could not shake the family's control of Nicaragua. Somoza García's eldest son, Luis, became president, and leadership of the Guardia passed to his youngest son, Anastasio Somoza Debayle. When Luis died of a heart attack in 1967, Anastacio (known as the "Last Marine" because of his training at the U.S. Military academy at West Point[18]) became president, and held on to his spot as jefe of the Guardia Nacional. Less politically astute than either his father or his brother, Anastacio Somoza Debayle was more inclined to rely on repressive force to maintain control. Yet under all the Somozas, Guardia recourse to violence and murder became routine. The Guardia became the controlling force of Nicaraguan life, combining all the powers of the military, police, and customs collection in one corrupt institution. Separated from the general population, with its own stores, schools, and even hospitals, it became an elite unto itself.

In reaction, a group calling themselves the Sandanistas (taking their name from the murdered leader) emerged in 1961. The original core was made up of young Marxist militants who, inspired by Cuba, left the old Soviet-affiliated socialist party, the PSN, and formed the Frente Sandanista de Liberación Nacional (Sandinista National Liberation Front), or FSLN, to wage guerrilla war. They had little success in the 1960s but gained traction in the 1970s as the Somoza regime became increasingly brutal and unpopular. In the end, the viciousness of the Somoza regime unified the growing opposition, and thus necessitated evermore repressive methods. As the Guardia turned more and more to indiscriminate murder and "disappearing," Argentine advisors and trainers were invited to teach the lessons of their own dirty war. (The Argentines even stayed on in the region after Somoza fell, and laid the foundations for the Contras.)

Pedro Joaquín Chamorro, scion of the old elite clan and editor of the opposition newspaper *La Prensa*, was assassinated in 1978 (even though Chamorro could in no way be called a leftist). Also, in September 1978, in the face of open revolt in the urban areas, the Guardia shifted its focus from the countryside, and resorted to bombing raids against the cities. Chomorro's murder, as well as the general heavy-handedness of Somoza Debayle's approach, helped create the final coalition that would bring the Somoza clan down, demonstrating the limits of political murder. An excellent example of the regime's actions at this tipping point was the murder on tape of a U.S.

television journalist, ABC correspondent Bill Stewart. He was taken from his car, laid on the ground, and shot in the back as his horrified camera crew watched (and filmed) from another car. The eighteen-month war in 1978–1979 produced an FSLN victory. Somoza fled. Over fifty thousand died in the struggle, or roughly 2 percent of the population.

Since the old regime had been defeated unconditionally, the role of creating and directing a counterrevolution fell to outsiders. Building on the work of the Argentine military, with their creation of the Legión 15 de Septimebre, the United States quite naturally took up the Nicaraguan challenge. In July 1979, the CIA sent a series of aircraft to Managua to transport select elements of the Guardia into exile in Miami and other points north (one bore Red Cross insignia). These men would serve as the foundation of the Contras. Under the Carter administration, the United States began by funneling over a million dollars to opposition groups in Nicaragua. But under the Reagan administration, which came into office in early 1981, the United States really began to play the game seriously. Reagan and his advisors were obsessed with preventing the creation of a "second Cuba." This was not a direct offensive (as against Sandino), but a proxy war, funded by plenty of cash from a compliant U.S. Congress, combined with extreme economic pressure. Vernon Walters was sent to Argentina and Honduras to drum up a "coalition" of support. Tens of thousands of dollars found their way through Argentine military intelligence channels to mercenary forces. The effort was meant to destabilize the Sandanista government, or even better, cause it to overreact and discredit itself by becoming the repressive regime Reagan and company claimed it was. The Sandanista government, led by Daniel Ortega, however, was overall rather pragmatic and moderate. It rebuilt the army and used a mixed economy and social reform to garner deep grass roots support.

Known among U.S. intelligence operatives as "the project," the covert war began to take shape in the spring of 1981. Drawing on anti-Sandinista groups of Nicaraguan exiles in Miami and parts of Central America, the CIA laid the foundation for a paramilitary apparatus. Training camps of questionable legality were established in Florida, Texas, and California, while command of the operation emanated from the U.S. embassy in Tegucigalpa, Honduras, under Ambassador John Negroponte. Generically code-named U.S. agents supervised Contra operations and put together the various groups. (Many landless peasants of the north were drawn into the Contras, who manipulated their long-standing distrust of the capital.) The two most important were the FDN (Fuerza Democrática Nicaraguense), based in Honduras, and the ARDE (Alianza Revolucionaria Democrática) in Costa

Rica. The ARDE was founded by former Sandinistas, and as such, was useful for U.S. propaganda purposes. Yet by April 1984 the CIA had cut it off for refusing to toe the line laid down in Langley. The larger FDN, recipient of most U.S. aid, had a leadership made up for the most part of former Guardia officers. Called "freedom fighters" by the Reagan administration, even its members later admitted that the organization followed CIA orders. From its bases inside Honduras, the FDN made raids into northern Nicaragua. Their strategy of counterrevolutionary harassment amounted to brutal attacks on Nicaraguan infrastructure and its citizens. Though never a true insurgent threat to the Sandanista government, since it could never point to broad popular support, the Contras' forte was decimating small villages and murdering unarmed civilians. By early 1986, the Nicaraguan government estimated that thirty-six hundred Nicaraguans had been killed, and four thousand more wounded. An additional five thousand had been kidnapped. Human rights organizations chronicled the FDN's tendency to murder medical volunteers and other aid personnel, and summarily execute prisoners. The CIA also carried out its own raids on infrastructure, using Latin American mercenaries from El Salvador, Honduras, Chile, Argentina, Ecuador, and Bolivia. These operations were then claimed by the Contras (at CIA insistence). The most infamous operation was the mining of Nicaragua's harbors in 1984.

Violeta Barrios Torres de Chamorro, wife of the murdered publisher, led a political opposition to the Sandinista government and finally won the presidential election of 1990. Ortega and the FSLN gave up power. In a similar pattern to El Salvador, political violence and repression created the conditions for an anti-Sandinista political victory at the polls.

PANAMA

Even more than Honduras, Panama has been known for its long and especially intimate relationship with the U.S. military.[19] During the nineteenth century Panama was a state and later a department of Colombia. It gained its independence in 1903 thanks to U.S. "assistance," provided because of Colombian government intransigence in the face of U.S. strategic plans. The United States was then free to build the canal it wanted. The United States controlled the Canal Zone and the commercial oligarchy-dominated politics. This cozy relationship endured until the Panamanian military, known predictably as the Guardia Nacional, began in the 1950s to challenge these forces for power. The 1967 election of Arnulfo Arias Madrid was a contest marked by fraud and violence. When he moved to reorganize the Guardia, it promptly ousted him after less than two weeks in office with a coup in October 1968. Lt. Colonel Omar Torrijos, who exhibited leftist but non-socialist pretensions, led the coup. Under its "Revolutionary Government," the Guardia carried out a number of measures designed to garner popular support—freezing prices on food, medicine, and other necessities, controlling rents, and recognizing squatters' rights to their property. Yet Torrijos could not abide any political dissent, and banned all political parties. The Guardia moved to crush all opposition, murdering and disappearing critics in the name of anticommunism. Torrijos had himself proclaimed "Maximum Leader of the Panamanian Revolution," but he died in a somewhat mysterious plane crash in 1981 (rumored by many to be a CIA assassination, and perhaps the work of his lieutenant, Manuel Noriega). Noriega, who Torrijos had called "my gangster," quickly gained control of the Guardia and renamed it the Panama Defense Forces, or PDF. Noriega had been trained in Peru and Panama (by U.S. operatives) in the arts of counterintelligence and psychological operations, and Torrijos had made him lieutenant colonel and chief of military intelligence. Noriega worked for the CIA in various capacities from the late 1950s through the 1980s, though he was never excited about working with the Contras. Noriega also became banker and money launderer to Colombian narcos, especially the Medellín cartel of Pablo Escobar. In 1983, Noriega promoted himself to general, and the Panamanian legislature declared him Chief Executive Officer of the government. Noriega allowed presidential elections in 1984, but when it was clear that former President Arias Madrid would win handily, Noriega blatantly ignored the count and installed his surrogate. His regime was infamous for its murder of government critic Hugo Spadafora, carried out as Noriega was becoming a less than stellar *cliente* for the Gringos.

Noriega's government was resisted politically by the Civic Crusade, a movement composed mostly of upper-class Panamanians, of largely European dissent, and backed by the George Herbert Walker Bush administration. Both Noriega and Torrijo were of "Zambo" dissent, local Panamanian parlance for mixed European, African, and Indian ancestry. Noriega and his followers mocked the Civic Crusade as the "*rabiblancos*," or "whitetails." He also sent PDF units, police, and paramilitaries to attack their rallies and kill their leaders. The "Dobermans" was the nickname for the "Company of Public Order," the special antiriot police squads, trained as paratroopers and special forces, who enjoyed "cracking heads." They wore green fatigues, blue berets, and shoulder patches depicting snarling Doberman Pinschers. The "Sapos" (Toads), as Noriega's intelligence agents and thugs were known, also acted as the "F-8" death squad. Finally, there were Noriega's "Dignity Battalions," paramilitary dirty war specialists in torture, kidnapping, and murder. Dobermans worked in tandem with the paras to harass Roberto Eisenmann, enemy of Noriega and publisher of *La Prensa*, and to attack and abduct other Civic Crusade leaders. In the 1989 presidential elections, all political groups united against Noriega in a unified ticket of Guillermo Endara for president, with Ricardo Arias Calderón and Guillermo "Billy" Ford as his first and second vice presidents. The Dignity Battalions, as stupidly brutal as Somoza's Guardia, attacked Endara's motorcade. Endara and vice president "Billy" Ford were beaten as journalists videotaped the encounter. After his bodyguards were killed, Ford fled on foot in a bloody shirt as Dignity Battalion members beat him with a metal pipe.

Noriega's man was outpolled by huge margins (even Noriega's own troops voted against him). Jimmy Carter, present as an election observer, denounced Noriega's efforts to steal the election. The United States recognized Endara, and soon thereafter ousted Noriega in 1989 with the massive U.S. invasion of Panama known as Operation Just Cause, in which as many as four thousand Panamanians died. Their bodies were quickly buried in mass graves by U.S. forces. After the establishment of U.S. control, political murders of dissidents and community leaders were rumored to continue with Gringo involvement.

PARAGUAY

Paraguay, much less surprisingly than, for example, Uruguay, has had significant experience with political murder, most notably under the military dictatorship of Alfredo Stroessner, which was itself a continuation of time-honored Paraguayan tradition. Before the 1990s, Paraguay knew little other than instability or dictatorial regimes, having long alternated between periods of chaos and authoritarian government. Paraguay is also somewhat more insular and culturally cohesive than other Latin American countries, given that most of its inhabitants, whether Indian, mestizo, or white, are bilingual in Spanish and Guaraní.[20]

Paraguay, even more than most Latin American nations, has historically had little real experience with democratic or constitutional governance. Beginning with its stable (even stagnant) period of postindependence rulers after 1811, dictatorial rule and absolute power became one pole of its norm, conforming to the most stereotypical Latin American extreme. Doctor José Gaspar Rodríguez de Francia, who held the office of president for life and took the title El Supremo, ruled for twenty-five years. His regime was followed by eighteen years under Carlos Antonio López, also a dictator for life and dubbed El Excelentisimo. López's son, Francisco Solano López was also an absolute dictator. He led Paraguay into the ruinous War of the Triple Alliance against Argentina, Brazil, and Uruguay and died in battle in 1870.

From 1870 to 1954 Paraguay conformed to another Latin American stereotype, with forty-four presidents in eighty-five years. Some came to power through fraudulent elections, but most just seized power, and were very likely thrown from power by force themselves. They typically ranged from slightly more popular, though still dictatorial, regimes that had some plebian support, to dictatorships that ruled in the service of the propertied elites. The years from 1904 to 1954 were particularly frothy; Paraguay had thirty-one presidents, and most were removed by coups and revolts. Lasting authoritarian stability was finally re-established under the regime of Alfredo Stroessner. The Stronato endured for over three decades, until it was finally overthrown in February 1989.

The period after Paraguay's victory over Bolivia in the Chaco war (1932–1935) was a time of potential social revolution, savage reaction, civil war, inept government, and political exhaustion. The country was ripe, especially given its history, for a strongman to step in and fill the void. Alfredo Stroessner was born in 1912. His father was a German immigrant from Bavaria, and his mother was from a wealthy Paraguayan family. The young Alfredo chose a military career, serving in the artillery during the Chaco War. After decisive action to save the government in the Civil War of 1947 (most of the professional officer corps went over to the unsuccessful rebels), he moved up the ranks quickly to become a very young brigadier in 1948. Stroessner was hard working, a soldier's soldier, a good leader of men, who was patient and skillful in the art of strategy. He came to control the military, and eventually (through intrigues and purges), the Colorado party, which served to mobilize civilian supporters. On these two pillars of power he could withstand all challengers for decades. His regime also deployed the selective use of repression and political murder.

In May 1954 Stroessner threw President Federico Chávez out in a coup. Running as the only candidate in a special election, Stroessner was elected president in July 1954. He was "elected" seven times in all, and he always won his contests by ridiculously huge margins. As the leader of the Colorado party, he rigged elections and dominated politics. In practice, Paraguay was a one-party state. After taking office for the first time, Stoessner declared what came to be a quasi-permanent state of siege (renewed every ninety days throughout his regime, and only nominally lifted during elections.) Stroessner was a strong anticommunist, and though perhaps a Nazi sympathizer, he became a devoted adjunct to United States. On balance, Paraguay became stable and economically prosperous under his rule. Stroessner encouraged economic growth and investment. He built the world's largest hydroelectric plant in Itaipu. Yet a huge percentage of Paraguayan GDP and the government's budget went to maintain the army and police, and he pursued very elite-friendly policies. (He also gave land to retired soldiers.) Under Stroessner, Paraguay had no income tax, and the smallest percentage of GDP spent on public projects in Latin America. He built roads and highways, and allowed a huge black market to operate, making the country a hub of smuggling.

Stroessner's regime employed illegal detention, torture, and political murder throughout. Waves of repression met periods of revolutionary activity, especially in the early 1960s and early to mid-1970s, given the influence of the Cuban revolution. The Stroessner system rested on a dual policy of political repression and murder to quiet any opposition (from the Right and the Left). He also successfully used bribes to tie other powerful interests to the status quo. This was the formula of most successful long-term caudillos. Evidence from the "Archive of Horror," discovered in 1992, detailed much of the history of Paraguay's participation in Operation Condor, as well as the activities of Pastor Coronel, chief of Stroessner's secret police, nicknamed the Pyragués ("hairy feet"). Stroessner reportedly listened on the phone as the secretary of the Paraguayan communist party was ripped apart with a chainsaw. It is important to note, however, that Stroessner and his long-in-power colleagues could rarely rely on coercion alone. Paraguay was never a total police state. While political murder was practiced fairly consistently, its use was somewhat random by design.

In 1988, after Stroessner had himself reelected yet again at age seventy-seven, fear in the military that one of his widely hated sons would succeed him led to a coup. Stroessner fled to Brazil, where he eventually died on August 16, 2006. Fittingly, this was the very day that the "Museum of Memory" opened in "La Técnica," the popular name of the secret torture facility housed at the old Dirección Nacional de Asuntos Técnicos in Asunción.

PERU

Peru presents an especially telling case. On the one hand, elites have stayed true to form and pursued repressive political murder to silence threats to their privileged role. This was especially evident during the administration of President Alberto Fujimori (1990–2000), under which the armed forces and other coercive elements of the Peruvian state moved against the typical messengers of change. These were killed, as in so many other countries, under the pretext of a righteous fight against subversion. On the other hand, Maoist guerrillas from the Sendero Luminoso (Shining Path) actually murdered a comparable number of people to the state security forces and their paramilitary allies.[21]

The late nineteenth and early twentieth century "Aristocratic Republic" in Peru gave way after the market crash of 1929 and the beginnings of the Great Depression to more earnest political struggles. The Alianza Popular Revolucionaria Americana, or APRA (also known as Aprismo), was founded by Victor Raúl Haya de la Torre in 1924 to be a pan-Latin American movement, but in the 1930s came to be a solidly Peruvian populist political party with nationalistic and anti-imperial leanings. On the left, Aprismo competed with the newly formed Peruvian Communist Party, the PCP, founded by intellectual José Carlos Mariátegui. Both parties faded in and out of legality from the 1930s to the 1950s. Haya de la Torre was elected president in 1962, but the military did not allow him to take office. Especially in its early years, Aprismo advocated democracy, equal rights for Latin America's indigenous peoples, and a grab bag of quasi-socialist economic policies—including state control of industry and land reform that would break up oligarchic latifundia in favor of communal land holdings. During its various periods of illegality, APRA was vigorously repressed and its adherents killed.

These currents on the left, however, were not without some influence. General Juan Velasco led a coup in 1968 that called its administration the Revolutionary Government of the Armed Forces. As president, he openly pushed a left-leaning program known as Peruanismo that sought social justice for Peruvians, recognized Quechua as an official language of the state, and advocated a land reform effort of expropriation and redistribution. Not in sync with most other Latin American military governments and their dirty wars, Peru's military regimes were (needless to say) rather atypical between 1968 and 1980. (Though while making space for leftist opinions, Velasco's government was known to harass his political opponents). His regime followed nationalistic and populist strategies more common in earlier decades, nationalizing some industries, installing protectionist trade barriers, and resisting draconian payment schedules for Peru's foreign debt. The Peruvian military also had much closer ties to the Soviet Union and Cuba than to the United States, purchasing more weapons and receiving more training from that quarter. Only in the 1990s did the War on Drugs finally bring Peru and the United States closer.

Peru also blazed its own trail in another important way. It was home to a revolutionary group that long practiced their own version of repressive political murder, with disastrous results. Strangely, the brutal Maoist guerrilla army of the Sendero Luminoso, led by Abimael Guzmán, a philosophy professor at San Cristóbal de Huamanga University in Ayacucho, actually began as a student organization and tiny breakaway group of former Communists in the 1970s. Known among his followers by his non de guerre, "Presidente Gonzalo," Guzmán expanded his influence to other universities, especially those in Huancayo and La Cantuta, as well as the National University of Engineering in Lima and the National University of San Marcos. After losing a series of student council elections, Guzmán and his followers began to look beyond the universities. In 1980, at the same moment that Peru's military government eased its grip and permitted elections for the first time since the late 1960s, the Shining Path chose to move in the other direction and began to pursue violent revolutionary struggle. Its first action was the symbolic seizure and burning of ballot boxes in Chuschi, a town in Ayacucho. The Shining Path expanded throughout the 1980s, particularly in the rural highlands of Ayacucho, Apurímac, and Huancavelica. It garnered early support among the largely subsistence peasantry by providing a political presence in regions historically ignored by state and federal government. It carried out so-called "popular" trials of cattle thieves and local merchants who were said to cheat farmers, often imposing bloody capital punishments. The newly elected civilian government first gave the impression that it was either uninterested in addressing the Shining Path's initiatives, or unable to do so. Then, when the government did react, the military intervened with its usual lack of finesse and arrested and tortured many local residents who had had nothing to do with Sendero. As the decade wore on, however, it became clear that the Shining Path's own brutality cost it popular support. It routinely assassinated leaders of rival leftist parties, as well as labor leaders, local politicians, and peasant leaders who opposed them. Sendero also carried out massacres, in retaliation against specific communities for attacks on their militants, such as the Lucanamarca massacre, in the province of Huancasancos, where they killed sixty-nine villagers, and the attack on Hauyllo, Ayacucho Department, where forty-seven peasants died, including fourteen children. Finally, Sendero also attacked the urban populations, especially of Lima, where they bombed electrical installations, political offices, government buildings, and even shopping malls.

On the political front, the first term of President Alan García (1985–1990, the first-ever APRA administration), was imploding. Elected at the age of thirty-six, García was the second youngest president in Latin American history. Hailed as the "Latin American John F. Kennedy," his early popularity quickly evaporated. Hyperinflation that went as high as 7,650 percent led to the repeated collapse of the Peruvian currency, while García's efforts to nationalize the insurance and banking sectors led to open warfare with the International Monetary Fund and financial isolation for Peru. As the situation became grave, with political crisis driven by scandals and talk of embezzlement, the García administration also seemed to opt for a political murder solution to the Sendero threat. At least sixteen hundred people were disappeared. Some reports linked the government to paramilitary forces of the Rodrigo Franco Command, though the extent of García's personal involvement was never clear. Yet despite the influence Sendero came to wield in large parts of Peru, especially in the center and south of the country, by the 1990s it was clearly unpopular with most Peruvians. Sendero murdered any who opposed them, including government administrators, local politicians, police officers, soldiers, workers, and peasants.

Enter President Alberto Fujimori, son of Japanese immigrants, whose government was broadly seen as a "civil dictatorship." His election in the 1990 election was post–Cold War, but Fujimori could still use the War on Drugs to cozy up to the United States in ways Peruvian governments had not done for decades. In conjunction with the military he carried out an "auto-coup" (self-coup) against his own government in 1992, closed down the Peruvian congress, purged the judiciary of judges he did not care for, and pushed through "antiterrorism" laws and amnesty for the armed forces. But Fujimori greatly benefited from the fact that, by 1991, 83 percent of Peruvians polled viewed the Sendero in exceedingly negative terms. Though this was clearly a more urban sampling, support was also soft in the countryside. Campesinos resented the Sendero's open disdain for indigenous traditions. The Sendero (who opposed any form of "capitalism") closed local markets in an attempt to economically strangle the cities and larger towns. These closures, however, severely affected small farmers. Rural folk also recoiled at the barbarity of the bloody punishments handed out by judges in the Sendero's "popular" trials, a feeling that was compounded by the Sendero's normal prohibition against the burial of anyone they executed. Finally, in a move that proved to be spectacularly hated, Sendero attempted to prohibit the consumption of alcohol in many communities.

Not surprisingly, Sendero's unpopularity led some campesinos to take up arms against them. Often with help from regional elites or the local and national government, they created paramilitary groups called "rondas" in the early 1980s. Though equipped only with castoff weapons from the military, rondas attacked the Senderistas. In 1991, President Fujimori legalized their status and, in a move reminiscent of the Colombian case, named them Comités de auto defense, or self-defense committees. Nevertheless, the bulk of the offensive against the Sendero fell to the Peruvian armed forces, which coordinated the work of their paramilitary proxies. In the early fighting, military operations were so heavy handed and rife with atrocities, with the massacre of whole villages and the murder of suspected guerrilla supporters, that Sendero did well by comparison. Peru's most infamous paramilitary death squad, known as the Grupo Colina, plied its trade from 1990 through 1994 under the Fujimori administration. Its most notable exploits were the Barrios Altos Massacre, the La Cantuta Massacre, and the murder of noted intellectuals such as Pedro Yauri, director of the "Punto Final" news program on Radio Universal in Huacho. Yauri was abducted in June 1992 by men wearing police uniforms, who also beat his father.

In September of 1992, Guzmán was captured, along with other Sendero leaders, at an apartment in Lima. Soon thereafter the movement was battered by "rondas" in a series of humiliating armed encounters that underscored how weak its rural support really was. Once in custody, Guzmán quickly pleased his captors' with calls for demobilization that splintered the movement. (Though portions of the Sendero soldiered on through the rest of the 1990s, it went into steep decline after the capture in 1999 of Oscar Ramírez, the leader who took over command after the capture of Guzmán.)

In 1993, anonymous members of the Peruvian military documented the Grupo Colina's involvement in the disappearances, and subsequent murders, of the La Cantuta victims. They also eventually disclosed their clandestine burial sites. Though the Supreme Council of Military Justice sentenced ten of the perpetrators of the murders to prison terms of various lengths in February of 1994, nothing happened because of the Amnesty Law (no. 26479) of 1995. The law granted general amnesty to members of the armed forces and their civilian proxies who had been accused or convicted of human rights violations committed in the years since 1980. The situation changed dramatically in 2000, however, when videotaped evidence surfaced of Fujimori's advisor, Vladimiro Montesinos, offering bribes to fellow politicians and military men. Fujimori fled to Japan. With the fall of the Fujimori government in 2000, and the repeal of the Amnesty Law, there were further arrests and prosecutions.

President Valentín Paniagua initiated a truth and reconciliation commission, the final report of which, in 2003, documented that, between 1980 and 2000, over sixty-nine thousand people were killed or disappeared. Using the commission's data, Human Rights Watch, a leading human rights organization, estimated that Sendero had killed about half of the victims.

URUGUAY

Known as it was for its well-established and stable democratic tradition and welfare state, Uruguay, like Chile, was seemingly not a candidate for inclusion in a discussion of political murder. Like Costa Rica, it was often compared to Switzerland. (Lots of countries in the region like to be compared to the Swiss; in Latin American eyes they represent the epitome of a small, stable, rich, and civilized nation). But in the 1970s Uruguay had its own experience with dictatorship and dirty war.[22]

In the nineteenth century, Uruguay had its share of power struggles among rural caudillos. But in the twentieth century it went in a dramatically new direction. Along with Argentina, Uruguay experienced massive European immigration, especially from Italy and Spain. The country's signature welfare state was ushered into existence by President José Batlle y Ordóñez early in the century. It gave Uruguayans, especially the middle class in Montevideo, a particularly high standard of living by Latin American standards. This new system was based on a general understanding of the state as the caretaker of society via political and economic paternalism. Yet Uruguay was a small country dominated by one city, and unfortunately, the underpinnings of Uruguayan stability in the agricultural export economy began a decline in the late 1950s, dooming the state's ability to continue its paternalistic policies. A series of economic shocks and deficits forced the reduction of government benefits. The traditional political parties faltered, while social and political conflicts increased. More than seven hundred strikes occurred in 1967, and the situation only worsened between 1968 and 1973. Massive outward migration siphoned off up to 10 percent of the population, especially of the most economically and politically active sectors. And an armed resistance movement emerged with utopian inclinations—the Movimiento de Liberación Nacional, or Movement of National Liberation, the so-called Tupamaros. The Tupamaro leaders were a diverse group of mostly middle-class leftists and labor organizers, the most noteworthy of whom was the sugar cane union leader, Raúl Sendic.

Through their early antics, the Tupamaros excelled at making the government and security forces look foolish and inept. When the regime reacted with a more repressive response to social problems, the Tupamaros became more violent. The Uruguayan military then began what amounted to a "slow-motion coup" (as it is often called) through more frequent use of states of emergency. These allowed for detentions without trials and, after 1970, reliance on Article 31 of the Constitution, which empowered the executive to carry out arrests and searches without warrants, open mail, muzzle the press, and eavesdrop on suspected subversives. In September 1971, a presidential decree allowed the military to take over the struggle against subversion from the police, and forced police officers to lend a hand in the dirty war operations. In April 1972, the congress declared a "state of internal war," after which seditious acts were tried in military law courts. Later in 1972 and early in 1973, civil rights were largely suspended, and severe restrictions were even passed against primary and secondary students. These increasingly repressive policies finally blossomed into the June 1973 dissolution of the national congress. A period of focused political murder and repression followed. In particular, special prisons were created for subversives, where torture was routinely employed. Uruguayans, in fact, made extreme use of clandestine imprisonment and torture, especially psychological manipulation. Political murder was used, though the number of disappearances was low in Uruguay. At least two hundred were killed, however, in Operation Condor.

A combination of internal developments and potent external influences had encouraged the weak, apolitical military, traditionally under civilian control, to impose a brutal dictatorship. After the Tupamaros were suppressed in the early 1970s, the armed forces moved on to attack the Uruguayan Communist Party and the Confederación Nacional de Trabajadores (National Confederation of Labor), and eventually, anyone who dared to defend the practice of democracy, including senators, a good number of lawyers, and even soldiers and police officers with constitutionalist inclinations. Yet after its flirtation with the use of political murder and dirty war, Uruguay returned to its more democratic traditions. Indeed it eventually elected as president José "Pepe" Mujica, who had been a member of the Tupamaros, was jailed for years (and escaped more than once), and had been tortured while in custody.

NOTES

INTRODUCTION: A POLITICAL CULTURE OF MURDER

1. García Márquez, *One Hundred Years of Solitude*, pp. 245, 380–381.

2. The Greek idea of "killing the bearer of ill tidings" (usually the "message" was a bad one) found its "locus classicus" in Herodotus, when the Spartans under King Leonidas killed messengers of Persia's King Xerxes, who demanded submission.

3. For a traditional take on the definitions and interpretations of assassination and political murder see Franklin Ford's *Political Murder: From Tyrannicide to Terrorism*. A common characteristic of books that treated political murder after the 1960s, both as general phenomena and in the U.S. context, is that they tended to focus on the assassin (be he or she part of a conspiracy, or a "lone individual," perhaps "deranged," perpetrating a "random act") taking aim at someone in power. This is true of many works right up to the present. See: Bowyer, *Assassin!*; Camellion, *Assassination: Theory and Practice*; Clarke, *American Assassins: The Darker Side of Politics*; Cooper, *On Assassination*; Crotty, *Assassinations and the Political Order*; Hudson, *Assassination*; Hickey, *Encyclopedia of Murder and Violent Crime*; Kirkham, *Assassination and Political Violence;* Lentz, *Assassinations and Executions: An Encyclopedia of Political Violence*; McConnell, *The History of Assassination*; Porter, *Assassination: A History of Political Murder*; Belfield, *The Assassination Business.*

4. Is there a relationship between personalized politics and the use of assassination and political murder? Does caciquismo, and the key role individuals play in Latin American politics, breed this kind of violence? Spreading fear is important, as a variation on the anarchist "propaganda by the deed," but does the importance of the individual enter into it? I thank Arif Dirlik for asking these questions.

5. A good starting point for exploring hegemony (and popular resistance to it) in Latin America is Joseph and Nugent, *Everyday Forms of State Formation*; See also various works by James Scott that have influenced Latinamericanists, especially *Weapons of the Weak*, and *Domination and the Arts of Resistance.*

6. Turits, *Foundations of Despotism*, p. 4.

7. This interplay of hegemony and coercion is at work most everywhere, well beyond Latin America. Gramsci's distinction has perhaps been taken too far in other settings as well.

8. Menjívar and Rodríguez, "State Terror in the U.S.-Latin American Interstate Regime," p. 4.

9. Rummel, *Death by Government*, pp. 1–2, 9, 17.

10. Duvall and Stohl, "Governance by Terror," 256–262; Gurr, "The Political Origins of State Violence and Terror," 46–48; Wolpin, *State Terrorism*, 42–44.

11. Campbell, "Death Squads: Definition," pp. 7–11, 13.

12. Ibid., p. 8.

13. Stanley, *The Protection Racket State*, p. 5.

14. C. Wright Mills, *The Power Elite*, p. 18. For echoes in other books on elites; see Rothkopf, *Superclass: The Global Power Elite and the World They are Making*; and Wedel, *Shadow Elite: How the World's New Power Brokers Undermine Democracy, Government, and the Free Market.*

15. Halperín Donghi, *The Contemporary History of Latin America*, p. 312.

16. Schwarz, *American Counterinsurgency Doctrine*, p. 72.

17. How important is social stratification in the propensity of a regime or a regional elite to turn to political murder? Or for it to succeed or endure? How does a country's degree of social and economic inequality and exclusion correlate to the use of political murder? The answer is still not clear.

18. For an example of this impulse toward dramatic popular mobilization, see James Sander's *Contentious Republicans: Popular Politics, Race, and Class in Nineteenth-Century Colombia.*

19. Roniger, "U.S. Hemispheric Hegemony," pp. 28–31.

20. Richani, *Systems of Violence*, chapter 5.

21. Why kill people? Are elites "murderous" because they are threatened, wounded, or declining? Or rather is it because they see utility in murder? Some seem pretty healthy and in control. These are open questions. Also, while this hypothesis (that it is a deep fear of social and economic change, and a desire to derail it, that drives political murder) explains why elites turn to the practice, it does not address the motives of the "muscle," those skilled in the practice of murder. This is a less interesting question; obviously there will always be individuals twisted enough to do the actual killing, and for lots of reasons, including hatred, fear, anger, money, power, patriotism, ego, or sadistic fun. Many works that examine murder fixate on the mechanics of assassination, from ninja shurikens and poisonous concoctions to plastique and automatic weapons. Many students of assassination (and undoubtedly many readers) are fascinated by the psychology of the individual assassin (or of the breed) and want to be brought up to date on the tricks of the trade. This study, in contrast, will focus more on the political causes and effects of murder as it is practiced in Latin America.

22. Kruijt and Koonings, "The Military and Their Shadowy Brothers-in-Arms," p. 27.

23. Esparza, "Introduction: Globalizing Latin American Studies of State Violence and Genocide," p. 4 citing Leo Kuper.

24. Roniger, "U.S. Hemispheric Hegemony," pp. 28–31.

25. McSherry, *Predatory States*, p. 11.

26. See Walter, *Terror and Resistance: A Study of Political Violence.*

27. Mason and Krane, "Political Economy of Death Squads," p. 178.

28. Kruijt and Koonings, "The Military and Their Shadowy Brothers-in-Arms," pp. 27, 16.

29. Latin Americans are no more intrinsically blood thirsty than people in the United States; the murderous elite is international, and includes good numbers of Gringos, though they tend to express themselves south of the border.

30. See Joseph and Nugent, *Everyday Forms of State Formation*, and Jacobsen and Aljovín de Losada, *Political Cultures in the Andes, 1750–1950*, among others.

31. Geertz, *The Interpretations of Culture*, p. 44.

32. See Kuhn's *The Structure of Scientific Revolutions.*

33. Dawkins, *The Selfish Gene.*

34. Lauria-Santiago, "The Culture and Politics of State Terror and Repression in El Salvador," pp. 105–106.

35. Knight, "Habitus and Homicide," pp. 107–108.

36. For a broader view of a similar phenomenon, see Corey Robin's *The Reactionary Mind.*

37. See Ford, *Political Murder: From Tyrannicide to Terrorism,* pp. 31, 46, 50–59. Other messengers killed might include Socrates; rich and powerful citizens of Athens did not like "subversive" truth tellers. And then there is the case of Jesus.

38. Campbell, "Death Squads: Definition," p. 8.

39. Warren, "Conclusion: Death Squads," p. 226.

40. Romero, *Paramilitares y autodefensas*, p. 89.

41. Torres-Rivas, "Epilogue: Notes on Terror," p. 287. A related question is the use of political murder by guerrilla groups, and by popular, leftist political movements. Of course violence can be a tool of change, social transformation, and revolution. Yet in Latin America political murder has been a more common tool in the war by the forces of the status quo against the forces of change. See Chapter 2.

42. Pécaut, "From the Banality of Violence to Real Terror," p. 145; see Robin Kirk *More Terrible than Death* for a more emotional version of this argument; on Mexico, see Charles Bowden, *Murder City.*

CHAPTER 1: TARGETS AND VICTIMS

1. Schirmer, *The Guatemala Military Project,* p. 168.

2. The sons of Colonel Aureliano Buendía once again point the way. At their one and only gathering, they were induced by the women in the family to go to mass on Ash Wednesday. "More amused than devout, they let themselves

be led to the altar rail where Father Antonio Isabel made the sign of the cross in ashes on them. Back at the house, when the youngest tried to clean his forehead, he discovered that the mark was indelible and so were those of his brothers. They tried soap and water, earth and a scrubbing brush, and lastly a pumice stone and lye, but they could not remove the crosses." As García Márquez would later reveal, they had been marked for slaughter. When their murders came, they "aimed at the center of their crosses of ash." García Márquez, *One Hundred Years of Solitude,* pp. 222 and 245. García Márquez is more of a realist than he is given credit for.

3. Sluka, "Introduction: State Terror," p. 3, 5–6.

4. Mason and Krane, "The Political Economy of Death Squads," pp. 179–181.

5. Joyce and Stover, *Witnesses from the Grave,* pp. 211–212.

6. Knight, "Political Violence in Post-revolutionary Mexico," p. 118; Mazzei, *Death Squads or Self-Defense Forces?* p. 47.

7. Koonings, "Shadows of Violence and Political Transition in Brazil," p. 206.

8. Kruckewitt, "U.S. Militarization of Honduras," p. 182; Americas Watch, "Human Rights in Honduras," pp. 12–14, 17.

9. Beggar, "The Path of State Terror in Peru," p. 252.

10. Hristov, *Blood and Capital,* pp. 117–126. See also Julie Mazzei, *Death Squads or Self-Defense Forces?* pp. 67–68, for a similar characterization of victims in Colombia.

11. Gleijeses, *Politics and Culture in Guatemala,* pp. 8, 12. See also Richard Adam's seminal *Crucifixion by Power,* for patterns manifesting themselves in the 1960s, as well as additional evidence presented in Norman Gall's review of Adam's work, "Slaughter in Guatemala," *New York Review of Books,* May 20, 1971.

12. Similar characterizations of victims can be found in (among many others): Amnesty International, *Getting Away with Murder: Political Killings and 'Disappearances' in the 1990s,* chapter 2; *Torture in Brazil,* chapters 9–12; Kohut and Vilella, *Historical Dictionary of the "Dirty Wars,"* pp. xxxix–lx; Stanley, *The Protection Racket State,* especially chapter 6, "Descent into Mass Murder;" Ball, et al., *State Violence in Guatemala,* pp. 37–78.

13. See Katz, *De Díaz a Madero,* and *The Life and Times of Pancho Villa;* López González, *La muerte del general Emiliano Zapata*; Brunk, *Emiliano Zapata*; Womack, *Zapata,* pp. 322–329; Damirón, *Asesinatos politicos en Mexico*; García, *Rojo: del asesinato politico en Mexico.*

14. See Walker, *Nicaragua,* pp. 20–24, 26; Miranda and Ratliff, *The Civil War in Nicaragua,* pp. 10, 71.

15. Sánchez, "An Interpretive Synthesis," p. 113.

16. Koster and Sánchez, *In the Time of Tyrants,* p. 28.

17. Dosal, "San Ernesto," pp.323–325.

18. See the cases of Luis Donaldo Colosio and José Francisco Ruiz Massieu in Mexico: Castañeda, *Sopresas te da la vida*; Gilly, *El poder, el dinero y la sangre*; García, *Rojo: del asesinato político en Mexico*; Trueba Lara, *Magnicidio: La muerte de un candidato*; Arreola, *Asi fue*; Fernández Menéndez, *De Chiapas a Colosio.*

19. The irony of García Márquez's take on the famous massacre in *One Hundred Years of Solitude* is that he portrays it as forgotten, dooming Colombians to relive their history; this is one of his major themes.

20. See Braun, *The Assassination of Gaitán,* pp. 186, note 57.

21. See Cortés Arévalo, *El asesinato de Galán.*

22. See Romero, *Paramilitares y autodefensas*; Dudley, *Walking Ghosts*; Lora, *Siembra vientos y recogerás tempestades: La historia del M 19*; Roa Rojas, *El asesinato de Carlos Pizarro.*

23. Verbitsky, *The Flight,* pp. 81–82; Walsh's daughter Victoria, also a member of the Montoneros, committed suicide to avoid capture.

24. See Edmisten, *Nicaragua Divided;* Vélez Bárcenas, *Dr. Pedro Joaquín Chamorro Cardenal, asesinado!* and *Porque mataron a Chamorro?*

25. See Erlick, *Disappeared: A Journalist Silenced.*

26. Representative works on murdered journalists include Camaño and Bayer, *Los periodistas desaparecidos*; Salomone, *Maten al mensajero: Periodistas asesinados y desaparecidos*; Rincón and Ruiz, *Bajo todos los fuegos: Los periodistas en el conflicto colombiano*; Guerrero, *Reportaje con la muerte: Biografía de Leonardo Henrichsen, el reportero que filmó su propio muerte.*

27. Oglesby, "Myrna Mack," pp. 254–256; and Sluka, "Introduction: State Terror," p. 24.

28. See the American Anthropological Association's response to his murder, June 8, 1999.

29. Hamill, Caudillos, p. 234. His disappearance was noted in *Time Magazine*, April 2, 1956, and Feb. 11, 1957. See also Crassweller, *Trujillo,* pp. 311–323; for his account of living in the DR, see Galíndez, "Inside a Dictatorship."

30. Izquierdo, Jamie Garzón: *El genial impertinente*, and Rivera and Lozano, *Edificio Colombia: Antología de los libretos del programa "Quac El Noticero."*

31. See Brookman, *The Word Remains;* Stanley, *The Protection Racket State,* pp. 196–198; White, *The History of El Salvador,* pp. 99–100; Didion, *Salvador,* p. 55.

32. See Moreno Valencia and Villasana, *Sangre de mayo*; Ramos, *Muerte de un príncipe.*

33. See Rico and de la Grange, *Quién mató al Obispo?* Goldman, *The Art of Political Murder: Who Killed the Bishop?*

34. See Didion, *Salvador,* pp. 23–24; Noone and Glavac, *Compañeras en el camino*; Stanley, *The Protection Racket State,* p. 214; Zaqano, *Ita Ford: Missionary Martyr;* Lernoux, *Hearts on Fire.*

35. Whitfield, *Paying the Price,* p. 4. For their work with the poor that put the Jesuits in harm's way see Carranza, *Mártires de la UCA;* for the later legal struggles to prosecute the kıllers see Doggett, *Death Foretold.*

36. See Diebel, *Betrayed: the Assassination of Digna Ochoa.*

37. See Policzer, *The Rise and Fall of Repression in Chile,* pp. 96–97; Constable and Valenzuela, *A Nation of Enemies,* p. 57; Cavallo et al., *La historia oculta del regimen militar,* p. 57; Muñoz, *The Dictator's Shadow,* p. 65.

38. See Dinges, *Assassination on Embassy Row.*

39. Ball, et al., *State Violence in Guatemala,* p. 18.

40. Anderson, *Politics in Central America,* pp. 93–94.

41. See "El asesinato de Rodrigo Lara Banilla," Semana Aug. 7, 1987; Kirk, *More Terrible than Death,* p. 87; Romero, *Paramilitares y Autodefensas.*

42. Americas Watch, "Human Rights in Honduras," pp. 15–18.

43. Manitzas, "All the Minister's Men," pp. 86–87.

44. Guzman Bouvard, *Revolutionizing Motherhood,* pp. 75–79, 83–84; Joyce and Stover, *Witnesses from the Grave,* p. 215; Marchak, *God's Assassins,* pp. 163, 266.

45. Lewis, *Guerrillas and Generals,* pp. 13–14, 19–20; Crassweller, *Perón,* pp. 323, 332, 335–336.

46. Gall, "Slaughter in Guatemala;" and Wilkinson, *Silence on the Mountain,* p. 227; see also Levenson-Estrada, *Trade Unionists Against Terror.*

47. Schirmer, *The Guatemalan Military Project,* p. 312, note 13; Military intel G-2 ordered the abduction and murder.

48. Hodges and Grandy, *Mexico Under Siege,* pp. 40–55. See also Padilla, *Rural Resistance in the Land of Zapata.*

49. See Crassweller, *Trujillo,* pp. 401–403; Turits, *Foundations of Despotism.*

50. See Luis Emilio Corrales Londoño, president of the community action committee of El Cedrón, Antioquia; Oscar Fernández Osorio, also president of a community action committee in Tuluá, Valle de Cauca; Joselito Bailarín, governor of the Embera Katio indigenous community of Cañavarales, Antioquia; Bacilides Quiroga, president of the peasant association of Bugalagrande, Valle de Cauca; Nelson Freddy Gallego, leader of the Peace Communities of San Francisco de Asís, Urabá, Chocó; Martha Circa Becoche, vice president of the community action committee of La Cohetera, Cauca; Gilberto Agudelo Martínez, president of the Union of University Employees of Colombia (SINTRAUNICOL); Mario Sierra Anaya, a leader of the Union of Workers of INCORA; Elizabeth Cañas Cano, a founder of the Association of Families of the Disappeared of Magdalena Medio; and Marta Cecilia Hernández Luque, president of the National Association of Peasant, Black, and Indigenous Women. Hristov, *Blood and Capital,* pp. 111–121.

51. Romero, *Paramilitares y autodefensas,* pp. 140–141; See also Dudley, *Walking Ghosts;* Gómez-Súarez, "Political Violence and the Onset of the Unión Patriótica Genocide;" Giraldo, *Colombia: The Genocidal Democracy;* Human Rights Watch, *Colombia's Killer Networks;* Hylton, *Evil Hour in Colombia;* Kirk, *More Terrible than Death;* Leech, *Killing Peace;* Matta Aldana, *Terrorismo del estado y genocidio contra la Unión Patriótica;* Rodríguez Navarrete, *Genocidio de la Unión Patriótica.* See Uribe, *Enterrar y callar,* pp. 38–40 for a breakdown of the different varieties of massacres.

52. See Grandin, *The Last Colonial Massacre;* Garrand-Burnett, *Terror in the Land of the Holy Spirit,* p 92; and Falla, *Massacres in the Jungle,* for other examples.

53. See Seoane and Ruis Nuñez, *La noche de los lápices.*

54. See Gutierrez, *Violencia en Guerrero,* pp. 119–131; Weinberg, *Homage to Chiapas,* pp. 244–246; Ulloa Bornemann, "Surviving Mexico's Dirty War," p. 11.

55. Rose, *The Unpast: Elite Violence and Social Control in Brazil, 1954–2000,* p. 271.

56. This argument does not include other forms of armed struggle that occur between combatants, guerrillas, military, police, etc. This type of killing cannot be called "murder" unless all forms of war are defined as such. States fighting insurgencies typically deny them belligerent status and legal legitimacy, making all their violent actions into "terrorism" and murder, but this is clearly a self-serving point of view. And it is still true that the summary and extrajudicial execution of captured guerrillas qualifies as murder under the rules of warfare.

57. Sulka, "Introduction: State Terror," pp. 1–3. His definition: "state terror refers to the use or the threat of violence by the state or its agents or supporters, particularly against civilian individuals and populations, as a means of political intimidation and control (i.e., a means of repression)."

58. Obando, "Civil-Military Relations in Peru," p. 406.

59. See Hodges, Argentina's "Dirty War," pp. 103–123; and Robben, *Political Violence and Trauma,* chapter 8, for reprisal killings in Argentina.

60. Earlier Liberal guerrilla leaders who emerged from the pueblo, such as "Sangrenegra" (Blackblood), "Capitán Desquite" (Captain Vengeance), and "Chispas" (Sparks), carried out their fair share of retaliatory sectarian murder during the Violencia. Yet these murders during the late "bandolero" stage were more like the big tradition in that Liberal elites were sending them out for little jobs, more like pájaros, killing people to take their land, like criminal capital accumulation of the narcos in later decades.

61. Chase, "The Trials: Violence and Justice in the Aftermath of the Cuban Revolution," p. 186.

62. Anderson, *Che Guevara.*

63. The case of his successor Nicolás Maduro, however, could be another matter. The jury is still out, of course, but his heavy-handed approach to the protests of February 2014, as well as his tolerance for the violence perpetrated by his armed followers in their "colectivos" could help earn Venezuela a place in any future edition of this book.

CHAPTER 2: DIRTY WAR MECHANICS

1. Guzman Bouvard, *Revolutionizing Motherhood*, pp. 24–25.

2. Sulka, "Introduction: State Terror," p. 3

3. Campbell, "Death Squads: Definition," pp. 1–2, 5.

4. Huggins, "The Making of Police Death Squads in Modern Brazil," pp. 205–207, 212.

5. Sánchez, "The Violence: An Interpretative Synthesis," p. 85; Roldán, *Blood and Fire,* pp. 127, 132, 221. The Violencia was "the result of repeated provocations by the regional authorities" and was "directly proportional to the presence of irregular forces" supported by the state; See also Betancourt and Garcia, *Matones y cuadrilleros.*

6. Sulka, "Introduction: State Terror," pp. 4–5.

7. Kruijt and Koonings, "The Military and Their Shadowy Brothers-in-Arms," p. 27. Campbell, "Death Squads: Definition," p. 1.

8. Lynch, *Argentine Caudillo*, pp. 99–102. Lynch quoting *Facundo*, p. 77.

9. *Mexico: An Encyclopedia*, p. 141.

10. Simpson, *Many Mexicos*, p. 289.

11. Simpson, *Many Mexicos*, pp. 288–289; *Mexico: An Encyclopedia*, p. 141; Díaz was supposed to have quipped that running for president in Mexico could be detrimental to one's health.

12. See the classic portrayal of personalist rule of "caciques" and their pistolero enforcers in Friedrich, "A Mexican Cacicazgo," p. 191.

13. Mazzei, *Death Squads or Self-Defense Forces?* pp. 132–133; and see Dunkerley, *The Long War*, p. 20.

14. Alicia García, *La doctrina de la seguridad nacional*, p. 18.

15. Zalvar, "Urban Violence and Drug Warfare in Brazil," pp. 140–143; Van Reenen, "Policing Extensions," p. 41; Graham, *Patronage and Politics*, pp. 144–145.

16. Rose, *The Unpast*, p. 231.

17. Arnson, "Window on the Past," p. 89; Lauria-Santiago, "Culture and Politics of State Terror and Repression," p. 99.

18. Anderson, *Matanza*, pp. 125–133.

19. Stanley, *The Protection Racket State*, p. 52.

20. Danner, *Massacre at El Mozote*, pp. 41; and see Stanley, *The Protection Racket State*; Binford, *The El Mazote Massacre*, pp. 13–48.

21. Drouin, "Understanding the 1982 Guatemalan Genocide," p. 84.

22. Ball et al., *State Violence in Guatemala*, pp. 26–29.

23. Grandin, *Empire's Workshop*, p. 90.

24. See Green, *Gaitanismo*, pp. 60–62.

25. Tate, *Counting the Dead*, pp. 45–47.

26. Henderson, *When Colombia Bled*, pp. 171–180.

27. Sánchez, "The Violence: An Interpretative Synthesis," p. 89.

28. Ibid., p. 108.

29. Hristov, *Blood and Capital*, pp. 38–44.

30. Grossman, "Blood of the People," pp. 69–72, 74–79.

31. Lewis *Guerrillas and Generals*, pp. 105–113; see also Anderson, *Dossier Secreto*, pp. 124–141.

32. See Turits, "A World Destroyed."

33. See Carey, *Plaza of Sacrifices*; Poniatowska, *Masacre in* Mexico; Scherer García and Monsivaís, *Los patriotas de Tlatelolco a la guerra sucia.*

34. Manitzas, "All the Minister's Men," pp. 90–91.

35. Hylton and Thomson, *Revolutionary Horizons*, p. 84; Lehman, *Bolivia and the United States*, p. 166.

36. Verdugo, *Chile, Pinochet, and the Caravan of Death*, p. v.

37. Dinges, *Condor Years,* pp. 64–72; see also Policzer, *The Rise and Fall of Repression in Chile.*

38. Almirón, *Campo Santo,* pp. 105, 135.

39. Lewis, *Guerrillas and Generals,* pp. 149–151, 157; McSherry, *Predatory States,* pp. 76–77.

40. Robben, "Terror in the Netherworld," p. 95.

41. Schirmer, *The Guatemala Military Project,* pp. 151–152, 157–159, 167. The designation "G-2" mimics U.S. military nomenclature, where G-2's were intelligence officers.

42. Arnson, "Window on the Past," pp. 89, 101

43. Kruckewitt, "U.S. Militarization of Honduras," pp. 183–188.

44. Huggins, *Violence Workers,* pp. 63–80.

45. Conaghan, *Fujimori's Peru,* pp. 68, 72–75, 105, 107; see also Burt, *Political Violence and the Authoritarian State in Peru,* pp. 49, 181–83, 203–04; Obando, "Civil-Military Relations in Peru," p. 399; Umberto, *Ojo por ojo.*

46. Van Reenen, "Policing Extensions," pp. 33–36.

47. Knight, "Habitus and Homicide," pp. 112–113.

48. Anderson, *Matanza,* p. 133. See Stanley as well.

49. Van Reenen, "Policing Extensions," p. 38; Pinheiro, "Police and Political Crisis," pp. 168–173.

50. Van Reenen, "Policing Extensions," pp. 38–40.

51. Betancourt and García, *Matones y cuadrilleros,* pp. 62–64; Sánchez, "An Interpretive Synthesis," pp. 79, 85–86; Guzmán Campos, Fals Borda, Umaña Luna, *La violencia en Colombia,* v. 1, p. 83.

52. Uribe, *Matar, rematar, contramatar.* p. 54; Massacres in Colombia during the Violencia were motivated by local alliances, old party hatreds, and the chain of vengeance for personal and family loses to political violence. Early massacres by Chulavitas in the coffee zone of Tolima (heavily Liberal areas) were a driving force, and led to retaliatory massacres by Liberal bands, but more people were killed by Conservative and government forces; pp. 115–116.

53. Roldán, *Blood and Fire,* pp. 73, 80, 92–95, 100, 177.

54. Betancourt and García, *Matones y cuadrilleros,* pp. 74–76, 94–96.

55. Roldán, *Blood and Fire,* p. 142.

56. Seri, "Vicious Legacies," p. 185; Van Reenen, "Policing Extensions," p. 43; Kruijt and Koonings, "The Military and Their Shadowy Brothers-in-Arms," p. 26.

57. Arnson, "Window on the Past," pp. 99–100. The PN had ties to ARENA and D'Aubuisson, who the CIA believed picked its leftist targets; the PH did not get along well with ARENA's death squads.

58. Huggins, "The Making of Police Death Squads in Modern Brazil," p. 215.

59. Pinheiro, "Police and Political Crisis," pp. 168–173.

60. Armony, "Producing and Exporting State Terror," p. 322.

61. Bowden, *Killing Pablo,* pp. 167–168, 172–173, 175–177, 182, 192–193.

62. Aranguren Molina, *Mi confesión,* pp. 123, 142–143, 149, 154.

63. Knight, "Habitus and Homicide," pp. 108, 113–115.

64. Schroeder, "To Induce a Sense of Terror," pp. 28, 31–33.

65. Guzmán Campos, Fals Borda, Umaña Luna, *La violencia en Colombia*, v. 1, pp. 165–169.

66. Betancourt and García, *Matones y cuadrilleros*, pp. 20–21, 74–76, 105, 116.

67. He was portrayed rather closely by Colombian novelist Gustavo Alvarez Gardeazábal in his highly regarded tale *Cóndores no entierran todos los días*.

68. Betancourt and García, *Matones y cuadrilleros*, pp. 121–123, 127–133, 106–110.

69. Quoted by Arnson, "Window on the Past," p. 92

70. Mazzei, *Death Squads or Self-Defense Forces?* pp. 153–162.

71. Lauria–Santiago, "Culture and Politics of State Terror and Repression," pp. 97–98.

72. Arnson, "Window on the Past," pp. 94–98.

73. Scobell and Hammitt, "Goons, Gunmen, and Gendarmerie," p. 219.

74. See Giraldo, *Colombia: Genocidal Democracy*, p. 77.

75. Scobell and Hammitt, "Goons, Gunmen, and Gendarmerie," pp. 220–221.

76. Kruijt and Koonings, "The Military and Their Shadowy Brothers-in-Arms," pp. 25–27.

77. Quoted in Scobell and Hammitt, "Goons, Gunmen, and Gendarmerie," p. 220.

78. Kruijt and Koonings, "The Military and Their Shadowy Brothers-in-Arms," pp. 25.

79. Scobell and Hammitt, "Goons, Gunmen, and Gendarmerie," pp. 221–224.

80. Hristov, *Blood and Capital*, pp. 24–27, 58.

81. McSherry, *Predatory States*, p. 8.

82. Romero, *Paramilitares y autodefensas*, pp. 16–19.

83. Mazzei, *Death Squads or Self-Defense Forces?*, pp. 5–12.

84. Stanley as well, in *The Protection Racket State*, noted a similar dynamic involved with D'Aubuisson and his crew around 1980 regarding their conflicts and collusions with the military government.

85. Anderson, *Matanza*, pp. 122–124.

86. Degregori, "Reaping the Whirlwind: The Rondas," p. 80; See also Fumerton and Remijnse, "Peru's Comites and Guatemala's Patrullas."

87. Kruijt and Koonings, "The Military and their Shadowy Brothers-in-Arms," p. 26.

88. Manitzas, "All the Minister's Men," p. 85.

89. Ulloa Bornemann, *Surviving Mexico's Dirty War*, pp. 9–10. Another parallel group, the "Francisco Villa Group" was also employed to threaten and murder student activists

90. Hodges asks, "could preparation for parapolice terrorism have taken place without Perón's knowledge and approval?" Clearly his "interests were being served" and "he did nothing to disarm them." Hodges, *Dirty War*, pp. 172–176. See also González Janzen, *La Triple A*, pp. 7–38.

91. McSherry, *Predatory States*, pp. 73–74.

92. Hodges, *Dirty War*, 172–173; contrast with Lewis, *Guerrillas and Generals*, on Ezeiza; see also Crassweller, *Perón*, pp. 357–358; and González Janzen, *La Triple-A*, pp. 107–108.

93. McSherry, *Predatory States*, pp. 74–75. Later, parts of Triple A morphed into "fascist" group Militia; McSherry, *Predatory States*, p. 70.

94. Grandin, *Empire's Workshop*, p. 115.

95. See month by month tally by Brody, *Contra Terror*, pp. 153–183; See also Schroeder, "To Induce a Sense of Terror," p. 45, who noted atrocities galore; their special targets were teachers, health care providers, government workers, any Sandinistas.

96. Schroeder, "To Induce a Sense of Terror," p. 47. Grandin, *Empire's Workshop*, 115. See also Dillon, *Comandos*, pp. 57–131.

97. Mazzei, *Death Squads or Self-Defense Forces?* pp. 31, 33–38. Mazzei makes fine distinctions between GBs and later paras; essentially GB defended property and specific prerogatives of their bosses, while paras defended the larger system; but she admits that the victims are the same, "peasant organizations, land reform advocates, critics of the established social order and power structure." This is perhaps too fine a distinction; in practice this is a messy and interconnected continuum; paras represent a ratcheting up of pressure, but not a fundamental change; still political murder.

98. Norget, "Caught in the Crossfire," pp. 131–133.

99. Mazzei, *Death Squads or Self-Defense Forces?*, pp. 25–28, 38, 45–47

100. Norget, "Caught in the Crossfire," pp. 116 and 123.

101. Mazzei, *Death Squads or Self-Defense Forces?* p. 26.

102. See Hirales, *Camino a Acteal*, pp. 111–126; Weinberg, *Homage to Chiapas*, pp. 169–175; Moguel, *Chiapas: la guerra de los signos*, pp. 163–182; Hodges and Gandy, *Mexico under Siege*, p. 201,

103. Mazzei, *Death Squads or Self-Defense Forces?*, pp. 67–69.

104. Betancourt and García, *Matones y cuadrilleros*, p. 21; Romero, *Paramilitares y autodefensas*, p. 88; see also Richani, *Systems of Violence*, pp. 93–132. The conflict became much more complex and unstable with the resurgence of the paramilitaries. Richani identifies "an unholy alliance" that arose in the 1983 in the Magdalena Médio between narcos, large landowners, multinational corporations, industrial groups, and the Colombian state with the foundation of Autodefensas Campesinas (102–103). He shows how three different paramilitary formations, those of the emerald mafias, the narcos, and the landed elite, "converged in the 1990s under a unified leadership and with a conservative political program in support of the state's armed forces" (104). He then examines the political economy

of paramilitary homicides and their impact on land struggles, arguing that "massacres became an effective tool in the process of concentration of land" and that they were also employed to eliminate the guerrillas' base of support (120). Richani demonstrates that with the "clear trend in the increase of homicides which took hold after 1985."

105. Romero, *Paramilitares y autodefensas,* p. 103, 119, 244–245.

106. Mazzei, *Death Squads or Self-Defense Forces?,* p. 87.

107. Romero, *Paramilitares y autodefensas,* p. 92.

108. Tate, *Counting the Dead,* p. 50; Her three phases of para history (leaving out the 1950s): "death squad operations in the 1970s and early 1980s, private armies funded by the drug trade in the late 1980s and early 1990s, and the consolidation of paramilitaries into a single coordinating body represented by a national spokesman claiming to share a political platform in the late 1990s." This is good as far as she goes, but she misses earlier phases. See also, Romero, *Paramilitares y autodefensas,* p. 240.

109. Romero, *Paramilitares y autodefensas,* pp. 55–57, 60.

110. Mazzei, *Death Squads or Self-Defense Forces?,* p. 111. See Human Rights Watch's reports, *The "Sixth Division"* and *Colombia's Killer Networks,* for close ties between the military and the paras.

111. Romero, *Paramilitares y autodefensas,* pp. 106–109.

112. Hristov, *Blood and Captial,* pp. 83–88. Examples are the Alto Naya Massacre, April 2000; Mapiripán Massacre 1997; Tibú 2000.

113. Mazzei, *Death Squads or Self-Defense Forces?,* pp. 111–114, 117.

114. Romero, *Paramilitares y autodefensas,* pp. 197–201.

115. Aranguren Molina, *Mi confesión,* p. 12.

116. Romero, *Paramilitares y autodefensas,* pp. 227 and 246. See also Mazzei, *Death Squads or Self-Defense Forces?,* pp. 81, 88.

117. Romero, *Paramilitares y autodefensas,* p. 241.

118. Mazzei, *Death Squads or Self-Defense Forces?,* p. 91.

119. Ibid., p. 118.

120. Romero, *Paramilitares y autodefensas,* p. 223.

121. Lauria-Santiago, "Culture and Politics of State Terror and Repression," p. 100.

122. Gleijeses, *Politics and Culture,* p. 10; Huggins, "The Making of Police Death Squads in Modern Brazil," p. 203; McSherry, *Predatory States,* p. 21.

123. Campbell, "Death Squads: Definition," pp. 5–6.

124. McSherry, *Predatory States,* p. 70.

125. Huggins, "The Making of Police Death Squads in Modern Brazil," pp. 212–214.

126. Van Reenan, "Policing Extensions," p. 36.

127. Quoted by Arnson, "Window on the Past," p. 101; see also Stanley *The Protection Racket* State for rivalries and splits.

128. Huggins, *Violence Workers,* pp. 77–80.

129. Betancourt and García, *Matones y cuadrilleros*, pp. 110–111.

130. Kruijt and Koonings, "The Military and Their Shadowy Brothers-in-Arms," p. 26; among its many death squads were the Comisionados Militares (after 1979, army counterintelligence force); Movimiento de Acción Naconalista Organizada (MANO, 1966); Hermandad Blanca (1970s and 80s); Comité de Resistencia de Guatemala (known as CRAG, late 1960s); Consejo Anticomunista de Guatemala (known as CADEG, late 1960s); Ejercito Secreto Anticomunista (ESA, created in 1977); Fuerza de Acción Armada (FADA); Frente Anticomunista del Nororiente (FANO, in the 1970s and 80s); Frente Estudantil Anticomunista (FEA); Liga Nacional de Protección Guatemalteca; Guerrilla Acción Libertadora Guatemalteca Antisalvedoreña (GALGAS, death squad specialized in killing Salvadoran refugees).

131. Almirón, *Campo Santo*, pp. 124–126, 219–221.

132. See *Nunca Mas*.

133. Roldán, *Blood and Fire*, pp. 132–133, 146. Yet the governor was pushed by Gómez and other Conservative leaders in Bogotá to counteract Liberal guerrillas, and create more Contrachusmas.

134. Ibid., p. 156.

135. Betancourt and García, *Matones y cuadrilleros*, p. 119.

136. Hristov, *Blood and Capital*, pp. 78–79.

137. Huggins, "The Making of Police Death Squads in Modern Brazil," pp. 208, 217–223.

138. Van Reenen, "Policing Extensions," pp.41–42.

139. Knight, "Political Violence in Post-revolutionary Mexico," pp. 110–113.

140. Roldán, *Blood and Fire*, p. 100.

141. Romero, *Paramilitares y autodefensas*, p. 90.

CHAPTER 3: BODIES OF THE SLAIN

1. Didion, *Salvador*, pp. 15–20, 45–46.

2. Casper and Moore, *Missing Bodies*, pp. 8–9. Casper and Moore are interested in why some bodies matter and others "fail to matter."

3. Though one should mention two very different books, Clea Koff, *The Bone Woman: A Forensic Anthropologist's Search for Truth in the Mass Graves of Rwanda, Bosnia, Croatia, and Kosovo*, and Mary Roach, *Stiff: the Curious Lives of Human Cadavers*.

4. There is practically no discussion of dead bodies, let alone their political uses and meanings, in mainstream theory books. See Bryan Turner's *The Body and Society*, and Lock and Farquhar's *Beyond the Body Proper*.

5. Verdery, *Political Lives of Dead Bodies*, pp. 1–3. Her main focus is on the political uses of famous dead in "postsocialist" countries of Eastern Europe and the former Soviet Union, the "bones and corpses" of those people who "have become political symbols."

6. Ibid., pp. 22 and 25, 51, 27–28. She agrees with Reinhart Koselleck that people's uses of dead bodies, digging them up and reburying them, though similar in form, have local political meaning, p. 22.

7. Johnson, "Why Dead Bodies Talk," pp. 2–3. They focus on Obregon's arm, Santa Anna's leg, and Perón's hands, among others.

8. Ibid., pp. 4–6, 8.

9. Scarry, *The Body in Pain,* pp. 72–73. She argues that the "language of 'by-product' denotes 'accidental,' 'unwanted,' 'unsought,' 'unanticipated,' and 'useless,'" though she also notes that soldiers understand the use "to which they have been summoned," to kill or to be killed. Certainly in the case of political murder, bodies of the slain are not "unanticipated" by-products.

10. *Good-Bye to All That,* p. 163. Graves admitted that he "vomited more than once while superintending the carrying."

11. As Koff notes in *The Bone Woman,* p. 11.

12. See Roach, *Stiff,* pp. 61–69

13. Verdery, *Political Lives of Dead Bodies,* pp. 31–32.

14. Elshtain, "Introduction: Bodies and Politics," p. xi–xii; Cloyd, "Torture, Human Rights, and the Body," p. 244.

15. Foucault, *Discipline and Punish,* p. 8.

16. Ekirch, *At Day's Close,* p. 141.

17. Verdery, *Political Lives of Dead Bodies,* p. 28.

18. Foucault, *Discipline and Punish,* p. 14; Casper and Moore, *Missing Bodies,* pp. 6–7

19. Taylor, *Body Horror,* pp. 138 and 140.

20. Ibid., pp. 141–142.

21. Lynch, *Argentine Caudillo,* p. 99; Schroeder, "To Induce a Sense of Terror," p. 28; Shapiro, *Invisible Latin America,* p. 77; Miranda, *The Stroessner Era,* p. 93; Aldama, "Violence, Bodies, and the Color of Fear," p. 3.

22. Didion, Salvador, p. 20; Rose, The Unpast, p. 246; Huggins "The Making of Police Death Squads in Modern Brazil," pp. The "EM" also had its own more official public relations man, Ivo Americano Alves Brito, a former Federal Police security agent, who boasted of assassinations on the radio, while death squad members often published accounts of their work in police newsletters.

23. Johnson, "Why Dead Bodies Talk," p. 20.

24. Brunk, "Mortal Remains of Emiliano Zapata," pp. 147–149.

25. Dosal, "San Ernesto," pp. 326, 328–330.

26. Torres, "Bloody Deeds," pp. 144–145. She looked at Prensa Libre, the national daily with the largest circulation in the period, 1978–1984. She noted that not all cadavers made it into the reports; in fact, the huge majority did not; it was a controlled sample; also, reports focused on individual deaths and avoided descriptions of massacres (even though most deaths were produced by massacres), p. 147.

27. Menchú, *I, Rigoberta Menchú,* pp. 229–235.

28. Haba, *The Language of Life,* pp. 133–135.

29. Forché, "The Poetry of Witness," pp. 137–138; Haba, *The Language of Life,* p. 135. Despite political murder that is often brutal and vicious, and perpetrated on such a huge scale and which generates lots of bodies, people just refuse to believe in it, despite abundant evidence; in fact, ear cutting is a common way to count the dead; see Doug Farrah "Salvadoran Soldiers Tell of Cutting Off Ears of Dead Rebels," *New York Times,* May 20, 1986; see also case of Colombia in the violencia, Uribe, *Matar, rematar, contramatar,* p. 173. U.S. GI's and Marines in the Pacific during World War II, and later in Vietnam, often kept gruesome "souvenirs." There was nothing new about this behavior.

30. John Dear, "The Road to Colombia," in *Colombia Diary,* March 2006; Chip Mitchell, "Down the River in Colombia," *The Progressive,* April 2000.

31. Taussig, *Law in a Lawless Land,* p. xii.

32. Verdery, *Political Lives of Dead Bodies,* p. 42. Verdery on proper burial: "Because the living not only mourn their dead but also fear them as sources of possible harm, special efforts are made to propitiate them by burying them properly."

33. Verbitsky, *The Flight,* pp. 146–147.

34. Elshtain, "Introduction: Bodies and Politics," p. xv.

35. García, *Micropolíticas del cuerpo,* p. 141.

36. Robben, "Terror in the Netherworld," p. 98.

37. Roach, *Stiff,* pp. 21, 37–57.

38. Uribe, *Matar, rematar, contramatar,* pp. 173–187.

39. Betancourt and García, *Matones y cuadrilleros,* pp. 77–78.

40. Schroeder, "To Induce a Sense of Terror," p. 34.

41. Menchú, I, Rigoberta Menchú, pp. 201–211. This famous account, part of the reason she won a Nobel Peace Prize, generated a later controversy because it was her family members who witnessed the scene, but it is written as if she did. See Arias, *The Rigoberta Menchú Controversy.*

42. Brody, *Contra Terror,* pp. 154, 160, 171–172, 178.

43. Uribe, *Matar, rematar, contramatar,* pp. 167–168.

44. Luz Maria Sierra, "Colombia busca a 10 mil muertos," *El Tiempo* (Bogotá) April 24, 2007.

45. Hristov, *Blood and Capital,* p. 83.

46. Gleijeses, *Politics and Culture in Guatemala,* p. 11.

47. Schirmer, *The Guatemalan Military Project,* p. 312, note 13.

48. Verdery, *Political Lives of Dead Bodies,* p. 28.

49. Ibid., pp. 28 and 33.

50. Torres, "Bloody Deeds," pp. 148–152; as noted in REMHI, 1998, publication, Proyecto Interdiocesano de Recuperación de la Memoria Histórica; Guatemala Nunca Más, vol.s I and II.

51. Gleijeses, *Politics and Culture in Guatemala,* p. 11.

52. Robben, "Terror in the Netherworld," pp. 93, 197–98, 103.

53. Lewis, *Guerrillas and Generals,* p. 5.

54. Joyce and Stover, *Witnesses from the Grave,* p. 206.

55. Robben, "Terror in the Netherworld," p. 95.

56. Anderson, *Matanza,* pp. 131–132.

57. Joyce and Stover, *Witnesses from the Grave,* pp. 213–214.

58. Sanford, *Buried Secrets.*

59. See Livingstone, *Inside Colombia* for bodies in rivers, among others.

60. Luz Maria Sierra, "Colombia busca a 10 mil muertos," *El Tiempo* (Bogotá) April 24, 2007.

61. Juan Manuel Echavarría, "Death and the River," *Virginia Quarterly Review,* Fall 2007.

62. Milagros Salazar, ""Police Are Throwing Bodies in the River,' Say Native Protesters," CommonDreams.org, June 9, 2009; See also, "Peru Police Concealing Bodies of Indian Dead, NGO Charges," *Latin American Herald Tribune,* July 13, 2009.

63. Rose, *The Unpast,* pp. 236–237, 246, 260; his effort is interesting, but somewhat problematic in its overarching assumptions.

64. Verbitsky, *The Flight,* pp. 7–8, 19, 21, 23, 25, 49.

65. Joyce and Stover, *Witnesses from the Grave,* p. 213.

66. Wright, *State Terrorism in Latin America,* p. 111.

67. Roach, *Stiff,* pp. 119–121. Roach reports that much of the data was produced in 1968 by Richard Snyder in his study of people who committed suicide by jumping off the Golden Gate Bridge.

68. From *Nunca Más,* p. 223; Sanford, *Buried Secrets,* p. 47.

69. Schirmer, *The Guatemalan Military Project,* pp. 167–168.

70. Mazzei, *Death Squads or Self-Defense Forces?,* p. 114.

71. Roach, *Stiff,* p. 50.

72. Robben, "Terror in the Netherworld," p. 105.

73. Johnson, "Why Dead Bodies Talk," p. 20.

74. Braun, *Assassination of Gaitán,* pp. 184–185, 188–189.

75. Dosal, "San Ernesto," pp. 322, 326, 331. Dosal points to bodies, ideas, and ambivalence; p. 317. All the houses in La Higuera, where Che was executed, have "some sort of shrine" dedicated to his person; p. 318. Many people throughout the world "still revere Che for what he was in life, a militant anti-imperialist and an atheist." Yet his cause of world revolution "has been displaced by a meaningless commodity, an image that sells as well in the capitalist West as in communist Cuba." (But who is buying it? How many are believers?) pp. 319–320. Dosal argues that Che's ideals are dead . . . p. 321. Quoting Che's "Message to the Tricontinental" on death, "Whenever death may surprise us it will be welcome," as long as others take up the fight and "intone our funeral dirge with the staccato of machine guns." Dosal seems to think that he died in vain and that his revolution is dead; perhaps but many people did take up his fight in the 1970s and 80s, in the Southern Cone, Central America, and Colombia, many carry on.

76. Verbitsky, *The Flight,* pp. 7–8, 19, 21, 23, 25, 49–50.

77. Ibid., pp p. 128.

78. Robben, "Terror in the Netherworld," pp. 91–92.

79. Koff, *The Bone Woman,* p. 262.

80. Koff, *The Bone Woman,* pp. 7–9; In Rwanda, for example, the evidence shows that police and militia forces were wont to herd people into buildings or confined spaces, and slaughter them with blunt or sharp implements, especially machetes, usually stopping only to eat. Churches were particularly favored; pp. 23–24.

81. Ibid., pp. 259, 261–262.

82. Anderson, *Matanza,* pp. 131–132.

83. Luz Maria Sierra, "Colombia busca a 10 mil muertos," *El Tiempo* (Bogotá) April 24, 2007.

84. Sanford, *Buried Secrets,* p. 17.

85. Ibid., pp. 44–45.

86. Joyce and Stover, *Witnesses from the Grave,* pp. 235, 258–261.

87. Sanford, *Buried Secrets,* pp. 30, 32–36.

88. Ibid., pp. 37–39, 42–43, 47. Yet for many in the murderous elite, even such murders were not a crime, since guerrilla "supporters" were valid targets in their view.

89. Joyce and Stover, *Witnesses from the Grave,* p. 243.

90. Robben, "Terror in the Netherworld," pp. 104–107.

91. Ibid., p. 101.

Chapter 4: Dirty Warriors on Dirty War

1. The quote, from 1976, reflected the "theory of the three circles," according to which, the struggle could not be restricted to the first circle (that of the subversives proper), but had to be pursued into the second and third circles, where the sympathizers and the merely suspicious dwelt. See Torres-Riva, "Epilogue," pp. 290–291. Saint-Jean's words were quoted in Lewis, *Guerrillas and Generals,* p. 143, Roniger, "U.S. Hemispheric Hegemony," p. 33, among many others. D'Aubuisson quoted by Loren Jenkins, "El Salvador," *The Washington Post Magazine,* Aug. 16, 1981; Rio Montt quoted in Gleijeses, *Politics and Culture in Guatemala,* p. 9; Castaño speaking in Aranguren Molina, *Mi confesión,* pp. 121–122.

2. Gill, *The School of the Americas,* pp. xiii–xviii. He insisted that "I have done nothing wrong, nothing more than serve my country." Her image harkens more to members of the old school, dictators such as Hernández Martínez in El Salvador, Trujillo in the Dominican Republic, Batista in Cuba, Stroessner in Paraguay, and Somoza García in Nicaragua, though more modern examples are also available.

3. Robben, "The Politics of Truth and Emotions," p. 83.

4. Clea Koff notes that this mentality is hardly confined to Latin America. Asking "why did those governments decide to murder their own people" she answers, "I think the answer is self-interest." Their single-minded goal was to "maintain power for themselves." "In each of the places I've worked, the official 'reasons' were in fact rhetoric-packaged justifications designed to dilute popular resistance to committing

crimes against humanity." "I don't believe government officials were materially concerned with ancient battles or religious or ethnic takeovers. Rather they were focused on real issues of sustainability and power." Koff, *The Bone Woman,* p. 262.

5. Richani conjectured (in hindsight prematurely at the beginning of the Uribe era) that given the growing instability of forces perpetuating Colombia struggles, as well as the maturing inclination of important parts of the elite for peace, that the time could be "ripe" to bring an end to the war system. Richani, *Systems of Violence,* p. 154.

6. Mazzei, *Death Squads or Self-Defense Forces?,* p. 144. See Stanley, *Protection Racket State* as well.

7. Lewis, *Guerrillas and Generals,* pp.134–135.

8. Mazzei, *Death Squads or Self-Defense Forces?* pp. 10–11, 134, 161.

9. Lechner, "Some People Die of Fear," p. 27

10. Romero, *Paramilitares y autodefensas,* p. 81.

11. Lauria-Santiago, "Culture and Politics of State Terror and Repression," pp. 92–95.

12. Anderson, *Matanza,* p. 131.

13. Lewis, *Guerrillas and Generals,* p. 4. Brazilian elite views were similar, as were those of the elite Colombian anti-Gaitanistas who also shared a pronounced antipathy for "la chusma," as Herbert Braun noted at various points; see *The Assassination of Gaitán.*

14. Fagan, "Repression and State Security," pp. 43, 39, 44.

15. Ruiz, *Colombian Civil War,* p. 169.

16. Díaz Bessone, *Guerra revolucionaria,* pp. 25, 60–75.

17. Romero, *Paramilitares y autodefensas,* pp. 19–23, 79, 122–123, 125, 129, 134.

18. Aranguren Molina, *Mi confesión,* pp. 94–97. Castaño and Ernesto Báez spoke of Guarín's importance.

19. Aranguren Molina, *Mi confesión,* p. 116–118. Was this group a figment of his imagination? Perhaps, but it represents what most Colombians believe exists behind it all, especially after April 9, 1948.

20. Guillermoprieto, "Confessions of a Killer." "His actual credibility is of course the central question. Castaño fails to mention a large number of civilian massacres with which the family name or his organization has been linked. He denies participation in those he does not mention, although in many cases survivors and eyewitnesses have implicated him, his brother, or his associates."

21. Mazzei, *Death Squads or Self-Defense Forces?* p. 128; Rosenberg, *Children of Cain,* p. 264.

22. Arnson, "Window on the Past," pp. 95 and 110.

23. So argued "General Falcón," in Marchak, *God's Assassins,* p. 284.

24. Joyce and Stover, *Witnesses from the Grave,* p. 216.

25. Etchecolatz, La otra campana, pp. 105–108.

26. Verbitsky, *The Flight,* pp. 67–68, 91–94, 70–71.

27. Ibid., pp. 13–14.

28. Aranguren Molina, *Mi confesión*, pp. 40, 43–45.

29. Guillermoprieto, "Confessions of a Killer."

30. Verbitsky, *The Flight*, p. 7.

31. Robben, "The Politics of Truth and Emotions," p.

32. Steven Dudley seems to do just that with the UP in Colombia when he faults them for their embrace of the "todas las formas de lucha" strategy. He overlooks the virtual inevitability, given Colombia's long history of repression against all parties of the left, that they would have been targeted for political murder no matter what they did. See *Walking Ghosts*.

33. See the Brazilian case, where the military was not mediocre, in which armed struggle by the Left in the 1960s and 1970s was a spectacular failure; Alves, *State and Opposition in Military Brazil*, pp. 104–105, 119.

34. Díaz Bessone, *Guerra revolucionaria*, pp. 29–39.

35. Etchecolatz, *La otra campana*, pp. 7–8, 19–21. He was also angry about being prosecuted, and devoted a large part of the book to his legal tribulations; he contended that many Argentine legislators were "integrated into the terrorist organizations" at the time, and were part of the Marxist, communist left; pp. 9, 43–45.

36. Almirón, *Campo Santo*, pp. 121–122.

37. Verbitsky, *The Flight*, pp. 18, 23. At first there was a good deal of support for the 1976 coup in the more well-heeled sectors of Argentine society, but many voices of protest were also silenced, such as Rodolfo Walsh.

38. Verbitsky, *The Flight*, pp. 11–12.

39. Betancourt and García, *Matones y cuadrilleros*, pp. 106–110.

40. Aranguren Molina, *Mi confesión*, pp. 96–97.

41. The author heard it from an old Conservative street speaker in Cali.

42. Lewis *Guerrillas and Generals*, pp. 142, 137.

43. Verbitsky, *The Flight*, p. 30.

44. Robben, "The Politics of Truth and Emotions," p. 81. He sounds very much like General Jack Ripper before he shot himself . . . completely justified, though Robben was not sure whether he was being truthful even with himself.

45. Etchecolatz, *La otra campana*, p. 11.

46. McSherry, *Predatory States*, p. 1.

47. Lewis *Guerrillas and Generals*, p. 131.

48. Frontalini and Caiati, *El mito de la guerra sucia*, p. 75.

49. Hodges, *Dirty War*, pp. 180–181; see also Duhalde, *El estado terrorista*.

50. Quoted in Kirk, *More Terrible than Death*, p. 62. See also General Fernando Landazábal's *Estrategia de la subversion y su desarrollo en la América Latina*.

51. In Marchak, *God's Assassins*, pp. 267–268. His clear implication, it predated the officers who served through the Proceso; they inherited the problem. Subversion was an old problem they had to clean up.

52. Ibid., pp. 268–269, 271, 275–276.

53. Ibid., pp. 273–74.

54. Aranguren Molina, *Mi confesión*, pp. 115–116, 120–121, 183, 227–226.

55. Hodges, *Dirty War*, p. 181.

56. Seri, "Vicious Legacies," pp. 186, 191.

57. Frontalini and Caiati, *El mito de la guerra sucia,* pp. 221–227.

58. Drouin, "Understanding the 1982 Guatemalan Genocide," p. 84.

59. Schirmer, *The Guatemalan Military Project,* pp. 125, 128.

60. Galuga, *Counterinsurgency Warfare,* p. 126.

61. Díaz Bessone, *Guerra revolucionaria.*

62. Schirmer, *The Guatemalan Military Project,* p. 136; interviews, 1990–1994.

63. Ibid., pp. 137 and 140.

64. Ibid., p. 137.

65. Dinges, *The Condor Years,* p. 119.

66. Manitzas, "All the Minister's Men," p. 89, opinion voiced in a January 1983 interview.

67. Gill, *The School of the Americas,* pp. xiii–xviii. The general complained that if a commandant were to do "the right thing in his operations" against the "subversives" and hit them "hard," then "it's easy to denounce him and to say that he was the one who disappeared such-and-such a person."

68. Aranguren Molina, *Mi confesión,* p. 100.

69. Note, for instance, the case of the hit squad sent to Europe to avenge the murders of the Israeli athletes killed by the PLO in Munich in 1972. It had many of the classic characteristics of Latin American paramilitary groups; see Jonas, Vengeance, pp. 77–81.

70. Huggins, "The Making of Police Death Squads in Modern Brazil," p. 210.

71. Aranguren Molina, *Mi confesión,* p. 142.

72. Schirmer, *The Guatemalan Military Project,* pp. 138 and 140. See Kubrick's *Doctor Strangelove* for another eerie parallel: [Turgidson advocates a further nuclear attack to prevent a Soviet response to Ripper's attack.] General "Buck" Turgidson: Mr. President, we are rapidly approaching a moment of truth both for ourselves as human beings and for the life of our nation. Now, truth is not always a pleasant thing. But it is necessary now to make a choice, to choose between two admittedly regrettable, but nevertheless *distinguishable,* postwar environments: one where you got twenty million people killed, and the other where you got a hundred and fifty million people killed. President Merkin Muffley: You're talking about mass murder, General, not war! General "Buck" Turgidson: Mr. President, I'm not saying we wouldn't get our hair mussed. But I do say no more than ten to twenty million killed, tops. Uh, depending on the breaks.

73. LeoGrande, *Our Own Backyard,* pp. 48–49.

74. Robben, "The Politics of Truth and Emotions," pp. 90–91.

75. Bowden, *Killing Pablo,* pp. 177–178.

76. The full title of Kubrick's 1964 film is *Dr. Strangelove, Or: How I Learned to Stop Worrying and Love the Bomb.*

77. Crahan, *Human Rights and Basic Needs in the Americas,* pp. 7 and 102.

78. Roniger, "U.S. Hemispheric Hegemony," pp. 31–33.

79. McSherry Predatory States, pp. 17 and 13. This no more true than the assertion that all repressive ideas emanate from Washington, DC.

80. McClintock, "American Doctrine," pp. 131–138; Lindsay quoted in Grandin, *Empire's Workshop,* pp. 98–99. Theodore Shackley was a CIA operative in Laos and Vietnam who worked with a paramilitary army of ethnic Meos and with the Phoenix Program published *The Third Option* in 1981, pushing counterinsurgency techniques and covert action.

81. McSherry *Predatory States,* pp. 10–11. Is counterinsurgency always conducted "illegally"?

82. See Walker, "Introduction," pp. 12–14.

83. Lewis, *Guerrillas and Generals,* p. 135.

84. Ibid., pp. 136–138.

85. Ibid., pp. 136–143.

86. Grandin, *Empire's Workshop,* pp. 89–94; see also Waghelstein, "Counterinsurgency Doctrine."

87. See *The Central American Crisis Reader,* pp. 506–509.

88. McClintock, "American Doctrine and Counterinsurgent State Terror," p. 121.

89. Kruijt and Koonings, "Introduction: Violence and Fear in Latin America," pp. 15–16. See also Hirstov, *Blood and Captial,* pp. 58–63.

90. Ryan, "Turning on Their Masters," pp. 295–296.

91. Perelli, "From Counterrevolutionary Warfare to Political Awakening," p. 28. Even McSherry, who generally stressed the U.S. role, noted that "each Latin American military blended the new security doctrine with its own historical traditions and perceptions of domestic threat. The form and extent of political repression differed in each country." McSherry, *Predatory States,* p. 51.

92. Betancourt and Garcia, *Matones y cuadrilleros,* p. 9.

93. Kirk, *More Terrible than Death,* pp. 47–49; Gulula, *Counterinsurgency Warfare,* p. 124.

94. See Dinges, *Condor Years,* p. 112, and Frontalini and Caiati, *El mito de la guerra sucia,* pp. 22 and 25.

95. Manitzas, "All the Minister's Men," p. 88.

96. Hodges, *Dirty War,* p. 179. "Besides identifying the enemy with international subversion, he likened the struggle against subversion to that of Nazi Germany against its own 'red menace.'" Duhalde, *El estado terrorista,* pp. 81–84.

97. Gleijeses, *Politics and Culture in Guatemala,* p. 6.

98. Wilkinson, *Silence on the Mountain,* p. 210. For an in depth analysis of the method, see Centro Internacioinal par Investigaciones en Derechos Humanos. *Draining the Sea: An Analysis of Terror in Three Rural Communities in Guatemala, 1980–1984.*

99. Danner, *Massacre at El Mozote,* p. 44.

100. Romero, *Paramilitares y autodefensas,* pp. 119–121; Kirk, *More Terrible than Death,* p. 48.

101. Hodges, *Dirty War,* pp. 176 and 178.

102. Schwarz, *American Counterinsurgency Doctrine,* p. 80; Schwarz, "Dirty Hands," pp. 108–109.

103. Policzer, *The Rise and Fall of Repression in Chile.*
104. Aranguren Molina, *Mi confesión,* pp. 98 and 104.
105. Robben, "Terror in the Netherworld," p. 94.
106. Knight, "Political Violence in Post-revolutionary Mexico," p. 118.

Chapter 5: International Collaborations and the Conflicted Roles of the United States

1. Dinges, *The Condor Years*, pp. 10–15.

2. To be discussed: Menjívar and Rodríguez, *When States Kill*; Gill, *School of the Americans*; Grandin, *Empire's Workshop*; McSherry, *Predatory States*; and most recently, Esparza, Huttenback, and Feierstein, and their authors, who "emphasize the 'U.S. factor' in shaping political violence," in their "Introduction," to *State Violence and Genocide in Latin America*, p. 9.

3. Kruijt, "Exercises in State Terrorism," pp. 43–44.

4. See Woodward, *The Veil.*

5. The U.S. role in encouraging political murder was certainly key in some smaller countries, e.g. Honduras and Uruguay; yet even in those two cases, other countries were also vital in training, especially the Argentines.

6. Grandin, *Empire's Workshop*, pp. 2, 42, 46–49. See also Schmitz, *Thank God They're on Our Side*, chapter 5.

7. Lindsay-Poland, *Emperors in the Jungle*, p. 6–7, 9.

8. McSherry, *Predatory States,* p. 50. The most balanced work on Phoenix is Moyer, *Phoenix and the Birds of Prey*; see also the extensive portrait in Valentine, *The Phoenix Program*; and Cook, *The Advisor* for the view of a participant.

9. Huggins, "U.S.–Supported State Terror," pp. 219–220.

10. Grandin, *Empire's Workshop*, p. 88; this of course assumes that what went on in those countries was "U.S." violence.

11. Gill, *School of the Americas,* pp. 6–9, 26; reasons for the existence of the SOA evolved from fighting communism to drugs ("narcoguerrillas") and on to the war on terror, p. 10.

12. Ibid., pp. 9, 46–49, 30–31, 73–75. Honduras (and other little places) fits her argument better than the big countries; it was also a special case as the U.S. staging area for Contra war.

13. McSherry, *Predatory States,* pp. 111–112.

14. Sikkink, *Mixed Signals*, pp. xiv–xv. She too noted that in 1976, Secretary of State Kissinger and Vice President Rockefeller "essentially gave" the Argentine military "a green light for repression."

15. Dinges, *Condor Years,* pp. 156–158.

16. LeoGrande, *Our Own Backyard,* pp. 580–589.

17. Grandin, *Empire's Workshop*, pp. 13–14, 178, 4–7, 154, 181.

18. Gill, *School of the Americas,* pp. 36–37.

19. Bowden, *Killing Pablo*, pp. 176–178.

20. Grandin, *Empire's Workshop*, pp. 46–48; see also Rabe *The Most Dangerous Area*.

21. Schmitz, *The U.S. and Right-Wing Dictatorships*, pp. 241–243.

22. LeoGrande, *Our Own Backyard*, pp. 582–584; Sikkink, *Mixed Signals*, pp. xiv–xv.

23. Schmitz, *The U.S. and Right-Wing Dictatorships*, pp. 242–243.

24. Roniger, "U.S. Hemispheric Hegemony," pp. 24–26; for Bolivia after 1952 see Lehman, *Bolivia and the United States*.

25. Grandin, *Empire's Workshop*, p. 49.

26. Roniger, "U.S. Hemispheric Hegemony," pp. 34–35.

27. Kruckewitt, "U.S. Militarization of Honduras," pp. 177–178, 188–191.

28. Bowden, *Killing Pablo*, pp. 194–196.

29. Grandin, *Empire's Workshop*, p. 115.

30. Dinges, *Condor Years*, pp. 165, 170, 193, 199.

31. Sikkink, *Mixed Signals*, pp. xiii–xix.

32. Armony, *Argentina and the U.S. in Central America*, pp. 39–41.p33. LeoGrande, *Our Own Backyard*, p. 585; Sikkink, *Mixed Signals*, pp. xvii–xviii; Schmitz, *The U.S. and Right-Wing Dictatorships*, p. 243.

34. Grandin, *Empire's Workshop*, p. 4; Gill, *School of the Americas*, pp. 236, 59–60.

35. Calloni, *Los Años del Lobo*, p. 16.

36. McSherry, *Predatory States*, pp. 249, 36.

37. Gill, *School of the Americas*, pp. 1, 3, 233–234.

38. McSherry, *Predatory States*, pp. 46, 48, 52, 58.

39. Gill, *School of the Americas*, pp. 233–234.

40. Latin Americans are very sensitive to such language. As the old saying goes, "el que coje no es maricón," which can be translated as "he who fucks is not the queer," or in this case, "the bitch."

41. See McClintock, *The American Connection*, vol. I, and *Instruments of Statecraft*.

42. Grandin, *Empire's Workshop*, pp. 86–88, 95–96.

43. McSherry, *Predatory States*, pp. 3, 35.

44. Gómez-Suárez, "U.S.-Colombian Relations in the 1980s," p. 162.

45. McSherry, *Predatory States*, pp. 11, 35, 253; Condor's operations "were consistent with U.S. counterinsurgency and counter terror doctrine and training;" p. 247. True, but they were consistent with French doctrine and training as well.

46. Grandin, *Empire's Workshop*, p. 13.

47. Gill, *School of the Americas*, pp. 60–61. But she still insists that the SOA took Latin American security forces and "molded them into proxy armies under U.S. tutelage."

48. Hristov, *Blood and Capital*, p. 43.

49. Menjívar and Rodríguez, "State Terror in the U.S.-Latin American Interstate Regime," pp. 3–5

50. Sluka, "Introduction: State Terror," pp. 7–9; Herman, *The Real Terror Network*, p. 132. One can ask, what about Soviet and Chinese use of terror? The real point is, all the big imperial powers use state terror at times, and certainly did so during the Cold War.

51. Sluka, "Introduction: State Terror," pp. 7–9.

52. Lewis, *Guerrillas and Generals*, p. 136.

53. Gill, *School of the Americas,* pp. 51–52.

54. Dinges, *Condor Years,* pp. 105–106.

55. Gill, *School of the Americas,* p. 50; Reimann, *Confesiones de un contra*, p. 29; Almirón, *Campo Santo*, pp. 151–152.

56. Haba, *The Language of Life,* p.133.

57. Gill, *School of the Americas,* pp. 72–73, 77.

58. Ibid., p. 110.

59. McSherry, *Predatory States,* pp. 1, 54, 17, 52. She notes Brazil's role in creating intel organizations (but still puts it under U.S.), p. 53.

60. Calloni, *Los Años del Lobo*, pp. 12, 17, 19–26.

61. See Nilson Cezar Mariano, *Operación Condor: Terrorismo del estado en el Cono Sur*, and Francisco Martorell, *Operación Condor: El vuelo de la muerte*, as well as Dinges, *The Condor Years.*

62. McSherry, *Predatory States,* pp. 45–46, 48–53.

63. Ibid., p. 6.

64. Dinges, *Condor Years,* p. 100.

65. McSherry, *Predatory States,* pp. 69, 78–94.

66. Dinges, *Condor Years,* pp. 72, 150–154.

67. McSherry, *Predatory States,* pp. 4–10.

68. Ibid., pp. 108, 115, 122.

69. Armony, "Producing and Exporting State Terror," pp. 305–306.

70. Kruckewitt, "U.S. Militarization of Honduras," pp. 177–178.

71. Americas Watch, "Human Rights in Honduras," pp. 8–12.

72. Armony, "Producing and Exporting State Terror," pp. 313, 320, 325.

73. Armony, *Argentina and the U.S. in Central America,* p. xvi.

74. McSherry, *Predatory States,* p. 56.

75. Ryan, "Turning on Their Masters," pp. 282–283, 286, 288, 290; but when Ryan argues that "it is obvious that without foreign, primarily U.S. assistance, the Uruguayan security forces would have been quite simply incapable of initiating a campaign of terror that was institutionalized, comprehensive, and technologically sophisticated" (pp. 295–297), he seems to be selling them a little short.

76. Armony, "Producing and Exporting State Terror," pp. 321–325.

77. Grandin, *Empire's Workshop*, pp. 113–117.

78. Armony, "Producing and Exporting State Terror," pp. 321–325.

79. Ibid., pp. 321–325. See also Armony, *Argentina and the U.S. in Central America*, pp. 122–123.

80. Eich and Rincón, *The Contras*, pp. 11–13, 30–39.

81. Yeves, *La contra: Una guerra sucia*, pp. 49–50, 52.

82. Armony, *Argentina and the U.S. in Central America*, pp. xx, 172–173, 8–9, 26.

83. Dinges, *The Condor Years*, pp. 10–11.

84. Armony, "Producing and Exporting State Terror," p. 325.

85. Gill, *School of the Americas*, p. 11.

Chapter 6: The Enduring Appeal and Continuing Challenge of Political Murder in Latin America and Beyond

1. Marchak, *God's Assassins*, p. 337; "El asesinato de Santillán," *Página/12*, June 27, 2002; "Max Kosteki: el artista que no dejaron ser," *El Naciente*, June 30, 2003; Seri, "Vicious Legacies," pp. 182–183.

2. Ford, *Political Murder: From Tyrannicide to Terrorism*, pp. 387, 2.

3. And much of Ford's evidence pointed to the effectiveness of repression, though he largely ignored it. It should also be remembered that Ford's long work was decidedly Eurocentric. In one of his last chapters he made a few waving gestures toward Latin America, but clearly was not prepared for the new campaign that would have been required to really deal with its implications. Rather unconvincingly he asserted that "little would be gained by simply enumerating the monotonous roll of Latin American assassination attempts in recent years, their heaviest concentrations occurring in El Salvador, Nicaragua, and Guatemala to the north and Bolivia as well as Argentina a the extreme south, with a generous scattering in between," Ford, *Political Murder*, p. 340.

4. Mazzei, *Death Squads or Self-Defense Forces?*, p. 139.

5. See Green, *Gaitanismo*.

6. Spencer, *Colombia's Paramilitaries*, pp. 22–23, 12.

7. Schwarz, "Dirty Hands," pp. 108–109.

8. Dinges, *The Condor Years*, p. 229.

9. Henderson, *When Colombia Bled*, pp. 180.

10. See the conflicting views of Paul Lewis and Thomas Wright on this point in *Guerrillas and Generals* and *Terrorism in Latin America*.

11. See Grandin, *Empire's Workshop*, Gill, *The School of the Americas*, and Klein, *The Shock Doctrine* for variations on this theme.

12. In the simultaneous globalization both of violence and legal norms, it is possible that the decline of political murder might ironically have something to do with the globalization of the economies. At the same time, violence might now be following a different dictate.

13. Drouin, "Understanding the 1982 Guatemalan Genocide," pp. 95–96.

14. Kruijt and Koonings, "Introduction: Violence and Fear in Latin America," pp. 1–2.

15. Van Reenen, "Policing Extensions," pp. 44–48.

16. Savenije and Van Der Borgh, "Youth Gangs," pp. 155, 157, 168–169.

17. Elízaga, "Terror and Violence in Mexican Political Culture," pp. 78–79.

18. Knight, "Political Violence in Post-Revolutionary Mexico," p. 120.

19. Chevigny, "Police Deadly Force," pp. 212–213.

20. Seri, "Vicious Legacies," pp. 183, 186, 188; see also McSherry, *Incomplete Transition,* pp. 182–186 on the "remnants of the grupos de tareas."

21. See Smith, *Killer Elite,* as well as Seahill, Blackwater, and Pelton, *Licensed to Kill.*

22. See Fontananrrosa, *Todo Boogie.*

23. Pelton, *Licensed to Kill,* pp. 17–41. For memoirs, see Herrington, *Stalking the Vietcong: Inside Operation Phoenix;* Walker, *Seal! From Vietnam's Phoenix Program to Central America's Drug Wars;* and Crowell, *ICEX Intelligence: Vietnam's Phoenix Program.*

24. Dahlia Lithwick, "The Fiction Behind Torture Policy," *Newsweek,* July 26, 2008.

25. From the August 22, 2005, broadcast of "The 700 Club."

26. Cited by Greg Sargent's "The Plum Line" in the WashingtonpostOnline, June 15, 2010; Broadcast report on Fox 5 Atlanta, Oct. 14, 2010; noted by *Washington Post* columnist Dana Milbank, Jan. 26, 2011.

27. Silva, "Collective Memories," p. 192.

28. See Mary Lacy, "4 Salvadorans Killed in a Way that Evokes 80s Conflict," NYTS, Feb. 21, 2007.

29. Seri, "Vicious Legacies," p. 188.

30. Mazzei, *Death Squads or Self-Defense Forces?* pp. 130, 201, 212.

31. Seri, "Vicious Legacies," p. 192.

32. Sanford, *Buried Secrets,* p. 46.

33. Robben, "Terror in the Netherworld," p. 96.

34. Garretón, "Fear in Military Regimes," p. 23.

35. The phrase "culture of fear" was coined by Guillermo O'Donnell in 1983; Garretón, "Fear in Military Regimes," p. 23.

36. Sluka, "Introduction: State Terror," pp. 22–23. See also, Taussig, *Law in a Lawless Land.*

37. Kruijt, "Exercises in State Terrorism," pp. 45, 47.

38. Koonings, "Shadows of Violence and Political Transition in Brazil," p. 203. See Stephan, *Rethinking Military Politics.*

39. Garretón, "Fear in Military Regimes," p. 23.

40. Corradi, et al., "Fear: A Cultural and Political Construct," p. 5.

41. Lechner, "Some People Die of Fear," p. 26.

42. Kruijt and Koonings, "Introduction: Violence and Fear in Latin America," pp. 18–19.

43. Piero Gleijeses, *Politics and Culture in Guatemala,* pp. 4, 6–7, 14–15.

44. Wilkinson, *Silence on the Mountain,* p. 60.

45. Silva, "Collective Memories, Fears, and Consensus," p. 176.

46. Fagen, "Repression and State Security," p. 40.

47. Rial, "Makers and Guardians of Fear," p. 99.

48. Robben, "Terror in the Netherworld," p. 96.

49. Torres-Rivas, "Epilogue: Notes on Terror," pp. 285–286.

50. Dinges *Condor* Years, p. 229.

51. McSherry, *Predatory States*, p. xvii.

52. Sikkink, *Mixed Signals*, p. xiv.

53. Rummel, *Death By Government*, p. 27.

54. Tate, *Counting the Dead*, pp. 8–10, 26, 72–75. See also the activism around the School of the Americas; Hodge and Cooper, *Disturbing the Peace*; and Nelson-Pallmeyer, *School of Assassins*.

55. Tate, *Counting the Dead*, pp 72–75. She could also have added the influence of the left Liberal tradition of the 1930s and 1940s, and the Gaitanistas. It is interesting to note that Uribe et al have a point, technically, when they equate human rights defenders with guerrillas in that there is a "family" connection; they are connected to the extent that both insurgents and human rights activists want to change the world. Of course, the fact that most human rights groups are not really in league with the insurgents (indeed, Amnesty International forcefully rejects and condemns rebel violence) is not important to practitioners of political murder, not that they believe the denials anyway. It fits in with their tendency to lump all voices for change together as legitimate targets; to them, it is logical and reasonable.

56. Ibid., pp. 107–108, 167–168.

57. Sikkink, *Mixed Signals*, pp. xviii, xix, 208.

58. Verdeja, "Political Violence, Justice, and Reconciliation," pp. 172–173.

59. Ibid., pp. 173–175.

60. Ibid., pp. 177–179.

61. Ibid., pp. 175–176.

62. Joyce and Stover, *Witnesses from the Grave*, pp. 251–252.

63. Dinges, *Condor Years*, pp. 230–232.

64. Her group of over thirty contributors included scholars, human rights activists, and diplomats.

65. Afflitto, "Homogenizing Effects of State-Sponsored Terror," pp. 115, 124–125.

66. Tate, *Counting the Dead*, p. 30.

67. Grandin and Klubock, "Editor's Introduction—Truth Commissions," p. 1.

68. Ibid., pp. 2–3.

69. Ibid., pp. 4–6. Grandin and Klubock are right to be skeptical about the "liberal" way, but in the end, they still seem to offer a version of it. The world does not seem to be plowing ahead towards a rosy postcapitalist future; more likely is a general collapse of the system, in which case the future is likely to be even more Hobbesian.

70. Ibid., p. 1.

71. Verdeja, "Political Violence, Justice, and Reconciliation," pp. 169–171.

72. Garretón, "Fear in Military Regimes," p. 24.

73. Sanford, *Buried Secrets*, p. 35.

74. Molina Mejía, "Bringing Justice to Guatemala," p. 232.

75. Torres-Rivas, "Epilogue: Notes on Terror," pp. 292–293.

76. Pécaut, "From the Banality of Violence to Real Terror," p. 148.

77. Gill, *School of the Americas,* pp. 12–15.

78. Ibid., 189–190.

79. Verbitsky, *The Flight*, pp. 69, 3–16. They were demonstrating the logic of impunity when in1994 Lt. Commanders Juan Carlos Rolón and Antonio Pernías wanted their promotions to full Captain, and were afraid the navy would abandon them. Their position was logical since, as they argued, most if not all naval officers were rotated through all duties during the dirty war; and they were just following orders (and indeed, had been pardoned by the "Full-Stop" and "Due Obedience" laws); finally, since the men who had issued their orders had been confirmed as admirals, the senate had no choice but to promote them. In their testimony, they acknowledged that torture was used on disappeared subversives, who were later executed. In the process, they admitted that the navy had been lying all along. Yes, they were chuckleheads who should have kept their mouths shut; but they were just being "logical" and "reasonable."

80. Kruijt and Koonings, "Introduction: Violence and Fear in Latin America," pp. 3, 5, 11.

81. Kruijt and Koonings, "The Military and Their Shadowy Brothers-in-Arms," pp. 16–19.

82. Hirstov, *Blood and Capital*, pp. 24–25; Torres-Rivas, "Notes on Terror."

83. Hirstov, *Blood and Capital*, p. 31.

84. Corradi, "Towards Societies without Fear," p. 285. Some argue that "transitional justice" though imperfect, may be the best way to go; see Pierre Hazan *Judging War, Judging History: Behind Truth and Reconciliation*; and see also Marth Minow *Between Vengeance and Forgiveness*, and Verdeja, *Unchopping a Tree.*

85. Tate, *Counting the Dead*, pp. 55–71.

86. Ibid., pp. 68–71.

87. Ibid., pp. 215–218, 255–256 [and other countries pp. 219–222].

88. See the trilogy of works by Steve J. Stern, his so-called *Memory Book of Pinochet's Chile*, that explores this question: Book 1, *Remembering Pinochet's Chile*; Book 2, *Battling for Hearts and Minds*; Book 3, *Reckoning with Pinochet.*

89. Grandin and Klubock, "Editor's Introduction—Truth Commissions," p. 3. See also Roniger and Sznajder, *The Legacy of Human Rights Violations in the Southern Cone.*

90. See C.J. Chivers, "Slain Exile Detailed Cruelty of Ruler of Chechnya," *The New York Times*, Jan. 31, 2009; Luke Harding, "Chechen President Threatened Murdered Campaigner, Human Rights Group Alleges," *The Guardian*, July 16, 2009; K. Anthony Appaih, "Russia's War on Words," *The New York Times*, Oct. 7, 2009; Editorial, "The Courage of Russia's Journalists," *The New York Times*, May 19, 2010; see also the case of the punk band "Pussy Riot;" Karin Brulliard, "In Pakistan, A Pattern of Disappearances," *The Washington Post*, Oct. 2, 2011; Austin Ramzy, "State Stamps Out Small 'Jasmine' Protests in China," *Time*, Feb. 21, 2011;

Scott Shane, "U.S. Decision to Approve Killing of Cleric Causes Unease," *The New York Times*, May 13, 2010.

91. Tate, *Counting the Dead*, pp. 22–23. As she acknowledged Taussig's point, Tate rejected those who insist that it is impossible to "pierce the veil" of the "hallucinatory terror that is endemic to Colombian life," and her objection is valid for the rest of Latin America as well.

92. See the collection edited by Craig Smith, *Silencing the Opposition*.

93. Cloyd, "Torture, Human Rights, and the Body," p. 243.

94. McSherry *Predatory States*, pp. 50–51; Horowitz, "The Rise and Fall of Project Camelot," p. 4; See also Pyle, *Military surveillance of Civilian Politics*; Halperin, *The Lawless State: The Crimes of U.S. Intelligence*.

APPENDIX: POLITICAL MURDER IN LATIN AMERICA: INDIVIDUAL COUNTRY NARRATIVES

1. During the 2002 attempted coup against Hugo Chávez, at the Llaguno Bridge Massacre, nineteen were shot dead, but by who is not clear. And during 1989 riots against the IMF austerity program, "by some accounts" there were more than one thousand murdered; see Grandin and Klubock, "Editors' Introduction," p. 2. The events of early 2014 could earn Venezuela a spot on the list. See Chapter 1.

2. Argentina's long history of political murder can be explored in Crassweller, *Perón*; Hodges, *Argentina's "Dirty War"*; Lewis, *Guerrillas and Generals*; Marchak, *God's Assassins*; Neilson, *En tiempo de oscuridad*; Anderson, *Dossier Secreto*; Duhalde, *El estado terrorista argentino*; Anzorena, *Tiempo de violencia y utopia*; Feinmann, *López Rega*; Frontalini and Caiati, *El mito de la guerra sucia*; Feitlowitz, *A Lexicon of Terror*; González Janzen, *AAA: La triple A*; Larraquy, *López Rega, el Peronismo y la Triple A*; Guest, *Behind the Disappearances*; Graham, *A State of Fear*; Guzman Bouvard, *Revolutionizing Motherhood*; Armony, *Argentina, the United States, and the Anti-Communist Crusade*.

3. On Bolivia, see Malloy and Gamarra, *Revolution and Reaction*; Sivak, *El asesinato de Juan José Torres*; Hylton and Thomson, *Revolutionary Horizons*, Lehman, *Bolivia and the United States*; Dunkerley, *Rebellion in the Veins*; Sanabria, *El crimen politico en Bolivia*; Gallardo Lozada, *De Torres a Banzer*; Sandoval Rodríguez, *El proyecto político military*; Salmón, *the Defeat of Che Guevara*.

4. Finally, for the case of Brazil, see Alves, *State and Opposition in Military Brazil;* Montero, *Brazilian Politics*; Huggins, "The Making of Police Death Squads in Modern Brazil;" Rose, *The Unpast*; Huggins, et al., *Violence Workers*; Koonings, "Shadows of Violence;" Williams and Weinstein, "Vargas Morto;" Archdiocese of São Paulo, *Torture in Brazil*; Cancelli, *O mundo da violencia*; Graham, *Patronage and Politics*; Zuluar, "Urban Violence and Drug Warfare in Brazil;" Human Rights Watch, *Police Brutality in Urban Brazil*; Pereira, "An Ugly Democracy?"; Power, *The Political Right in Postauthoritarian Brazil*.

5. Montero quoting Anthony Pereira, *Brazilian Politics*, p. 48; see Pereira, "An Ugly Democracy?" pp. 220–221.

6. Huggins, *Violence Workers*, p. 75.

7. Chile's detour into the realm of political murder is depicted in Dinges, *The Condor Years*, as well as his *Assassination on Embassy Row*; Policzer, *The Rise and Fall of Repression in Chile*; Klein, *The Shock Doctrine*; Constable and Valenzuela, *A Nation of Enemies*; Cavallo, Salazar, and Sepúlveda, *La historia oculta del régimen military*; Escalante, *La mission era matar*; Houser, *The Execution of Charles Horman*; Kornbluh, *The Pinochet File*; Muñoz, *The Dictator's Shadow*; Verdugo, *Los zarpazaos del puma* and *Chile, Pinochet, and the Caravan of Death*; Wright, *State Terrorism in Latin America.*

8. Representative (though varying) portraits of Colombia's experience with political murder can be found in Leal Buitrago, "Armed Actors in the Colombian Conflict"; Richani, *Systems of Violence*; Romero, *Paramilitares y autodefensas*; Dudley, *Walking Ghosts*; Bergquist and Sánchez, eds, *Violence in Colombia*; Braun, *The Assassination of Gaitán*; Betancourt and García, *Matones y cuadrilleros*; Fluharty, *Dance of the Millions*; Green, *Gaitanismo*; Henderson, *When Colombia Bled*; Hristov, *Blood and Capital*; Hylton, *Evil Hour in Colombia*; Kirk, *More Terrible than Death*; Palacios, *Entre la legitimidad y la violencia*; Roldán, *Blood and Fire*; Taussig, *Law in a Lawless Land*; Uribe, *Matar, rematar, contramatar*; Tate, *Counting the Dead*; Human Rights Watch, "The Rise and Growth of Successor Groups;" Carroll, *Violent Democratization.*

9. Different interpretations of the Cuban experience can be found in Fontaine, "Communism in Latin America;" A.Chomsky, *A History of the Cuban Revolution* (for a more balanced view, acknowledging the accomplishments of the revolutionary regime); Arboleya, *The Cuban Counter-Revolution*; Shapiro, *Invisible Latin America*; Faber, *Revolution and Reaction in Cuba*; see also Chase, "The Trials: Violence and Justice in the Aftermath of the Cuban Revolution."

10. Works that outline the relevant history of the Dominican Republic include Turitis, *Foundations of Despotism*; Drederich, *Trujillo: Death of the Goat*; Aquino García, *Holocaust in the Caribbean*; Atkins and Wilson, *the Dominican Republic and the United States*; Crassweller, *Trujillo*; Franco, *La era de Trujillo*; Galíndez, *The Era of Trujillo*; Hicks, *Blood in the Streets*; Mencía Lister, *Trujillo y su época*; Roorda, *The Dictator Next Door.*

11. For Ecuador, see Becker, *Indians and Leftists*, and his electronic appendix.

12. Different accounts of El Salvador's ordeal can be found in Anderson, *Matanza*; Stanley, *The Protection Racket State*; Mazzei, *Death Squads or Self-Defense Forces?* Lauria-Santiago, "Culture and Politics of State Terror and Repression in El Salvador;" Schwarz, "Dirty Hands;" LeoGrande, *Our Own Backyard*; Doggett, *Death Foretold*; Menzel, *Bullets Versus Ballots*; Arnson, "Window on the Past;" Byrne, *El Salvador's Civil War*; Danner, *The Massacre at El Mozote*; Binford, *The El Mozote Massacre*; Lungo Velés, *El Salvador en los 80*; McClintock, *The American Connection, Vol. I*; Whitfield, *Paying the Price*; White, *The History of El Salvador*; Santiago, *The Social-Historical Construction of Repression in El Salvador.*

13. Versions of Guatemala's story are told in Drouin, "Understanding the 1982 Guatemalan Genocide;" Ball, *State Violence in Guatemala*; Centro Internacional para Investigationes en Derechos Humanos, *Draining the Sea*; Cullather, *Secret History*; Delli Sante, *Nightmare or Reality: Guatemala in the 1980s*; Garrard-Burnett, *Terror in the Land of the Holy Spirit*; Gleijeses, *Politics and Culture in Guatemala*; Jonas, *The Battle for Guatemala*; Kruijt, "Exercises in State Terror;" May, *Terror in the Countryside*; Sanford, *Buried Secrets*; Grandin, *The Last Colonial Massacre*; McClintock, *The American Connection, Vol. II*; Levenson-Estrada, *Trade Unionists Against Terror*; Streeter, *Managing the Counterrevolution*.

14. For Honduras, see Kruckewitt, "U.S. Militarization of Honduras;" LaFeber, *Inevitable Revolutions*; Méndez, *Human Rights in Honduras*; Pine, *Working Hard, Drinking Hard*; Schulz and Schulz, *The United States, Honduras, and the Crisis in Central America*; Morris, *Honduras: Caudillo Politics and Military Rule*.

15. Mexico's telling history of political murder can be followed in Simpson, *Many Mexicos;* Knight, "Habitus and Homicide," and "Political Violence in Post-revolutionary Mexico;" Sherman, *The Mexican Right*; Aguayao Quezada, *La charola*; López Astrain, *La guerra de baja intensidad en Mexico*; Sierra Guzmán, *El enemigo interno*; Damirón, *Asesinatos políticos en Mexico*; Ronquillo, *La guerra oculta*; Smith, *Pistoleros and Popular Movements*; Gutiérrez Moreno, *Violencia en Guerrero*; Bobrow-Strain, *Intimate Enemies*; Hernández Navarro, *Chiapas: La guerra y la paz*; Hirales, *Camino a Acteal*; Moguel, *Chiapas: La guerra de los signos*; Weinberg, *Homage to Chiapas*.

16. Knight, "Political Violence in Post-revolutionary Mexico," pp. 116–118.

17. For views of Nicaragua's ordeal see MacAulay, *The Sandino Affair*; Walker, *Nicaragua: Living in the Shadow of the Eagle*; Kinzer, *Blood of Brothers*; Grossman, "The Blood of the People;" Schroeder, "To Induce a Sense of Terror;" Miranda and Ratliff, *The Civil War in Nicaragua*; Brody, *Contra Terror*; Yeves, *La contra*; Maera, *Contra Cross*; Eich and Rincón, *The Contras*; Dickey, *With the Contras*; Dillon, *Comandos*; Dixon and Jonas, *Nicaragua Under Siege*; Kagen, *A Twilight Struggle*; Cabestrero, *Blood of the Innocent*.

18. Nicaraguans were unaware that graduates of West Point tended to go into the U.S. Army, while Marine Corps officers were more likely to be graduates of the Naval Academy at Annapolis Maryland. It was simply the case that their experience with U.S. military personnel came largely from Marines.

19. On Panama, see Alodier Zárate, "Muertos y desaparecidos durnate la época military," *La Prensa* November 9, 2003; Mike Billington, *Sun Sentinel*, March 12, 1988; Buckley, *Panama*; Kester and Sánchez, *In the Time of Tyrants*; Lindsay-Poland, *Emperors in the Jungle*; Dinges, *Our Man in Panama*.

20. Regarding Paraguay, see Lewis, *Paraguay under Stroessner*; Miranda, *The Stroessner Era*; Almada, *Paraguay, la cárcel olvidada*; Boccia Paz, *Es mi informe*, *En los sótanos de los generals*, and *La década inconclusa*; Meilinger de Sannemann, *Paraguay en el operative Cóndor*.

21. For the interesting case of Peru, see Beggar, "The Path of State Terror in Peru;" Burt, *Political Violence and the Authoritarian State in Peru*; Conaghan,

Fujimori's Peru; Amnesty International, *Peru: La Matanza de Cayara*; Degregori, "Reaping the Whirlwind;" Human Rights Watch, *Into the Quagmire*; Manitzas, "All the Minister's Men;" Nelson, *El tiempo de miedo*; Poole and Renique, *Peru: Time of Fear*; Umberto, *Ojo por ojo*; Stern, "Introduction: Beyond Enigma."

22. For the case of Uruguay, consult Rial, "Makers and Guardians of Fear;" Ryan, "Turning on their Masters;" Caetano and Rilla, *Breve historia de la dictadura*; Cores, *Memorias de la resistencia*; Fernández Huidobro, *Historia de los tupamaros (vol.s 1–3)*; Gardo, *Confesiones para un genocidio*; Markarian, *Left in Transformation*; Myers, *Los años oscuros.*

Bibliography

General Works on Political Violence, Murder, Genocide, Assassination, Culture, and the Human Body

Aldama, Arturo J. "Violence, Bodies, and the Color of Fear." In *Violence and the Body: Race, Gender, and the State.* Ed. Arturo J. Aldama. Bloomington: Indiana University Press, 2003. 1–15.

Belfield, Richard. *The Assassination Business: A History of State-Sponsored Murder.* New York: Carroll & Graf Publishers, 2005.

Bell, J. Bowyer. *Assassin!* New York: St. Martin's Press, 1979.

Bergquist, Charles W. *Labor in Latin America: Comparative Essays on Chile, Argentina, Venezuela, and Colombia.* Stanford, CA: Stanford University Press, 1986.

Camellion, Richard. *Assassination: Theory and Practice.* Boulder, CO: Paladin Press, 1977.

Campbell, Bruce B. "Death Squads: Definition, Problems, and Historical Context." In *Death Squads in Global Perspective: Murder with Deniability.* Eds. Bruce B. Campbell and Arthur D. Brenner. New York: Palgrave Macmillan, 2000. 1–26.

Campbell, Bruce B., and Arthur D. Brenner, Eds. *Death Squads in Global Perspective: Murder with Deniability.* New York: Palgrave Macmillan, 2000.

Casper, Monic J., and Lisa Jean Moore. *Missing Bodies: the Politics of Visibility.* New York: New York University Press, 2009.

Chirot, Daniel, and Clark McCauley. *Why Not Kill Them All? The Logic and Prevention of Mass Political Murder.* Princeton, NJ: Princeton University Press, 2006.

Clarke, James W. *American Assassins: The Darker Side of Politics.* Princeton, NJ: Princeton University Press, 1982.

Cloyd, J. Timothy. "Torture, Human Rights, and the Body." In *Politics and the Human Body: Assault on Dignity.* Eds. Jean Bethke Elshtain and J. Timothy Cloyd. Nashville, TN: Vanderbilt University Press, 1995. 243–257.

Cook, John L. *The Advisor: The Phoenix Program in Vietnam.* Atglen, PA: Schiffer Publishing, 2000.

Cooney, Mark. *Is Killing Wrong? A Study in Pure Sociology*. Charlottesville: University of Virginia Press, 2009.

__________. "The Decline of Elite Homicide." *Criminology*, 1997 (35)3:381–407.

Cooper, H.H.A. *On Assassination*. Boulder, CO: Paladin Press, 1984.

Cromell, G. LaVerne. *ICEX Intelligence: Vietnam's Phoenix Program*. Baltimore: PublishAmerica, 2006.

Crotty, William J., Ed. *Assassinations and the Political Order*. New York: Harper & Row, 1971.

Dawkins, Richard. *The Selfish Gene*. New York: Oxford University Press, 2nd ed. 1990.

Du Preez, Peter. *Genocide: The Psychology of Mass Murder*. New York: Boyars/Bowerdean, 1994.

Duvall, Raymond D., and Michael Stohl. "Governance by Terror." In *The Politics of Terrorism*, 3rd ed. Ed. Michael Stohl. New York: Marcel Dekker, 1988. 231–271.

Ekirch, A. Roger. *At Day's Close: Night in Times Past*. New York: W.W. Norton and Company, 2005.

Elshtain, Jean Bethke. "Introduction: Bodies and Politics." In *Politics and the Human Body: Assault on Dignity*. Eds. Jean Bethke Elshtain and J. Timothy Cloyd. Nashville, TN: Vanderbilt University Press, 1995. ix–xvi.

Elshtain, Jean Bethke, and J. Timothy Cloyd, Eds. *Politics and the Human Body: Assault on Dignity*. Nashville, TN: Vanderbilt University Press, 1995.

Fein, Helen, Ed. *Genocide Watch*. New Haven: Yale University Press, 1992.

Forché, Carolyn. "The Poetry of Witness." In *The Writer in Politics*. Eds. William H. Gass and Lorin Cuoco. Carbondale: Southern Illinois University Press, 1996. 135–161.

Ford, Franklin L. *Political Murder: From Tyrannicide to Terrorism*. Cambridge, MA: Harvard University Press, 1985.

Galula, David. *Counterinsurgency Warfare: Theory and Practice*. New York: Praeger, 1964.

Gibney, Mark, et al., Eds. *The Age of Apology: Facing Up to the Past*. Philadelphia: University of Pennsylvania Press, 2008.

Geertz, Clifford. *The Interpretation of Culture: Selected Essays*. New York: Basic Books, 1973.

Grandin, Greg, and Thomas Miller Klubock. "Editor's Introduction—Truth Commissions: State Terror, History, and Memory," *Radical History Review* Issue 97 (Winter 2007), pp. 1–10.

Gurr, Ted Robert. "The Political Origins of State Violence and Terror: A Theoretical Analysis." In *Government Violence and Repression: An Agenda for Research*. Eds. Michael Stohl and George A. López. Westport, CN.: Greenwood Press, 1986. 46–48.

Haba, James, Ed. *The Language of Life: A Festival of Poets/Bill Moyers*. New York: Doubleday, 1995.

Halperin, Morton H., et al. *The Lawless State: The Crimes of the U.S. Intelligence Agencies*. New York: Penguin Books, 1976.

Havens, Murray C., Carl Leiden, and Karl M. Schmitt. *The Politics of Assassination.* Englewood Cliffs, NJ: Prentice-Hall, 1970.

Hayner, Priscilla B. *Unspeakable Truths: Facing the Challenge of Truth Commissions.* New York: Routledge, 2002.

Herman, Edward S. *The Real Terror Network: Terrorism in Fact and Propaganda.* Boston: South End Press, 1982.

Herrington, Stuart. *Stalking the Vietcong: Inside Operation Phoenix: A Personal Account.* New York: Presidio Press, 2004.

Hewitt, William L. *Defining the Horrific: Readings on Genocide and Holocaust in the Twentieth Century.* Upper Saddle River, NJ: Pearson Prentice Hall, 2004.

Hickey, Eric, Ed. *Encyclopedia of Murder and Violent Crime.* Thousand Oaks, CA: Sage Publications, 2003.

Horowitz, Irving Louis. "The Rise and Fall of Project Camelot." In *The Rise and Fall of Project Camelot: Studies in the Relationship Between Social Science and Practical Politics.* Ed. Irving Louis Horowitz. Cambridge, MA: MIT Press, 1967. 3–44.

Hudson, Miles. *Assassination.* Phoenix Mill, UK: Sutton Publishing, 2002.

Jacobson, Matthew Frye. *Barbarian Virtues: The United States Encounters Foreign Peoples at home and Abroad, 1876–1917.* New York: Hill and Wang, 2000.

Jonas, George. *Vengeance: The True Story of an Israeli Counter-Terrorist Team.* New York: Simon and Schuster Paperbacks (1984) 2005.

Joyce, Christopher, and Eric Stover. *Witnesses from the Grave: The Stories Bones Tell.* New York: Ballantine Books, 1991.

Kirkham, James F., et al. *Assassination and Political Violence, Vol. 8: A Report to the National Commission on the Causes and Prevention of Violence.* Washington, D.C.: U.S. Government Printing Office, 1969.

Klein, Naomi. *The Shock Doctrine: The Rise of Disaster Capitalism.* New York: Metropolitan Books/Henry Holtz, 2007.

Koff, Clea. *The Bone Woman: A Forensic Anthropologist's Search for Truth in the Mass Graves of Rwanda, Bosnia, Croatia, and Kosovo.* New York: Random House Trade Paperbacks, 2004.

Kuhn, Thomas S. *The Structure of Scientific Revolutions, Second Edition, Enlarged.* Chicago: The University of Chicago Press, 1970.

Lentz, Harris M. *Assassinations and Executions: An Encyclopedia of Political Violence, 1865–1986.* Jefferson, NC: McFarland and Company, 1988.

Lindsay-Poland, John. *Emperors in the Jungle: The Hidden History of the U.S. in Panama.* Durham, NC: Duke University Press, 2003.

Lock, Margaret, and Judith Farquhar, Eds. *Beyond the Body Proper: Reading the Anthropology of Material Life.* Durham, NC: Duke University Press, 2007.

Mason, T. David, and Dale A. Krane. "The Political Economy of Death Squads: Toward a Theory of the Impact of State-Sanctioned Terror." *International Studies Quarterly*, 1989, 33: 175–198.

McClintock, Michael. "American Doctrine and Counterinsurgent State Terror." In *Western State Terrorism*. Ed. Alexander George. Cambridge: Polity Press, 1991. 121–154.

———. *Instruments of Statecraft: U.S. Guerrilla Warfare, Counterinsurgency, and Counterterrorism, 1940–1990.* New York: Pantheon Books, 1992.

McConnell, Brian. *The History of Assassination.* Nashville, TN: Aurora Publishers, 1970.

Mills, C. Wright. *The Power Elite.* New York: Oxford University Press, 1956.

Moyer, Mark. *Phoenix and the Birds of Prey: Counterinsurgency and Counterrevolution in Vietnam.* Lincoln: University of Nebraska Press, 2007.

Payne, Leigh A. *Unsettling Accounts: Neither Truth nor Reconciliation in Confessions of State Violence.* Durham, NC: Duke University Press, 2008.

Pelton, Robert Young. *Licensed to Kill: Hired Guns in the War on Terror.* New York: Crown Publishers, 2006.

Porter, Lindsay. *Assassination: A History of Political Murder.* New York: The Overlook Press, 2010.

Pyle, Christopher H. *Military Surveillance of Civilian Politics, 1967–1970.* New York: Garland Publishing, 1986.

Roach, Mary. *Stiff: the Curious Lives of Human Cadavers.* New York: W.W. Norton and Company, 2003.

Robin, Corey. *The Reactionary Mind: Conservatism From Edmund Burke to Sarah Palin.* Oxford: Oxford University Press, 2011.

Rummel, R.J. *Death by Government.* New Brunswick, NJ: Transaction Publishers, 1994.

Scahill, Jeremy. *Blackwater: The Rise of the World's Most Powerful Mercenary Army.* New York: Nation Book, 2007

Scarry, Elaine. *The Body in Pain: The Making and Unmaking of the World.* Oxford: Oxford University Press, 1985.

Schmitz, David F. *Thank God They're on Our Side: The United States and Right-Wing Dictatorships, 1921–1965.* Chapel Hill: University of North Carolina Press, 1999.

Schmitz, David F. *The United States and Right-Wing Dictatorships, 1965–1989.* Cambridge: Cambridge University Press, 2006.

Scobell, Andrew, and Brad Hammitt. "Goons, Gunmen, and Gendarmerie: Toward a Reconceptualization of Paramilitary Formations." *Journal of Political and Military Sociology,* 1998, (26)2 (Winter): 213–227.

Scott, James C. *Domination and the Arts of Resistance: Hidden Transcripts.* New Haven: Yale University Press, 1990.

———. *Weapons of the Weak: Everyday Forms of Peasant Resistance.* New Haven: Yale University Press, 1985.

Shackley, Theodore. *The Third Option: An American View of Counterinsurgency Operations.* New York: Dell Publishing, 1981.

Sluka, Jeffrey A., Ed. *Death Squad: The Anthropology of State Terror.* Philadelphia: University of Pennsylvania Press, 2000.

Sluka, Jeffrey A. "Introduction: State Terror and Anthropology." In *Death Squad: The Anthropology of State Terror.* Ed. Jeffrey A. Sluka. Philadelphia: University of Pennsylvania Press, 2000. 1–45.

Smith, Craig R. *Silencing the Opposition: Government Strategies of Suppression of Freedom of Expression.* Albany, NY: SUNY Press, 1996.

Smith, Michael. *Killer Elite: The Inside Story of America's Most Secret Special Operations Team.* New York: St. Martin's Press, 2007.

Taylor, John. *Body Horror: Photojournalism, Catastrophe, and War.* New York: New York University Press, 1998.

Trinquier, Roger. *Modern Warfare: A French View of Counterinsurgency.* New York: Praeger, 1964.

Turner, Bryan S. *The Body and Society: Explorations in Social Theory.* Third Edition. London: Sage Publications, 2008.

Valentine, Douglas. *The Phoenix Program.* Lincoln, NE: An Authors Guild Backin-Print.com Edition (1990) 2000.

Valentino, Benjamin A. *Final Solutions: Mass Killing and Genocide in the 20th Century.* Ithaca, NY: Cornell University Press, 2004.

Verdery, Katherine. *The Political Lives of Dead Bodies: Reburial and Postsocialist Change.* New York: Columbia University Press, 1999.

Waghelstein, John D. "Counterinsurgency Doctrine and Low-Intensity Conflict in the Post-Vietnam." In *The American War in Vietnam: Lessons, Legacies, and Implications for Future Conflicts,* Eds. Lawrence E. Grinter and Peter M. Dunn. New York: Greenwood Press, 1987. 127–137.

Walsh, Michael J., and Greg Walker. *Seal!: From Vietnam's Phoenix Program to Central America's Drug Wars.* New York: Pocket Books, 1995.

Walter, E.V. *Terror and Resistance: A Study of Political Violence, with Case Studies of Some Primitive African Communities.* New York: Oxford University Press, 1969.

Warren, Kay B. "Conclusion: Death Squads and Complicities: Dilemmas for the Anthropology of Violence." In *Death Squad: The Anthropology of State Terror.* Ed. Jeffrey A. Sluka. Philadelphia: University of Pennsylvania Press, 2000. 226–247.

Wolpin, Miles D. *State Terrorism and Death Squads in the New World Order.* Peace Research Reviews XII, No. 3. Dundas, Canada: Peace Research Institute, 1992.

Woolf, Greg. *Et Tu, Brute? The Murder of Caesar and Political Assassination.* Cambridge, MA: Harvard University Press, 2007.

Zellner, Harold M., Ed. *Assassination.* Cambridge, MA: Schenkman Publishing Company, 1974.

Political Violence and Murder in Latin America as a Region

Amnesty International. *Getting Away with Murder: Political Killings and "Disappearances" in the 1990s.* New York: Amnesty International, 1993.

Bohning, Bon. *The Castro Obsession: U.S. Covert Operations Against Cuba, 1959–1965.* Washington, D.C.: Potomac Books, 2005.

Brockett, Charles D. *Political Movements and Violence in Central America.* Cambridge: Cambridge University Press, 2005.

Brown, Cynthia, Ed. *With Friends Like These: The Americas Watch Report on Human Rights and U.S. Policy in Latin America.* New York: Pantheon Books, 1985.

Calloni, Stella. Los años del lobo: Operación Cóndor. Buenos Aires: Ediciones Continente, 1999.

Chevigny, Paul G. *Edge of the Knife: Police Violence in the Americas.* New York: New Press, 1997.

__________ "Police Deadly Force as Social Control: Jamaica, Brazil, and Argentina." In *Vigilantism and the State in Modern Latin America: Essays on Extralegal Violence.* Ed. Martha Huggins. New York: Praeger, 1991. 189–217.

Corradi, Juan E. "Toward Societies without Fear." In *Fear at the Edge: State Terror and Resistance in Latin America.* Eds. Juan E. Corradi et al. Berkeley: Univ. of California Press, 1992. 267–292.

Corradi, Juan E., et al., Eds. *Fear at the Edge: State Terror and Resistance in Latin America.* Berkeley: Univ. of California Press, 1992.

Corradi, Juan E., Patricia Weiss Fagen, and Manuel Antonio Garretón. "Fear: A Cultural and Political Construct." In *Fear at the Edge: State Terror and Resistance in Latin America.* Eds. Juan E. Corradi et al. Berkeley: Univ. of California Press, 1992. 1–10.

Crahan, Margaret. *Human Rights and Basic Needs in the Americas.* Washington, D.C.: Georgetown University Press, 1982.

Dinges, John. *The Condor Years: How Pinochet and His Allies Brought Terrorism to Three Continents.* New York: The New Press, 2004.

Escalante, Fabián. *Executive Action: 634 Ways to Kill Fidel Castro.* Melbourne: Ocean Press, 2006.

Esparza, Marcia. "Introduction: Globalizing Latin American Studies of State Violence and Genocide." In *State Violence and Genocide in Latin America: The Cold War Years.* Eds. Marcia Esparza, et al. New York: Routledge, 2010. 1–19

Esparza, Marcia, et al., Eds. *State Violence and Genocide in Latin America: The Cold War Years.* New York: Routledge, 2010.

Fagen, Patricia Weiss. "Repression and State Security." In *Fear at the Edge: State Terror and Resistance in Latin America.* Eds. Juan E. Corradi et al. Berkeley: Univ. of California Press, 1992. 39–71.

Feierstein, Daniel, and Guillermo Levy, Eds. *Hasta que la muerte nos separe: Poder y prácticas socials genocidias en América Latina.* La Plata, AR: Ediciones Al Margen, 2004.

Fontaine, Pascal. "Communism in Latin America." In *The Black Book of Communism: Crimes, Terror, Repression.* Eds. Stéphane Courtois et al. Cambridge, MA: Harvard University Press, 1999. 647–682.

Fowler, Will, and Peter Lambert, Eds. *Political Violence and the Construction of National Identity in Latin America.* New York: Palgrave Macmillan, 2006.

García, Raúl. *Micropolíticas del cuerpo: de la conquista de América a la última dictadura militar.* Buenos Aires: Editorial Biblos, 2000.

Garretón, Manuel Antonio. "Fear in Military Regimes: An Overview." In *Fear at the Edge: State Terror and Resistance in Latin America.* Eds. Juan E. Corradi et al. Berkeley: Univ. of California Press, 1992. 13–25.

Gill, Lesley. *The School of the Americas: Military Training and Political Violence in the Americas.* Durham, NC: Duke University Press, 2004.

Godoy, Angelina Snodgrass. *Popular Injustice: Violence, Community, and Law in Latin America.* Stanford: Stanford University Press, 2006.

Grandin, Greg. *Empire's Workshop: Latin America, the United States, and the Rise of the New Imperialism.* New York: Owl Books, 2006.

Guest, Iain. *Behind the Disappearances.* Philadelphia: University of Pennsylvania Press, 1990.

Halperín Donghi, Tulio. *The Contemporary History of Latin America.* Durham, NC: Duke University Press, 1993.

Hamill, Hugh M., Ed. *Caudillos: Dictators in Spanish America.* Norman: University of Oklahoma Press, 1992.

Hodge, James, and Linda Cooper. *Disturbing the Peace: The Story of Father Roy Bourgeois and the Movement to Close the School of the Americas.* New York: Orbis Books, 2004.

Huggins, Martha. *Political Policing: The United States and Latin America.* Durham, NC: Duke University Press, 1998.

__________ "U.S.-Supported State Terror: A History of Police Training in Latin America." In *Vigilantism and the State in Modern Latin America: Essays on Extralegal Violence.* Ed. Martha Huggins. New York: Praeger, 1991. 219–242.

Huggins, Martha, Ed. *Vigilantism and the State in Modern Latin America: Essays on Extralegal Violence.* New York: Praeger, 1991.

Johnson, Lyman L., Ed. *Body Politics: Death, Dismemberment, and Memory in Latin America.* Albuquerque: University of New Mexico Press, 2004.

Joseph, Gilbert M. "Close Encounters: Toward a New Cultural History of U.S.-Latin American Relations." In *Close Encounters of Empire: Writing the Cultural History of U.S.-Latin American Relations.* Eds. Gilbert M. Joseph, Catherine LeGrand, and Ricardo D. Salvatore. Durham, NC: Duke University Press, 1998. 3–46.

Joseph, Gilbert M., Catherine LeGrand, and Ricardo D. Salvatore, Eds. *Close Encounters of Empire: Writing the Cultural History of U.S.-Latin American Relations.* Durham, NC: Duke University Press, 1998.

Kohut, David, and Olga Vilella. *Historical Dictionary of the "Dirty Wars."* Lanham: The Scarecrow Press, Inc., 2010.

Koonings, Kees, and Dirk Kruijt, Eds. *Armed Actors: Organised Violence and State Failure in Latin America.* New York: Zed Books, 2004.

Koonings, Kees, and Dirk Kruijt, Eds. *Societies of Fear: The Legacy of Civil War, Violence, and Terror in Latin America.* New York: Zed Books, 1999.

Kruijt, Dirk, and Kees Koonings. "Introduction: Violence and Fear in Latin America." In *Societies of Fear: The Legacy of Civil War, Violence, and Terror in Latin*

America. Eds. Kees Koonings and Dirk Kruijt. New York: Zed Books, 1999. 1–30.

Kruijt, Dirk, and Kees Koonings. "The Military and Their Shadowy Brothers-In-Arms." *In Armed Actors: Organised Violence and State Failure in Latin America.* Eds. Kees Koonings and Dirk Kruijt. New York: Zed Books, 2004. 16–32.

LaFeber, Walter. *Inevitable Revolutions: The United States in Central America.* New York: Norton, 1983.

Lechner, Norbert. "Some People Die of Fear: Fear as a Political Problem." In *Fear at the Edge: State Terror and Resistance in Latin America.* Eds. Juan E. Corradi et al. Berkeley: Univ. of California Press, 1992. 26–35.

Leiken, Robert S., and Barry Rubin, Eds. *The Central American Crisis Reader.* New York: Summit Books, 1987.

LeoGrande, William M. *Our Own Backyard: The United States in Central America, 1977–1992.* Chapel Hill: The University of North Carolina Press, 1998.

Lernoux, Penny. *Cry of the People: The Struggle for Human Rights in Latin America—The Catholic Church in Conflict with U.S. Policy.* New York: Penguin Books, 1982.

Lewis, Paul H. *Authoritarian Regimes in Latin America: Dictators, Despots, and Tyrants.* New York: Rowman and Littlefield, 2006.

Mariano, Nilson Cezar. *Operacíon Cóndor: Terrorismo de estado en el cono sur.* Buenos Aires: Ediciones Lohlé-Lumen, 1998.

Martorell, Francisco. *Operación Cóndor: El vuelo de la muerte, La coordinación represiva en el cono sur.* Santiago: Colección Septiembre, 1999.

Mashkin, Valentin. *Operación Cóndor: Su rastro sangriento.* Buenos Aires: Editorial Cartago, 1985.

Mazzei, Julie. *Death Squads or Self-Defense Forces? How Paramilitary Groups Emerge and Challenge Democracy in Latin America.* Chapel Hill: University of North Carolina Press, 2009.

McCuen, Gary E. *Political Murder in Central America: Death Squads and U.S. Policies.* Hudson, WI: GEM Publications, 1985.

McSherry, J. Patrice. *Predatory States: Operation Condor and Covert War in Latin America.* New York: Rowman and Littlefield, 2005.

Menjívar, Cecilia, and Nestor Rodríguez, Eds. *When States Kill: Latin America, the U.S., and Technologies of Terror.* Austin: University of Texas Press, 2005.

———. "State Terror in the U.S.-Latin American Interstate Regime." In *When States Kill: Latin America, the U.S., and Technologies of Terror.* Eds. Cecilia Menjívar and Nestor Rodríguez. Austin: University of Texas Press, 2005. 3–27.

Mina, Gianni. *Un continente desaparecido.* Mexico: Editorial Diana, 1996.

Nelson-Pallmeyer, Jack. *School of Assassins: The Case for Closing the School of the Americas and for Fundamentally Changing U.S. Foreign Policy.* New York: Orbis Books, 1997.

Nieto, Clara. *Masters of War: Latin America and U.S. Aggression from the Cuban Revolution through the Clinton Years.* New York: Seven Stories Press, 2003.

Payne, Leigh A. *Uncivil Movements: The Armed Right Wing and Democracy in Latin America.* Baltimore: The Johns Hopkins University Press, 2000.

Roniger, Luis. "U.S. Hemispheric Hegemony and the Descent into Genocidal Practices in Latin America." *In State Violence and Genocide in Latin America: The Cold War Years.* Eds. Marcia Esparza, et al. New York: Routledge, 2010. 23–43.

Roniger, Luis, and Mario Sznajder. *The Legacy of Human-Rights Violations in the Southern Cone: Argentina, Chile, and Uruguay.* Oxford: Oxford University Press, 1999.

Rosenberg, Tina. *Children of Cain: Violence and the Violent in Latin America.* New York: Penguin Books, 1992.

Sánchez Gómez, Gonzalo, and Eric Lair, Eds. *Violenicas y estrategias colectivas en la región andina: Bolivia, Colombia, Ecuador, Perú y Venezuela.* Bogotá: Grupo Editorial Norma, 2004.

Sikkink, Kathryn. *Mixed Signals: U.S. Human Rights Policy and Latin America.* Ithaca, NY: Cornell University Press, 2004.

Snodgrass Godoy, Angelina. *Popular Injustice: Violence, Community, and Law in Latin America.* Stanford, CA: Stanford University Press, 2006.

Sosa Elízaga, Raquel, Ed. *Sujetos, víctimas y territories de la violencia en América Latina.* México: Universidad de la Ciudad de México, 2004.

Stern, Steve J. "The Decentered Center and the Expansionist Periphery: The Paradoxes of Foreign-Local Encounter." In *Close Encounters of Empire: Writing the Cultural History of U.S.-Latin American Relations.* Eds. Gilbert M. Joseph, Catherine LeGrand, and Ricardo D. Salvatore. Durham, NC: Duke University Press, 1998. 47–68.

Sznajder, Mario, and Luis Roniger. *The Politics of Exile in Latin America.* Cambridge: Cambridge University Press, 2009.

Torres-Rivas, Edelberto. "Epilogue: Notes on Terror, Violence, Fear, and Democracy." In *Societies of Fear: The Legacy of Civil War, Violence, and Terror in Latin America.* Eds. Kees Koonings and Dirk Kruijt. New York: Zed Books, 1999. 285–300.

Van Reenen, Piet. "Policing Extensions in Latin America." In *Armed Actors: Organised Violence and State Failure in Latin America.* Eds. Kees Koonings and Dirk Kruijt. New York: Zed Books, 2004. 33–51.

Verdeja, Ernesto. "Political Violence, Justice, and Reconciliation in Latin America." In *State Violence and Genocide in Latin America: The Cold War Years.* Eds. Marcia Esparza, et al. New York: Routledge, 2010. 169–181.

Wright, Thomas C. *State Terrorism in Latin America: Chile, Argentina, and International Human Rights.* New York: Rowman and Littlefield, 2007.

ARGENTINA

Abós, Alvaro, *El poder carnivoro.* Buenos Aires: Editorial Legasa, 1985.

Abraham, Tomás. *Historias de la Argentina deseada*. Buenos Aires: Editorial Sudamericana, 1995.

Abuelas de Plaza de Mayo. *Niños desaparecidos, jóvenes localizados en la Argentina desde 1976 a 1999*. Buenos Aires: Temas Grupo Editorial, 1999.

Actis, Munú, Cristiana Aldini, Liliana Gardella, Miriam Lewin, and Elisa Tokar. *Ese infierno: Conversaciones con cinco mujeres sobrevivientes de la ESMA*. Buenos Aires: Editorial Sudamericana, 2001.

Almirón, Fernando. *Campo Santo: Los asesinatos del ejercito en Campo de Mayo, Testimonios del ex-sargento Víctor Ibañez*. Buenos Aires: Editorial 21 SRL, 1999.

Andersen, Martin Edwin. *Dossier Secreto: Argentina's Desaparecidos and the Myth of the "Dirty War."* Boulder, CO: Westview Press, 1993.

Anzorena, Oscar. *Tiempo de violencia y utopía: Del golpe de Onganía (1966) al golpe de Videla (1976)*. Buenos Aires: Ediciones del Pensamiento Nacional, 1998.

Armony, Ariel C. *Argentina, the United States, and the Anit-Communist Crusade in Central America, 1977–1984*. Athens, OH: Ohio University Center for International Studies, 1997.

———. "Producing and Exporting State Terror: The Case of Argentina." In *When States Kill: Latin America, the U.S., and Technologies of Terror.* Eds. Cecilia Menjívar and Nestor Rodríguez. Austin: University of Texas Press, 2005. 305–331.

Asociación Madres de Plaza de Mayo. *Historia de las madres de Plaza de Mayo*. Buenos Aires: Ediciones Asociación Madres de Plaza de Mayo, 1999.

———. *Massera: el genocida*. Buenos Aires: Editorial Página 12, 1999.

———. *Nuestros hijos*. Editorial Contrapunto SRL, 1987.

Asociación de Periodistas de Buenos Aries. *Periodistas desaparecidos: Con vida los queremos*. Buenos Aires: Unión de Trabajadores de Prensa de Buenos Aires, 1987.

Ballester, Horacio P. *Memorias de un coronel democrático: Medio siglo de historia política argentina en la óptica de un militar*. Buenos Aires: Ediciones de la Flor SRL, 1996.

Baschetti, Roberto, compilador. *Documentos 1973–1976, Vol. I: De Cámpora a la ruptura*. La Plata: Editorial de la Campana, 1996.

———. *Documentos 1973–1976, Vol. II: De la ruptura al golpe*. La Plata: Editorial de la Campana, 1999.

———. *Documentos 1976–1977, Vol I: Golpe militar y resistenica popular*. La Plata: Editorial de la Campana, 2001.

Bermúnez, Norberto, and Juan Gasparini. *El testigo secreto*. Buenos Aires: Javier Vergara Editor, 1999.

Bonasso, Miguel. *Recuerdo de la muerte (Edición Definitiva)*. Buenos Aires: Planeta/Espejo de la Argentina (1994) 2001.

Bousquet, Jean-Pierre. *Las locas de la Plaza de Mayo*. Buenos Aires: El Cid Editor, 1982.

Brysk, Alison. *The Politics of Human Rights in Argentina: Protest, Change, and Democratization.* Stanford, CA: Stanford University Press, 1994.

Calveiro, Pilar. *Poder y desaparición: Los campos de concentración en Argentina*. Buenos Aires: Ediciones Colihue SRL, 2001.

Caraballo, Liliana, Noemí Charlier and Liliana Garulli. *La dictadura, 1976–1983: Testimonio y documentos.* Buenos Aires: Eudeba, 1996.

———. *Documentos de historia argentina, 1955–1976.* Buenos Aires: Eudeba, 1998.

Centro de Estudios Legales y Sociales, Buenos Aires and Human Rights Watch. *La inseguridad policial: Violencia de las fuerzas de seguridad en la Argentina.* Buenos Aires: Eudeba, 1998.

Cheren, Liliana. *La masacre de Trelew, 22 de agosto de 1972: Institucionalización del terrorismo de estado.* Buenos Aires: Ediciones Corregidor, 1997.

Cohen Salama, Mauricio. *Tumbas anónimas: Informe sobre la identificación de restos de víctimas de la represión ilegal, Equipo Argentino de Antropología Forense.* Buenos Aires: Catálogos Editora, 1992.

Comisión Nacional sobre la Desaparición de Personas. *Nunca Más: Informe de la Comisión Nacional sobre la Desaparición de Personas.* Buenos Aires: Eudeba (1984) 2001.

Crassweller, Robert D. *Perón and the Enigmas of Argentina.* New York: W.W. Norton and Company, 1987.

D'Andrea Mohr, José Luis. *Memoria debida.* Buenos Aires: Ediciones Cohihue, 1999.

De Riz, Liliana. *La política en suspenso, 1966–1976.* Buenos Aires: Paidós, 2000.

Díaz Bessone, Rámon Genaro. *Guerra revolucionaria en la Argentina, 1959–1978.* Buenos Aires: Editorial Fraterna, 1986.

Discursos del Comandante en Jefe de la Fuerza Area Argentina Brigadier General Orlando Ramón Agosti. Author's edition, 1978.

Duhalde, Eduardo Luis. *El estado terrorista argentino: Quince años después, una mirada crítica.* Buenos Aires: Eudeba, 1999.

Dujovne Ortíz, Alicia. *Quién mató a Diego Duarte? Crónicas de la basura.* Buenos Aires: Aguilar, 2010.

Dussel, Inés, Silvia Finocchio, and Silvia Gojman. *Haciendo memoria en le país de nunca más.* Buenos Aires: EUDEBA, 1997.

Etchecolatz, Miguel O. *La otra campana del Nunca Más.* Argentina: s.n., 1988.

Feinmann, José Pablo. *López Rega: La cara oscura de Perón.* Buenos Aires: Editorial Legasa, 1987.

———. *La sangre derramada: ensayo sobre la violencia política.* Buenos Aires: Ariel, 1999.

Feitlowitz, Marguerite. *A Lexicon of Terror: Argentina and the Legacies of Torture.* Oxford: Oxford University Press, 1999.

Frontalini, Daniel, and Maria Cristina Caiati. *El mito de la guerra sucia.* Buenos Aires: Centro de Estudios Legales y Sociales (CELS), 1984.

Funes, Carlos "Chango." *Perón y la guerra sucia.* Buenos Aires: Catálogos, 1996.

Gelman, Juan, and Mara La Madrid. *Ni el flaco perdón de Dios: Hijos de desaparecidos.* Buenos Aires: Planeta/Espejo de la Argentina, 1997.

González Janzen, Ingnacio. *AAA: La triple A.* 2a Edición. Buenos Aires: Editorial Contrapunto, 1986.

Graham Yooll, Andrew. *A State of Fear: Memories of Argentina's Nightmare.* London: Eland, 1986.

Grupo de Iniciativa Por Una Convención International Sobre la Desaparición Forzada de Personas. *La desaparición: Crimen contra la humanidad.* Buenos Aires: Asamblea Permanente por los Derechos Humanos, 1987.

Guest, Iain. *Behind the Disappearances: Argentina's Dirty War Against Human Rights and the United Nations.* Philadelphia: University of Pennsylvania Press, 1990.

Guzman Bouvard, Marguerite. *Revolutionizing Motherhood: The Mothers of the Plaza de Mayo.* New York: SR Books, 2004.

Guzzetti, Ana. *Maders: El crímen de Córdoba.* Montevideo: Ediciones de la Urraca, 1993.

Hagelin, Ragnar. *Mi hija Dagmar: Una víctima del terrorismo del Estado que conmocionó a la comunidad internacional.* Buenos Aires: Sudamericana/Planeta, 1984.

Hodges, Donald C. *Argentina's "Dirty War": An Intellectual Biography.* Austin: University of Texas Press, 1991.

Invernizzi, Hernán, and Judith Gociol. *Un golpe a los libros: Represión a la cultura durante la última dictadura militar.* Buenos Aires: Eudeba, 2002.

Jauretche, Ernesto. *Violencia y política en los 70: No dejés que te la cuenten.* Buenos Aires: Ediciones del Pensamiento Nacional, 1997.

Kimel, Eduardo. *La masacre de San Patricio.* Buenos Aires: Ediciones Lohlé-Lumen (1989) 1995.

Larraquy, Marcelo. *López Rega, El Peronismo, y la Triple A.* Buenos Aires: Aguilar (2004) 2011.

Leonidas Chaves, Gonzálo, and Jorge Omar Lewinger. *Los del 73: Memoria Montonera.* La Plata: Editorial de la Campana, 1999.

Lewis, Paul H. *Guerrillas and Generals: The "Dirty War" in Argentina.* Westport: Praeger, 2002.

López Echague, Hernán. *El enigma del general Bussi: De la Operación Independencia a la Operación Retorno.* Buenos Aires: Editorial Sudamericana, 1991.

Lynch, John. *Argentine Caudillo: Juan Manuel de Rosas.* Lanham, MD: SR Books, 2006.pMarchak, Patricia. *God's Assassins: State Terrorism in Argentina in the 1970s.* Montreal and Kingston: McGill-Queen's University Press, 1999.

McSherry, J. Patrice. *Incomplete Transition: Military Power and Democracy in Argentina.* New York: St. Martin's Press, 1997.

Méndez, Eugenio. *Alte. Lacoste: Quién mató al Gral. Actis?* Cordoba: El Cid Editor, 1984.

———. *Aramburu: el crimen imperfecto.* Buenos Aires: Sudamericana/Planeta, 1987.

———. *Santucho: Entre la inteligenica y las armas.* Buenos Aires: Ediciones de La Toma, 2001.

Mittelbach, Federico and Jorge. *Sobre áreas y tumbas: Informe sobre desaparecedores.* Buenos Aires: Editorial Sudamericana, 2000.

Neilson, James. *En tiempo de oscuridad, 1976–1983.* Buenos Aires: Emecé Editores, 2001.

Neuman, Elías. *Crónica de muertes silenciadas: Villa Dovoto, 14 de marzo de 1978.* Buenos Aires: Editorial Bruguera Argentina, 1985.

Otero, Daniel. *Maten a Gutiérrez: Un crimen de la Aduana paralela*. Buenos Aires: Planeta, 1998.

Paoletti, Alipio. *Como los Nazis, como en Vietnam: Los campos de concentración en la Argentina*. Buenos Aires: Ediciones Asociación Madres de Plaza de Mayo, 1996.

Pla, Alberto J., et al. *La Década trágica: Ocho ensayos sobre la crísis argentina*. Buenos Aires: Editorial Tierra del Fuego, 1984.

Pozzi, Pablo. *Por las sendas argentinas: El PRT-ERP, La guerrilla marxista*. Buenos Aires: Eudeba, 2001.

Robben, Antonius C. G. M. *Political Violence and Trauma in Argentina*. Philadelphia: University of Pennsylvania Press, 2005.

———. "Terror in the Netherworld: Disappearance and Reburial in Argentina." In *Death Squad: The Anthropology of State Terror*. Ed. Jeffrey A. Sluka. Philadelphia: University of Pennsylvania Press, 2000. 91–113.

———. "The Politics of Truth and Emotion among Victims and Perpetrators of Violence." In *Fieldwork Under Fire: Contemporary Studies of Violence and Survival*. Eds. Carolyn Nordstrom and Antonius C.G.M. Robben. Berkeley: University of California Press, 1995. 81–103.

Rojas, Diego. *Quién mató a Mariano Ferreyara?* Buenos Aires: Grupo Editorial Norma, 2011.

Salomone, Franco. *Maten al mensajero: Periodistas asesinados y desaparecidos desde Mariano Moreno hasta José Luis Cabezas*. Buenos Aires: Editorial Sudamericana, 1999.

Sarmiento, Domingo Faustino. *Facundo: Civilization and Barbarism*. Trans. Kathleen Ross. Berkeley: University of California Press, 2004.

Seoane, María, and Vicente Muleiro. *El dictador: La historia secreta y pública de Jorge Rafael Videla*. Buenos Aires: Editorial Sudamericana, 2001.

Seoane, María, and Hector Ruiz Nuñez. *La noche de los lápices*. Buenos Aires: Editorial Contrapunto, 1986.

Seri, Guillermina S. "Vicious Legacies? State Violence(s) in Argentina." In *State Violence and Genocide in Latin America: The Cold War Years*. Eds. Marcia Esparza, et al. New York: Routledge, 2010. 182–196.

Siwak, Pedro. *Víctimas y mártires de la década del setenta en la Argentina*. Buenos Aires: Editorial Guadalupe, 2000.

Taylor, Diana. *Disappearing Acts: Spectacles of Gender and Nationalism in Argentina's "Dirty War."* Durham, NC: Duke University Press, 1997.

Troncoso, Oscar. *Cronología y documentación: El proceso de reorganización nacional/1 (De marzo de 1976 a marzo de 1977)*. Buenos Aires: Centro Editor de América Latina, 1984.

Unión de Trabajadores de Prensa de Buenos Aires. *Periodistas desaparecidos: Las voces que necesitaba silenciar la dictadura*. Buenos Aires: Grupo Editorial Norma (1986) 1998.

Verbitsky, Horacio. *El vuelo*. Buenos Aires: Planeta/Espejo de la Argentina, 1995.

Vezzetti, Hugo. *Pasado y presente: Guerra, dictadura y sociedad en la Argentina*. Buenos Aires: Siglo Veintiuno Editores Argentina, 2002.

BOLIVIA

Aguiló, Lic Federico. *"Nunca Más" Para Bolivia.* Cochabamba: Colorgraf Rodríquez, 1993.

Dosal, Paul J. "San Ernesto de la Higuera: The Resurrection of Che Guevara." In *Death Dismemberment, and Memory: Body Politics in Latin America.* Ed. Lyman L. Johnson. Albuquerque: University of New Mexico Press, 2004. 317–341.

Dunkerley, James. *Rebellion in the Veins: Political Struggle in Bolivia.* London: Verso, 1984.

Gallardo Lozada, Jorge. *De Torres a Banzer: Diez meses de emergencia en Bolivia.* Buenos Aires: Ediciones Periferia, 1972.

Harris, Richard L. *Death of a Revolutionary: Che Guevara's Last Mission.* New York: W.W. Norton & Company, 2000.

Hylton, Forrest, and Sinclair Thomson. *Revolutionary Horizons: Past and Present in Bolivian Politics.* London: Verso, 2007.

Lehman, Kenneth D. *Bolivia and the United States: A Limited Partnership.* Athens: University of Georgia Press, 1999.

Malloy, James M., and Eduardo Gamarra. *Revolution and Reaction: Bolivia, 1964–1985.* New Brunswick: Transaction Books, 1985.

Pardo Salmón, Gary. *The Defeat of Che Guevara: Military Response to Guerrilla Challenge in Bolivia.* New York: Praeger Publishers, 1987.

Sanabria, Floren. *El Crimen político en Bolivia.* La Paz: Empresa Editora Proinsa, 1988.

Sandoval Rodriguez, Isaac. *El Proyecto político militar, 1971–1982: El estado de la seguridad nacional en Bolivia.* Santa Cruz: Editorial Universidad Autónoma "Gabriel r. Moreno," 1987.

Sivak, Martín. *El asesinato de Juan José Torres: Banzer y el Mercosur de la muerte.* Buenos Aires: Ediciones del Pensamiento Nacional, 1998.

BRAZIL

Alves, Maria Helena Moreira. *State and Opposition in Military Brazil.* Austin: The University of Texas Press, 1985.

Archdiocese of São Paulo. *Torture in Brazil: A Shocking Report on the Pervasive Use of Torture by Brazilian Military Governments, 1964–1979.* Trans. Jaime Wright. Austin: University of Texas Press, 1998.

Cancelli, Elizabeth. *O mundo da violência: A policía da era Vargas.* Brasília: Editora Universidade de Brasília, 1993.

Cano, Ignacio. *The Use of Lethal Force by Police in Rio de Janeiro.* Rio de Janeiro: ISER, 1997.

Graham, Richard. *Patronage and Politics in Nineteenth-Century Brazil.* Stanford, CA: Stanford University Press, 1990.

Huggins, Martha K. "Modernity and Devolution: The Making of Police Death Squads in Modern Brazil." In *Death Squads in Global Perspective: Murder with Deniability*. Eds. Bruce B. Campbell and Arthur D. Brenner. New York: Palgrave Macmillan, 2000. 203–228.

Huggins, Martha K., et al. *Violence Workers: Police Torturers and Murders Reconstruct Brazilian Atrocities*. Berkeley: University of California Press, 2002.

Human Rights Watch. *Police Brutality in Urban Brazil*. New York: Human Rights Watch, 1997.

Koonings, Kees. "Shadows of Violence and Political Transition in Brazil: From Military Rule to Democratic Governance." In *Societies of Fear: The Legacy of Civil War, Violence, and Terror in Latin America*. Eds. Kees Koonings and Dirk Kruijt. New York: Zed Books, 1999. 197–234.

Montero, Alfred P. *Brazilian Politics: Reforming a Democratic State in a Changing World*. Cambridge: Polity Press, 2005.

Pereira, Anthony W. "An Ugly Democracy? State Violence and the Rule of Law in Postauthoritarian Brazil." In *Democratic Brazil: Actors, Institutions, and Processes*. Eds. Peter R. Kingstone and Timothy J. Power. Pittsburgh, PA: University of Pittsburgh Press, 2000. 217–235.

Pinheiro, Paulo Sérgio. "Police and Political Crisis: The Case of the Military Police." In *Vigilantism and the State in Modern Latin America: Essays on Extralegal Violence*. Ed. Martha Huggins. New York: Praeger, 1991. 167–188.

Power, Timothy J. *The Political Right in Postauthoritarian Brazil: Elites, Institutions, and Democratization*. University Park: Pennsylvania State Press, 2000.

Rose, R.S. *The Unpast: Elite Violence and Social Control in Brazil, 1954–2000*. Athens, OH: Ohio University Center for International Studies, 2005.

Stephan, Alfred C. *Rethinking Military Politics: Brazil and the Southern Cone*. Princeton, NJ: Princeton University Press, 1987.

Williams, Daryle, and Barbara Weinstein. "Vargas Morto: The Death and Life of a Brazilian Statesman." In *Body Politics: Death, Dismemberment, and Memory in Latin America*. Ed. Lyman L. Johnson. Albuquerque: University of New Mexico Press, 2004.

Zaluar, Alba. "Urban Violence and Drug Warfare in Brazil." In *Armed Actors: Organised Violence and State Failure in Latin America*. Eds. Kees Koonings and Dirk Kruijt. New York: Zed Books, 2004. 139–154.

CHILE

Constable, Pamela, and Arturo Valenzuela. *A Nation of Enemies: Chile Under Pinochet*. New York: W.W. Norton & Company, 1991.

Cavallo, Ascanio, Manuel Salazar and Oscar Sepúlveda. *La historia oculta del régimen militar: Chile, 1973–1988*. Santiago: Editorial Grijalbo, 1997.

Dinges, John, and Saul Landau. *Assassination on Embassy Row: The Shocking story of the Letelier-Moffitt Murders*. New York: McGraw-Hill Book Company, 1980.

Escalante, Jorge. *La misión era matar: El juicio a la caravana Pinochet-Arellano.* Santiago: LOM Ediciones, 2000.

Frazier, Lessie Jo. Salt in the Sand: Memory, Violence, and the Nation-State in Chile, 1890 to the Present. Durham, NC: Duke University Press, 2007.

Garcés, Joan E., and Saul Landau. Orlando Letelier: Testimonio y vindicación. Madrid: Siglo Veintiuno Editores, 1995.

Guerrero, Modesto Emilio. *Reportaje con la muerte.* Buenos Aires: Javier Vergara Editor, 2002.

Hauser, Thomas. *The Execution of Charles Horman: An American Sacrifice.* New York: Harcourt, Brace, Jovanovich, 1978.

Kornbluh, Peter. *The Pinochet File: A Declassified Dossier on Atrocity and Accountability.* New York: The New Press, 2003.

Martín de Pozuelo, Eduardo, and Santiago Tarín. *España acusa.* Barcelona: Plaza Janés, 1999.

Muñoz, Heraldo. *The Dictator's Shadow: Life Under Augusto Pinochet.* New York: Basic Books, 2008.

O'Shaughnessy, Hugh. *Pinochet: The Politics of Torture.* New York: New York University Press, 2000.

Policzer, Pablo. *The Rise and Fall of Repression in Chile.* Notre Dame: University of Notre Dame Press, 2009.

Silva, Patricio. "Collective Memories, Fears and Consensus: The Political Psychology of the Chilean Democratic Transition." In *Societies of Fear: The Legacy of Civil War, Violence, and Terror in Latin America.* Eds. Kees Koonings and Dirk Kruijt. New York: Zed Books, 1999. 171–196.

Sorensen, Kristin. *Media, Memory, and Human Rights in Chile.* New York: Palgrave Macmillan, 2009.

Stern, Steve J. *Remembering Pinochet's Chile: On the Eve of London 1998.* Durham, NC: Duke University Press, 2006.

———. *Battling for Hearts and Minds: Memory Struggles in Pinochet's Chile, 1973–1988.* Durham, NC: Duke University Press, 2006.

———. *Reckoning with Pinochet: The Memory Question in Democratic Chile, 1989–2006.* Durham, NC: Duke University Press, 2010.

Verdugo, Patricia. *Los zarpazos del puma: La caravan de la muerte.* Santiago: Ediciones ChileAmérica CESOC, 1989.

———. *Chile, Pinochet, and the Caravan of Death.* Miami, FL: North-South Center Press at the University of Miami, 2001.

Wright, Thomas C. *State Terrorism in Latin America: Chile, Argentina, and International Human Rights.* Lanham, MD: Rowman and Littlefield, 2007.

COLOMBIA

Aranguren Molina, Mauricio. *Mi confesión: Carlos Castaño revela sus secretos.* Bogotá: Editorial Oveja Negra, 2001.

Archila N., Mauricio, et al. *Conflictos, poderes e indentidades en el Magdalena medio, 1990–2001*. Bogotá: Colciencias Colombia/CINEP, 2006.
Ardila Galvis, Constanza. *The Heart of the War in Colombia*. London: Latin American Bureau, 2000.
Arnson, Cynthia, Ed. *The Peace Process in Colombia with the Autodefensas Unidas de Colombia–AUC*. Washington D.C.: Woodrow Wilson International Center for Scholars, 2005.
Arregi, Ion. *Colombia: un pueblo sentenciado a muerte*. San Sebastián: Tercera Prensa, 1998.
Baud, Michiel, and Donny Meertens, Eds. *Colombia from the Inside: Perspectives on Drugs, War and Peace*. Amsterdam: Centre for Latin American Research and Documentation, 2004.
Bergquist, Charles, and Gonzalo Sánchez, Eds. *Violence in Colombia: The Contemporary Crisis in Historical Perspective. SR.*
Betancourt, Darío, and Maria Luz García. *Matones y cuadrilleros: Orígen y evolución de la violencia en el occidente colombiano*. Bogotá: Tercer Mundo Editores, 1991.
Bouvier, Virginia M., Ed. *Colombia: Building Peace in a Time of War*. Washington D.C.: United States Institute of Peace Press, 2009.
Bowden, Mark. *Killing Pablo: The Hunt for the World's Greatest Outlaw*. New York: Penguin Books, 2001.
Braun, Herbert. *The Assassination of Gaitán: Public Life and Urban Violence in Colombia*. Madison: University of Wisconsin Press, 1985.
———. *Our Guerrillas, Our Sidewalks: A Journey into the Violence of Colombia*. Second Edition. New York: Rowman & Littlefield Publishers, 2003.
Carroll, Leah Anne. *Violent Democratization: Social Movements, Elites, and Politics in Colombia's Rural War Zones, 1984–2008*. Notre Dame, IN: University of Notre Dame Press, 2011.
Cañón M., Luis. *El patrón: Vida y muerte de Pablo Escobar*. Bogotá: Editorial Planeta Colombiana, 1994.
Castaño, José Alejandro. *Cuánto cuesta matar a un hombre? Relatos reales de las comunas de Medellín*. Bogotá: Grupo Editorial Norma, 2006.
Contreras, Joseph, with Fernando Garavito. *Biografía no autorizada de Alvaro Uribe Vélez: El señor de las sobras*. Bogotá: Editorial Oveja Negra, 2002.
Corporación Observatorio Para La Paz. *Las verdaderas intenciones de los paramilitaries*. Bogotá: Intermedio Editores, 2002.
Cortés Arévalo, Fernando. *El asesinato de Galán*. Bogotá: Planeta, 1994.
Crandall, Russell. *Driven by Drugs: U.S. Policy Toward Colombia*. Boulder, CO: Lynne Rienner Publishers, 2002.
Dudley, Steven. *Walking Ghosts: Murder and Guerrilla Politics in Colombia*. New York: Routledge, 2004.
Fluharty, Vernon Lee. *Dance of the Millions: Military Rule and Social Revolution in Colombia, 1930–1956*. Pittsburgh: University of Pittsburgh Press, 1957.
Franco Isaza, Eduardo. *Las guerrillas del llano*. Bogotá: Editorial Planeta Colombiana, 1994.

Gardeazábal, Gustavo Alvarez. *Condores no entienrran todos los días*. Medellín: Editorial Victor Hugo, 1990.

Giraldo, Javier. *Colombia: The Genocidal Democracy*. Monroe, ME: Common Courage Press, 1996.

Gómez Nadal, Paco. *Los muertos no hablan*. Bogotá: Aguilar, 2003.

Gómez-Suárez, Andrei. "U.S.-Colombian Relations in the 1980s: Political Violence and the Onset of the Unión Patriótica Genocide." In *State Violence and Genocide in Latin America: The Cold War Years*. Eds. Marcia Esparza, et al. New York: Routledge, 2010. 152–165.

Green, W. John. *Gaitanismo, Left Liberalism, and Popular Mobilization in Colombia.* Gainesville: University Press of Florida, 2003.

Guillermoprieto, Alma. "Confessions of a Killer," *New York Review of Books*, (49)15, Oct. 10, 2002.

Gutiérrez, Francisco, María Emma Wills, and Gonzalo Sánchez Gómez, Eds. *Nuestra guerra sin nombre: Transformaciones del conflicto en Colombia.* Bogotá: Grupo Editorial Norma, 2006.

Henderson, James D. When *Colombia Bled: A History of the Violencia in Tolima.* University, Alabama: The University of Alabama Press, 1985.

Hilarión, Alfonso. *Balas de la ley*. Bogotá: Editorial Santafé, 1953.

Hristov, Jasmin. *Blood and Capital: The Paramilitarization of Colombia.* Ohio University Press, 2009.

Human Rights Watch. *Colombia's Killer Networks: The Military-Paramilitary Partnership and the United States.* New York: Human Rights Watch, 1996.

———. "III. The Rise and Growth of Successor Groups." In *Paramilitaries' Heirs: The New Face of Violence in Colombia.* New York: Human Rights Watch, 2010.

———. *State of War: Political Violence and Counterinsurgency in Colombia.* New York: Human Rights Watch, 1993.

———. *The "Sixth Division": Military-Paramilitary Ties and U.S. Policy in Colombia.* New York: Human Rights Watch, 2001.

Hylton, Forrest. *Evil Hour in Colombia.* London: Verso, 2006.

Izquierdo, Germán. *Jamie Garzón: El genial impertinente.* Bogotá: Planeta, 2009.

Jaramillo, Ana María, Marta Inés Villa, and Luz Amparo Sánchez. *Miedo y desplazamiento: Experiencias y percepciones*. Medellín: Corporación Región, 2005.

Kirk, Robin. *More Terrible than Death: Massacres, Drugs, and America's War in Colombia*. New York: Public Affairs, 2003.

Landazábal, Fernando. *Estrategia de la subversion y su desarrollo en la América Latina.* Bogotá: Editorial Pax, 1969.

Lara, Patricia. *Siembra vientos y recogerás tempestades: La historia del M-19, sus protagonistas y sus destinos*. Bogotá: Editorial Planeta Colombiana, 2002.

Leal Buitrago, Francisco. "Armed Actors in the Colombian Conflict." In *Armed Actors: Organised Violence and State Failure in Latin America*. Eds. Kees Koonings and Dirk Kruijt. New York: Zed Books, 2004. 87–105.

Leech, Garry M. *Killing Peace: Colombia's Conflict and the Failure of U.S. Intervention*. New York: Information Network of the Americas, 2002.

Livingstone, Grace. *Inside Colombia: Drugs, Democracy and War*. New Brunswick, NJ: Rutgers University Press, 2004.

Mariño Macías, María Alejandra. *Sangre de mártires, semilla de esperanza: Construcción de las nociones de cuerpo y memoria tras la massacre de Trujillo*. Bogotá: Editorial Universidad del Rosario, 2011.

Martínez Osorio, Glenda (Compiladora). *Hablan los generales: Las grandes batallas del conflicto colombiano contadas por sus protagonistas*. Bogotá: Grupo Editorial Norma, 2006.

Martínez Osorio, Glenda. *Salvatore Mancuso, su vida: Es como si hubiera vivido cien años*. Bogotá: Grupo Editorial Norma, 2004.

Matta Aldana, Luis Alberto. *Poder captialista y violencia política en Colombia: Terrorismo de estado y genocidio contra la Unión Patriótica*. Bogotá: Edición Ideas y Soluciones Gráficas, 2002.

Medina Gallego, Carlos. *Autodefensas, paramilitaries y narcotráfico en Colombia: Origen, desarrollo y consolidación. El caso "Puerto Boyacá."* Bogotá: Editorial Documentos Periodisticos, 1997.

Méndez, Juan E. *Political Murder and Reform in Colombia: The Violence Continues*. New York: Human Rights Watch, 1992.

Molano, Alfredo. *Los años del tropel: Crónicas de la violencia*. Bogotá: CEREC/El Ancora Editores (1985) 1991.

Morales Riveira, Antonio, and Miguel Angel Lozano. *Edificio Colombia: Antología de los libretos del programa "Quac El Noticero."* Bogotá: Revista Número Ediciones, 2006.

Palacios, Marco. *Entre la legitimidad y la violencia: Colombia, 1875–1994*. Bogotá: Grupo Editorial Norma, 1995.

Pardo Rueda, Rafael. *La historia de las guerras*. Bogotá: Ediciones B Colombia, 2004.

Pécaut, Daniel. "From the Banality of Violence to Real Terror: The Case of Colombia." In *Societies of Fear: The Legacy of Civil War, Violence, and Terror in Latin America*. Eds. Kees Koonings and Dirk Kruijt. New York: Zed Books, 1999. 141–167.

Rangel, Alfredo, Ed. *El poder paramilitar*. Bogotá: Editorial Planeta Colombiana, 2005.

Rangel, Alfredo. *Guerreros y políticos: Diálogo y conflicto en Colombia, 1998–2002*. Bogotá: Intermedio Editores, 2003.

Richani, Nazih. *Systems of Violence: The Political Economy of War and Peace in Colombia*. Albany: State University of New York Press, 2002.

Rincón, Omar, and Marta Ruiz, Eds. *Bajo todos los fuegos: Los periodistas en el conflicto colombiano*. Bogotá: Proyecto Antonio nariño, 2002.

Roa Rojas, Mónica. *El asesinato de Carlos Pizarro*. Bogotá: Editorial Planeta Colombiana, 1995.

Rodríguez Navarrete, Martín Emilio. *Podrán matar la flor pero no la primavera: Genocidio de la Unión Patriótica*. Bogotá: Martín Emilio Rodríguez Navarrete, 2005.

Roldán, Mary. *Blood and Fire: La Violenica in Antioquia, Colombia, 1946–1953*. Durham, NC: Duke University Press, 2002.

Romero, Mauricio. *Paramilitares y autodefensas, 1982–2003*. Bogotá: Editorial Planeta Colombiana, 2003.

Romero, Mauricio, et al. *Parapolítica: La ruta de la expansión paramilitar y los acuerdos políticos*. Bogotá: Corporación Nuevo Arco Iris, 2007.

Ruiz, Bert. *The Colombian Civil War*. Jefferson, NC: McFarland & Company Publishers, 2001.

Salazar Palacio, Hernando. *Desaparecidos: El drama de las familias*. Bogotá: Intermedio Editores, 1999.

Sánchez Gómez, Gonzalo. *Guerras, memoria e historia*. Medellín: La Carreta Editores E.U., 2006.

———. "The Violence: An Interpretative Synthesis." In *Violence in Colombia: The Contemporary Crisis in Historical Perspective*. Eds. Charles Bergquist, Ricardo Peñaranda, and Gonzalo Sánchez. Wilmington, DE: SR Books, 1992. 75–124.

Sánchez Gómez, Gonzalo, and Donny Meertens. *Bandoleros gamonales y campesinos: El caso de la Violencia en Colombia*. Bogotá: El Ancora Editores (1983) 1985.

Sánchez Gómez, Gonzalo, and Donny Meertens. *Bandits, Peasants, and Politics: The Case of "La Violencia" in Colombia*. Austin: University of Texas Press, 2001.

Sanders, James. *Contentious Republicans: Popular Politics, Race, and Class in Nineteeth-Century Colombia*. Durham, NC: Duke University Press, 2004.

Simons, Geoff. *Colombia: A Brutal History*. London: Saqi Books, 2004.

Spencer, David. *Colombia's Paramilitaries: Criminals or Political Force?* Carlisle, PA: Strategic Studies Institute, 2001.

Stokes, Doug. *America's Other War: Terrorizing Colombia*. London: Zed Books, 2005.

Tate, Winifred. *Counting the Dead: The Culture and Politics of Human Rights Activism in Colombia*. Berkeley: University of California Press, 2007.

———. "Paramilitaries in Colombia," *The Brown Journal of World Affairs* 2001, Winter/Spring, Vol. VIII, Issue 1: 163–176.

Taussig, Michael. *Law in a Lawless Land: Diary of a Limpieza in Colombia*. New York: The New Press, 2003.

Uribe, María Victoria. *Antropología de la inhumanidad: Un ensayo interpretativo del terror en Colombia*. Bogotá: Grupo Editorial Norma, 2004.

———. *Enterrar y callar: Las masacres en Colombia, 1980–1993*. Bogotá: Comité Permanente por la Defensa de los Derechos Humanos, Fundación Terres des Hommes, 1995.

———. *Matar, rematar contramatar: Las masacres de la violencia en el Tolima, 1948–1964*. Bogotá: CINEP, 1990.

Vargas, Alejo. *Las fuerzas armadas en el conflicto colombiano: Antecedentes y perspectivas*. Bogotá: Intermedio Editores, 2002.

CUBA/PANAMA/ECUADOR

Anderson, John Lee. *Che Guevara: A Revolutionary Life*. New York: Grove Press (1997) 2010.

Arboleya, Jesús. *The Cuban Counter-Revolution.* Trans. by Rafael Betancourt. Athens, OH: Ohio University Center for International Studies, 2000.

Becker, Marc. *Indians and Leftists in the Making of Ecuador's Modern Indigenous Movements.* Durham, NC: Duke University Press, 2008.

Buckley, Kevin. *Panama: The Whole Story.* New York: A TOUCHSTONE BOOK, 1992.

Casey, Michael. *Che's Afterlife: The Legacy of an Image.* New York: Vintage Books, 2009.

Chase, Michelle. "The Trials: Violence and Justice in the Aftermath of the Cuban Revolution." In *A Century of Revolution: Insurgent and Counterinsurgent Violence During Latin America's Long Cold War.* Eds. Greg Grandin and Gilbert M. Joseph. Durham, NC: Duke University Press, 2010. 163–198.

Comsky, Aviva. *A History of the Cuban Revolution (Viewpoints/Puntos de Vista).* Chichester: Blackwell Publishing, 2011.

Dinges, John. *Our Man in Panama: the Shrewd Rise and Brutal Fall of Manuel Noriega.* New York: Random House, 1990.

Faber, Samuel. *Revolution and Reaction in Cuba, 1933–1960.* Middletown, CT: Wesleyan University Press, 1976.

Koster, R.M., and Guillermo Sánchez. *In the Time of Tyrants: Panama, 1968–1990.* New York: W.W. Norton and Company, 1990.

Lindsay-Poland, John. *Emperors in the Jungle: The Hidden History of the U.S. in Panama.* Durham, NC: Duke University Press, 2003.

McBeth, Brian S. *Dictatorship and Politics: Intrigue, Betrayal, and Survival in Venezuela, 1908–1935.* Notre Dame, IN: University of Notre Dame Press, 2008.

Shapiro, Samuel. *Invisible Latin America.* Boston: Beacon Press, 1963.

DOMINICAN REPUBLIC

Atkins, G. Pope, and Larman C. Wilson. *The Dominican Republic and the United States: From Imperialism to Transnationalism.* Athens: University of Georgia Press, 1998.

Crassweller, Robert D. *Trujillo: The Life and Times of a Caribbean Dictator.* New York: The Macmillan Company, 1966.

Drederich, Bernard. *Trujillo: Death of the Goat.* Boston: Little, Brown, 1978.

Franco, Franklin J. *La era de Trujillo.* Santo Domingo: Fundación Cultural Dominicana, 1992.

Galíndez Suárez, Jesús de. *The Era of Trujillo: Dominican Dictator.* Tucson: University of Arizona Press, 1973.

———. "Inside a Dictatorship." In *Cuadillos: Dictators in Spanish America.* Ed. Hugh Hamill. Norman: University of Oklahoma Press, 1992. 234–245.

García, Miguel Aquino. *Holocaust in the Carribean: The Slaughter of Twenty-Five Thousand Haitians on One Week.* (Translation by International Studies Institute of Rhode Island). Waterbury, CT: Emancipation Press, 1977.

Hicks, Albert C. *Blood in the Streets: The Life and Rule of Trujillo.* New York: Creative Age Press, 1946.

Mencía Lister, Rafael. *Trujillo y su época.* Santo Domingo: Taller, 1992.

Roorda, Eric Paul. *The Dictator Next Door: The Good Neighbor Policy and the Trujillo Regime in the Dominican Republic, 1930–1945.* Durham, NC: Duke University Press, 1998.

Turits, Richard Lee. *Foundations of Despotism: Peasants, The Trujillo Regime, and Modernity in Dominican History.* Stanford, CA: Stanford University Press, 2003.

———. "A World Destroyed, A Nation Imposed: The 1937 Haitian Massacre in the Dominican Republic." *Hispanic American Historical Review,* 2002, (82)3: 589–635.

El Salvador

Amnesty International. *El Salvador's "Death Squads"—A Government Strategy.* 1988.

———. *Political Killings by Governments.* 1983.

Anderson, Thomas. *Matanza: E Salvador's Communist Revolt of 1932.* Lincoln: University of Nebraska Press, 1971.

Arnson, Cynthia J. "Window on the Past: A Declassified History of Death Squads in El Salvador." In *Death Squads in Global Perspective: Murder with Deniability.* Eds. Bruce B. Campbell and Arthur D. Brenner. New York: Palgrave Macmillan, 2000. 85–124.

Binford, Leigh. *The El Mozote Massacre: Anthropology and Human Rights.* Tucson: The University of Arizona Press, 1996.

Brockman, James R. *The Word Remains: A Life of Oscar Romero.* Maryknoll, NY: Orbis Books, 1982.

Byrne, Hugh. *El Salvador's Civil War: A Study of Revolution.* Boulder, CO: Lynne Rienner, 1996.

Carranza, Salvador. Ed. *Mártires de la UCA.* San Salvador: UCA Editories, 1990.

Danner, Mark. *The Massacre at El Mozote.* New York: Vintage Books, 1994.

Didion, Joan. *Salvador.* New York: Vintage International, 1983.

Dogget, Martha. *Death Foretold: The Jesuit Murders in El Salvador.* Washington D.C.: Georgetown University Press, 1993.

Dunkerley, James. *The Long War: Dictatorship and Revolution in El Salvador.* London: Junction Books, 1982.

Lauria-Santiago, Aldo A. "The Culture and Politics of State Terror and Repression in El Salvador." In *When States Kill: Latin America, the U.S., and Technologies of Terror.* Eds. Cecilia Menjívar and Nestor Rodríguez. Austin: University of Texas Press, 2005. 85–114.

Lernoux, Penny, et al. *Hearts on Fire: The Story of the Maryknoll Sisters.* Maryknoll NY: Orbis Books, 1995.

"Los escuadrones de la muerte en El Salvador." Editorial Jaraguá, 1994.

Lungo Uclés, Mario. *El Salvador in the Eighties: Counterinsurgency and Revolution.* Amelia F. Shogan Trans. Philadelphia: Temple University Press, 1996.

Mason, David T., and Dale A. Krane. "The Political Economy of Death Squads: Toward a Theory of the Impact of State-Sanctioned Terror." *International Studies Quarterly*, 1989, 33, 175–198.

Menzel, Sewall H. *Bullets Versus Ballots: Political Violence and Revolutionary War in El Salvador* (1979–1991). New Brunswick, NJ: Transaction Publishers, 1994.

McClintock, Michael. *The American Connection, Volume I: State Terror and Popular Resistance in El Salvador.* London: Zed Books, 1985.

Noone, Judith M., and Cynthia Glavac. *Compañeras en el camino: Mártires de El Salvador.* San Salvador: Impreso en Talleres Gráficos, 1999.

Santiago, Aldo Laurie. *The Social-Historical Construction of Repression in El Salvador.* New York: Columbia University, 1991.

Savenije, Wim, and Chris Van Der Borgh. "Youth Gangs, Social Exclusion, and the Transformation of Violence in El Salvador." In *Armed Actors: Organised Violence and State Failure in Latin America.* Eds. Kees Koonings and Dirk Kruijt. New York: Zed Books, 2004. 155–171.

Schwarz, Benjamin C. *American Counterinsurgency Doctrine and El Salvador: The Frustrations of Reform and the Illusions of Nation Building.* Santa Monica, CA: Rand, 1991.

———. "Dirty Hands." *The Atlantic Monthly*, December 1993.

Stanley, William. *The Protection Racket State: Elite Politics, Military Extortion, and Civil War in El Salvador.* Philadelphia: Temple University Press, 1996.

White, Christopher M. *The History of El Salvador.* Westport, CT: Greenwood Press, 2009.

Whitfield, Teresa. *Paying the Price: Ignacio Ellacuría and the Murdered Jesuits of El Salvador.* Philadelphia: Temple University Press, 1996.

Zaqano, Phyllis. *Ita Ford: Missionary Martyr.* New York: Paulist Press, 1996.

GUATEMALA

Afflitto, Frank M. "The Homogenizing Effects of State-Sponsored Terrorism: The Case of Guatemala." In *Death Squad: The Anthropology of State Terror.* Ed. Jeffrey A. Sluka. Philadelphia: University of Pennsylvania Press, 2000. 114–126.

Afflitto, Frank M., and Paul Jesilow. *The Quiet Revolutionaries: Seeking Justice in Guatemala.* Austin: University of Texas Press, 2007.

Arias, Arturo. Ed. *The Rigoberta Menchú Controversy.* Minneapolis: University of Minnesota Press, 2001.

Ball, Patrick, et.al. *State Violence in Guatemala, 1960–1996: A Quantitative Reflection.* New York: American Association for the Advancement of Science, 1999.

Centro Internacioinal par Investigaciones en Derechos Humanos. *Draining the Sea: An Analysis of Terror in Three Rural Communities in Guatemala, 1980–1984.* Translation by Gretta Tovar-Siebentritt. Grupo de Apoyo Mutuo, 1996.

Cullather, Nick. *Secret History: The CIA's Classified Account of its Operations in Guatemala, 1952–1954*. Stanford: Stanford University Press, 1999.

Delli Sante, Angela. *Nightmare or Reality: Guatemala in the 1980s*. Amsterdam: Thela Publishers, 1996.

Drouin, Marc. "Understanding the 1982 Guatemalan Genocide." In *State Violence and Genocide in Latin America: The Cold War Years*. Eds. Marcia Esparza, et al. New York: Routledge, 2010. 81–103.

Erlick, June Carolyn. *Disappeared: A Journalist Silenced: The Irma Flaquer Story*. Emeryville, CA: Seal Press, 2004.

Falla, Ricardo. *Massacres in the Jungle: Ixcán, Guatemala, 1975–1982*. Trans. Julia Howland. Boulder, CO: Westview Press, 1994.

Garrard-Burnett, Virginia. *Terror in the Land of the Holy Spirit: Guatemala under General Efraín Ríos Montt, 1982–1983*. Oxford: Oxford University Press, 2010.

Gleijeses, Piero. *Politics and Culture in Guatemala*. Ann Arbor: Center for Political Studies, Institute for Social Research, University of Michigan, 1988.

Goldman, Francisco. *The Art of Political Murder: Who Killed the Bishop?* New York: Grove Press, 2007.

Grandin, Greg. *The Last Colonial Massacre: Latin America in the Cold War*. Chicago: University of Chicago Press, 2004.

Jonas, Susanne. *The Battle for Guatemala: Rebels, Death Squads, and U.S. Power*. Boulder, CO: Westview Press, 1991.

Kruijt, Dirk, "Exercises in State Terrorism: Counter-insurgency Campaigns in Guatemala and Peru." In *Societies of Fear: The Legacy of Civil War, Violence, and Terror in Latin America*. Eds. Kees Koonings and Dirk Kruijt. New York: Zed Books, 1999. 33–62.

Levenson-Estrada, Deborah. *Trade Unionists Against Terror: Guatemala, 1954–1985*. Chapel Hill: University of North Carolina Press, 1994.

May, Rachel. *Terror in the Countryside: Campesino Responses to Political Violence in Guatemala, 1954–1985*. Athens, OH: Ohio University Center for International Studies, 2001.

McClintock, Michael. *The American Connection, Volume II: State Terror and Popular Resistance in Guatemala*. London: Zed Books, 1985.

Menchú Tum, Rigoberta. *I, Rigoberta Menchú: An Indian Woman of Guatemala*. Ed. Elisabeth Burgos-Debray. Trans. Ann Wright. London: Verso (1984) 2009.

Molina Mejía, Raúl. "Bringing Justice to Guatemala: The Need to Confront Genocide and other Crimes Against Humanity." In *State Violence and Genocide in Latin America: The Cold War Years*. Eds. Marcia Esparza, et al. New York: Routledge, 2010. 209–234.

Nelson, Diane M. *A Finger in the Wound: Body Politics in Quincentennial Guatemala*. Berkeley: University of California Press, 1999.

Oglesby, Elizabeth. "Myrna Mack." In *Fieldwork Under Fire: Contemporary Studies of Violence and Survival*. Eds. Carolyn Nordstrom and Antonius C.G.M. Robben. Berkeley: University of California Press, 1995. 254–259.

Ortiz, Dianna. *The Blindfold's Eyes: My Journey from Torture to Truth*. Maryknoll, NY: Orbis Books, 2006.

Peacock, Susan C., and Adriana Beltran. *Hidden Powers in Post-Conflict Guatemala: Illegal Armed Groups and the Forces Behind Them*. Washington, D.C.: Washington Office on Latin America, 2003.

Rico, Maite, and Bertrand de la Grange. *Quién mató al Obispo? Autopsia de un crimen político*. Mexico: Editorial Planeta Mexicana, 2003.

Sanford, Victoria. *Buried Secrets: Truth and Human Rights in Guatemala*. New York: Palgrave Macmillan, 2003.

Saxon, Dan. *To Save Her Life: Disappearance, Deliverance, and the United States in Guatemala*. Berkeley: University of California Press, 2007.

Schirmer, Jennifer. *The Guatemalan Military Project: A Violence Called Democracy*. Philadelphia: University of Pennsylvania Press, 1998.

Streeter, Stephen M. *Managing the Counterrevolution: The United States and Guatemala, 1954–1961*. Athens, OH: Ohio University Center for International Studies, 2000.

Torres, M. Gabriela. "Bloody Deeds/*Hechos Sangrientos*: Reading Guatemala's Record of Political Violence in Cadaver Reports." In *When States Kill: Latin America, the U.S., and Technologies of Terror*. Eds. Cecilia Menjívar and Nestor Rodríguez. Austin: University of Texas Press, 2005. 143–169.

Wilkinson, Daniel. *Silence on the Mountain: Stories of Terror, Betrayal, and Forgetting in Guatemala*. New York: Houghton Mifflin Company, 2002.

HONDURAS

Kruckewitt, Joan. "U.S. Militarization of Honduras in the 1980s and the Creation of CIA-backed Death Squads." In *When States Kill: Latin America, the U.S., and Technologies of Terror*. Eds. Cecilia Menjívar and Nestor Rodríguez. Austin: University of Texas Press, 2005. 170–197.

Méndez, Juan E. *Human Rights in Honduras: Signs of "The Argentine Method."* New York: An Americas Watch Report, 1982.

Morris, James A. *Honduras: Caudillo Politics and Military Rulers*. Boulder, CO: Westview Press, 1984.

Pine, Andrienne. *Working Hard, Drinking Hard: On Violence and Survival in Honduras*. Berkeley: University of California Press, 2008.

Schulz, Donald E., and Deborah Sundloff Schulz. *The United States, Honduras, and the Crisis in Central America*. Boulder, CO: Westview Press, 1994.

MEXICO

Aguayo Quezada, Sergio. *La charola: Una historia de los servicios de inteligencia en México*. Mexico: Editorial Grijalbo, 2001.

Arreola, Federico. *Así fue: La historia detrás de la bala que truncó el futuro de México*. Mexico: Nuevo Siglo/Aguilar, 2004.

Barrera Bassols, Jacinto. *El caso Villavicencio: Violencia y poder en el porfiriato.* México: Extra Alfaguara, 1997.

Blancornelas, Jesús, et al. *El tiempo pasa: De Lomas Taurinas a Los Pinos.* México: Océano, 1997.

Bobrow-Strain, Aaron. *Intimate Enemies: Landowners, Power, and Violence in Chiapas.* Durham, NC: Duke University Press, 2007.

Brunk, Samuel. *Emiliano Zapata! Revolution and Betrayal in Mexico.* Albuquerque: University of New Mexico Press, 1995.

———. "The Mortal Remains of Emiliano Zapata." In *Death Dismemberment, and Memory: Body Politics in Latin America.* Ed. Lyman L. Johnson. Albuquerque: University of New Mexico Press, 2004. 141–178.

Carey, Elaine. Plaza of Sacrifices: *Gender, Power, and Terror in 1968 Mexico.* Albuquerque: University of New Mexico Press, 2005.

Carpizo, Jorge, and Julián Andrade. *Asesinato de un cardenal: Ganancia de pescadores.* Mexico: Nuevo Siglo/Aguilar, 2002.

Castañeda, Jorge G. *Sorpresas te da la vida: México 1994.* Mexico: Nuevo Siglo/Aguilar, 1994.

Coerver, Don M., Suzanne B. Pasztor, and Robert M. Buffington. *Mexico: An Encyclopedia of Contemporary Culture and History.* Santa Barbara, CA: ABC-CLIO, 2004.

Condés Lara, Enrique. *El 10 de junio no se olvida!* (halcones, paras) Benson -Q- LA 428.7 C66 2001 GET

Coordination of Non-Governmental Organizations for Peace (CONPAZ). *Militarization and Violence in Chiapas.* Mexico: CONPAZ, 1997.

Damirón, M.G. *Asesinatos Político en México, 1910–1994.* México: Planeta, 2008.

Diebel, Linda. *Betrayed: The Assassination of Digna Ochoa.* New York: Carroll & Graf Publishers, 2006.

Elízaga, Raquel Sosa. "Terror and Violence in Mexican Political Culture at the End of the Twentieth Century." In *Citizens of Fear: Urban Violence in Latin America.* Ed. Susana Rotker. New Brunswick: Rutgers University Press, 2002. 72–86.

Fernández Menéndez, Jorge. *De Chiapas a Colosio: El año que vivimos en peligro.* Mexico: Rayuela Editores, 1994.

———. *El otro poder: Las redes del narcotráfico, la política y la violencia en México.* Mexico: Nuevo Siglo/Aguilar, 2001.

Friedrich, Paul. A Mexican Cacicazgo. *Ethnology,* 1965, (4) 2: 190–209.

García, Clara Guadalupe. *Rojo: de el asesinato político en Mexico.* Barcelona: Plaza and James, 1997.

Gilly, Adolfo. *México: El poder, el dinero y la sangre.* Mexico: Nuevo Siglo/Aguilar, 1996.

Gutiérrez Moreno, Maribel. *Violencia en Guerrero.* Mexico: La Jornada Ediciones, 1998.

Hernández Navarro, Luis. *Chiapas: La guerra y la paz.* Mexico: ADN Editores, 1995.

Hirales, Gustavo. *Camino a Acteal.* Mexico: Rayuela Editores. 1998.

Hodges, Donald, and Ross Gandy. *Mexico: The End of the Revolution.* Westport CT: Praeger, 2002.

———. *Mexico Under Siege: Popular Resistance to Presidential Despotism.* London: Zed Books, 2002.

Huchim, Eduardo. *México 1994: La rebelión y el magnicidio.* Mexico: Nueva Imagen, 1994.

Joseph, Gilbert, and Daniel Nugent eds. *Everyday Forms of State Formation: Revolution and Negotiation of Rule in Modern Mexico.* Durham: Duke University Press, 1994.

Katz, Friedrich. *De Díaz a Madero.* Mexico, D.F.: Ediciones Era, 2004.

———. *The Life and Times of Pancho Villa.* Stanford, CA: Stanford University Press, 1998.

Knight, Alan. "Habitus and Homicide: Political Culture in Revolutionary Mexico." In *Citizens of the Pyramid: Essays on Mexican Political Culture.* Ed. Wil G. Pansters. Amsterdam: Thelma Publishers, 1997. 107–129.

———. "Political Violence in Post-revolutionary Mexico." In *Societies of Fear: The Legacy of Civil War, Violence, and Terror in Latin America.* Eds. Kees Koonings and Dirk Kruijt. New York: Zed Books, 1999. 105–124.

López Astrain, Martha Patricia. *La guerra de baja intensidad en México.* Mexico: Plaza y Valdés Editores, 1996.

López González, Valentín. *La muerte de General Zapata.* Cuernavaca: Instituto Estatal de Documentación de Morelos, 2001.

Loret de Mola, Rafael. *Denucia: Presidente sin palabra.* Mexico: Editorial Grijalbo (1987) 1995.

Moguel, Julio. *Chiapas: La guerra de los signos, del amanecer Zapatista de 1994 a la masacre de Acteal.* Mexico: La Jornada Editores, 1998.

Moreno, Norberto. *Genocidio: La verdadera noche de Tlatelolco.* México: s.n., 2008.

Moreno Valencia, Héctor, and José Alberto Villasana. *Sangre de mayo: El homicidio del cardenal Posandas Ocampo.* Mexico: Oceano, 2002.

Norget, Kristin. "Caught in the Crossfire: Militarization, Paramilitarization, and State Violence in Oaxaca, Mexico." In *When States Kill: Latin America, the U.S., and Technologies of Terror.* Eds. Cecilia Menjívar and Nestor Rodríguez. Austin: University of Texas Press, 2005. 115–142.

Padilla, Tawalís. *Rural Resistance in the Land of Zapata: The Jaramillista Movement and the Myth of the Pax Priísta, 1940–1962.* Durham, NC: Duke University Press, 2008.

Poniatowska, Elena. *Massacre in Mexico.* Trans. Helen R. Lane. Columbia: University of Missouri Press, 1992.

Ramírez, Carlos. *El asesor incómodo: Joseph-Marie Córdoba Montoya.* Mexico: Oceano, 1997.

Ramos, Víctor M. *Muerte de un principe.* Guadalajara: Editorial Conexión Gráfica, 1993.

Ronquillo, Victor. *La guerra oculta: Impunida y violencia política.* Mexico: Espasa-Calpe Mexicana, 1996.

Scherer García, Julio, and Carlos Monsiváis. *Los patriotas de Tlatelolco a la guerra sucia.* Mexico: Nuevo Siglo/Aguilar, 2004.

Sierra Guzmán, Jorge Luis. *El enemigo interno: Contrainsurgencia y fuerzas armadas en México.* Mexico: Plaza y Valdés Editores, 2003.

Simpson, Lesley Byrd. *Many Mexicos.* Berkeley: University of California Press, 1967.

Smith, Benjamin, and T. Pistoleros. *Popular Movements: The Politics of State Formation in Postrevolutionary Oaxaca.* Lincoln: University of Nebraska Press, 2009.

Trueba Lara, José Luis. *Magnicidio: La muerte de un candidato.* Mexico: Editorial Posada, 1994.

———. *Rául Salinas de Gortari: El abuso del poder.* Mexico: Grupo Editorial Planeta, 1996.

Weinberg, Bill. *Homage to Chiapas: The New Indigenous Struggles in Mexico.* New York: Verso, 2000.

Womack, John, Jr. *Zapata and the Mexican Revolution.* New York: Vintage Books, 1968.

NICARAGUA

Brody, Reed. *Contra Terror in Nicaragua.* Boston: South End Press, 1985.

Cabestrero, Teófilo. *Blood of the Innocent: Victims of the Contras' War in Nicaragua.* Maryknoll, NY: Orbis Press, 1985.

Dickey, Christopher. *With the Contras: A Reporter in the Wilds of Nicaragua.* New York: Simon and Schuster, 1985.

Dillon, Sam. *Comandos: The CIA and Nicaragua's Contra Rebels.* New York: Henry Holt and Company, 1991.

Dixon, Marlene, and Susanne Jonas, Eds. *Nicaragua Under Siege.* San Francisco: Synthesis Publications, 1984.

Dunbar-Ortiz, Roxanne. *Blood on the Border: A Memoir of the Contra War.* Cambridge, MA: South End Press, 2005.

Edmisten, Patricia Taylor. *Nicaragua Divided: La Prensa and the Chamorro Legacy.* Gainesville: University of West Florida Press, 1990.

Eich, Dieter, and Carlos Rincón. *The Contras: Interviews with Anti-Sandinistas.* San Francisco: Synthesis Publications, 1984.

Grossman, Richard. "'The Blood of the People': The Guardia Nacional's Fifty-Year War against the People of Nicaragua, 1927–1979." In *When States Kill: Latin America, the U.S., and Technologies of Terror.* Eds. Cecilia Menjívar and Nestor Rodríguez. Austin: University of Texas Press, 2005. 59–84.

Kagan, Robert. *A Twilight Struggle: American Power and Nicaragua, 1977–1990.* New York: The Free Press, 1996.

Kinzer, Stephen. *Blood of Brothers: Life and War in Nicaragua.* New York: G.P. Putnam's Sons, 1991.

Kornbluh, Peter. "The Covert War." In *Reagan versus the Sandinistas: The Undeclared War on Nicaragua.* Ed. Thomas W. Walker. Boulder, CO: Westview Press, 1987. 21–38.

———. "The U.S. Role in the Counterrevolution." In *Revolution and Counterrevolution in Nicaragua*. Ed. Thomas W. Walker. Boulder, CO: Westview Press, 1991. 323–349.

MacAulay, Neil. *The Sandino Affair.* Chicago: Quadrangle Books, 1967.

Miranda, Roger, and William Ratliff. *The Civil War in Nicaragua: Inside the Sandinistas.* New Brunswick, NJ: Transaction Publishers, 1993.

Navarro-Genie, Marco Aurelio. *Augusto "César" Sandino: Messiah of Light and Truth.*

Omang, Joanne, and Aryeh Neier. *Psychological Operations in Guerrilla Warfare: The CIA's Nicaragua Manual.* New York: Vintage Books, 1985.

Reimann, Elisabeth. *Confesiones de un contra: Historia de "Moisés" en Nicaragua.* Buenos Aires: Editorial Legasa, 1986.

Schroeder, Michael J. " 'To Induce a Sense of Terror': Caudillo Politics and Political Violence in Northern Nicaragua, 1926–34 and 1981–95." In *Death Squads in Global Perspective: Murder with Deniability*. Eds. Bruce B. Campbell and Arthur D. Brenner. New York: Palgrave Macmillan, 2000. 27–56.

———. "The Sandino Rebellion Revisited: Civil War, Imperialism, Popular Nationalism, and Sate Formation Muddied Up Together in the Segovias of Nicaragua, 1926–1934." In *Close Encounters of Empire: Writing the Cultural History of U.S.-Latin American Relations*. Eds. Gilbert M. Joseph, Catherine LeGrand, and Ricardo D. Salvatore. Durham, NC: Duke University Press, 1998. 208–268.

Vélez Barcenas, Jacinto. *Dr. Pedro Joaquín Chamorro Cardenal, asesinado!* Managua: SN, 1979.

———. *Porque mataron a Chamorro?* Nicaragua, 1986.

Walker, Thomas W. *Nicaragua: Living in the Shadow of the Eagle*. Fourth Edition. Boulder, CO: Westview Press, 2003.

———. "Introduction." In *Reagan versus the Sandinistas: The Undeclared War on Nicaragua*. Ed. Thomas W.Walker. Boulder, CO: Westview Press, 1987. 1–17.

———. Ed. *Reagan versus the Sandinistas: The Undeclared War on Nicaragua*. Boulder, CO: Westview Press, 1987.

———. Ed. *Revolution and Counterrevolution in Nicaragua*. Boulder, CO: Westview Press, 1991.

———. "The Armed Forces." In *Revolution and Counterrevolution in Nicaragua*. Ed. Thomas W. Walker. Boulder, CO: Westview Press, 1991. 77–100.

Yeves, Enrique. *La contra: Una guerra sucia*. Barcelona: Ediciones B, 1990.

PARAGUAY

Almada, Martín. *Paraguay, la cárcel olvidada: El país exiliado*. Asunción: Intercontinental Editora, 1993.

Boccia Paz, Alfredo. *La década inconclusa: Historia real de la OPM*. Asunción: Editorial El Lector, 1997.

Boccia Paz, Alfredo, et al. *Es mi informe: Los archivos secretos de la policía de Stroessner.* Asunción: Centro de Documentación y Estudios, 1994.

Boccia Paz, Alfredo, et al. *En los sótanos de los generales: Los documentos ocultos del Operativo Cóndor*. Asunción: Expolibro/Servilibro, 2002.

Lewis, Paul H. *Paraguay under Stroessner.* Chapel Hill: The University of North Carolina Press, 1980.

Meilinger de Sannemann, Gladys. *Paraguay en el Operativo Cóndor: Represión e intercambio clandestino de prisioneros políticos en el cono sur*. Asunción: Ministerio de Educación y Culto, 1994.

Miranda, Carlos R. *The Stroessner Era: Authoritarian Rule in Paraguay.* Boulder, CO: Westview Press, 1990.

PERU

Amnesty International. *Perú: La matanza de Cayara.* London: 1989.

Beggar, Abderrahman. "The Path of State Terror in Peru." In *When States Kill: Latin America, the U.S., and Technologies of Terror.* Eds. Cecilia Menjívar and Nestor Rodríguez. Austin: University of Texas Press, 2005. 252–277.

Bracamonte, Jorge, et al. *Para no olvidar: Testimonios sobre la violencia política en el Peru.* 2003.

Burt, Jo-Marie. *Political Violence and the Authoritarian State in Peru: Silencing Civil Society.* New York: Palgrave Macmillan, 2007.

Comisión Investigadora de los Asesinatos de los Señores Diputados Eriberto Arroyo Mío y Pablo Norberto Li Ormeño, así como de las Actividades Desarrolladas por el Grupo Terrorista que Desarolla Acciones Criminales Incompatibles con la Vida Democrática del País y de Indebidamente Utiliza el Nombre de un Mártir, "Informe final." Lima, 1989.

Conaghan, Catherine M. *Fujimori's Peru: Deception in the Public Sphere*. Pittsburgh, PA: University of Pittsburgh Press, 2005.

Degregori, Carlos Iván. "Reaping the Whirlwind: The *Rondas Campesinas* and the Defeat of the *Sendero Luminoso* in Ayacucho." In *Societies of Fear: The Legacy of Civil War, Violence, and Terror in Latin America*. Eds. Kees Koonings and Dirk Kruijt. New York: Zed Books, 1999. 63–87.

Human Rights Watch. *Into the Quagmire: Human Rights and U.S. Policy in Peru.* New York: Human Rights Watch, 1991.

Manitzas, Elena S. "All the Minister's Men: Paramilitary Activity in Peru." In *Vigilantism and the State in Modern Latin America: Essays on Extralegal Violence.* Ed. Martha Huggins. New York: Praeger, 1991. 85–103.

Nelson, Manrique. *El tiempo del miedo: La violencia política en el Peru, 1980–1996.* 2002.

Obando, Enrique. "Civil-Military Relations in Peru, 1980–1996: How to Control and Coopt the Military (and the Consequences of Doing So.)" In *Shining and Other Paths: War and Society in Peru, 1980–1995*. Ed. Steve J. Stern. Durham, NC: Duke University Press, 1998. 385–410.

Poole, Deborah, and Gerardo Renique. *Peru: Time of Fear.* Latin America Bureau, 1992.

Stern, Steve J. "Introduction: Beyond Enigma: An Agenda for Interpreting Shining Path and Peru, 1980–1995." In *Shining and Other Paths: War and Society in Peru, 1980–1995.* Ed. Steve J. Stern. Durham, NC: Duke University Press, 1998. 1–9.

Umberto, Jara. *Ojo por ojo: La verdadera historia del Grupo Colina.* Lima: Grupo Editorial Norma, 2003.

Una lucha contra la impunidad. Lima, 1989.

URUGUAY

Caetano, Gerardo, and José Rilla. *Breve historia de la dictadura, 1973–1985.* Montevideo: Ediciones de la Banda Oriental, 1987.

Caula, Nelson, and Alberto Silva. *Alto el fuego 2: la logia de los tenientes de Hitler.* Montevideo: Rosebud Ediciones, 1997.

Cores, Hugo. *Memorias de la resistencia.* Montevideo: Ediciones de la Banda Oriental, 2002.

Faraone, Roque, and Robin Cheesman. *El caso Berrios: Estudio sobre información errónea, desinformación y manipulación de la opinión pública.* Montevideo: Editorial Nordan-Comunidad, 2002.

Fernández Huidobro, Eleuterio. *Historia de los tupamaros, tomo I, Los orígenes.* Montevideo: Ediciones de la Banda Oriental, 1986.

———. *Historia de los tupamaros, tomo II, El nacimiento.* Montevideo: Ediciones de la Banda Oriental, 1986.

———. *Historia de los tupamaros, tomo III, El MLN.* Montevideo: Ediciones de la Banda Oriental, 1986.

———. *La tregua armada.* Montevideo: TAE Editorial, 1990.

Gardo, Mauricio Lee. "Confesiones para un genocidio." Montevideo: TAE Editorial, 1987.

Israel, Sergio. *El enigma Trabal.* Montevideo: Ediciones Trilce, 2002.

Markarian, Vania. *Left in Transformantion: Uruguayan Exiles and the Latin American Human Rights Networks, 1967–1984.* New York: Routledge, 2005.

Myers, Scott L. *Los años oscuros, 1967–1987.* Montevideo: Editorial Latina, 1997.

Perelli, Carina. "From Counterrevolutionary Warfare to Political Awakening: The Uruguayan and Argentine Armed Forces in the 1970s." *Armed Forces and Society,* 1993, 20 (Fall): 25–49.

Rial, Juan. "Makers and Guardians of Fear: Controlled Terror in Uruguay." In *Fear at the Edge: State Terror and Resistance in Latin America.* Eds. Juan E. Corradi et al. Berkeley: Univ. of California Press, 1992. 90–103.

Rosencof, Mauricio, and Eleuterio Fernández Huidobro. *Memorias del calabozo, tomo I.* Montevideo: Ediciones de la Banda Oriental, 1987.

Ryan, Jeffrey J. "Turning on Their Masters: State Terrorism and Unlearning Democracy in Uruguay." In *When States Kill: Latin America, the U.S., and Technologies of Terror.* Eds. Cecilia Menjívar and Nestor Rodríguez. Austin: University of Texas Press, 2005. 278–304.

———. *Memorias del calabozo, tomo II.* Montevideo: Ediciones de la Banda Oriental, 1987.

———. *Memorias del calabozo, tomo III.* Montevideo: Ediciones de la Banda Oriental, 1987.

Servicio Paz y Justicia Uruguay. *Uruguay Nunca Más: Human Rights Violations, 1972–1985.* Translation by Elizabeth Hampsten. Philadelphia: Temple University Press, 1992.

Turiansky, Wladimir. *Apuntes contra la desmemoria.* Montevideo: ARCA Editorial, 1988.

Uruguayos desaparecidos en Argentina. Enero, 1985.

Index